Women's Test Cricket –
The Golden Triangle 1934–1984

THE BOOK GUILD LIMITED

WOMEN'S TEST CRICKET

The Golden Triangle

1934-84

JOAN L. HAWES

THE
BOOK GUILD LIMITED
Lewes

To them all
Old women cricketers never die,
they simply change their stance.

Cover photograph:
England's prolific opener Jan Brittin executes a square cut in fine style
during the Jubilee Test Series in Australia 1984–85.

The Book Guild Ltd
25 High Street,
Lewes, Sussex

First published 1987
© Joan Lillian Hawes 1987

Set in Linotron Bembo
Typeset by CST, Eastbourne
Printed in Great Britain by
Antony Rowe Ltd
Chippenham, Wilts

ISBN 0 86332 274 3

CONTENTS

Alec (L) and Eric Bedser with Jim Laker at a Reception at Qantas in London, where an exhibition of Cricketana was staged. Everyone smiles as the 1963 Australian Captain Mary Allitt tries out an old-fashioned bat. Janice Wady is the team member with her.

FOREWORD

My first realisation of the keenness of women cricketers was in 1938 when I coached a Ladies cricket team at a Cricket School in Kingston. Since then I have greatly admired the dedication and effort of women cricketers.

With hardly any help teams representing England have toured to many parts of the world. The Women's Cricket Association has raised money by all manner of means to enable their trips to be made. What is more each player has contributed a great deal to enable herself to make the trip. This shows a wonderful spirit in these days of ultra commercialization in sport. One could say the last genuine amateur team sport left. It took a long time and hard work for women's cricket to be recognised. Now it is well and truly "On the Map" throughout the world.

Not a lot is known of the history of women's cricket so it gives me great pleasure to welcome this book which will fill that gap. I wish it and women's cricket every success and may it go from strength to strength.

Alec Bedser.

ACKNOWLEDGEMENTS

This book would not have been possible without Cricket Society Statistician Arthur Stanford's devotion to his hobby. For it was his compilation of Women's Test Matches from 1934 to 1979 which came into my hands in August 1984 and sparked off the idea of celebrating the Golden Jubilee with a book. My task has been eased considerably by WCA Archivist Marion Collin who had always responded to my calls for help with patience and encouragement.

Many friends, as well as past and present cricketing colleagues, have come to my aid with illustrations, scrap books and pictures. Certain of them have entertained me to board and lodge and added inspiration and stories to that. I take pleasure in publicly thanking all of them here.

Molly Hide, Netta Rheinberg, Betty Snowball, Myrtle Maclagan, Dorothy McEvoy and Cecilia Robinson have done me proud in all respects. Netta's published reminiscences of 1957-8 and Robbie's personal diary of the 1948-9 Tour made those eras pleasurable writing. Shirley Dixon was also kind enough to loan me her memoirs for 1957-8. Polly Marshall has been a continual source of encouragement, never failing to respond generously to any request for anything. Eileen Vigor's picture album filled a worrying gap for 1966. Edna Barker's scrap books for both 1957-8 and 1968-9 were an invaluable source as was many a discussion. Enid Bakewell and Shirley Hodges wrote their reminiscences, and loaned and gave photographs and other vital material to take me to 1976. Carole Hodges' scrap books and her file of statistics helped me through to New Zealand's Tour of 1984, and Janet Aspinall's 1984-5 newspaper cuttings collection – rendered chronological by the ever-thorough Marion Collin – supplied the rest. I'm also grateful to Norma Izard for allowing me to read her personal diary, other papers and the team-effort "Jubilee Tour Diary".

Obtaining suitable photographs formed the major problem. Almost all the above helped out – particularly Molly, Netta, Myrtle and Betty S – and latterly I have also to thank Lynne Thomas and June Stephenson. But for the recent era I owe much to the kindness of Gill McConway.

England proved difficult enough but getting pictures of Australians and New Zealanders was a trial indeed. Fortunately I seem to have one or two friends 'Down There', or friends who have friends anyway.

In Australia, I don't know what I'd have done without the generosity of Marjorie Whincup, Menna Davies, Sylvia Faram and Kate McGready. In New Zealand, Trish McKelvey, spurred on by her good friend Audrey Disbury, came up trumps.

Those who helped on diverse ways, perhaps simply with advice and entertainment, were Pat Sheringham, Dorothy Macfarlane and Helene Hegarty. To the photographic expertise of Messrs Alex Matusiczky and John Brocksopp I owe much indeed.

For his knowledgeable, kind and encouraging Foreword, my very sincere thanks go to Alec Bedser.

Every effort has been made to check on the copyright owners of the material used, and I include them here even where both firms and individuals have proved untraceable. The attempt has been made to mention in the text every magazine, journal or newspaper from which quotations have been taken. Otherwise acknowledgements are due to:

The Adelaide Advertiser
The Daily Telegraph/Morning Post
The Sydney Morning Herald
The Manchester Guardian/Guardian
The Daily Mirror
The Evening News
Marjorie Pollard Publications

Birmingham Post & Mail
Yorkshire Evening Post
The Melbourne Advertiser
The Age (Melbourne)
Evening Post (Wellington)
The Times
The Cricketer

For photographs in particular:
Ken Kelly
Pippa Levett
Michael Rayner Impressions (Aust,)
Derek Rowe (Photos) Ltd
The Photo Source Ltd
Women's Cricket
Sport & General

The Author bowling at The Oval in 1957 under the watchful eye of the first woman to obtain an ACU qualification. Mrs Doris Coysh, formerly Turner, also registered a Test Cricket "first" since she toured Australia and New Zealand in 1934–5.

INTRODUCTION

December 1984 marked the Golden Jubilee of women's cricket internationally. It all began in Queensland, Australia, on the 28th of that month when in response to the generous hospitality offered them, England's tourists did the unladylike thing in thoroughly beating their hostesses by the large margin of nine wickets. The first Test match ever to be staged was the occasion for a remarkable record when opening bat and off-spin bowler Myrtle Maclagan followed her demoralising 7 wickets for 10 runs in Australia's first innings by scoring the first Test 50 in a total of 72. That performance, at the now defunct Exhibition Ground, still stands as an all-time record for Test matches in Brisbane. Since that time, Test match arenas have straddled the globe. From Manchester to Melbourne, Canterbury to Cape Town, Worcester to Wellington, England's women cricketers have carried their enthusiasm, along with bag and baggage, and shown themselves to be talented exponents of the game displaying guts as well as guile and grace.

The portrayal of women cricketers in action seems an appropriate way to commemorate the first fifty years. The title WOMEN'S TEST CRICKET – THE GOLDEN TRIANGLE 1934–1984, points to the fact that those first years were three-cornered tussles between England, Australia and New Zealand. Only in more recent times have South Africa, West Indies and India become part of the Test scene.

An ex-England player writing about Test cricket will naturally emphasise England's role, but the book also includes personalities from all three countries. The record holders, grounds remarkable for achievements or not, the Captains and others more humble – but all players of calibre, these are what the book highlights. It is a celebration of the noble art of cricket as *she* is played.

ENGLAND IN AUSTRALIA and NEW ZEALAND 1934–1935

More, perhaps, than on any other subsequent occasion, the adventurous band of fifteen women cricketers who self-financed their way to the Antipodes, were in October 1934 putting womanhood on world-view in an unfamiliar sporting guise. The common purpose, repeated by each one it has been possible to ask, was to play cricket in such a way as to give pleasure to all who cared to watch it as well as the players themselves; and that way had necessarily to be one that incorporated the skills and finesse of the game.

Could women actually wield the blade of willow though? Of course, provided it didn't weigh "a Botham". Could they turn an arm, tweak the fingers, catch a hard leather ball and fling it in from the boundary? Certainly, provided that ball was not impossibly difficult to hold and less than express speed – with consequently greater accuracy – was acceptable. And could they run? They could indeed, provided what they wore to play in did not hamper movement unduly. And, interestingly enough, it was the clothes question that featured most prominently in newspaper comment of the times – before, that is, the reality that women could actually play *cricket* began to hit the headlines.

AUSTRALIA 1934/35

Before the time came for Women's Test Cricket to make its debut, the width of the Australian Continent had been travelled by the tourists. And everywhere they stopped to play, the greeting was enthusiastic and mostly they won with ease: But it was not quite so in the State games.

In Perth, the West Australians were outclassed by technique – but managed to hold on for a draw. The Victorians at Melbourne themselves showed class, especially in the spin bowling department, and this time it was England who hung on for a draw. After that match the players were the wiser for knowing what good, fast wickets could do as well as realising that practice against spin bowling was a dire necessity.

Against New South Wales, at the Sydney Cricket Ground, England met with the strongest batting thus far and it was only an extremely sporting declaration by the Australian Captain elect that gave England her winning chance. She took it with flashing bat and scored 57 runs in 30 minutes. And so to Queensland, where wet weather interfered with the game against the State side – the match actually starting in rain. The visitors won the match by 201 runs. Perhaps this augured well for England because Brisbane, Queensland, was to stage the first Test.

Brisbane: The Exhibition Ground, December 28, 29 & 31

In perfect weather conditions, the pitch dry, though the outfield somewhat slow because of recent rain, the Australian opening pair, Hazel Pritchard and Ruby Monaghan, took firm steps, and historic

A relaxed touring party 1934-5 taken in Australia. Back Row L-R: Doris Turner, Mary Burletson, Mollie Child, Molly Hide, Joy Liebert, Mary Taylor, Mary Richards, Mary Spear Sitting L-R: Myrtle Maclagan, Betty Snowball (Vice-capt.), Betty Archdale (Capt.), Betty Green (Manager), Joy Partridge
In Front L-R: Carol Valentine, Grace Morgan

ones, towards the waiting England fielders. At 1.20 pm Pritchard faced slow bowler Maclagan and with straight bat blocked the good length ball. And if both players were relieved to get the very first Test Match under way, after the next delivery Pritchard was even more relieved because her snick through the slips was a chance that Partridge missed.

Assuredly, in the presence of some 1,500 spectators, the nervous tension of the occasion had communicated itself to the members of both teams.

The first over ended with Pritchard scoring a single to leg and she then had to face fast bowler Mary Taylor. A firm strike to the off brought Monaghan in the firing line and she too got off the mark with a single. When, however, it was her turn to face Maclagan, she rashly went down the wicket, missed the ball but so too did the wicketkeeper. This tentative play looked to be at an end when a three came off Maclagan but two balls later Pritchard played back and she was unfortunate enough to hit the stumps. At 8 for 1 Nell McLarty joined Monaghan and safely played out the over.

After a maiden from Taylor, McLarty faced Maclagan and hit a firm lofted straight drive which the bowler held. Essie Shevill was next at the crease and witnessed the demise of Monaghan, who was also caught and bowled Maclagan, before she herself was clean bowled by the same bowler. At this stage Maclagan had taken all the wickets to fall and her tally was 4 for 5 runs. In going from 9 for 3 to 10 for 4, Australia had put up stubborn resistance while pace bowlers, Taylor and Spear had sent down eight consecutive maidens between them. Nor was the position for Australia helped when wicket-keeper Hills, after pulling Maclagan to leg for 2, was struck on the nose by a ball which ran up the bat and consequently had to retire from the field. Her place was taken by the Captain, Margaret Peden, who scored a single off second change bowler Hide and was subsequently clean bowled by Taylor.

Kath Smith, who had been at the crease some 35 minutes for her one run, was joined by Lorna Kettels. These two then made something of a stand, seeing both Doris Turner and Joy Partridge brought into the bowling attack, before Kettels became another Maclagan victim. She was brilliantly caught in the slips by Partridge for 9. The score sheet then recorded two more Partridge catches, one wicket to each of Maclagan and Taylor: Maclagan had then taken 7 for 10 runs. Australia's innings closed at 47 for 9 wickets because the unfortunate Hills was unable to resume batting.

England opened their innings with Myrtle Maclagan taking strike and Vice Captain Betty Snowball at number 2. Fast bowler Fern Blade started proceedings, with Pritchard deputising as wicketkeeper. Maclagan took a single off Blade's second ball and Snowball also scored a single from the over, so each had got off the mark. Soon the runs came freely despite some rapid changes of bowling. Within half an hour of the start, the usually reticent Maclagan had scored 25 and in 40 minutes 50 was on the scoreboard but with one wicket down. It was Snowball's that went when, after scoring 15, she skied a ball to Shevill at mid-off, the bowler being canny spinner Peggy Antonio.

Hide at number three survived a chance the ball before she was caught by Kettels off Palmer for 9. The left-handed Palmer then spun out Child and Partridge, so that England were 99 for 4. But Maclagan was still there, having brought up her 50 in 80 minutes, when Captain Betty Archdale came to the wicket. Archdale presented a safe bat and when play ended for the day, as a consequence of Palmer clean bowling Maclagan for 72, she was 12 not out. England had scored 116 for 5 and were therefore a comfortable 69 runs ahead with 5 wickets in hand.

The second day's play began with Palmer, who at that time had taken 4 wickets for 15 runs, finishing off the over against new bat Doris Turner. McLarty took the other end and Archdale added two to her score from that over. Palmer then bowled a maiden to Turner who looked to have difficulties with the spin and, in the next Palmer over, she was out to catch taken by McLarty at silly mid-on having scored just two runs.

At 120 for 6, England looked to be losing her advantage. And when Liebert came and went – to McLarty for 1 – the tailenders were needed for a few runs. It was the Captain, however, who kept these coming while Taylor made a duck and Spear and Valentine both became Palmer victims. The latter ended with a superb 7 for 18. England's closing score was 154 and her Captain carried her bat for 32.

England's last five wickets had taken only 50 minutes to fall so that Australia had some two and a half hours to play to attempt to cancel the 107 run deficit. But they also had to dismiss England again if a win was to result. It seemed a daunting task and yet, when Pritchard and Monaghan opened against Maclagan and Taylor, it was with confidence and no sign of their first innings nervousness.

Monaghan opened the score for Australia with a well-placed cover drive for 2. Until Child ran out Monaghan with a throw to the bowler's end, after misfielding a Pritchard hit to leg, the Australian openers seemed to have no problems with the bowling. Shevill, too, looked confident, while Archdale switched bowling ends with the trio of Maclagan, Taylor and Spear and also brought Turner into the attack.

There were a good few maiden overs bowled and the score crept along only slowly.

The second wicket fell when Snowball took a good catch behind off Spear to dismiss Pritchard for 20. After the tea interval Smith joined Shevill, both of them raised in the batting order, and was sound in defence. These two had put on some 20 runs before Smith was comprehensively bowled by Valentine who was the sixth bowler to be brought into action.

At 58 for 3, the 50 having been brought up in 85 minutes, McLarty went in at number 5. She provided Snowball's second catch of the innings, also off Spear's good length bowling, and was out for a well struck 8. When Kettels was bowled by Spear for a duck after being at the crease for 13 minutes, Peden was required to see out the end of play with the stalwart Shevill. At stumps Australia was 99 for 5 and still 8 runs behind, with Peden on 2 and Shevill not out 46.

Essie Shevill, the only Australian player to score a half-century in the 1934-5 series, executes an off drive on her way to her 63 not out in the second innings of the Brisbane Test.

The final afternoon's play was almost a foregone conclusion. England, obviously in a winning position, needed just 4 wickets since Hills was still unable to bat. Taylor and Partridge opened the bowling and Peden seemed bemused by the slow bowler's lobs. It was Spear, however, who had Peden caught in the slips by Partridge for 12. But the latter got her wicket, that of Palmer whose was the last wicket to fall, for Spear bowled Antonio and Hide got Blade's wicket from a catch by Child. Australia were all out for 138, leaving England to score 29 to win. This was done with the loss of Maclagan's wicket. The inaugural Test Match was, therefore, a resounding win to England by nine wickets.

Summary of the First Test 1934–35

England won by 9 wickets

Australia:	47 and 138
England:	154 and 34 for 1

Best Batting

1st Innings

Australia:	K Smith	25
	L Kettels	9
England:	M Maclagan	72
	E Archdale	32 n o

2nd Innings

Australia:	E Shevill	63 n o
	H Pritchard	20
England:	E A Snowball	18 n o

Best Bowling

1st Innings

England:	M Maclagan	7 – 10
	M Taylor	2 – 9
Australia:	A Palmer	7 – 18
	N McLarty	1 – 12

2nd Innings

England:	M Spear	5 – 15
	J Partridge	1 – 6
	C Valentine	1 – 9

Highlights

On a wicket that seemed to favour the bowlers, the maiden 50s by Maclagan and Shevill were examples of patience and graft. While Maclagan's 17 – 11 – 10 – 7, and Palmer's 13.2 – 4 – 18 – 7 showed what could be done on a drying pitch, Spear's pace bowling produced 34 – 24 – 15 – 5 on the third day. England's fielding was of a high standard throughout. There were only five boundaries scored: Smith got three of them.

DOUR FIGHT

Our Own Kath Smith Only One To Hit Boundary

Left-Hander Palmer Is The Best In Home Side

(By H. M. THURLOW).

Things were at a low ebb in the second innings of the match between the Australian girls and England yesterday until McLarty, the Aussie fast bowler came in and made the spectators, of whom there were about 5000, sit up and take delight in almost everything with a healthy action. The Scores lifte The p old lift

AUSTRALIA.

first Innings.

H. Pritchard. hit wkt., b. Maclagan	...	4
P. Monaghan, c. and b. Maclagan	...	4
M. McLarty, c. and b. Maclagan	...	0
E. Shevill, b. Maclagan	..	9
H. Hills, retired hurt	..	2
M. Peden, b. Taylor	..	1
K. Smith, c. Spear, b. Maclagan ..	..	25
K. Kettles, c. Partridge, b. Maclagan		9
A. Palmer, c. Partridge, b. Maclagan	..	1
P. Antonio, c. Partridge, b. Taylor	..	0
F. Blade, not out	..	0
Sundries	..	1
		—
Total	..	47

BOWLING.

	O.	M.	R.	W.
Maclagan	17	11	10	7
Taylor	14.3	8	9	2
Spear	8	2	2	0
Hide	4	0	6	0
Turner	4	1	7	0
Partridge	2	0	12	0

Innings lasted 141 minutes.

Shevill specialised in glides through the slips, a shot that is fraught with danger. Pritchard showed good form in making 20 in good style before being caught on the leg-side by Snowball, off Spear.

Kath. Smith had bad luck when shaping soundly to drag one into her wicket. She started cautiously and was on the lookout for runs when the accident happened.

CRISP BATTING

Australia started batting at about 2.30, and the rate of run-getting fluctuated. The openers set about their task crisply, until Monaghan had the misfortune to be run-out through a bad misunderstanding, and the scoring rate slowed down to a funeral pace.

The advent of Spear, Turner, and Hide at the bowling crease caused this, per medium of good, accurate bowling, which was always on the dot, the deliveries possessing plenty of guile; in fact, maiden overs were the order of the day.

Maclagnan bowled well, without repeating her success of Friday. She is keenness personified. Taylor is the fast bowler, and has a good action, with a bound into the air at the end, somewhat reminiscent of Jack Gregory, though to a lesser degree. Our bowlers compared very favorably with the visitors, though lacking somewhat in their accuracy.

With five wickets down for 116, England resumed play very confidently, but good bowling and fielding upset their ideas and they were all soon out for 154. Archdale got the not out, with 32 to her credit, and she played some attractive shots, her difficulty being that the others would not, or could not, stick with her.

The game at present is still in a fairly open state, as with some good bats still to come, England may be set a stiff hurdle to overcome in their second knock. This, however, mainly depends on the batting of Shevill, if she gets going again she may tot up a respectable total.

NO PLAY IN WOMEN'S MATCH

SYDNEY. Jan. 5.—Rain prevented play to-day in the second women's match between England and Australia. In order to make up for the loss of to-day's play the match has been extended until Tuesday. Australia has so far made 147 for the loss of nine wickets in her first innings.—

K. Smith by Joy Liebert

If We May Say So

By TOM WEBSTER

THE LATTER DID THIS WITHOUT ANY HELP FROM THE M.C.C.

THIS IS PROBABLY WHY THEY DID IT.

CRICKET.

THE AUSTRALIAN WOMEN WERE BEATEN IN THE SECOND TEST MATCH BY THE ENGLISH WOMEN

Sydney: Sydney Cricket Ground January 4, (5), 7 & 8, 1935

The second Test on the famous Sydney Cricket Ground was remarkable in several ways. From the cricket tradition point of view its interest lay in the omission of a weekend afternoon that was not a Sunday. There were, therefore, two 'rest days' in the match – no doubt due to the requirements of the men's game for Saturday play. However, it was a privilege to play on the ground and one which was appreciated by all; the all on this occasion being the two Test sides and an average of 4,500 spectators over the three days.

Another unusual feature was that Australia's team included two pairs of sisters: Margaret and Barbara Peden and Essie and Rene Shevill. The latter had joined the team as a wicketkeeper in place of Hilda Hills, and Barbara Peden as a specialist slip fielder who could also turn an arm. The other replacement in the team was Joyce Brewer and the two omitted were Lorna Kettels and Fern Blade. There was just one change in the England team, Mary Richards came in for Carol Valentine.

Play was scheduled for a 1.15 pm start on Friday the 4th, and began at 1.17 with the Australian openers Monaghan and Pritchard facing up to Maclagan's slows and Taylor's pace. The perfect playing conditions and wicket were not enjoyed for long by Pritchard, however, because Maclagan's second ball hit the leg stump and Australia were 2 for 1; the two coming off the first ball as leg byes. Though Monaghan had obviously deferred to Pritchard on taking strike the prompt dismissal of her partner did not affect her composure when she faced Taylor. In fact, 8 of the 9 runs she scored came off that first Taylor over and included a boundary. At the other end Essie Shevill saw through a maiden over from Maclagan, and Taylor found a better length in her second, giving away just the single to bring Monaghan into Maclagan's firing line. She survived just one ball and was then bowled.

The situation that Australia now faced was treated in complete contrast by the two bats Shevill and Smith, who needed to retrieve the sorry plight of 11 for 2. Shevill offered stolid and unenterprising defence, while Smith attempted to hit her way out of the problem, starting with two boundaries off Maclagan. The dullness of Shevill's batting – when she was out it was for a duck that had taken 47 minutes to 'acquire' – at least had the effect of removing Maclagan from the bowling scene. In fact, several bowling changes had been tried and it was Hide who finally got Shevill caught behind.

Newcomer Brewer joined Smith at number 5, and though somewhat fortunate at times, stemmed a possible Australian collapse (as at Brisbane) with the more forceful Smith. Their partnership had put on a crucial 44 runs when Smith was lbw to Spear just 3 short of her half century. Barbara Peden was the next in and she and Brewer saw play to the tea break. After that the 100 was brought up (in 168 minutes) but then with the addition of only 1 run, Brewer was caught by Hide off Spear's bowling for 34.

The sixth wicket to fall was McLarty's. She had hit two good clouts, for 3 and 4 runs respectively, and then took a foolish run from a hit direct to mid-on; Snowball summarily swept off the bails from a sharp Spear return. Captain Margaret Peden joined Peden B. and the partnership looked secure until the latter was lbw to Turner for 12. At 127 for 7, Rene Shevill joined her captain and the did the unforgiveable by running her out. The attempted run was again improbable and the keen England fielding – this time in the shape of Liebert – re-emphasised that such risky runs were an affront.

Perhaps Shevill's mistake could be accredited to first match nerves. The next bat in, however, had no such qualms. Peggy Antonio, young in her years but now quite experienced against England, struck the ball with confidence from the start. Shevill did not keep her company for long, falling to Maclagan. Palmer was last in and attacked merrily with her co-spinner to see out play which ended with Australia 147 for 9 wickets.

The second day began as it had ended two days previously with Antonio and Palmer in attacking mood. Their spirited play produced a further 15 runs before Maclagan trapped Palmer lbw for 14. Antonio was not out 18 in Australia's final score of 162.

England's innings opened at 1.40 pm, customarily, with Maclagan and Snowball. Pace bowlers McLarty and the left-armer Smith were used in short spells, so that after only the first eight overs spinner Antonio, and medium pace bowler, B. Peden, were in the attack. The bowling, however, lacked penetration even though Snowball took some while to get off he mark. In real terms only two chances were put down by the Australians, while Snowball now galloped along soon overtaking Maclagan as run-getter. The 50 was up in 47 minutes, and by tea the century. During the second session, play slowed somewhat when Snowball lost her wicket, lbw to the accurate Smith, she had scored 71 runs and England's score was 145.

The Australian total was passed with Maclagan still there and Hide flashing an attractive bat. When her wicket went, bowled by Smith for 34, her total included four successive boundaries. At around 5 pm Maclagan was out lbw to Antonio having made 119 runs and became the first ever century scorer for England. Her going brought Archdale to the wicket, but after scoring just three, the England Captain was bowled by Smith.

Australia's competent fielding, still not yet England class however, was further put to the test when Mollie Child struck the ball well to keep up the pace of England's run getting. She saw Turner bowled by Antonio for 9, and was joined by Partridge before play ended for the day with the score an amazing 301 runs for 5 wickets, accumulated in some 230 minutes.

On the third and final afternoon, England declared at the overnight score and set about removing the Australians promptly. Archdale, for once, deserted the usual tactic of a slow-fast attack, and even more shrewdly, gave Maclagan second bowl to the high-lobbed slows of Partridge. This move was yet to reap its full benefit, though, as in the first innings, Maclagan clean bowled Pritchard for a duck, and Australia was 0 for 1 wicket. Clearly, Maclagan was becoming Pritchard's *bete noir.*

Shevill was next in and looked to have the situation under control, taking a four off the first ball of Maclagan's second over and continuing steadily. Understandably, however, the pace of scoring was

Myrtle Maclagan becomes the first woman to score a Test century with a four through the covers. It was part of a magnificent 119 at the Sydney Cricket Ground in January 1935.

slow and not without mishap, a near stumping and run out being survived. The next wicket fell to the tantalising Partridge, still going strong in her twelfth over. Monaghan jumped down the wicket to despatch Partridge to the boards, missed the ball and provided Snowball with the first stumping in Test cricket. By then Australia had progressed to 34 for 2. Vice-Captain Smith, the accomplished Queensland all-rounder, then joined Shevill and the two of them cracked on the pace as well as runs; the fifty came up in 60 minutes. They saw off several bowlers, even the beguiling Partridge, and a promising partnership ended when Shevill was run out for 36 trying to sneak a risky run. Her partner soon followed, going lbw to the recalled Partridge. Joyce Brewer, who had done well in the first innings, looked as though she would make a few but with only 9 against her name she was out to a low delivery from Spear which rebounded from the wicketkeeper's pads and found her outside the crease.

Barbara Peden scored 4 and was then caught by Hide making a running catch, the bowler being Partridge. Next, at 99 for 6, Partridge was the bowler when Rene Shevill, raised to 7 in the batting order, hit

Fast bowler Nell McClarty stumped Snowball bowled Partridge for 8 in the second Test at Sydney Cricket Ground.

her wicket. McLarty, too, went to Partridge – another stumping to Snowball. This successful pair also took the final wicket, that of the courageously determined Palmer, who scored 23, after Maclagan had bowled Antonio for 8. The not out bat was Margaret Peden who had captained her side to a 10 run lead over England.

For the winning of the Second Test, Archdale changed the opening pair from the established Maclagan and Snowball to the lower order Mary Richards and Joy Liebert. Unfortunately they managed only 3 between them and it was left to Snowball and Hide to see England safely home by 8 wickets.

Summary of the Second Test 1934-5

England won by 8 wickets

Australia:	162 & 148
England:	301 for 5 wickets dec. & 10 for 2

Best Batting

1st Innings

Australia:	K Smith	47
	J Brewer	34
England:	M Maclagan	119
	E A Snowball	71

2nd Innings

Australia:	E Shevill	36
	K Smith	27

Best Bowling

1st Innings

England:	M Maclagan	4 – 33
	M Spear	2 – 19
Australia:	K Smith	3 – 42
	P Antonio	2 – 53

2nd Innings

England:	J Partridge	6 – 96
	M Maclagan	2 – 35

Highlights

To follow her 4 – 33 in 33 overs with the first century in Test cricket was a brilliant achievement by Maclagan. The first wicket partnership of 145 with Snowball remained a record against Australia until 1976. The latter's 4 stumpings in an innings has never been bettered for England. Partridge's 6 – 96 came off 35.4 overs in two spells of 14 and 21.4 overs with 6 maidens.

Melbourne: Melbourne Cricket Ground, January 18, 19 & 20 1935

Three not very challenging matches and some 800 miles of road and rail travel preceded the third and final Test Match on the Australian Continent. The venue was the Melbourne Cricket Ground where, on the occasion of the game against the Victorian State side, England had come within range of a beating, having failed miserably against the spin of Peggy Antonio. Now, though, Antonio was not the unknown youngster of six weeks earlier and experience for already accomplished players counts a lot. But on home ground – and on a pitch already known to help the spin bowlers – would Antonio do it again, aided by the able Palmer? And if so, would Maclagan, Partridge and Hide have a ready answer?

For the first time Archdale won the toss and elected to bat on a perfect wicket. Maclagan and Snowball were together just on ten minutes before the latter was clean bowled by opener Smith in her third over. Smith had already been unlucky to see Maclagan missed in the slips off the very first ball bowled, but now Hide was at the wicket to face the two remaining balls. She scored a single which gave her the

Australia's line-up for the final Test at Melbourne C G in 1935: Back Row L-R: Nell McLarty (12th), Lorna Kettels, Margaret Peden (Capt.), Amy Hudson, Barbara Peden. Front row L-R: Hazel Pritchard, Essie Shevill, Kath Smith, Rene Shevill (Wkt.), Joyce Brewer, Ann Palmer. (Missing from the line-up: Peggy Antonio) The Umpires were Messrs W R Wettenhall and H E Nichols.

strike against Kettels. But Kettels was bowling tidily and produced her second consecutive maiden.

In her fourth over Smith gave away 7 runs and consequently was removed from the attack to be replaced by Amy Hudson making her debut. Hudson's medium pacers kept both batswomen quiet, and when Antonio replaced Kettels, Hide became the first to be spun out in a sequence of three by her. Hide went for 7, to be followed by Child and Partridge who contributed 3 and 0 respectively. England was 48 for 4 when Archdale joined Maclagan. At that stage Antonio had taken 3 for 5 in 8 overs.

In the backs-to-the-wall situation, Archdale turned in one of her Captain's innings and with Maclagan moved the score along steadily until the latter was out, bowled by Hudson for 50. Number seven, Turner, who made 5, was Antonio's fourth scalp, but Richards saw the bowling safely through to tea. After the interval Kettels was given a second spell and was unlucky not to get Archdale in the slips. The

Left-arm bowler and right-hand bat Kath Smith, the most successful Australian player of the 1934-5 series against England, still has her hat on when she bowls Betty Snowball for a single in the first innings of the third Test at Melbourne. Partner Myrtle Maclagan, with eye-shield, went on to make 50, and in the second innings Betty made 83 not out.

England Captain's survival was soon emphasised when she brought up the century with a cover drive off Smith for 3. This seemed to signal a bowling change for the Australians and Barbara Peden and Antonio were brought into the attack.

Off the first Antonio over Richards hit two fours making the most of the occasion. It looked as though the partnership was going to settle to accumulating much needed quick runs, but in her second over, Peden clean bowled Archdale for 32. Liebert joined Richards and the eighth wicket put on 23 before Antonio claimed another wicket, that of Liebert for 13. Next out was Richards whose 31 runs had taken a brisk 54 minutes, but she too went to Antonio, caught by Palmer. Mary Taylor was run out, in an over in which she and Spear had scored 12 runs off Antonio, leaving Spear not out 7 and Antonio with the fine tally of 6 wickets for 49 runs.

England had scored their 162 in just on three and a quarter hours, so that Australia had an hour to play to the close. On this occasion newcomer Hudson opened with her Captain to the bowling of Maclagan and Hide. After only two overs, however, Maclagan was replaced by pace bowler Taylor. Spear was also given a spell and Maclagan then had a second bowl. Success for England eventually came off Hide's seventh over when she had Margaret Peden caught behind for 10. When play ended for the day Australia was 31 for 1 wicket.

The second afternoon's play began with Hudson and Essie Shevill facing Partridge and Spear. Hudson opened her account with a 3 off Partridge's first over, and Shevill got a single in the same over. Spear, however, was giving nothing away and her spell of consecutive maidens eventually caused Shevill to attempt to hit her way out of the doldrums. The result was a spooned-up catch which Maclagan made no mistake in holding. Smith joined Hudson who, without adding to the score, was run out by a good return from Turner to Snowball. Pritchard, at number 5 instead of her customary opening role, was now faced with the task of stabilising an Australian innings which was not looking too healthy at 37 for 3. Unfortunately though, when she had been only a few minutes at the crease, there was a misunderstanding with Smith and the latter was another run out casualty. Even now, it seemed, the Australians were not able to judge a run in the face of the keen and accurate England fielding. Pritchard herself lasted only 11 minutes, being caught at mid-on off Hide for 5.

At 45 for 5 Antonio and Barbara Peden were together and made every attempt to get runs. They brought up the 50 (in a pathetically slow 2 hours) but the pace of scoring increased only marginally. When

Antonio was bowled by Maclagan just before the tea interval, her 16 runs had taken 80 minutes to accumulate. Peden was joined by Kettels but became another wicket for Spear when Richards took a well-caught catch in the slips. A total of 78 for 7 was certainly looking good England's way but then Brewer, at number 9, began to put a bit of spark into the Australian attack. When she was joined by Ann Palmer, Kettels going for 9 to a Hide catch off Maclagan, the tail really wagged valiantly. The last two wickets put on 59 runs and the result was that the Australian score reached a respectable 150, only 12 short of England's total.

With just 25 minutes of play left, Archdale sensibly kept her opening pair in abeyance for a refreshed view of things for the third and final day. She herself opened, with Mollie Child taking first strike against pace bowler Smith. They saw out play for the day with England's score on 8 and 20 runs ahead.

Play began at 1.19 pm on the last day and after only a few minutes the first English wicket went as a result of a mishap. Child, going for a short run dropped her bat, hesitated, and was run out by a quick return from Pritchard to Rene Shevill. Snowball joined Archdale who soon fell lbw to Smith, having added 5 runs to her overnight score. The old firm of Snowball and Maclagan were now together with Snowball looking in good form. Her first six scoring shots included 3 boundaries and two threes. Maclagan, on the other hand, was as restrained as Snowball was vigorous and though Antonio conceded 10 runs off her first over of the day, in her third she had Maclagan lbw. With England 3 wickets down for 40 runs, Hide joined Snowball.

Never a laggard in the hunt for runs in such circumstances, Hide attacked the bowling and placed the ball well. The partnership brought up the 50 in 65 minutes and, when Hide was bowled by the slow left-armer Palmer, had added 46 runs. Hide's 26 had taken 25 minutes. But Snowball was still going well in her 40s. It was not until she was joined by Mary Richards, however, that her second 50 of the series was on the scoreboard. Meanwhile, England had lost another wicket; that of Partridge who scored a single.

When Richards was out for 18, caught by Kettels off Antonio, England was some 146 runs ahead with about 150 minutes of playing time to go. It was clear that a declaration would soon need to be made if England wanted to win. On the other hand, with nothing to lose, the Australians might just achieve such a run-rate. In the event, the 15 minutes before tea saw Taylor and Turner at the wicket. Taylor was bowled by Palmer for 5 and at tea, when England declared, Turner was 1 not out and Snowball an expertly played 83 not out. The England total was 153 for 7 wickets and Australia required 166 runs to win in 132 minutes.

Hudson and Pritchard opened for the Australians against the bowling of Maclagan and Hide. Disaster came for the home side in the shape of three wickets down to Maclagan for 28 after 50 minutes play. First Hudson was caught and bowled for 8, then Smith was caught by Partridge for 9 and finally Pritchard holed out to Child for 5. Some juggling of the batting order brought Antonio and Palmer together at the wicket; a partnership which looked to be full of runs. Just on 25 minutes together though, and both fell victim to the pace attack; Antonio lbw to Spear for 14 and Palmer bowled Taylor for 11. Taylor also bowled Essie Shevill for a duck.

With Australia 51 for 6, England had victory clearly in their sights, but that was to reckon without the dogged spirit of Barbara Peden and Joy Brewer. At 7 and 8 respectively, these two put on 44 runs before Brewer was bowled by the resolute Maclagan for 31. Although Kettels was only able to contribute a single to the total, Captain Margaret Peden joined sister Barbara to see Australia through to the close of play with the score 104 for 8 wickets. The drawn match nevertheless left England victorious in the series with the wins at Brisbane and Sydney to their credit.

Farewell to Australia as the England tourists depart from Melbourne. Here a charming picture of L-R: Mary Spear, Peggy Antonio and Betty Snowball.

Summary of the Third Test 1934-5

Match Drawn

England:	162 and 153 for 7 dec.
Australia:	150 and 104 for 8

Best Batting

1st Innings

England:	M Maclagan	50
	E Archdale	32
	M Richards	31
Australia:	A Palmer	39
	J Brewer	26

2nd Innings

England:	E A Snowball	83 n o
	M E Hide	26
Australia:	J Brewer	31
	B Peden	24 n o

Best Bowling

1st Innings

Australia:	P Antonio	6 – 49
	A Hudson	1 – 7
	B Peden	1 – 9
England:	M Spear	3 – 21
	M Maclagan	3 – 32
	M E Hide	2 – 24

2nd Innings

Australia:	A Palmer	3 – 17
	P Antonio	2 – 55
England:	M Maclagan	4 – 28
	M I Taylor	2 – 13

Highlights

Her third consecutive match 50 and bowling analysis of 7 for 60, put the seal on this series being Maclagan's triumph, with Snowball a close second. Once again, on her home ground, Antonio showed herself a force in Australia's future with a match analysis of 8 for 104 off 36.5 overs.

NEW ZEALAND 1935

The tourists set sail from Melbourne on the *Wanganella* the day after the third Test. Some six days later they were again adorning the cricket field; this time at Eden Park in Auckland. From the start it was obvious that the New Zealanders were no match for the England women. Even their representative sides showed a raw inexperience which could not be counteracted by keenness, though plenty of the latter was evident. So England romped through the preliminary matches, never looking to be troubled by the opposition. They beat Auckland by 167 runs in a one-day game; Wanganui was similarly beaten by 123 runs; they over-whelmed Wellington by an innings and 75 runs, and the story was not very different against Canterbury and Otago. The Test Match which took place at Christchurch had about it the air of a foregone conclusion. Nevertheless, press coverage and attendance at the matches had been very favourable to England, the former unanimously realising the extent to which such a tour could boost women's cricket in the home country.

The tourists of 1934-5 with Maori guides and children reflected in a pool among the hot springs at Whakarewarewa.

THE NEW ZEALAND WOMEN'S REPRESENTATIVE CRICKET TEAM.—From right: Misses R. Symons, M. Hollis, M. Bishop, P. Taylor, H. Miller, P. Savin, N. Browne, M. Marks, A. Ell, M. Corby and H. Buck.

CRICKET.

WOMEN'S   CRICKET.
WOMEN'S   CRICKET.

ENGLAND   v.   NEW   ZEALAND
ENGLAND   v.   NEW   ZEALAND
ENGLAND   v.   NEW   ZEALAND
ENGLAND   v.   NEW   ZEALAND
ENGLAND   v.   NEW   ZEALAND

LANCASTER   PARK
LANCASTER   PARK
LANCASTER   PARK
LANCASTER   PARK
LANCASTER   PARK

TO-DAY (MONDAY)
TO-DAY (MONDAY)
TO-DAY (MONDAY)

COMMENCES 11 A.M.

Luncheon: 1-1.45 p.m

2/-.   1/-.
2/-.   1/-.

School Children Half Price.
School Children Half Price.

9624F.P.

CHRISTCHURCH, N.Z.: SATURDAY, FEBRUARY 16, 1935.

NEW ZEALAND WOMEN PLAY THEIR FIRST TEST MATCH.

Cricket as played by the gentler sex, according to our caricaturist, who gives an impression above of Miss Betty Archdale, the English captain.

N.Z. Team Soon Dismissed and English Players Knock Up Big Score.

TWO CENTURIES IN AFTERNOON.

AFTER DISMISSING the New Zealand women cricketers for 44 runs to-day, the English team knocked up a big score, and at stumps had 431 runs for the loss of four wickets. E. Snowball made 189 and M. Hide 110.

Christchurch: Lancaster Park Cricket Ground, February 16 & 18

Although a chill southerly wind was blowing, weather prospects were settled for the first day's play in New Zealand's inaugural Test and the final match of the Australasian Tour for England. Ruth Symons, the New Zealand Captain, won the toss and elected to bat on a firm, true wicket. It was Hilda Buck and Margaret Marks who had the privilege of facing up to Maclagan and Taylor.

Just one minute after the start of play, Buck was out caught at silly mid-on by Spear off Maclagan. Two overs later Marks suffered a similar fate and New Zealand were 3 runs for 2 wickets. When the wicketkeeper Savin was clean bowled by Maclagan, having added 3 to the score, it began to look as though Test Match nerves and Maclagan were going to effect a rout. It was Taylor, however, who was to take the next two wickets, forcing Mabel Corby back on her stumps and aided by Snowball in the dismissal of Marjorie Bishop. With wickets tumbling about her, Symons maintained an effective resistance, and

Betty Snowball (L) and Molly Hide going out to resume their record breaking stand of 235 at Lancaster Park, Christchurch on 16 February 1935.

when joined by Merle Hollis kept her end up while the latter made every effort to score runs. A change of bowler was required to dismiss Hollis who, when caught by Liebert off Spear, had made 24. Thus Hollis, batting ninth in the order, had seen the score go from 16 for 7 to 44 for 8. The last wicket to fall was that of Hazel Miller after her captain had been run out by a return from substitute Valentine. Unfortunately, no further addition to the score was made, Symons having stayed over 50 minutes for her 5 runs, and New Zealand were all out at 12.21 for 44.

In the 25 minutes of play remaining before lunch, Maclagan and Snowball suffered no discomfort against the bowling of openers Miller and Browne, nor did the other four bowlers used worry them. The tactics of the New Zealand Captain seemed almost to be aimed at giving everyone a bowl in an attempt to curb the run rate. After the three overs bowled by each of the openers, 29 runs had been scored; the 50 came up in 20 minutes. Bowling inexperience was up against the most experienced opening partnership in Test cricket which, at the

The scoreboard that tells almost all the story of the only Test between England and New Zealand on the 16th and 18th February 1935. In overwhelming the opposition, Betty Snowball recorded England's highest ever individual score of 189 which took 222 minutes. That total included the fastest Test century on record: 115 minutes.

interval, looked invincible.

Shortly after the break, however, Maclagan snicked one to slips and the catch was held by Symons off the bowling of Miller. For a modest 26, Maclagan's going must have provided hope for the New Zealanders because they knew it was a valuable wicket to capture. But next in was Molly Hide whose stroke play was soon to be displayed in all its ease and power. She and Snowball saw the hundred up in 68 minutes. At an ever accelerating pace, the boundaries flowed and when Snowball reached her century in 115 minutes, she had scored thirteen of them. The only bowler who seemed able to retain a length in the batting onslaught was Symons, and it was she who claimed Snowball's wicket. The latter, however, had by that time made 189 and the tea interval had long gone. England were 372 for 3.

The second wicket down was Hide's, who was caught at square leg by substitute Norman off the bowling of Hollis, having made a fine 110. Her going had brought Mollie Child to the crease and she too collared the bowling. Partridge joined her when Snowball was out but stayed only 13 minutes for 6 runs, caught by Bishop off Symons. At 395 for 4, Archdale joined Child and the two of them took England through to close of play without further loss, and with the addition of 56 runs.

In just on one hour after the start of play on the second and final day, Archdale declared England's innings closed. She did not manage to add to her overnight score, but replacement Mary Richards knocked up quick runs to end 48 not out, and Child had put on a further 24 to finish up with a splendid 86 not out. With England an unimpeachable 503 for 5, a lead of 459, the most New Zealand could hope for was to improve on the first innings total of 44. Only one incident marred the satisfactory outcome to the game for England and that was the absence through injury of the opposing captain Symons. With one bat short, New Zealand totalled 122 runs, Partridge taking most of the wickets. The final result was an overwhelming win for England by an innings and 337 runs.

Summary of the Test 1934-5

England won by an innings and 337 runs

New Zealand:	44 and 122
England:	503 for 5 declared

Best Batting

1st Innings

New Zealand:	M Hollis	24
	R Symons	5
England:	E A Snowball	189
	M E Hide	110
	M Child	86 n o

2nd Innings

New Zealand:	M Bishop	27
	M Marks	23

Best Bowling

1st Innings

England:	M Maclagan	5 – 22
	M I Taylor	3 – 6
New Zealand:	R Symons	2 – 71
	P Taylor	1 – 62
	H Miller	1 – 77

2nd Innings

England:	J Partridge	4 – 60

Highlights

Maclagan's 5 – 22 in 14.2 overs, 6 of which were maidens gave her two five-wicket analyses in four Tests. Her overall total produced an average of 8.69. Snowball's 189 not only remains the highest score by an England player in any position, it provided the fastest century, in 115 minutes, and the highest second wicket partnership of 235 with Hide. It was the latter's first Test century. Not only did Snowball achieve success with the bat but she also took two catches and made two stumpings in the match.

AUSTRALIA IN ENGLAND 1937

Months before the Australian team were to arrive for the second ever Test Series to get under way, the official journal of Women's Cricket Association in England, *Women's Cricket*, had many a page devoted to speculation and information about the likely visitors and their accomplishments. Almost as soon as the 1934/35 tourists returned, a hospitality fund was launched in preparation for the event, and the expectations that this summer of 1937 would see an Aussie side of cricket maturity based on previous potential were mooted. And so – certainly in the four representative matches leading to the first Test at Northampton – it proved to be; the tourists convincingly overcoming the opposition in both the East and Midlands.

Northampton: Northants Cricket Ground June 12, 14 & 15

Rain had threatened and the skies were grey when Molly Hide led an England team with six newcomers onto the field the first Test Match held in England. On winning the toss, Margaret Peden, the Australian Captain, was first to the wicket, accompanied by a now seasoned campaigner, Peggy Antonio. Unfortunately, in her opening role, Antonio soon went to the speed of Betty Belton seeing only three overs for her duck. The early breakthrough by England brought another 'veteran' to the wicket: The stylish Hazel Pritchard.

Pritchard opened her account with a boundary off Maclagan, the spin bowler who caused her most anguish in Australia, and continued to make fine strokes, solidly supported by her captain. These two were still together at the lunch interval, having passed the hundred partnership and moved the total from 0 for 1 wicket to 126 for 1. Soon after the interval, however, Pritchard, whose runs had flowed mostly from elegant drives, made an uncharacteristic heave at a full toss from Belton and was easily caught off a skier by Hide at mid-on. She had added just one to her lunchtime score of 86. Her 87 runs included 10 boundaries. Wicketkeeper Winnie George replaced Pritchard but was not at the crease long before Peden was trapped lbw by Hide for an invaluable 34.

Pat Holmes at number 5 seemed to find the wicket to her liking and she and George saw Australia to 150 before the latter was clean bowled by Maclagan for 18. Next in was the strong hitter and opening fast bowler, Kath Smith, who, after a steady start, laid about the bowling in determined fashion. She saw Holmes go for 21, caught by Snowball off Hide, and Barbara Peden dismissed with an excellent slip catch by M. E. Haddelsey off Belton.

The 200 was brought up in some 210 minutes, largely due to Smith's powerful performance and, though eight bowlers were tried, the Queenslander seemed immovable. Before Hide finally removed Smith after tea, clean bowling her when the latter seemed set on scoring a six, she had made 88 and Australia were 286 for 8. With some 45 minutes left for play, Australia went on batting, adding 14 runs for the last two wickets and finishing with a fine total of 300, the last three wickets falling to Whelan. Fortunately the England bowlers, who appeared to lack penetration at times, were supported by good fielding. Had it been otherwise they might have been facing a much more daunting

Lord Spencer, late Grandfather of HRH The Princess Diana, shaking hands with Amy Hudson as he is presented to the first Australian Touring team to England by their Captain, Mrs Margaret Peden. With him at the Northampton County Cricket Ground in June 1937 is the Club President, Mr S Schilizzi.

Australian score.

There were around 35 minutes of batting before play ended in which England lost a wicket in an unfortunate and unnecessary run out. In failing light, which had never been exactly bright all day, Hide sent in Mollie Child and Muriel Lowe to face the fast bowlers Mollie Flaherty and Kath Smith, thus saving the established pair Maclagan and Snowball for the Monday. With the score on 12, Child misjudged a run from a push to mid-on. Flaherty, the bowler, fielded the ball herself and threw down the wicket. This sharp piece of fielding resulted in a very good day for Australia who crowned their 300 runs with England on 14 for 1 at the close of play.

On a rain affected wicket, Lowe and M. J. Haddelsey resumed for England on the Monday morning. Australia were without Flaherty who had damaged a knee, and opened the attack with Nell McLarty and Smith. With an attacking field the England players found runs difficult to obtain and after an hour's batting only ten runs had been added to the weekend score. Gradually, however, the scoring rate increased and the second wicket fell at 41; Haddelsey being caught by Pritchard off the spin of Antonio for 8. Lowe, who was going well, was then joined by Maclagan who opened with a four off Antonio's last ball. And Maclagan, batting at an unaccustomed number 4, looked to be prepared to settle in.

With the score on 70, Lowe was beaten by McLarty and clean bowled. Her score of 42 had provided a firm foundation on which Maclagan, and now Snowball, could build. For a while it looked as though the renowned pair would do just that, for the runs came steadily. But, on the last ball of Antonio's final over before lunch, Snowball was bowled for 13. At this stage in the game the drying wicket became the spinner's ally, and it was against both Antonio and Walsh, whose flighted off breaks needed watchful concentration, that the players were finding most difficulty.

After lunch Joan Davis gave able support to the resolute Maclagan, and made 19 before she was bowled by Walsh. Hide came and went without scoring, another Walsh victim but brilliantly snapped up by McLarty fielding close in at short leg. Of the last four batsmen, only M. E. Haddelsey and Eileen Whelan required a second hand for counting runs and they, together with Mary Taylor and Betty Belton, were spun out by Antonio who was virtually unplayable and ended with 6 wickets for 51 runs. England were dismissed for 204, 96 runs behind the Australians, with a staunch Maclagan undefeated on 89.

At 3.55 pm Australia opened their second innings with the same pair, Antonio and M. Peden, but this time Peden took first strike. Although both players found runs hard to come by and, indeed, Antonio did not last long enough at the crease in going to Joyce Haddelsey for 1. It was clear that the wicket was still not an encouraging one for fast bowlers. After Pritchard ran herself out for 17, Lowe with her leg breaks, Hide, Davis and Maclagan, spinners all, together with Whelan, carried the bowling and shared the wickets. But for McLarty's robust 23, Australia could have been whittled down to a much lower total than 91 for 9 at the close of play. Although this was heartening for England, there was still a lead of 187 to combat, and the final wicket to take.

After just 8 minutes of play on the third and final day, Australia were all out for 102, the valiant Flaherty being not out 12. The latter was again absent from the field, however, and it was McLarty and Smith who opened the Australian bowling against Maclagan and Snowball.

Progress was good for England, and when Maclagan was caught behind off the bowling of McLarty for 28, a sound opening stand of 58 registered on the scoreboard. At lunch, Davis and Snowball were

Molly Hide (R) captains England against Australia for the first time. She is with Muriel Haddelsey (M E). Vice-captain Betty Snowball (R) shares a smile with newcomer Eileen Whelan. Next are the fast bowling pair Mary Taylor and Betty Belton. Myrtle Maclagan rubs her eye and Joan Davis looks on. Mollie Child talks to hidden players Muriel Lowe or Joyce Haddelsey (M J).

Hazel Pritchard making an off drive during her 87 in the first innings at Northampton. With partner Margaret Peden (34) she established the Australian record 2nd wicket partnership of 127 which still stands. Wicket-keeper Betty Snowball and Betty Belton at slip keenly watch the outcome of the shot.

together with no further loss of wickets and the prospect of getting the necessary runs to win was very possible.

Soon after the interval with the score of 97, Davis was bowled by Smith who was getting the ball to rise disconcertingly off a length. Hide went the same way for only 4, and Child was bowled by Antonio for a single. Meanwhile, Snowball kept the runs coming, cutting and driving as well as giving the slow bowling of Walsh the full treatment.

The situation began to look more dismal for England when 106 for 4 became 106 for 5, the loss being M. E. Haddelsey for a duck, and the bowler Antonio. But Muriel Lowe, stalwart of the first innings, was next to the wicket and appeared confident. She though, and M. J. Haddelsey who followed, fell victim to the fielding skill of McLarty at close short leg, off the bowling of Smith. Taylor and Whelan helped Snowball and the score along, but when Snowball was out lbw to Holmes for a splendid 72, England still had a shortfall of 36 runs. It was Antonio who took the last wicket, bowling Belton for 1, and giving her side victory by a margin of just 31 runs with an hour to spare.

Summary of the First Test 1937

Australia won by 31 runs

Australia:	300 and 102
England:	204 and 167

Best Batting

	1st Innings	
Australia:	K Smith	88
	H Pritchard	87
England:	M Maclagan	89 n o
	M Lowe	42
	2nd Innings	
Australia:	N McLarty	23
	H Pritchard	17
England:	E A Snowball	72
	M Maclagan	28

Best Bowlings

	1st Innings	
England:	M E Hide	3 – 50
	E Whelan	3 – 56
	E Belton	3 – 65
Australia:	P Antonio	6 – 51
	A Walsh	2 – 52
	2nd Innings	
England:	M E Hide	2 – 10
	J Davis	2 – 11
	M Lowe	2 – 40
Australia:	K Smith	4 – 50
	P Antonio	3 – 40
	N McLarty	2 – 11

Highlights

With three players topping the eighties, the Australian pair Smith and Pritchard achieving a first 50, Maclagan her third, and Snowball's valiant 72 giving her a third half-century, honours were even. Antonio's match figures of 38.4 – 9 – 91 – 9: 10.11 was an outstanding effort. If England had the fielding edge in this match it was Australian Nell McLarty who shone by taking 3 catches to add to her 3 wickets at 14.33 apiece.

Blackpool: Stanley Park Cricket Ground, June 26, 28 & 29

With the defeat at Northampton to avenge and the wicket looking good for runs, it was no surprise to see Maclagan and Snowball out in the middle when Hide won the toss. But though Maclagan seemed to settle quite quickly, against the bowling of Flaherty and particularly Smith, Snowball was uncomfortable. On the last ball of Smith's fourth over, a tentative hook which Walsh took easily at square leg, saw the demise of Snowball for 1 run. Davis, too, only managed a single before being bowled by Flaherty and this brought Hide to the crease. After a subdued start, Hide seemed to absorb some of Maclagan's confidence and both players began to score more freely.

At lunch Maclagan had scored 68, her 50 taking some 85 minutes, while Hide was on 19. When play restarted Hide demonstrated her easy style to good effect and both she and Maclagan found boundaries easier to come by. The hundred partnership was not long past before Hide was bowled by McLarty for 34. Two wickets later when 139 for 3 had become 151 for 5, Maclagan was batting fluently on. Hers, however, was the sixth wicket to fall as she played forward to one from Alicia Walsh which beat the bat. Wicketkeeper Alice Wegemund, making her debut in this match, whipped off the bails and Maclagan was stumped for 115; her second Test hundred against Australia had included 15 fours.

With England now looking less secure Lowe came to the wicket and again proved her steadying influence by scoring adroit runs whilst wickets tumbled at the other end. Going in at 155 for 6, Lowe's was the last wicket to fall, she and Belton making a lively stand of 25 while the Australians tried everything they had to capture the last wicket. Success was theirs when Lowe was caught by Barbara Peden off McLarty's bowling for 43, and England had mustered 222 runs.

At 5.05 pm Australia's innings opened with Margaret Peden and Antonio facing up to Belton's pace with Maclagan's spin. A quick breakthrough by Maclagan in her second over was the result of Joyce Haddelsey (M. J.) snapping up a low down catch at extra cover. With a further 20 runs added, Snowball caught Antonio off Belton; 23 for 2, but dangerwoman Pritchard was cruising along confidently. Holmes too, true to current form, kept her head down and scored well. Having resisted all the bowler's efforts, at the close of play Pritchard and Holmes had moved Australia's score along by some 80 runs to put their side in the very comfortable position of 108 for 2.

As though Saturday's weather had just tempted all and sundry to believe that this was one Test Match that would proceed uninterrupted,

Cricket

AUSTRALIA WELL PLACED

Women's Test Match

From our Special Correspondent

NORTHAMPTON, SATURDAY

The first women's Test match ever played in this country was begun here to-day in dull, grey weather. The amount of interest aroused was shown by the attendance, which was a record for the ground, more than six times as great as on any ...... the recent match between ...... New Zealand ...... presid ...... Club, order ...... will ...... at the ...... at the sides ......

A ...... cau ...... the ...... Eng ...... Mi ...... wit ...... Be ...... At ...... M ...... ca ......

luncheon ...... still for one wicket ...... quietly and defensively, while ...... Pritchard showed once again a form which one can confidently say has never before been seen in women's cricket in this country. The only bowler who appeared to give her any trouble was Miss Maclagan, who during the tour of 1934 had her constantly in difficulties. A century, the first of the tour, seemed certain, ... over after lunch prevent ...... rather feats ...... fini ...... al ...... she ...... the ...... sho ...... the ...... broug ...... over ...... Hide, and us ......

The ...... made b ...... girl, w ...... left-hand ...... carefree ...... on both ...... strong ...... noticeab ...... of runs ...... in front ...... glance ...... innings ...... total. The ...... out the d ...... snowball ...... and sale ...... Oldfield an ...... In the d ...... were unfort ...... who allowed ...... needlessly r ......

PEGGY ANTONIO—the Austra-lian "Miss Grimmett"

AUSTRALIA First Innings
...... [scorecard partially illegible] ......

Australian Women Collapse in the Second Innings

MISS HIDE BOWLS WELL FOR ENGLAND

From our Special Correspondent

BLACKPOOL, TUESDAY

At ten past six to-day under blue skies and bright sunshine England won the second women's Test match against Australia by 25 runs. An hour and a half before such a result would have ...... inconceivable the best En ...... for would) ......

beau ...... soon have made ...... in the team t ...... her bowling in ...... been encourag ...... favourite strok ...... unusual one in th ...... is one of the few indeed ...... nod give to her attempts at glancing to leg an air of uncertainty and flukiness. She played a sturdy innings, cutting and gliding the faster bowlers and hitting the slow bowling of Miss Walsh over square-leg's head. Miss Walsh has an excellent action which somehow fails to affect her bowling itself. Her arms describe a perfect cartwheel which reminds those who remember th great bowlers of the past of Col Blythe. But Blythe did not give leap into the air as he delivered th ball, and this may be where Mi Walsh makes her mistake. Natu ...... given her the physique a ...... ural action of a slow bowler, ... adds to them the leap of a fas ...... er, with the result that she loses ...... rol of the ball.

...... ss M. Hide showed again he ...... ful style, cutting and driving ...... ease and elegance. The last ball ...... lunch bowled her, with the ...... 176 for four wickets. After ...... two more wickets fell in quic ...... tion, but after that Miss Child ...... ss Belton by vigorous hitting ...... and sound defence helped to put ...... together the respectable total of 231.

It was decided not to have an interval for tea, and an Australian win seemed almost certain. The Australians began their second

innings and at once set about the bowling. Miss Antonio was guilty in Miss Whelan's second over of a stroke which it was as well her trainer in Australia could not see. Three of the English fielders stood together, but in the end it was decided that the ball when at length it was seen descending should be left for the large white gloves of ...... Miss H. Pritchard ...... another of ...... arefree ...... anship. ...... wicket ...... if wry-

We hav ...... final match of the series ...... e Oval a fortnight hence will be full of interest. Scores

ENGLAND'S CENTURY-MAKER

First innings **ENGLAND** Second innings
...... [scorecard partially illegible] ......

ENGLAND WIN BY 25 RUNS

THRILLING FINISH TO SECOND "TEST"

Total 220	Total	231

First innings **AUSTRALIA** Sec. innings
...... [scorecard partially illegible] ......

THE WOODFULL AND THE BRADMAN TOUCH AT THE OVAL

By J. G. ORANGE
OVAL. Saturday.

The women cricketers of England and Australia played for their Ashes at the Oval to-day. It was the final of the series of three Tests, and each had won one.

It was the Oval's first women's Test, and, though among a fair-sized crowd the electric atmosphere of a men's Test was missing, it was patent to all that it existed out there in the field among the women

For as soon as the Australians had won the toss, M. Peden, their captain, who went out to open with P. Holmes, started to dig herself in in the best Woodfull manner.

She had evidently studied the methods of the men who bat for days in a Test out in Australia. She put the full face of the bat to every ball—slow off-spinners from M. Maclagen, medium-paced right-handers from K. Whelan, and slow left-arm stuff from J. Davis

And while she was plodding along, P. Holmes, with more enterprise and much more freedom, ran up the runs

Men, Please Note

It was noticeable that the field was set to stop all strokes in front of the wicket. There was only one slip, and it was obvious that drives were expected more than anything else.

Evidently women are in-front-of-the-wicket cricketers, and mere man might well make a note of it.

M. Peden looked safe for about a week's batting when she was suddenly out l.b.w. (new rule, I thought!) to J. Davis. This was at 39

In came Hazel Pritchard, star of Australia's batting this tour in spite of that record innings of 200 by P Holmes the other day.

But she was only in for a minute when a junior cloudburst swamped everyone and everything.

Merry Hitting

After two and a half hours' delay and various consultations on the pitch, play was resumed and Miss Holmes at once earned ap------- from the large crowd that was ------
J. Davis to th------
Hazel Pritchar------
aggression and ------
the expense of ------
Australian won ------
lost time.

The spectat------
Hazel Pritchar------
man, and the ------
She had the ------
the same quic------
She really cl------
ing. mainly w------
express rate to the Pavilion rails.

Just Reward

The fieldswomen, for all their fleetness of foot were powerless to stop them.

After the resumption, England ha resorted only to slow spin bowler who got no response from the pitch.

But Miss Hide, England's captain with a little more pace than the other.. met with her due reward for a nice spell of bowling by disturbing the stumps of Australia's captain, Hazel Pritchard, with a beautiful ball, the second wicket falling at 84.

Peggy Antonio, dark and frizzy, made a couple of lucky snicks in her 15; and Miss Holmes was still going strong with 55 at tea, when the score was 124 for 3.

Miss Holmes was Australia's stylist to-day, and she was also Australia's lucky batsman. She was missed off an easy catch in the slips early in her innings, and Miss Lowe fumbled a good chance of running her out at 46.

THE WOMAN BRADMAN   By Harold Gittins

HOW'S THAT?

Those women cricketers were full of "Pep" ... Even in a thunderstorm ... Run out at 99 ... and what Bob Wyatt said.

TO return for a minute to the Pavilion, it was amusing to notice how the lady spectators for the most part had the sense to slip away about 5.30 p.m.

They knew, bless them, that their men-folk must have at least one hour in which to tell each other, in their own words, what they thought of it all!

A word of sympathy for Miss Snowball, of England, who was run out at 99!

MY most vivid impression of the lady cricketers at the Oval, apart from the brilliant footwork and wrist of Miss Pritchard, of Australia—a mirror of Bradman here—was their gay determination to continue play even if it hailed frogs or brimstone.

On the first morning, when a tremendous thunderstorm burst on the ground, the two umpires—who looked, by the way, strangely like two little surgeons at an exciting operation!—stayed out, almost arguing with providence, as once Ajax, they say, defied the lightning!

Then, with a sudden burst they did almost even time to the Pavilion.

AN INTERESTING MATCH DRAWN

FROM OUR CRICKET CORRESPONDENT

The third, and last, Test Match between the women of England and Australia was left drawn at the Oval yesterday, and so each side must remain content with one victory. Every effort possible was made by both sides to obtain a definite result, but too much time had been lost by rain during the first two days, and yesterday there was never a chance of one side beating the other.

Monday gave the players just another facet to contend with: It blew a gale. In very blustery conditions, then, Pritchard and Holmes batted on and saw out the opening few overs without too many qualms. But then medium pacer, Eileen Whelan beat Pritchard completely, taking the middle stump, when the latter's score was 67 and she had added only 5 to her total.

At 121 for 3, it was Kath Smith who joined Holmes. Always a lusty hitter, her first four scoring strokes contained two boundaries, both off the bowling of Haddelsey who was then removed from the attack in favour of Maclagan. Encouraged perhaps, by Smith's vigour, Holmes attempted to do likewise to Maclagan, but either the gale or a mishit sent the ball high to Hide fielding at long off. Despite the cold wind, Hide hung on to the catch and Holmes was out for 44. Not long after Winnie George arrived at the crease, rain stopped play.

When play resumed at 1.40 lunch had been taken. Both George and Smith pushed the score along, though George was the more cautious of the two. Caution paid off, however, because when the next wicket fell, that of Smith, the score was 198 for 5.

Next in was Nell McLarty who failed to add to the total when she was caught and bowled first ball by Maclagan. The seventh wicket, however, with George still there and ably assisted by Barbara Peden, put on 81 runs before the latter was bowled by Hide. The next two wickets, of Walsh and Wegemund, also went similarly to Hide, and Davis disposed of Flaherty with the assistance of a catch by Mollie Child at square leg. The Australian total of 302, with George not out 62, gave a deficit of 80 for England on the first innings.

With a strong wind blowing and the conditions grey and very cold indeed, Hide changed the batting order, sending in Mona Greenwood and Muriel Lowe. Against Flaherty and Smith there were some anxious moments for both players. And when Greenwood was caught behind off Flaherty for 13, her flirtations with the ball rising just outside the off stump were over. Maclagan joined Lowe, and gritting their teeth in the face of the gale and an Australian attack encouraged by the fall of the wicket – 28 for 1 – they settled to see through to the close of play some ten runs ahead and 9 wickets standing.

Grey skies still accompanied the resumption of the England innings on the final day. Lowe and Maclagan continued batting soundly until, with nine runs added to her overnight score of 40, Maclagan was beaten by Flaherty's pace to be clean bowled. Snowball joined Lowe but was soon caught at square by substitute Elsie Deane (replacing an injured Barbara Peden) off the medium pace bowling of Holmes. Hide was next in and she and Lowe continued in good form until just before lunch when Antonio was brought into the attack. With the first ball of her third over she bowled Hide for 31, and the England score was 176 for 4 wickets.

If England were to have any chance of winning it was clear that quick runs were needed. Past experience had shown how the Aussies could stick at it when under pressure. And yet, the second innings at Northampton had indicated that they were also vulnerable. But things were certainly going England's way when all too quickly after lunch Antonio continued to spin her way through the wickets. After McLarty bowled Lowe for 57, Antonio dismissed Davis for a duck aided by Wegemund's stumping skill. This combination was also responsible for Haddelsey's wicket and three wickets were down for 8 runs. But Child and Belton managed to stay there and put on a few runs until the latter holed out to Antonio for a more than useful 25 runs. Both Taylor and Whelan failed to score, leaving Child not out 19 and Australia about 165 minutes to make 152 runs.

Margaret Peden obviously knew her capabilities when, instead of opening herself, she sent in Holmes with Antonio; it was hardly the time for slow scoring but possibly wickets for runs were a tolerable beginning. First to go was Antonio for 4, caught behind off Whelan in the first bowling change. Pritchard, who replaced her, struck the ball as well and confidently as ever, and the initial setback was soon changed to a bright outlook as the 50 partnership was passed.

Another change of bowling which again brought Whelan into the attack resulted in Pritchard's wicket; she was clean bowled for 41. Kath Smith was only at the crease briefly before Whelan had her caught by Snowball for a duck. Australia were then 68 for 3, but time was still on their side. For a while it looked as though Winnie George and Pat Holmes would see their team through to victory but then, in the fourth over of her second spell, Hide had Holmes lbw. Again and a quick wicket followed when Flaherty was clean bowled in Hide's subsequent over for a duck. Walsh was next in and soon out, this time caught by Lowe off Hide. In this inspired spell Hide had taken 3 wickets for 5 runs and Australia had collapsed from 68 for 3 to 93 for 6. This was soon 93 for 7 when McLarty repeated her first innings first ball demise – this time caught Davis bowled Hide.

It was at this stage of the game that the Australian Captain batted. Her stay at the wicket was short, however, being caught in the slips by Belton off Maclagan for 3. Belton was again the catcher and Maclagan the bowler when Wegemund went – also for 3. The Australian score was then 110 for 9 and it was the turn of injured Barbara Peden to bat. Valiantly the last wicket partnership, Winnie George was still there, battled on for the runs but finally, and fittingly, the last wicket went to Hide when Peden was lbw for 2. George was not out 34 in the Australian total of 126. England had won this exciting and tantalising Test by 25 runs with twenty minutes left for play.

Summary of the Second Test 1937

England won by 25 runs

England:	222 and 231
Australia:	302 and 126

Best Batting

	1st Innings	
England:	M Maclagan	115
	M Lowe	43
	M E Hide	34
Australia:	H Pritchard	67
	K Smith	63
	W George	62 n o

	2nd Innings	
England:	M Lowe	57
	M Maclagan	49
	M E Hide	31
Australia:	H Pritchard	41
	W George	34 n o
	P Holmes	33

Best Bowling

1st Innings

Australia:	P Antonio	3 – 34
	N McLarty	2 – 29
	M Flaherty	2 – 45
	K Smith	2 – 57
England:	M E Hide	3 – 38
	M Maclagan	3 – 78

2nd Innings

Australia:	P Antonio	5 – 31
	N McLarty	2 – 25
England:	M E Hide	5 – 20
	E Whelan	3 – 35

Highlights

For Maclagan another triumph with the bat – over half of her 115 came in boundaries – and a creditable performance with the ball with a match analysis: 50-19-107-5. Another 50 for Pritchard confirmed her quality, but without George, Smith (the latter notching up her second 50) and Holmes, Australia's position would have been more vulnerable. Antonio's bowling was superb, her 8 match wickets coming off only 23 overs. For England Hide was outstanding, averaging 7.25 for her 8 wickets. Although England triumphed by the margin of 'extras', wicketkeeper Wegemund made a record 7 dismissals in the match with 5 stumpings and 2 catches: A magnificent Test debut.

Kennington, London: The Oval, July 10, 12 & 13, 1937

The third and final Test Match which took place on the famous turf of the Surrey County Cricket Club was one full of the promise that a so far drawn series between two equally balanced sides could produce. It had the potential to be as exciting, thrilling and rewarding to watch as any game of cricket with the same ingredients anywhere. This is how women followers of cricket saw it, and in particular, a pioneering enthusiast for the game: author, journalist and broadcaster Marjorie Pollard. An exceptionally brilliant hockey player who represented England from 1921-28 and 1931-33 and twice scored all the goals in winning matches (13 against Wales and 8 against Germany), cricket for Marjorie Pollard was very much a second game. Although an excellent player, she did not represent her country but did more – in the communication field – to promote cricket for women than anyone since, with the exception perhaps of Netta Rheinberg.

Without doubt, Pollard would have played in a Test Match had the series in England been even five years earlier. As it was, she followed the 1937 Tour writing on most of the matches in the official magazine *Women's Cricket*, which she founded and edited for some 19 years. This unique record in diary form shows much of the character of a great sportswoman and entertaining writer. Not only that, it gives some-

Marjorie Pollard (1899–1982): outstanding sportswoman, pioneering journalist and broadcaster for both hockey and cricket, and a woman of resolute qualities and unfailing friendship.

HRH The Duchess of Gloucester seen here shaking hands with Audrey Collins, the current President of the Women's Cricket Association, who was then making her début for England. It is The Oval on a gloomy day in July 1936 and Captain Molly Hide, presents her team to the Duchess. The series against the Australians is even. Rain won the day, however, and the match and the series was drawn.

thing of the flavour of 'the times'. For all these reasons it seems apposite to let Marjorie Pollard tell the story of the Third Test, with the hope that it loses nothing in some necessary, but slight, editing.

"For months now we have been saying to each other 'See you at the Oval,' and the first of three great days has gone. History was being made all day, and because 6,123 people paid to see the match the fact was evidently appreciated. But it is not my intention in this diary to talk of fulfilment and such things, rather to give my idea of the game as I saw it. Here I would like to make a thing clear. These views and thoughts I set down are my views. I do not expect anyone to believe them or take them as 'official' truth. I give you my impression of what I saw and set out for you my reactions. This is not an infallible chronicle, it is just my diary.

"This morning after Molly Hide tossed a coin, a great notice appeared, 'Toss won by Visitors,' and so Australia were going to bat. The wicket looked perfect, but who could say what the weather was going to do. Great clouds lolled about in a bluish sky – but the visibility was too good. The great gasometer looked within poking distance (I'd love to give it a poke), and I could see the spire of Westminster Cathedral just as if it was a hundred yards away.

The English team took the field, followed by Mrs. Peden and Pat Holmes (sans chapeau), and the third Test Match had begun. B. Belton bowled to Mrs. Peden from the Vauxhall end, and for twenty minutes I felt that Australia and England were sparring for openings, everything seemed tentative. Then came a short, sharp shower, and the players ran in. After a quarter of an hour out they came.

"Runs came steadily, bowlers were changed, the fielding was excellent, and when the score was 39, Mrs Peden was lbw to Mrs Davis. That was a good start because Mrs. Peden is one of those batsmen who can stay for hours, and often does.

"So Hazel Pritchard arrived and she and Pat Holmes scored a run or two, and then the blackest cloud imaginable came up from Westminster, and in less than no time the Oval was afloat. Rain, hail and wind swept across it, and the dismals said no more cricket today.

"But at 3.0 o'clock the players were out again, after the umpries had harried Martin the groundsman, who at first gave the impression as he walked his sacred turf, that on no account should the Oval be used for cricket.

"Now, what was this pitch going to do? Before the covers were rushed on, rain had soaked it.

"A ball popped here and there, but Holmes and Pritchard went quite gaily on. They both made lovely strokes but when Pritchard had made 28 (5 fours and the rest singles), she was clean bowled by Hide, a grand ball to which Pritchard went neither forward not back, she draped her bat and, I feel, hoped for the best and got the worst. That was 2 wickets for 84.

"Peggy Antonio was next, and she was cautious – very. Holmes was going on nicely and quite confidently now. She passed her fifty with a sumptuous clout to the on boundary and then Antonio, who was as comfortable as a cat on griddle, cocked up an easy catch to Lowe in the slips and that was 3 for 120.

"This was a good score we felt, and there were George, Smith, Hudson, still to come. George was in next, and she is a grand bat to watch. She has a watchful period, and then just when least expected, she cracks the ball through the covers in anything but mincing style.

She hit three 4's in a row, gorgeous shots they were, and then closed the shutters again, and then later, had another outburst.

"Things were getting a bit serious. It was 5.30 (the light was shocking) and 150 was on the board. 160 went up and then Hide put Mrs. Davis on to bowl.

"The first ball she tossed up, George hit quite peacefully into the air and it came to rest in the hands of square leg. That was 4 for 167 and about time, too, we said, still not dreaming what was about to happen.

"In came Kath Smith and we expected fireworks. The score went to 175 and in her next over Mrs. Davis clean bowled Smith for 3. There was no denying that it was a good ball – it pitched on the leg stump and took the off bail and Smith, whose defence is as sound as England's will be after the rearmament, was beaten. 5 for 174. Pat Holmes, who had made 70 very precious runs, was the next to go; two balls later Mrs. Davis got her lbw and that was 6 for 175.

"Here, excitement must not let us forget that this innings of Holmes was a little masterpiece. It was made through many interruptions – rain, rain, tea – and she had been at the wickets since 11.30. I am glad

Maclagan, caught and bowled McLarty 34, Australian fast bowler Nell McLarty, still wearing her hat, makes this spectacular dive to dismiss opener Myrtle Maclagan at The Oval in 1937. Alicia Walsh is at slip and the wicketkeeper is Alice Wegemund.

she has done so well. She will play for Australia for a very long time.

"Nell McLarty had several fruitless goes at Mrs. Davis and then she hit one up that we thought would go for four. But no! Up went Mrs Davis' hand, and she held a superb catch, and that was 7 for 179.

"The air was now electric, the fielding magnificent and the game a complete thrill.

"A. Hudson and A. Walsh were together and it was six o'clock.

"Taylor came on to bowl and in her thrid over she got Walsh snapped up by Greenwood at point and the scoreboard said 8 for 198.

"Such a game is cricket: 4 for 167 to 8 for 198 in half an hour, and in four overs Mrs. Davis took four wickets for 10 runs – a wonderful performance.

"Mollie Flaherty and Amy Hudson then gently and firmly led the game to its close. A. Hudson resisted all endeavours from the crowd to 'have a go' – her bat was straight, her smile was brilliant. Flaherty, living dangerously and precariously, survived and so Australia will bat again on Monday. The score is 201 for 8 wickets.

"It is three hours since I broadcast from London in the ten o'clock news. What a burden keeping a diary is, to be sure.

"This in a way has been a grand day for England and of course not so good for Australia. Play before lunch was ruined by drizzle which turned to rain, and when it was over Australia, seeing that time was very precious, declared with their score at 207 for 9.

"England had to bat just before lunch. The light was shocking, but the pitch had rolled out into an easy paced wicket, and Maclagan and Snowball found no great difficulty in scoring 19 runs in 20 minutes.

"After lunch, still with a drizzle of rain falling, the game went on. Maclagan was making the runs and was showing us what an accomplished batsman she is. Then with her score at 34 and the total at 50, she was c and b McLarty.

"At 59 Mrs. Davis was clean bowled by Walsh; and then Hide came in and she and Snowball put on 134 runs before they were parted. These two made hay of the Australian bowling and Hide certainly did give us a fascinating display of driving. She hit the ball with tremendous power and it was really good to see freshness and spontaneity back again in her batting. When she had made as good a 60 as ever she has made, she was bowled by Walsh, and the score was 193 for 3.

"At about 4 o'clock, amidst all this grand run getting by Hide and Snowball the Duchess of Gloucester arrived. Both teams were presented to her on the field, and later she took tea with them.

"After tea Greenwood and Snowball took the score along to 227,

Snowball had then reached 96. She had been cutting and hooking in great style, and on her really, had been built up the England total. The Australian bowlers with the exception of McLarty (who seemed to bowl nothing but maidens) were not at their best. The fielding also was scrappy, but Amy Hudson was throwing the ball immense distances with that lovely easy action of hers. So the day ended with England in a very strong position having scored 227 for 3 wickets.

"I wonder why Mrs. Peden did not use Antonio more? I wonder why Walsh was not put on earlier? I wonder – so we (the knowalls) go on. What a life it must be to be a captain. If England can proceed until lunch time like they did this afternoon, they will be in a winning position. But, will the Australian attack be as blunt and leisurely as it was to-day? I wonder.

"The situation after two days of cricket is this: Australia 207 for 9 dec. England 227 for 3.

"So, England must go for runs like mad in the morning, establish a lead of about 180, if possible, and then set about getting Australia out ; but I feel Australia will not be dictated to like this. They will have more than a say in the matter. So we must wait and see.

"A lovely, sunny day, with a blue sky; in fact, a day that was made for cricket. And we saw a grand game go to a tame draw. A game full of incident just tailed off and we have lived to see Whelan and Taylor open for England. But here is the story.

"England 227 for 3, had as their plan of campaign a rapid 130 odd runs before lunch. Splendid thought. But, the plan miscarried, for the very simple reason that Australia this morning were a totally different side as compared with yesterday afternoon. If I live to see more accurate bowling than that of McLarty's, I shall be surprised. If I see a cleverer spin bowler than Antonio I shall not only be surprised, but a genuine disbeliever. Well at the end of an hour's toil England had harvested – with pain and tribulation – 40 runs, and there, had we but known it was one of the several reasons why the game turned into a draw.

"Snowball missed her century by 1 run, just 1 miserable run. She was run out by that accurate thrower Flaherty, who from 30 yards wrecked the wicket. When Archdale and Collins were together things did look up, and the law and the scholar (there is nothing subtle intended there) put on 55 runs in half an hour, and retrieved, as far as they were able, a desperate situation. Just about 1 o'clock Hide declared. The score was 308 for 9, and McLarty had bowled 37 overs – 20 maidens and taken 3 wickets for 29. Can you beat that? (NO! even the knowalls couldn't).

"So England were 101 runs on and a whole side still ready to bat.

"Australia batted for the miserable twenty minutes before lunch, and off the first ball of the innings Belton got Mrs. Peden caught at the wicket – 1 for 0.

"But Holmes and Pritchard stayed put, and came into lunch, after the English Team. Why do the English players always come off before the batsmen? (Now we, the knowalls, were taught at school . . .)

"After lunch Holmes was bowled by Whelan for 6. Well, we'll let that pass. The score was 2 for 18 and we had strong visions of an innings victory for England. But Hazel Pritchard, who drove with perfect ease and grace, hit the first ball she received for 4, went on to make 66, and the Oval Old Boy' Association said they'd never seen anything like it before. We certainly are fostering women's cricket among Oldish Gentlemen (and young gentlemen also), it's a pity there were not a few more girls and young women about, to be so impressed that they straightway wanted to go home and play cricket.

"Peggy Antonio had a great hand in this stand. She was a noble soul, and she certainly kept her end going while Pritchard put on the runs. When Pritchard went the score was 94 for 3. Antonio went at 119. She had made 37. W. George went at 128, the result of a marvellous piece of stumping by Snowball, much approved by a certain section of the O.O.B.A.

"Kath Smith put paid to all hopes of a win for England, and I must admit up till 5 o'clock I still hoped it could be done. She, with that cracking off drive, and lightning pull shot, made 45, and fairly burned up the grass on the Oval. She went at 176, and now we could see only a draw ahead.

"Australia just went on playing cricket, calmly and sensibly to plan. England were still in the field, aching to be batting, but Australia were not out till 6.10, and by that time they had scored 224. A. Walsh made a quick 24, and she proved me to be untruthful, because she can drive and hook as well as cut. Good for Alicia. The last I saw of her at the Oval was when she was blushingly receiving compliments from a veteran O.O.B.

"England went in to bat at 6.20, and E. Whelan and M. Taylor opened the innings. Flaherty and McLarty bowled, and in the next ten minutes England made 9 runs and lost three wickets – and that was that.

Summary of the Third Test 1937

Match Drawn

Australia: 207 for 9 dec and 224
England: 308 for 9 and 9 for 3 wickets

Best Batting

	1st Innings	
Australia:	P Holmes	70
	W George	34
England:	E A Snowball	99
	M E Hide	64
	M Maclagan	34

	2nd Innings	
Australia:	H Pritchard	66
	K Smith	45
	P Antonio	37

Best Bowling

	1st Innings	
England:	J Davis	5 – 31
Australia:	N McLarty	3 – 29
	P Antonio	2 – 56
	A Walsh	2 – 58

	2nd Innings	
England:	J Davis	3 – 55
	M Maclagan	3 – 58
	B Belton	2 – 26
Australia:	M Flaherty	2 – 4

Highlights

Holmes registered her first Test fifty and Pritchard her third in Tests and in the series, giving her top of the averages status with 51.00. George was the runner up with 42.50. As to the bowling, the magnificent Antonio finished with 19 in the series at 11.15 apiece. Here, though, McLarty did very well to end up with a match average of 11.33 off 38 overs, 20 of which were maidens.

The most unfortunate run-out of Snowball robbed her of her only Test century against Australia but, nevertheless, provided her fourth 50 in Test cricket and her second of the series. Interestingly this was Hide's first 50 against Australia and her highest score against that country in Tests. Bowling honours in this match belonged to Davis who, apart from the outstanding first innings feat of 5 wickets, had her 8 – 86 off 30.4 overs. She topped the series averages with 11.36, though Hide took more wickets, 14 to Davis's 11, for her 12.64.

ENGLAND IN AUSTRALIA AND NEW ZEALAND 1948 – 1949

Britain in 1948 might still be suffering the post-war pangs of rationed goods though bread had just, in July, been reprieved, but in the things that really mattered, optimism was uppermost. So it was that the Women's Cricket Association team, several of whom had been selected for the aborted 1939 Tour, held high hopes that good cricket as well as a cut of the good life awaited them down under.

Molly Hide captained a formidable squad in Betty Snowball (Vice Captain), Myrtle Maclagan, Grace Morgan (all four veterans of 1934/35), Dorothy McEvoy, Mary Johnson, Megan Lowe, Netta Rheinberg (Manager/Player), Aline Brown, Barbara Wood, Joan Wilkinson, Eileen Whelan, Betty Birch, Mary Duggan, Nancy Joy, Cecilia Robinson and Hazel Sanders. These representatives, covering all territories but largely from the South and North of England, left Tilbury on October 14, at 9 pm on the Orient Line *Orion*. They were facing ship-board life for the better part of a month.

First stop for cricket – Colombo, Ceylon (now Sri Lanka). Overwhelming success here despite shaky sea legs. Not only does the team win by 111 runs, but Molly Hide scores a century, and the spin bowler Lowe manages a hat trick in her 3 for 2; capturing the last three wickets. Was it to be this way in Australia though?

AUSTRALIA 1948/49

The *Orion* docked at Fremantle on November 9, and by midday the tourists were installed in their Perth hotel. Is it any wonder that diarists of the times, among records of the kindness and good nature of hosts who became friends, cannot help mention the pleasure of scenery unravaged by war, tables laden with many varieties of food, and of menus promising even more. But the serious stuff of cricket practice, which followed and preceded receptions and speeches galore, was essential if the team were to be fit and not fat.

With the first Test over a month away, quite a few matches were

The tour of Australia and New Zealand was cancelled when war was declared in 1939. The touring party would have been, standing L-R: Aline Brown, Grace Morgan, Peggy Sulman, Audrey Collins, Betty Belton, Freda Iredale, Dorothy McEvoy, Megan Lowe, Margaret Williamson. Sitting: Eileen Whelan, Betty Snowball (v-Capt.), Betty Archdale (Capt.), E Parish (Manager), Barbara Blaker, Muriel Lowe.

scheduled, and these covered the Western and Southern States as well as Queensland and New South Wales. And travelling those vast distances can be very tiring. Nevertheless, England's happy band of tourists survived to do battle with the full strength Australian side without losing a match. The tally up to that time was: played 11, won 7, drawn 4.

Adelaide: The Adelaide Oval, January 15, 17 & 18, 1949

Overnight rain was succeeded by a cloudy, windy morning but this did not prevent play starting promptly at 10.30 in sunshine, nor did it cause Mollie Dive to contemplate anything other than batting when she won the toss for Australia. Who knows whether she began to doubt these tactics when after just twenty eight minutes, three wickets were down for only 19 runs; her own included in an unfortunate run out? That, together with the dismissal of Schmidt and Hudson by fast bowler McEvoy, brought Una Paisley and Betty Wilson together, batting at 4 and 5. But drama followed drama as Wilson offered a comparatively straight-forward catch to Rheinberg in the slips before she had scored; a chance the unhappy Netta failed to grasp. Maclagan was the bowler and how she must have lamented the sight of the arch-rival spinner getting away with it so easily before she had the opportunity to settle. Settle Wilson did, however, and with her a sound Paisley. When lunch was taken at 12.30 the Australian score was 95 for 3.

Soon after the interval Wilson's 50 came up and was greeted by an appreciative crowd. She raced on to her century batting brilliantly. Meanwhile, Paisley, who stayed to make the 100 partnership in 111 minutes, was out leg before to Hide for 46. The next two bats, McLintock and Larter stayed a total of 17 minutes at the crease for 3 and

Safely arrived at Fremantle, Western Australia, the England's 1948-9 tourists are: Back Row L-R: Aline Brown, Eileen Whelan, Nancy Joy, Dorothy McEvoy, Mary Johnson, Mary Duggan, Barbara Wood, Hazel Sanders, Betty Birch. Middle Row L-R: Cecilia Robinson, Myrtle Maclagan, Megan Lowe, Joan Wilkinson, Grace Morgan. Front: Betty Snowball, Molly Hide, Netta Rheinberg.

The first post-war England Test Team to tour Australia and New Zeland in 1948/9. Standing L-R: Hazel Sanders, Mary Johnson, Cecilia Robinson, Eileen Whelan, Nancy Joy (12th), Megan Lowe, Netta Rheinberg. Sitting: Dorothy McEvoy, Betty Snowball (Vice-capt. & Wkt) Molly Hide (Capt.), Myrtle Maclagan, Mary Duggan.

1 respectively, both going to Hide. At this stage the Australian score was 154 for 6. Joyce Christ came to the wicket and made a sprightly 12 before being the first to be run out in a sequence of three such dismissals which finally included the wicket of Betty Wilson.

Tea was taken as a result of play being stopped by rain; the total was 204 for 5, of which Wilson had scored 111. Play recommenced in proper time, but Alma Vogt was soon lbw to pace bowler Johnson who had toiled well for this one wicket, appearing to have borne the brunt of a Wilson in full flow. The not out batsman was Myrtle Craddock who had added 9 runs towards the total of 213.

With 84 minutes to go before play ended for the day, England openers Maclagan and Robinson had no need to feel hurried into precipitate action. As this suited the temperaments of both players admirably, consolidation was undoubtedly the name of the game. When Maclagan was at the wrong end of a run out decision some 40 minutes later, she'd made 4. At close of play, England were a dreary 21 for 2. Mary Duggan who had stonewalled for 40 minutes for her single, was out caught by Hudson off the bowling of Wilson, having lashed out just five minutes before time. Nightwatchman Sanders managed to hold things together, all, that is, except for losing a piece of tooth which was removed when the last ball of the day disconcertingly popped up to hit her in the mouth. The sign of a changing wicket perhaps?

Conditions on the Monday after the rest day were perfect for cricket. It was sunny; the wicket was considered easy to good for batting. In only 14 minutes England advanced her score by 16 runs – but, unfortunately, with the loss of Sanders' wicket. Now Molly Hide came to the crease and treated the full toss from Whiteman with suitable disrespect, but had to run the resulting four. After playing a very watchful Wilson over, however, Hide was bowled by a beautiful off-break from Craddock. England's score was 41 for 4 when Vice-Captain Snowball joined Robinson. Yet again, however, Robbie was to see a salutary departure; Snowball adding just 1 in her 16 minutes at the

Pictured at the famous Adelaide Oval in 1949, the Australian team which won the first Test by 186 runs. Back Row (L-R): Lorna Larter, Myrtle Craddock, Amy Hudson, Joan Schmidt, June Ingham (12th), Joyce Christ. Sitting (L-R): F McLintock, Betty Wilson, Mollie Dive (capt.), Una Paisley (Vice-capt.), Norma Whiteman, Alma Vogt. Australia won the series 1-0: two Tests were drawn.

wicket. But worse was to follow when Rheinberg was stumped by Larter off Wilson for a duck. England at 46 for 6 was succumbing to the spin bowling, particularly that of Wilson who had taken 3 for 14 at this stage.

And nor did the tail manage to wag with any conviction. Though the last four wickets fell with the addition of 26 runs, the very last to go was Robinson's. Her stolid 34 in 215 minutes was hardly the debut any opening bat would wish to remember, but it represented just over half of England's scoring shots in the total of 72. Betty Wilson, Australia's spinning genius, ended the innings with 6 for 23.

Though England too had her share of better than average spinners in Maclagan, Hide, Lowe and Sanders, surprisingly, Hide chose not to use the first innings opening attack of McEvoy and Maclagan, one fast one slow, but put on Johnson with McEvoy in an all-pace attack. These two did very well in restraining Schmidt and Hudson, giving away only 24 runs in their first total spell of 17 overs. True, it took the Australians just under half as long to bring up the 25 (45 as opposed to

The inimitable Betty Wilson on her way to a classic 111 at Adelaide in 1949 with this glide to mid-wicket off the bowling of Mary Duggan. The fielders are: Dorothy McEvoy third man, second slip Eileen Whelan, first slip Netta Rheinberg, wicketkeeper Betty Snowball and, back to camera, Cecilia Robinson.

The last wicket falls in the 1st Test at the Adelaide Oval, January 1949, when Una Paisley bowls Eileen Whelan for a duck. Australian wicketkeeper, Lorna Larter, in suspended animation speaks for the whole side.

England's 104 minutes) and without loss of wickets. Even so, to make certain of winning, Australia needed to ensure that she didn't bat on the last day.

The first change bowler was Maclagan who started with a maiden. With the second ball of her second over she saw Schmidt well caught at square leg by Hide, and Australia had made 24 for 1. Next to go was Mollie Dive who, in playing back to Maclagan, stepped on her wicket. At 28 for 2, Paisley joined Hudson who was batting cautiously but solidly. The two of them withstood the efforts of Maclagan and second medium-pace bowler Duggan until tea, and for nearly an hour after tea they resisted all other attempts to remove them. Then their 66 run partnership ended when Paisley was bowled by Johnson for 29. With Australia on 94 and 235 ahead, the fielding side, who'd not made the most of some very possible chances, could hardly have greeted the sight of Betty Wilson's approach to the wicket with other than fortitude. But this was the time for Australia to make quick runs – there was just under an hour to close of play – and Wilson wasted no time in getting on with the job. Hudson, too, hit out and the pair of them cruised along until the wicket was thrown down by Sanders to run out

Wilson.

At 140 for 4 and 281 ahead, Australia were still in the hunt for runs. McLintock knocked up a speedy 11 and was then caught and bowled, hitting a skier to Duggan. Wicketkeeper Larter played out the last quarter of an hour for four not out and Hudson ended the day 81 not out. Australia finished with 173 for 5, scored in 195 minutes, to be a splendid 314 ahead.

More fine, warm weather greeted England's attempt to score 315 to win in 330 minutes, when Dive declared on the morning of the third and final day. Once again the established pair of Maclagan and Robinson opened, but thereafter, with the first wicket falling at 24, the batting order was adjusted. Hide went in at number 3 when Maclagan was bowled by Whiteman for 10 with a ball that hit the pitch and never looked up. But Hide played well, making 30 in 29 minutes before going, again, to Craddock. This time, however, the catch which dismissed her was one brilliantly taken by Whiteman fielding at close mid-off. Whiteman appeared to pluck the hard hit, lofted drive out of the air. Robinson was next out, well caught in the slips after moving her feet in an attempt to get Wilson away. Snowball, batting 4, supported an aggressive Duggan in a short stand of 21 runs, before she was bowled by Whiteman for 1. Rheinberg was next at the wicket, staying there for 5 minutes without receiving a ball. She was then clean bowled first ball by Wilson.

At 77 for 5 England was beginning to look hard pressed to make up the 238 run deficit; the heroine of the Australian hour being Norma Whiteman who had a hand in three of the five wickets to fall. But at lunch, Duggan and Sanders were still there.

Just five minutes after the break, Sanders became Whiteman's third bowled victim, having made 10 runs. Ten minutes later Duggan was caught at square leg by Paisley off Craddock. And then though first McEvoy followed by Lowe and Johnson hit out well, within the hour after lunch Australia became victorious by the large margin of 186 runs.

Summary of the First Test 1948-9

Australia won by 186 runs

Australia:	213 and 173 for 5 dec.
England:	72 and 128

Best Batting

1st Innings

Australia:	B Wilson	111
	U Paisley	46
England:	C Robinson	34

2nd Innings

Australia:	A Hudson	81 n o
	U Paisley	29
England:	M E Hide	30
	M B Duggan	24

Best Bowling

1st Innings

England:	M E Hide	3 – 24
	D McEvoy	2 – 43
Australia:	B Wilson	6 – 23
	M Craddock	1 – 15

2nd Innings

England:	M Maclagan	2 – 42
Australia:	N Whiteman	4 – 33
	B Wilson	3 – 39
	M Craddock	2 – 22

Highlights

Wilson's century represented the first in a Test v England and her 6 – 23 remains the best analysis for The Adelaide Oval. All the honours are Australia's here for the 115 partnership between Wilson and Paisley took only 129 minutes. Whiteman, too, did nobly in being a participant in 6 dismissals in England's second innings.

Melbourne: Melbourne Cricket Ground, January 28, 29 & 31

In the ten days lapse between the first and second Tests, only two matches were played. Though these provided a comparative run bonanza for the tourists, who amassed some 500 in a total of about ten hours play, the going was easy and perhaps not the serious, demanding kind of practice that a run up to a Test match warranted.

The England team that took to the field, for once again Mollie Dive won the toss, was without an unfit McEvoy but included Wilkinson who had completely recovered from the eye problem which had kept her out of the first Test. Medium-fast bowler Barbara Wood replaced McEvoy and the Australians too had switched fast bowlers; Flaherty was in replacing Vogt.

In very hot, humid conditions Johnson and Maclagan opened the attack against Schmidt and Hudson, and they toiled in opposition to a pair unwilling to take risks with the steady bowling. In all, six bowlers were used in the 2 hours before lunch, only Megan Lowe bowling more than 9 overs at a stretch. The more pacey bowlers were used in much shorter spells owing, no doubt, to the sultry weather and the unyielding pitch. But such tactics brought little reward, except in the accumulation of maidens – Lowe totalled 8 in her first 10 overs – so that at lunch Australia was around the seventy mark without loss. Schmidt was on 26 and Hudson 38.

After the interval, however, the intrepid Lowe made the break-through by getting Hudson lbw; thereby achieving a wicket maiden. Johnson, who'd bowled steadily thus far, was hit to the boundary by Dive who looked as though she meant business. But she was next to go, another Lowe victim, for 10 runs. 85 for 2, became 90 for 3 when Schmidt was bowled – again by Lowe. Things were beginning to look better for England but then Wilson joined Paisley who was already batting comfortably.

A noticeable increase in the scoring rate was the first sign of the confidence this pair seemed to exude, no matter what the bowling. But it was a careless call that severed the partnership when Wilson was run out by a controlled Robinson return to the bowler's end. Wilson had made 33 of the 49 that the fourth wicket partnership put on. But Paisley did not survive her for long, being caught behind off Johnson for 23 just on the tea interval.

In a temperature not far short of a 'ton' (for so the Aussies like to term 100°F) England stuck to their bowling guns and fielded admirably. McLintock and 'keeper Larter totted up a few, however, and Christ, batting 8, defied the England attack with spirit in her 42 scored in 52 minutes. The last two Australian wickets put on 31, and the side was all out six minutes before the close with 265 on the board.

The familiar sight of Maclagan and Robinson heralded the start of England's innings the following day. In the same sultry conditions as hitherto, Flaherty and Whiteman opened the Australian attack. For 15 overs 'Mac' and Robbie battled it out and kept their ends up for some time against the spin of Wilson and Craddock. The pace of scoring was not too rapid, though Maclagan, when stumped by Larter off Wilson for 36, was going at more than twice Robinson's rate. 50 for 1, however, was not too bad a basis from which to build a reasonable score. Hide started her innings somewhat shakily and soon went to a gift of a catch taken by Flaherty off Wilson at square. With the score at 64 for 2, real disaster followed when Wilkie and Snowball were out to Wilson, Christ taking both catches.

At 64 for 4, Duggan entered the arena and managed to stay put until lunch. The middle order collapse was not staved off for long, for when Christ caught Duggan – her third successive catch – off Paisley's spinners, Sanders was subsequently caught and bowled by the same bowler for a duck. 82 for 6 soon became 86 for 7. And still the gallant Robbie, repeating her role in the Adelaide Test, held up one end. But it was now that she saw the need to put on a few – for want of partners – and she was stumped off the bowling of Hudson, newly brought into the attack. Johnson, who'd effected something of a stand with Robbie, was out in the same over, having contributed 11 useful runs. Whelan remained the not out batsman with 6 when the England innings closed at 118.

In the half-hour after tea, Maclagan removed both Australian openers to make the score 10 for 2; a brighter prospect for England. But Wilson was sent in as first wicket down and captain Mollie Dive joined her at number 4. These two then scored freely off all the bowling, so that at close of play Australia was 106 for 2, with Wilson on 51 and Dive 46. The hundred had come up in 101 minutes.

Just on 30 minutes into play on the morning of Monday, January 31, saw Dive declare the Australian innings closed at 158 for 4 wickets; a lead of 305.

With England needing 306 to win, the portents were all in Australia's favour when, in her second over, Whiteman bowled a yorker to remove Robinson for a duck. Hide took her now customary number 3 position and, after a tentative start, hit out well. Maclagan, too, was going steadily and the pair of them brought up the 50 in 60 minutes. At lunch they were still together with Hide on 31 and Maclagan 20.

Needing not only to score with the clock, but to consolidate the good start, it looked as though England had managed just that when Hide was out to a dolly, taken by Whiteman off Wilson, at short leg. Wilkinson scored one boundary in the thirteen runs it took 40 minutes to acquire, before being lbw to Dive. Snowball stayed even longer for 7 before becoming Wilson's second victim. Meanwhile, as the pace became too nearly a non-winning one, Maclagan remained steadfastly at the wicket. Both Duggan and Sanders made 2, but when the latter was out, only 29 minutes remained for play. Australia, requiring 4 wickets, could afford give-away runs since England was still 143 behind. It was definitely time for stonewall tactics if the visitors were not to lose the series. But that goal was not achieved without the loss of Maclagan's wicket. Her 77 was scored in 266 minutes, the not out bats Lowe and Johnson made 4 and 1 respectively, and the final score was 171 for 7.

Summary of the Second Test 1948-9

Match Drawn

Australia:	265 and 158 for 4 dec
England:	118 and 171 for 7

Best Batting

1st Innings

Australia:	J Christ	42
	A Hudson	39
England:	C Robinson	41
	M Maclagan	36

2nd Innings

Australia:	B Wilson	74
	M Dive	51
England:	M Maclagan	77
	M Hide	51

Best Bowling

1st Innings

England:	M Lowe	3 – 34
	M Hide	2 – 30
Australia:	B Wilson	4 – 25
	A Hudson	3 – 9
	U Paisley	3 – 10

2nd Innings

England:	M Maclagan	3 – 69
	M Johnson	1 – 40
Australia:	B Wilson	2 – 37
	A Hudson	2 – 37

Highlights

In the highest innings total as yet, no Australian made 50. In dismissing England for less than half their first innings total, no-one was bowled. Larter got three stumpings and Christ made three catches. The third wicket partnership of 123 between Wilson and Dive was a new Australian record. The similar second innings stand between Maclagan and Hide raised 79 runs.

Sydney: Sydney Cricket Ground, February 19, 20 & 21

Now fast approaching their last few days in Australia, the England representatives still had only the one lost match to offset an impressive eleven wins in the total of 18 played. The importance of the one loss, however, was that it was a Test. As such, the need to win at Sydney became imperative if Australia were not to gain the "ashes" that England had held since 1934.

At full strength for the final fray, with McEvoy restored to the team, it was a cloudy but warm day when Molly Hide at last won the toss for England. Maclagan and Robinson (of course) opened the innings and Flaherty and Whiteman made every attempt to remove them with their aggressive attack. Flaherty, in particular, started in fine style; accurate and determined. Whiteman it was, though, who had the first success by

Lt-General Northcott Governor of New South Wales is presented to members of the England Touring Team at Sydney Cricket Ground by Molly Hide. He is shaking hands with Eileen Whelan. To her left are Cecilia Robinson, Grace Morgan, Mary Johnson, Barbara Wood, Hazel Sanders and Betty Birch. To her right: Dorothy McEvoy, Betty Snowball, Aline Brown, Netta Rheinberg.

getting Maclagan with an inswinger, and England were 19 for 1.

Hide, somewhat restrained at first, soon settled into her stride and things began to look well for the tourists until Robinson edged a low full toss into the ready hands of Dive fielding at slip. This unfortunate dismissal, off the bowling of left arm spinner Craddock, brought Wilkinson to the wicket. She and Hide were together at lunch with the score not far short of the 100 mark, and two wickets down.

Wilkie, who had been off-driving impressively, was clean bowled by Whiteman for 27, forty minutes after lunch. Seven minutes later it was 122 for 4 when Hide was caught in the slips by Schmidt off Paisley, having made 63. Due to keen fielding and bowling, England's numbers 5, 6 and 7 bats managed to add only 20 to the score and it again looked as though a middle-order collapse was to ruin the good start. Though Sanders batted well for a bright 20 runs, no-one after he did anything much to stem a useful spell of bowling by Amy Hudson. Finally, Whelan was stumped off Wilson for 7 and the England innings closed at 172.

In the 65 minutes left for play, the left-handed Schmidt and partner Hudson did well to fend off England's openers, McEvoy and Mclagan, in poor light. Just ten minutes before close of play, second change bowler Lowe got Schmidt caught at slip by Wilkinson for 21. At stumps Australia had totalled 32 for 1 wicket.

Rain had fallen for most of the Sunday break, but on the Monday morning it was sunny, hot and humid. Hudson and Paisley, unworried by all but Hide's bowling, slowly accrued runs and when the first wicket went down another 90 had been added to the Aussie score. Paisley's was the wicket to fall, for 45, bowled Duggan.

At this stage Australia were some 80 runs ahead of England at the same position of one wicket down. Throughout the rest of the innings the England bowlers and fielders worked hard to reduce the difference at each fall of wicket. McEvoy bowled Wilson for a moderate 28, after Hudson had gone for 55 to a brilliant running catch that Sanders at backward point picked off her toes. Dive, batting 5, was bowled by Maclagan for 7. But then, just at England might have been hoping to dismiss the Aussies for around the 200 mark, Dot Laughton, making her debut in this Test, made a stand. She was ably abetted by first Larter, then Christ, and finally Whiteman. When out at the eighth wicket to fall, Laughton had made 47 and the score was 256. Duggan dismissed Flaherty, lbw for 3, and Maclagan brought her bag of wickets to four by getting Craddock to offer a catch to Wilkinson. Whiteman, whose 21 runs had taken 28 minutes, was the not out bat in Australia's final total of 272.

England had 35 minutes to begin to knock off the 100 first innings deficit. Robinson survived an lbw appeal off Wilson's bowling and that was the only incident to add further excitement to a fine day's play. At the close, England was 16 for no wicket.

The uncertain weather that so far had dogged the match did not let up for the final day's play. Tuesday, February 22, started off cold with occasional rain borne on a southerly wind. Against the accurate bowling of Whiteman and Wilson and the unpleasant weather conditions, England's scoring was slow, almost amounting to a run every three minutes. Just on half-and-hour's play had passed, however, when Whiteman produced exactly the same ball as dismissed Maclagan in the first innings. Hide was next to the crease with her side 26 for 1 wicket.

Somewhat fortunate at first, Hide took time to settle down to some steady batting. Robbie, too, was lucky not to be out to a catch at square; a difficult chance offered to Paisley. But then Hudson was put on to bowl and found it difficult to get her length with the result that 17 runs were conceded in two overs – Hide doing the necessary scoring. After this runs came freely from her bat and both her 50 and the century were brought up before lunch; the score being 107 for 1 wicket.

Only four overs after the interval, steady rain stopped play for about 40 minutes; time that England desperately needed if they were to hope to win. Shortly after play restarted, Robbie was out to a catch at long leg by Laughton without adding to the score at which rain intervened. At 114 for 2, Wilkie joined Hide and was lbw to Craddock for 0 in the first over she received. Next in was Snowball, who stayed with Hide until tea when the score was around 140 for 3 and the scoring rate achieving one a minute.

At this stage England were some 40 runs ahead with 105 minutes of play left. In an impossible winning position herself, Hide could have been intending to give Dive the chance to win in the line of sporting, but challenging, declarations, which had typified the spirit of the game throughout the tour. As it happened, however, rain decided the issue. Rain not only extended the tea interval but also, after just 22 minutes play, stopped it again for a further ten minutes. The only result possible from then on was a draw. At some 70 runs ahead, Hide made her century. When play ended she was an exemplary 124 not out and England had scored 205 for 4.

Summary of the Third Test 1948-9

Match Drawn

England:	172 and 205 for 4
Australia:	272

Best Batting

1st Innings

England:	M E Hide	63
	J Wilkinson	27

Australia:	A Hudson	55
	D Laughton	47
	U Paisley	45

2nd Innings

England:	M E Hide	124 n o
	C Robinson	30

Best Bowling

1st Innings

Australia:	A Hudson	3 – 11
	N Whiteman	2 – 31
	M Craddock	2 – 33

England:	M Maclagan	4 – 67
	M B Duggan	2 – 20

2nd Innings

Australia:	N Whiteman	1 – 29
	M Craddock	1 – 31

Highlights

Hide's 63 and 124 n o was the first 50/100 consecutive Test innings' achievement for England. Hudson made her second 50 of the series. Laughton's crucial 47, as well as taking the catch which dismissed Robinson in the second innings, was an impressive 'one and only' representation for Australia.

MOTHER OF FOUR TO PLAY IN 'TEST MATCH HERE

By Roy Colmer

*F*LORENCE McLintock, mother of four children, will play for Australia in the first Test match against the English women's cricket team at Adelaide Oval on Saturday.

McLintock is the only member of the side whose occupation is given as home duties.

Molly Dive, Australian captain, holds a science degree, and the team includes office workers, a lock assembler, salesgirl in a sports store, a packer, and a machinist.

Una Paisley, vice-captain, is one of three Victorian girls who gave the English bowlers a trouncing in Perth. She scored 102 and Betty Wilson 106 both not out. From 4/35 the score was taken to 5/304.

Amy Hudson, NSW allrounder, is the most experienced player in the eleven. She toured England with the 1937 Australian team. She is an opening batswoman and is regarded as the best spin bowler in women's cricket.

This Test is the first between

According to reports, many of the Australian team have developed fast returns from the field. This is due to their development of the under-arm whip throw used in baseball.

English players went to Port Pirie today and will play a match against a country team tomorrow.

The uniform worn by the touring side gives them a neat appearance on the field. Their cream skirts cost £5/10/ each in England, and they had to have three in their outfit.

Women's Cricket
ENGLAND CHASING RUNS

With a total of 423 to its credit, Australia declared its second innings with four down for 168 in the second Women's Test against England at the MCG today.

The Australian captain, Molly Dive, declared after 31 minutes' play. Australia resumed its second innings with an almost unbeatable lead of 305. This leaves England with 289 minutes to make 306 runs to win.

England opened its second innings badly when Cecilia Robinson was dismissed by a good-length ball from Whiteman without scoring. With only six on the English captain Hide, and Myrtle took the offensive against Australia's accurate bowling.

Play broadcast by woman

Listeners throughout Australia heard a woman describing play in the women's Test match at Adelaide Oval today. The voice was that of Mrs. Dot Emery, secretary of the Australian Women's Cricket Council, and an Australian commentator.

She conducts a session on women's sport at a Melbourne station, but she said today this was the first time she had given a ball-to-ball description.

English Spin Bowler Keeps Runs Down

Megan Lowe, English spin bowler, took three wickets for 34 runs yesterday in the women's cricket Test against Australia

The willow's in feminine hands today, so here's a . . .

Close-up of the English women

JUST nine years ago a 25-year-old English girl exchanged her cricket skirts for overalls and her bat for a plough. For four years she managed a 200-acre farm and temporarily forgot her cricket days at Surrey.

That's tall, dignified Molly Hide, one of the world's greatest batswomen, now in Perth as skipper of the English women's Test team which opened its Australian tour today. Just 14 years ago she made a century here.

Rather reserved conversation turns smartly dressed admired and others in her

Like all the married. Her ket; and aft When she retu hopes to make agricultural di ing University

Most of the started out by with boys, and at some of th schools that d as unwomanly

Let's look at

A glamour

23-year-old Betty Birch, a Middlesex physical education teacher. About 5ft. 6in. tall, blue-eyed and curly-haired, she has a delightful smile and charming personality.

Several of the women have been coached by leading English Test men. Vice-captain Betty Snowball (she was also here in 1934) has been helped by Leary Constantine.

Stocky five-footer Myrtle MacLagan, ("Mac" to her friends) was a senior commandant in the ATS during the war. She is the star slow bowler, also has a first-class National Council domestic science certificate.

Tall Yorkshire lass Barbara Wood, who leads the attack with fast outswingers, helps her brother, a veterinary surgeon. Few have played a bigger part on the organising side of cricket for women in England, for she has started 28 clubs in the last few years.

Hat trick specialist is fast left-hander Mary Duggan, who once took 7 for 2 off 11 overs, including 10 maidens.

Before they left England the players each got 100 special clothing coupons. Here they are delighted to find they don't need

M. Johnson, Megan Lowe and Norma Whiteman (Australia) with Sir Don Bradman.

Grimmett amazed by women at cricket

Hassett Victim Of 'Hat' Trick

By H. A. DE LACY

Lindsay Hassett was a victim of the "hat" trick today to Miss Eileen Whelan, a member of the English cricket team now in Australia.

Miss Whelan took a great fancy to a Gunn and Moore autographed bat belonging to Hassett.

"I will give you a pound for it," she said.

"A quid?" replied Hassett. "I'll sell it to you for a quid and a hat."

Snatching her hat off her head and handing it to Hassett, Miss Whelan said, "Sold!"

Hassett handed over the bat and Miss Whelan then got members of the English team to autograph her hat for Hassett. Meanwhile Hassett autographed the bat "sold for a quid, a hat and a smile."

Men Watch Women

Men predominated in the outer portion of the Cricket Ground yesterday when a crowd of 5,272 applauded the English and Australian women's cricket teams for efficient batting, bowling, and fielding.

Women for the first time were permitted to occupy the men's

ENGLAND WINS TEST CRICKET MATCH

GRIMMETT ... men will have to stop sneering.

TWO ACROBATIC SLIP CATCHES

Dominion Women's Team Easily [Beate]n by 185 Runs

By CANTAB

match be[ing...] [...]and which [...]rk yester[day...] [...]ngland by its second [...]ight score [...]ving New [...] to win. [...] a few [...]n tea ad[journment] as double the first

strong sun breeze. Although England watched the attendance during the Freyberg, interested [...]d to and both teams

when six [...]ew Zealand well. This [...]et partner[...]. Lamason

[...]ed to play freely and [...]ngs for 34. the wickets sound and shots when [...]ough some [...]were quite [...]nt in going [...]cked fairly [...]e in each[...] [...]advised to [...] across a[...]

[...]g from a[...] [...]for 19 in [...]and out to [...]o play some [...]ere only cut off [...]ptain. M. Hide, had [...]laced field.

[...]ngs E. Blackie opened [...]nd with more confidence [...]elop into a very sound [...]aland's last woman, G. [...]ceedings with a quickly- [...]two fours, one of these [...]well timed shot past

[...]ew Zealanders' display [...]g than that in the first [...]oaching and big match [...]ears to be plenty [...]eeds to be developed

[...]urs for England w[...] [...]and Hide, who finish[ed] [...]each. A left-hander [...]an has a good run [...]e easy action, while she

turned the ball appreciably and flighted it well. Hide, of the off-spin type, also bowled steadily, but her length was not as accurate as that of the left-hander.

The English fielding all round was quite good and Morgan gave a neat display of wicketkeeping.

Scores:—

ENGLAND

First Innings 204
Second Innings: Seven wickets, dec. 164

NEW ZEALAND

First Innings 61

Second Innings

J. Hatcher, lbw, b Johnson	..	..	1
I. Lamason, lbw, b Maclagan	..	..	15
D. Bailey, c and b McEvoy	..	..	5
V. Robinson, c Sanders, b Maclagan	..		4
P. Blackier, c Robinson, b Duggan	..		0
U. Wickham, lbw, b Hide	..	..	34
P. Batty, b Duggan	..	..	1
J. Lamason, b Hide	..	..	19
J. Francis, b Duggan	..	..	1
E. Blackie, not out	..	..	13
G. Gooder, b Hide	..	..	11
Extras	..	..	15
Total	..	..	122

Bowling.—McEvoy, 24 overs, 10 maidens, 30 runs, 1 wicket; Johnson, 16, 10, 8, 1; Duggan, 22, 9, 21, 3; Maclagan, 10, 4, 8, 2; Hide, 9.3, 2, 28, 3; Lowe, 5, 1, 12, 0.

STANDARD IMPROVED

VIEWS OF ENGLAND CAPTAIN

"I am rather surprised at the standard of women's play in New Zealand, which is better than I have been led to believe," said Miss M. Hide, captain of the English women's touring team, in an interview yesterday. "Although the New Zealand players did not perform too well in the test match, they [...] [...]who [...] de[...] velo[...] [...]nd, [...] [...]she be was bly [...]nce now [...]ents. the

WE'D RATHER WATCH THAN FACE McEVOY'S OVERS

JOAN SCHMIDT, fielding in the slips for Australia in the women's Test match at the Sydney Cricket Ground yesterday, took three brilliant catches. LEFT: She dives to catch Sanders off Amy Hudson's bowling. RIGHT: A left-handed catch dismisses Lowe, also from Hudson's bowling.

H. Sanders and P. Batty Stars Of First Day at Eden Park

Largely because of a sixth-wicket partnership of 75 runs, England scored 204 in five hours' batting when the first day of the women's test cricket match with New Zealand was held at Eden Park on Saturday. In 20 minutes' batting before stumps, New Zealand scored five runs but lost a wicket when D. Bailey played on a ball pitched well

one to Blackier on the leg side and departed, having batted 126 minutes.

M. Lowe hit one or two fortuitous boundaries on the leg side, but was always vigorous and her 25 in 46 minutes was highly useful to her team. She was given out to a catch behind and by appearance pondered the famous phrase, "Was it, or was it not?" all the way back to the pavilion. Johnson hooked one of U. Wickham's numerous full tosses grandly to the boundary and D. McEvoy, no Bradman, made some violent and humorous swishes. She even managed from a forward stroke to hit one to leg between the

NEW ZEALAND 1949

In New Zealand Britain's cricketing women met with hospitality no less welcoming than that in Australia, and found a landscape of great contrasts. Their tour started in Nelson, a coastal town in the north-western prong of the cleft that marks the tip of the South Island. From there they travelled down the west coast, renowned for its magnificent lakes, rivers and mountains, and then eastwards and northwards. En route they played cricket against teams that found it difficult to offer substantial opposition. Even against the District sides, Otago and Canterbury, the tourists had overwhelming wins, and were not to meet tougher resistance until they arrived in the North Island. Both Wellington and Auckland held England to a draw, and thus indicated that the one Test, which was to be the penultimate match of the entire tour, would be more closely fought.

New Zealand's team at Eden Park, Auckland against England in 1949. Standing L-R: Doreen Bailey, Phyl Blackler, Una Wickham, Joan Francis, Esther Blackie (Wkt), Peg Batty. Sitting: Joy Lamason, Grace Gooder, Ina Lamason (Capt.), J Yeatman (Manager), Joyce Fulford (12th), Joan Hatcher, Vera Robinson.

Auckland: Eden Park Cricket Ground, March 26, 28 & 29

The first day, which was bright but threatened showers, started at 10.30 with England's openers Maclagan and Robinson squaring up optimistically to the bowling of Joan Francis and Una Wickham on a soft, inviting wicket. Before the wicket had time to belie its appearance, however, Maclagan once again demonstrated her vulnerability on the leg side when she was lbw to Wickham for 15, having missed a full toss aimed at the leg stump.

Hide joined Robbie and started confidently but was out to a well taken catch by Peg Batty off a full-blooded cover drive at her legs. at 31 for 2, Wilkie presented a cautious bat to the slower-paced Joy Lamason and accurate off-spinner Gooder for the better part of half-an-hour. It was then a drying wicket and one of the consequences was that the ball kept low and turned slowly, with the occasional shooter. Caution was, therefore, politic, but when Blackler replaced Lamason, Wilkie was tantalised by her slow lobbed leg-spinners, went down the wicket to pull one and was clean bowled. Ten minutes later, Robbie snicked one off Gooder and was caught behind. With the score at 58 for 4, wicketkeeper Morgan, making her England debut in this Test (consequent on Snowball's return to home and work), joined Duggan. At lunch both were still there and England's score had moved on to 65 with no more wickets down.

Soon after lunch Duggan was caught by Batty, having made 3. At this stage, with the score on 73 for 5, Sanders joined her Surrey colleague and the two of them began to attack the ball, driving it hard and well. Their 74 partnership ended when Morgan was caught off Gooder for 37. Lowe who was next at the wicket carried on the momentum of run-getting, saw Sanders through her 50, and when she herself was out, had added 25 runs to the England total of 191 for 8.

With just 48 minutes left to play, Whelan, the number 10, joined Johnson. But she went for only 1 run to become Gooder's fifth victim. Last player McEvoy was not out 4 when Johnson was given out to an unlikely lbw appeal. England's final score was 204, off-spinner Gooder having taken 6 for 42. In the 25 minutes left for play, New Zealand lost the wicket of Dot Bailey who was unfortunate enough to play on a ball from Maclagan. The final score was 4 for 1.

Play on Monday, 28th March, started promptly in bright, sunny conditions after overnight frost, but a cold wind caused the England fielding side to pile on their sweaters. They also piled on the pressure. After Johnson had bowled Hatcher in her fourth over, the score moved from 6 for 2 to 8 for 3; and it was only Captain Ina Lamason's stubborn resistance which allowed New Zealand to reach double figures before the fourth wicket fell. McEvoy and Johnson were in rampant form, causing New Zealand to collapse to 19 for 7. It was then that Joan Francis joined Lamason to stem the flood of wickets for 17 courageous minutes – scoring four fours and a three in her 19 runs. She too left Lamason still at the crease, however, to be joined by wicketkeeper Blackie who stayed 33 minutes for her 8 runs to become the third highest scorer for her team. She was eventually bowled by McEvoy who completed the near-massacre by dismissing Gooder for a duck. At the end, Lamason remained an undefeated 14 in 130 minutes at the crease and New Zealand's score of 61 was sufficient to avoid the follow-on.

England opened their innings at 1.38 pm, conventionally. New Zealand attacked with fast bowler Francis and medium-pacer Joy Lamason who successfully appealed to dismiss Robinson lbw for 1. Hide and Maclagan took the score from 6 for 1 to 31 for 2 before Hide was bowled by first change Wickham for 13. Wilkinson stayed only 3 minutes before being caught behind off Gooder for 1 run, but replacement Duggan kept Maclagan company until the tea break.

Though England were nigh on 160 runs ahead, the scoring rate remained disappointingly slow, the variable wicket no doubt a contributory factor. It took 136 minutes to bring up 75 runs, and when Duggan was bowled by Lamason for 18, she had been at the crease for 68 minutes. It was clearly time for England to put on runs, despite the numerous bowling changes effected by Captain Ina Lamason. At 85 for 5 Maclagan went, bowled Blackler for 47. Blackler had another wicket 8 runs later, that of Morgan, and then Sanders and Lowe were together. They put on 39 for the seventh wicket before Lowe was stumped off Gooder. In the last 25 minutes of play, Sanders and Johnson achieved an aggressive rate of one a minute to be not out 26 and 14 respectively when England finished at 164 for 7.

On the Tuesday morning, Hide declared leaving her side ten minutes short of 6 hours to bowl New Zealand out. For their part, New Zealand required 308 to win. This daunting task was tackled uncertainly by openers Hatcher and Ina Lamason and even more disconcertingly, the first wicket went down for 7, Hatcher going lbw to Johnson for 1. Bailey, at number 3, was caught and bowled by McEvoy, and once again it looked as though the fast bowlers were to re-enact the first innings drama. But Captain Lamason also looked to be repeating her previous role until Maclagan trapped her lbw for 15, having dismissed Vera Robinson in the previous over.

The score of 27 for 4 soon became 27 for 5 when promoted Blackler was out to a catch by Cecilia Robinson off Duggan. Wickham and Batty were then together but after only 8 minutes – and a rare boundary – Batty was clean bowled by Duggan. At lunch, New Zealand was 36 for 6 and another rout looked ominously likely.

After the interval, however, Una Wickham and Joy Lamason made an enterprising stand, though this was somewhat blighted by the fact that Lamason was hit on the foot and had to have a runner. (It was Captain I. Lamason who assisted sister-in-law J. Lamason.) Nevertheless, when the latter finally hobbled off the field, bowled by Hide, she'd made 19 runs towards the doubling of the lunchtime score.

The intrepid Wickham went battling on seeing the departure of fast bowler Francis – dismissed by opposite number Duggan for 1 – but not managing to stay with wicketkeeper Blackie long before going lbw to Hide for her hard-earned 34 runs.

An encouraging stand of twenty was put on by Blackie and spin-bowler Gooder, but once again Hide broke through to bowl Gooder for 11, leaving Blackie not out 13 and the final New Zealand score at 122. England had defeated New Zealand by 185 runs.

Summary of the Test 1948-9

England won by 185 runs

| England: | 204 and 164 for 7 dec |
| New Zealand: | 61 and 122 |

Best Batting

1st Innings

England:	H Sanders	54
	G Morgan	37
New Zealand:	J Francis	19
	I Lamason	14

2nd Innings

England:	M Maclagan	47
	H Sanders	26 n o
New Zealand:	U Wickham	34
	J G Lamason	19

Best Bowling

1st Innings

New Zealand:	G Gooder	6 – 42
	U Wickham	2 – 33
England:	D McEvoy	5 – 23
	M Johnson	4 – 18

2nd Innings

New Zealand:	P Blackler	2 – 16
	J G Lamason	2 – 23
	G Gooder	2 – 31
England:	M B Duggan	3 – 21
	M E Hide	3 – 28

Highlights

Sanders first Test 50 took 109 minutes. Gooder, in her only Test appearance for New Zealand, had a match analysis of 8 – 73 in 39.2 overs. Blackie's 3 catches and 1 stumping represented a New Zealand best, and was also her only Test appearance.

AUSTRALIA IN ENGLAND 1951

Although it was just over three years since the clash of the oldest adversaries in women's cricket had taken place, fourteen years had elapsed since the Australians were last in the British Isles. They came expecting – who knew what? – of the 'Old Country' in its "Festival of Britain" year, but they also came as holders of the mythical "ashes".

England, then, had all to play for, and she knew that *these* Aussies would be no pushover. They never were, of course, but on this occasion the all-round talents of the visiting players were emphasised by experience. No fewer than seven of the 16-strong squad represented their country against the 1948/9 Touring Team and several others had been promising youngsters who'd played against England in State and minor games. They were led by the able Mollie Dive who also captained all the Tests in 1948/9.

For two of the Tests the Women's Cricket Association were breaking new ground: These were Scarborough and Worcester. The third match was to take place at The Oval, which was by way of becoming the traditional final Test venue.

Scarborough, Yorkshire: Scarborough Cricket Ground, June 16, 18 and 19

The bad news for England was not only that the Australians had romped their way round the country playing sporting and winning cricket, but also that appointed captain Molly Hide was unfit to play. Her deputy Myrtle Maclagan, veteran of eleven Tests, took the responsibility of captaincy and of opening the innings when she won the toss.

On a perfect summer's day with a cool breeze fanning the enthusiastic crowd of thousands of holidaymakers, Maclagan and Cecilia Robinson started steadily and confidently against the hostile pace attack of Mavis Jones and Norma Whiteman. It was not until the spinner Betty Wilson took over from Jones, however, that either batsman looked vulnerable. Even so, the only real chance was put down by

Another pair of famous openers for England, Myrtle Maclagan (L) and Cecilia Robinson (Robbie). The occasion is the Scarborough Test against the Australians in 1951, where Robbie scored her first Test Century with flowing strokes in a chanceless innings of 105.

Wilson when she dropped a difficult snick to slips by Maclagan off Whiteman. The opening pair therefore survived to lunch at which time the score was 76.

After the interval the Australian attack noticeably increased its accuracy of line and length and this, together with excellent fielding by Dive, restricted the England run-rate considerably. When Maclagan hit out at an Amy Hudson leg break and was well caught in the deep by Joan Schmidt, she had made 56 but the score had only increased by 19 in the 47 minute post-lunch period. At 95 for 1, Winnie Leech made her England debut taking the number 3 position which, customarily, was Hide's.

Although Leech was out for just 15 runs, lbw to left arm, medium pace leg-spinner Myrtle Craddock, she helped to accelerate the run-rate. In her 47 minutes at the crease 41 runs were added. Mary Duggan followed but was out for 4, brilliantly caught by Jones at silly mid-on when she dived to intercept a full-blooded drive. It was Joan Wilkinson (Wilkie) who kept Robinson (Robbie) company until tea, and then the score was around the 150 mark with 4 wickets down.

After half-an-hour at the crease, however, Wilkie was lbw to a flighted Paisley off-break for just 8 runs. With the score on 171 for 5, it was Hazel Sanders who joined Robbie. There then began an exhilarating partnership with Sanders hitting the ball all round the ground. She was there to see Robbie on 97 for several tense overs before urging her to run three off a Wilson full toss which, no doubt, had a different intention behind it. When she had made 105, however, Robbie was out to a low diving catch at square leg by Paisley off Hudson.

Mary Johnson (Johnnie) joined Sanders but made only 2 before being stumped by Larter off Wilson. At 249 for 6 and with 20 minutes to the close Mary Spry came to the wicket and played out the over.

Drama ensued in the continued hunt for runs when, firstly, Sanders was run out from a sharp throw in by Wilson having made 53, and then Barbara Murrey was lbw to Wilson for 2. It was suddenly 257 for 8 but Spry and Ann Geeves saw out the last 8 minutes circumspectly, leaving England with 260 on the scoreboard.

Playing conditions were still perfect for cricket on the Monday and England resumed batting at precisely 11.30 am. When the innings closed just over an hour later it was with the addition of only 23 runs. Spry, who was making her England debut, remained 21 not out.

Reward was quick for England when the left-handed opener Schmidt got a touch to a good ball from Duggan which was well taken by wicketkeeper Margaret Lockwood (Lockie). At 4 for 1 it was Hudson, a renowned sticker, who joined Mary Allitt. At lunch they were still together with the score on 13.

After the interval the scoring rate increased measurably with both players more assured against the pace attack. It was still Duggan who succeeded in getting Allitt clean bowled for 30, however, and England maintained her advantage when vice-captain Una Paisley provided Leech with her first Test wicket.

England were definitely in control with the Australians on 67 for 3, but Hudson was still there. When newcomer Val Batty also got her head down, the partnership looked threatening even though the scoring rate declined. A brief shower of rain had interrupted play for some 6 minutes after which Leech and Maclagan kept up a restricting bowling spell. Eventually Maclagan broke through to see Batty caught at backward point by Murrey for 31, and with the total at 135 for 4 Wilson joined Hudson.

Though the England attack was now without an injured Duggan it would probably have made little difference to the flow of shots and ease of despatch that Wilson applied to all bowlers alike. In her 86 minutes at the crease she scored 81 runs, including nine boundaries, while the wickets tumbled at the other end.

Except for a run out, all the wickets that fell during Wilson's innings went to Maclagan. Hudson was caught behind just on 45 minutes after tea for 70. Captain Mollie Dive, batting number 7, was caught by substitute Jean Cummins, and Larter and Whiteman were respectively bowled and lbw. When Wilson was out to the last ball of the day, caught by Geeves off pace bowler Johnson, the Australian innings was over with the score at 248.

The final day was obviously one in which a declaration had to feature since the weather remained perfect. On a hard wicket, Maclagan and Robinson made good ground against the pace of Jones and Whiteman: 25 runs were on the board in 25 minutes. The scoring rate altered only little when spinners Craddock and Wilson took over, but their efforts, allied to keen fielding, looked more threatening.

It was Craddock who made the breakthrough bowling Maclagan for 35 and then getting Leech caught and bowled for 2. A change in the batting order, necessitated by Duggan's pulled muscle, brought Wilkie in at number 4. She was still there at lunch with Sanders, Robbie having departed for 36 caught behind off Hudson.

Resuming at 95 for 3, now 130 runs ahead with just under four hours playing time left, quick runs were still needed. Wilkinson failed to add to her score and was caught by Schmidt off Whiteman in the first over after lunch for 20. Spry stayed 24 minutes for 7 and then Sanders was run out for 14. It was 115 for 6 and then 137 for 7, Johnson making 9 in 21 minutes, before Murrey and Duggan were together. They put on a sprightly 41 runs before Murrey was run out. The England innings was then declared closed at 178 for 8 wickets with Duggan remaining not out 21.

The Australians having been left to score a winning total of 214 in

Play in progress at Scarborough in 1951 shows Australia's Val Batty sweeping a ball from pace bowler Mary Johnson. Val scored 31 before being caught by Winnie Leech off Myrtle Maclagan. The 5th wicket stand with Betty Wilson, who made 81, realised 70 runs. Jean Cummins is in the gully, Margaret Lockwood behind the stumps and Winnie Leech at mid-on.

just under 2 hours lost a quick wicket when Allitt was caught by Geeves off Leech for 8. The only other wicket to fall was that of Schmidt who was run out for 31. Hudson, who was the other opener, remained undefeated on 48 with Batty not out 22. When time ran out, the final total was 111 for 2 and the well-fought first Test ended in a draw.

Summary of the First Test 1951

Match Drawn

England:	283 and 178 for 8 dec
Australia:	248 and 111 for 2

Best Batting

1st Innings

England:	C Robinson	105
	M Maclagan	56
	H Sanders	53
Australia:	B Wilson	81
	A Hudson	70

2nd Innings

England:	C Robinson	36
	M Maclagan	35
	B Murrey	33
Australia:	A Hudson	48 n o
	J Schmidt	31
	V Batty	22 n o

Best Bowling

1st Innings

Australia:	A Hudson	2 – 21
	U Paisley	2 – 34
	M Craddock	2 – 56
	B Wilson	2 – 59
England:	M Maclagan	5 – 43
	M B Duggan	2 – 28

2nd Innings

Australia:	M Craddock	2 – 39
	B Wilson	2 – 55
England:	W Leech	1 – 23

Highlights

Robinson's century, scored in some 270 minutes, was the first of her Test career and 105 her highest score. Maclagan's illustrious career was here capped by yet another half-century allied to her first innings analysis of 28 – 13 – 43 – 5. This was the third time that Maclagan had taken 5 wickets in an innings. It was Sanders' second half-century in five Tests.

This was veteran Amy Hudson's third half-century against England and she was playing in her seventh Test. It was Wilson's fifth Test match appearance and in 7 innings she had one century and three half-centuries to her credit.

England's team for the second Test at Worcester in 1951. Back Row L-R: Margaret Lockwood (Wkt.), Mary Spry, Mary Johnson, Winnie Leech, Dorothy McEvoy, Jean Cummins, Barbara Murrey. Front row L-R: Hazel Sanders, Cecilia Robinson, Myrtle Maclagan (Capt.), Mary Duggan, Joan Wilkinson.

Worcester: Worcester County Ground, June 30, July 2 and 3

It was an unchanged Australian side that took the field for the first time to admire the lovely setting of the home of Worcestershire County Cricket. England had made one change bringing in pace bowler Dorothy McEvoy in the place of Ann Geeves. Maclagan once again led the team and, on winning the toss yet again, decided to bat on a hard wicket.

The game was 15 minutes old and Maclagan had taken two boundaries off Whiteman when the Australians got their first wicket. In her third over she had Maclagan caught behind for 9 runs. Next to the wicket was Leech who also scored 9 before she was run out and, suddenly, things were looking tricky for England with the score at 29 for 2. But Robbie was still there and when Duggan joined her, runs mounted steadily. Before the fifty was up, however, Robinson had holed out to Whiteman off Craddock's bowling, and it was 46 for 3. At lunch the position had further worsened to a depressing 61 for 4, Wilkinson having come and gone – lbw to Wilson for 7 runs.

After the interval the Australians kept up the pressure by fine fielding and bowling and just on 10 minutes into the afternoon session Duggan was bowled by Wilson for 20. Spry joined Sanders but offered a simple catch to Whiteman at silly mid-on, thus making a duck and becoming Wilson's third victim in a tally of 3 for 16 off 13 overs.

Not until Murrey entered the forum did England look likely to reach 100 runs that day. Obviously too low in the batting order at number 9, the fluency and delight of her strokes restored a failing innings. Only McEvoy assisted materially and when she was out for 16, caught by Jones off Whiteman, their partnership had put on 45 runs for the 9th wicket. At 3.50 pm England finally capitulated with the score on 158 and Murrey a well sustained 39 not out.

In the short time before tea England had the encouraging sight of the

Mollie Dive leads out the Australian team for the second Test at Worcester in 1951. In a low-scoring match on a tricky pitch Australia won by 2 wickets.

Sixteen girls set sail for the battle of the 'Cinders

By GEORGE POLLOCK

SIXTEEN Australian girls set sail from Sydney yesterday and, if they put on a stone in weight during the voyage here, England's women cricketers will be secretly delighted.

Last time an Australian women's cricket "Test" team came over, that's what the boat trip did for them.

If it happens again, then England's women cricketers will have even higher hopes of eclipsing men at their own game and winning the "Ashes."

Three Tests, at Scarborough, Worcester and the Oval, will decide who wins the "Ashes"—actually, the women have no trophy, and in Australia the victors are usually credited with winning the "Cinders."

England's prospects? Miss Netta Rheinberg, secretary of the 6,000-strong Women's Cricket Association, says cautiously: "I think we stand a fairly good chance."

So far, on the three series of Test, England leads by one Test, but during their last visit to Australia in 1948, they lost one match and drew two, giving Australia the "Cinders."

☆

ENGLAND'S team have not yet been decided, but a short list of seventeen players have been in pretty strict training all winter.

For eight of the likely members, keeping fit is not too troublesome—they are sent a women's physical training instructors.

Others have cut out smoking, gone track running, kept a strict eye on what they ate and firmly

[...] side to though captain Molly Dive is a scien... Britain in 1937. biggest crowd w Miss Rheinber reasons for g pectations : w better known.

First Women Cricketers Go to Lord's

NO SCORN FROM OLD FAITHFULS

By ROLAND HURMAN

FEMININE emancipation marches on. It is now publicly admitted among decent chaps that women actually play cricket.

True, women can pay money at the turnstiles and pass through to watch the game at Lord's. But until yesterday none had ever swung bat above the sacred turf of the practice nets there.

Sixteen members of the Australian women's touring team got to Lord's in the morning, long before Middlesex and Sussex supporters arrived to watch the performances of Compton and Co.

To loosen up after a long sea voyage, they trotted round the ground. Then, off to the nets to get their eyes in for the team's opening game. That will be against Kent, at Sevenoaks, on Saturday.

There were raised eyebrows among Lord's faithfuls strolling by to favourite resting-places. There were also murmurs of : "Can this be true?"

But there was no scorn. For the women quickly proved that they knew their business.

They drove, they cut, they spun, and they swerved in the same efficient way that their menfolk have taught the gentlemen of Lord's to fear and respect.

Miss Mollie Dive, the team's captain was not satisfied. Said she : "I didn't know whether we were coming or going."

"All our gear was locked up on the ship and we had to practise there with string balls and toy bats. We were out of touch. We must keep at it. We shall be here again first thing tomorrow."

Cecilia hit Test 100

A CENTURY which took nearly 5 hours, made 26-year-old Cecilia Robinson, games mistress at Roedean, the star of the England women's side that made 260 for 8 in the first Test match against Australia at Scarborough.

Cecilia was never an aggressive player, but dealt confidently with the Australian bowlers.

When nearing her century, she was unruffled by appeals and an all-out bid to get her run out.

With Myrtle McLaglan, deputising for injured Molly Hide as captain, Robinson put on 95 for the first wicket. This was a laborious affair.

The first 100 took 2 hours 35 minutes but it tired the Australian attack, which received no encouragement from the pitch.

Robinson was dismissed by Paisley making an acrobatic catch at deep square leg, after she had been joined by Surrey's Hazel Sanders in a fifth wicket partnership which contributed 70 runs in 55 minutes.

Hudson, the only Australian who was in the 1937 tour, lived up to her reputation as partnership breaker, for it was she who had both McLaglan and Robinson caught off her spinners.

Dreary End to Women's Test

By TOM BRANDON

The women cricketers of England and Australia yesterday demonstrated that they can be just as dreary in Test cricket as the men. They allowed their first Test at Scarborough to fizzle out as a miserable draw.

England killed the final day by delaying their declaration until ten minutes to four, when they led by 213. They had taken three hours 20 minutes to score 178 runs yet left Australia only two hours to bat.

The Australians not only refused to go for the runs : they made little effort to keep the crowd entertained. Amy Hudson, who hit ... in ... for 48, which could have ... century but for the ... ...souvenirs with the Australians ...for two wickets

---

ENGLAND BAT IN WOMEN'S TEST

HALF-CENTURIES FOR THE OPENING PAIR

THOUGH the England batsmen were always on top in the first women's test against Australia at Scarborough today, they had to fight for runs against a keen attack backed by sound fielding. Myrtle Maclagan and Cecilia Robinson, England's opening pair, each scored a half-century, and by mid-afternoon a 6,000-crowd saw England score 130 for the loss of one wicket.

Myrtle Maclagan, deputising as England's skipper for the injured Molly Hide, kept out of the game by a sprained ankle, won the toss and opened the inning with Robinson against a medium-pace attack of Jones and Whiteman.

Maclagan, who has played in every test so far, opened the scoring too, and in a quiet half hour both batsmen took leg-side fours off full tosses from Jones.

ENGLAND—First Innings	
M. Maclagan c Schmidt b Hudson	56
C. Robinson not out	60
W. C. Leech not out	12
Extras	2
Total (one wkt)	**130**

mid-on in Hudson's third over, and Schmidt, running in, held the catch safely.

Maclagan had hit three fours in her stay of 2 hours 30 minutes, and England were still five short of the hundred when she left. Five minutes later the 100

Australian Women Cricketers

NO PRE-TEST NERVES FOR MOLLY'S XI

'HARDLY TIME TO WASH HAIR' SAYS CAPTAIN

THE biggest problem of the Australian women's cricket team, who opened their second Test match against England at Worcester to-day, is how to find time to write home, wash their hair and do other personal chores.

Australians Call The Tune at Worcester

ENGLAND LOSE 4 BATSMEN FOR 61 RUNS

In spite of cautious methods, the England women cricketers fared badly on a perfect pitch in their second Test match against the Australian women, which is being played on the County Ground, Worcester.

In glorious sunshine approximately 2,000 spectators watched a well-varied Australian attack always calling the tune

EVENING NEWS & TIMES, SATURDAY JUNE 30, 1951

minutes, had gathered ... ature of the play fielding. Their

WOMEN'S TEST MATCH

The fourth Test match at Leeds was washed out to-day and the game abandoned as a draw. But at the Oval it was a case of . . .

CAPS OFF TO THE TEST MATCH GIRLS

"Evening News" Reporter

AN elderly lady sitting in the stands at the Oval this evening put down her knitting, a young man in the Pavilion marked up his score-card. "Well done, Mary!" they exclaimed simultaneously.

For out there in the middle, Mary Duggan, 25-year-old P.T. instructress at a Highgate girls' school, had just dismissed Australia's opening-batswoman—and England had a chance of winning the Third Women's Test match. And here was half her family to support her.

"I'm so glad Mary is doing well," said Mother. "I've come down from our home in Worcester specially to watch her in this match. I see as many of her games as I can. Not that I

ENGLAND FINISH ALL SQUARE

By MARJORIE POLLARD

England women cricketers won the third Test match and so have drawn the rubber. Australia were set 221 runs to get in three hours at the Oval. So brilliantly did Mary Duggan, the left-hander, bowl that she took the first five wickets for five runs and the best of the Australian batting had gone for a mere 26 runs.

One player, Amy Hudson, defied England for nearly two hours and was undefeated in the end. Victory came with only 14 minutes when D. McEvoy clean bowled Jones. This match had a triumph for English fast bowling.

ENGLAND.—First Innings: 65. M. Maclagan 59). Second 174 for 7 dec. (Hide 42).

AUSTRALIA.—First Innings Whiteman 36 n.o.). Second (M. Duggan 5-30)

A lesson for the Australians

'Tops' in the Tests

Two fours for England

Peter May (left) plays South Africa's Chubb to leg for four—a boundary on the road to a hundred on his first appearance in a Test match. He was England's top scorer at the close with 110 not out. Molly Hide also scores four to leg—off Australia's Una Paisley. In the women's Test match at the Oval Miss Hide was England's top scorer with a useful 65.

THE name is Duggan—Mary Duggan, games mistress at a Hampstead Garden Suburb school, who played the star part in bringing England's women cricketers the first Test victory over Australia since 1937.

Bowling left arm, medium pace, she disposed of the first five Australians in the last innings for five runs out of 26.

She did not take another wicket —but made a catch and well earned the gift of the ball from the England captain in the end-of - the - match scramble for souvenirs.

Mary took nine wickets in the match for 104 ; equalled a woman's cricket record by taking 20 wickets in the Test series.

GRAND BOWLING BY MISS DUGGAN

ENGLAND TEST VICTORY

By A Special Correspondent

Inspired bowling by Mary Duggan, who at one time had taken five wickets for five runs, enabled England to beat Australia in the third and last women's Test match of the season by 137 runs at the Oval yesterday.

But it was a near thing. A last-wicket partnership which added 24 runs in 35 minutes kept England in the field until there were only 15 minutes to spare.

Honours are even on the series, each side winning one match and the other being drawn. The Ashes remain with Australia.

Molly Hide and Mary Spry batted well when England continued their innings adding 67 for the third wicket before Hide was caught when a lofted drive did not carry as far as she intended.

Spry left shortly afterwards and then both Sanders and Duggan made useful scores at a run a minute before England declared at 174 for seven, leaving Australia to get 221 in just over three hours.

HEAVY ATMOSPHERE

The heavy atmosphere helped Duggan's in-swingers. She had Schmidt caught in the slips off the second ball, Allitt l.b.w. with the total only three and had taken three more wickets when the score reached 26.

The match now looked all over, but Amy Hudson came in to play a sturdy defensive innings and she found capable partners in Batty, Larter and Whiteman. It took her half an hour to break her duck and she was dropped at the wicket almost immediately afterwards, but continued unperturbed.

With 50 minutes to go, fast bowler Jones came in, and by resolute defence these two made a last stand which proved the longest of the innings and had the England side on tenterhooks before McEvoy disposed of the courageous Jones.

ENGLAND.—First Innings: 238 (M. E. Hide 65, M. Maclagan 59; Whiteman 4-56, Wilson 3-27).

Second Innings		
M. Maclagan, lbw, b Paisley	16	
C. Robinson, b Whiteman	10	
M. E. Hide, c Whiteman, b Wilson	32	
M. Spry, c Schmidt, b Wilson	24	
H. Sanders, c Wills, b James	23	
M. Duggan, c Larter, b Paisley	20	
B. Murray, lbw, b James	14	
B. D. Birch, not out	4	
G. Morgan, not out	6	
Extras		

Total (7 wkts. dec.) 174

Bowling: Jones 4-2-12-0; Whiteman 15-7-26-1; James 16-4-33-2; Wilson 17-2-44-2; Paisley 19-5-34-2; Hudson 3-0-19-0.

AUSTRALIA.—First Innings: 192 (Duggan 4-74).

Second Innings		
J. Schmidt, c Hide, b Duggan	0	
M. Allitt, lbw, b Duggan	4	
M. Dive, c Morgan, b Duggan	0	
B. Wilson, b Duggan	11	
U. Paisley, b Duggan	14	
V. Batty, b Hide	17	
A. Hudson, not out	17	
L. Larter, c Duggan, b Hide	2	
N. Whiteman, c Johnson, b Maclagan	3	
J. James, c Sanders, b Johnson	5	
M. Jones, b McEvoy	17	
Extras	6	

Total 83

Bowling: Duggan 20-10-30-5; McEvoy 14-0-3-1; Maclagan 10-6-8-1; Johnson 16-5-21-1; Hide 10-3-15-2; Sanders 2-2-0-0.

umpire's finger raised to answer the lbw appeal which removed Allitt for 2 runs. The bowler was left-arm medium-pacer Duggan who had opened the attack with Johnson. Some 60 minutes of playing time later, Australia lost their second wicket when Hudson was also lbw – this time to McEvoy – having scored 10 runs. At 33 for 2, Dive joined opener Schmidt and was soon caught behind off Maclagan without adding to the score. In conditions of increasingly bad light with a thunderstorm in the offing, Paisley remained 49 minutes at the crease for 8 runs before being caught by Spry off Leech. It was 5 minutes to close of play when night-watchman Larter, at number 6, presented a straight bat to prevent the disaster – almost exactly emulating England's efforts – of finishing the day more than 4 wickets down for 63 runs. To say the least, there was enough food for thought at the fall of 14 wickets in 5½ hours play to concern both teams over the weekend break.

On the Monday there was no hint of other than perfect weather in which to continue this evenly-poised game. But England soon struck when McEvoy took Larter's wicket with the third ball of their first over. At that stage she had taken 2 wickets for 8 runs. It was then that Betty Wilson joined Schmidt and, once again, the apparently fiendish wicket began to look as though it was made for batting.

Unfortunately for the Australians, sheet anchor Schmidt became the third lbw victim just as the partnership was showing promise. She had made 42 and the score was on 81 for 6 when Batty joined Wilson. But Duggan, having taken Schmidt, followed one wicket maiden with another and Batty went, caught behind, without scoring. Amazingly, after Whiteman was run out for 5 and the total had reached 106 for 8, no incoming bat scored. 106 for 8 became 106 for 9 and yet when the innings closed, Duggan being responsible for the last two wickets, the Australian score had reached 120 with Wilson on 41 not out. There remained just 7 minutes for England to survive to lunch an unexpected, but well earned, 38 runs ahead.

Soon after the interval Robinson received what was probably the best delivery of the day and was clean bowled by Jones for 3. Leech replaced her but after 34 minutes was lbw to Wilson for 12. At 41 for 2 Duggan joined Maclagan and again made a useful 23 runs while, firstly Maclagan departed for 23 and then both Wilkie and Sanders came and went without scoring. She must have wondered if anyone could stay with her because Spry, too, departed before tea having made only 7. However, at 74 for 6, Murrey came to the crease and seemed intent on picking up where she left off in the first innings. Unfortunately, they were together only 5 minutes before Duggan was lbw to Wilson.

Tea intervened in the partnership of Murrey and number 9 Johnson, but afterwards, in almost a repeat of the Australian innings, when Johnson was bowled by Whiteman for 5, no-one added significantly to the score. 101 for 8 became 102 for 9 and then Murrey herself was bowled by Wilson for 34 out of the final total of 120. The England innings had taken 140 minutes and this left Australia in the comfortable position of having a day and 65 minutes in which to make 159 to win.

Schmidt and Allitt began confidently enough and had 25 on the board in 25 minutes. But then Maclagan came on as first change and got Allitt caught and bowled in her third over. With half-an-hour to go Wilson joined Schmidt, only to see the latter depart just 6 minutes before play was due to end. Schmidt was lbw to Leech and made 27. Hudson joined Wilson to play out the last few minutes but was also given out lbw to Leech without scoring, making the overnight total 59 for 3.

The third day started at 11 am with the Australians needing a century with 7 wickets in hand to go one up in the series. It looked an inevitable victory but there was still this extraordinary low-scoring wicket to take into account. An obviously determined Mollie Dive was having none of that nonsense however. In 30 minutes she and Wilson added 30 runs before the latter was caught behind off Duggan for 35. It was 89 for 4.

The Australian captain was not allowed freedom from trauma, though, since, she was at the crease to see Paisley come and go for a single before she too was given out lbw after a crucial 33 runs. At 117 for 6 Larter joined Batty who was going well. Another throat catching moment followed though when, after Batty was bowled by Duggan for 14, Larter fell similarly for just 3 runs. At 131 for 8, Craddock joined Whiteman and these two took the responsibility of seeing Australia through to a winning finish by two wickets. At least the Australians enjoyed their lunch.

Summary of the Second Test 1951

Australia won by two wickets

England:	158 and 120
Australia:	120 and 160 for 8

Best Batting

	1st Innings	
England:	B Murrey	39 n o
	H Sanders	24
	M B Duggan	20

| Australia: | J Schmidt | 42 |
| | B Wilson | 41 n o |

2nd Innings

England:	B Murrey	34
	M Maclagan	23
	M B Duggan	23

Australia:	B Wilson	35
	M Dive	33
	J Schmidt	27
	N Whiteman	25 n o

Best Bowling

1st Innings

Australia:	B Wilson	3 – 40
	M Craddock	2 – 24
	N Whiteman	2 – 48

| England: | M B Duggan | 5 – 40 |
| | D McEvoy | 2 – 33 |

2nd Innings

| Australia: | B Wilson | 4 – 42 |
| | N Whiteman | 3 – 34 |

England:	M B Duggan	4 – 67
	W Leech	2 – 10
	M Maclagan	2 – 51

Highlights

An unusual feature of this low-scoring match was the unprecedented number of lbws. These accounted for 12 wickets in all, eight of them favouring England.

Duggan took 5 wickets in an innings for the first time in her career, and her 9 match wickets for 11.89 each off 46.2 overs was excellent. Wilson, too, did well for a match analysis of 7 for 82 off 35.3 overs which, as top scorer with a batting average of 76, showed her to be the outstanding all-rounder.

Kennington, London: The Oval, July 28, 30 and 31

After what was, in all respects, probably the most strenuous month of their tour the Australians arrived at The Oval for the last Test secure in the knowledge that defeat in the series was out of the question. Being Aussies, however, and led by such a captain as Dive, playing for a draw was certainly not their style. No-one would be more aware of that than Molly Hide, now restored to fitness and captaining the England side, and since a win would be her single intention too, changes were made in the side to strengthen both the batting and fielding. Leech, an out of from Wilkinson and Lockwood were replaced by all-rounder Hide, specialist deep-field and middle order bat Betty Birch, an experienced player but here making her Test debut, and wicketkeeper Grace Morgan. Australia were forced to make one change – a crucial one – when the successful left arm spinner Myrtle Craddock was unfit. Pace

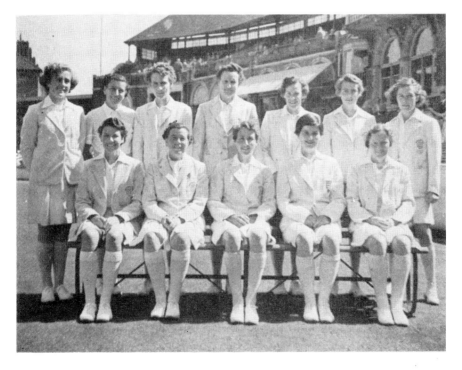

The line up for the final Test against the Australians at The Oval in 1951, which Molly Hide led to a win by 137 runs and drew the series. Standing L-R: Mary Johnson, Jean Cummins, Mary Spry, Dorothy McEvoy, Barbara Murrey, Betty Birch, Hazel Sanders. Sitting L-R: Cecilia Robinson, Myrtle Maclagan, Molly Hide, Mary Duggan, Grace Morgan (Wkt).

bowler June James, making her Test debut, was brought in to replace her.

England were again fortunate in winning the toss and took strike with the redoubtable opening partnership of Maclagan and Robinson facing up to Jones and Whiteman. In what was probably their fastest ever partnership 25 – it took 20 minutes – the England opening pair and The Oval wicket looked full of runs. Indeed, having seen off the Australian pace attack they also treated, after a few maidens, Paisley's off-spin and James's pace to the full face of the bat. They looked well set for the century partnership before lunch but with just 25 minutes to go James nipped one back from the off to remove Robbie's bails. She had made 32 and the score was 72 for 1.

Hide joined Maclagan and, for the ten minutes before lunch, Dive tempted both players with Hudson's slow flighted leg-breaks. This ploy served only to provide Hide with a couple of boundaries and at lunch the score was 99 without further loss.

The first ball after the break provided Maclagan with a chance to cut and bring up the 100. Not long afterwards a leg-glance saw her to 50. With Hide at the other end taking uncharacteristic swishes at the ball, frequently playing and missing, Maclagan's rock-like approach was a necessary antidote. By the time she was out, mistiming a pull to mid-wicket resulting in an easy catch by Jones off Whiteman, the score was 144 and Hide's uneasy patch a thing of the past.

Spry at number 4 soon gave way to Sanders; Hide had made her 50 and Wilson was now featuring in the Australian attack. It was the spinners who won through before tea, Paisley turning one the other way to bowl Hide for 65, and Wilson getting Sanders caught and bowled for 26. At 202 for 5 Murrey joined Duggan only to see the latter caught behind off Whiteman soon after tea. Birch became Whiteman's fourth wicket when she failed to score. Morgan offered some resistance but was run out for 3. When Murrey was out, bowled by Wilson for 19, there was no further addition to the score and England's innings ended at 5.30 pm with 238 on the board.

With 47 minutes to go the Australian openers Schmidt and Allitt played safely, only throwing the bat at the loose balls. At the close, 17 overs had been bowled by Duggan and McEvoy and the opening pair had scored 24.

Slow scoring epitomised the state of watchful play before lunch on the Monday, for when Allitt was lbw to Johnson she had added just 12 runs in 47 minutes. Hudson replaced her only to see left-hander Schmidt fall at last to left-hander Duggan with the addition of two runs. At 56 for 2 Dive joined Hudson but was out shortly before lunch having made 7 and seen the Australian score to 73 for 3.

After the interval Hudson kept her end up while first Paisley and then Batty attacked the bowling. But Paisley played back to a ball from Duggan and was given out lbw, and then Batty had the misfortune to be struck on the head by a throw in from Birch which caused her to retire.

Hudson's was the next wicket to fall, her 30 having taken 136 minutes, and the score of 133 for 5 brought Larter to join Wilson at the wicket. The partnership was short-lived, however, an unfortunate run-out dismissing Wilson for 7. Just before tea wicketkeeper Larter was caught and bowled by Maclagan for 10 and Batty returned to continue her innings. The score was 174 for 7.

In a situation where they were well behind the clock Whiteman set about scoring some runs. Batty stayed only 7 minutes without adding to her score though, and was replaced by James. In a stirring 59 minutes Whiteman put on 36 runs and remained not out when the innings

An incident during the Oval Test in 1951 where Betty Wilson almost ran out Hazel Sanders. The bowler is June James and the striker is Mary Duggan. Wicketkeeper Lorna Larter and first slip, Joan Schmidt, look on.

closed. James was dispatched by McEvoy, having contributed 7, and Jones was bowled by Duggan without scoring. Australia finished with 192.

Despite the fact that Australia gained the wickets of Maclagan and Robinson in the final hour, England finished 85 runs ahead at the end of the second day's play.

The final day looked to be very much more of the same when it was discovered that overnight thunderstorms had affected the pitch but little. Hide and Spry began on 12 and 0 respectively and pushed the score along very agreeably until Hide skied one to Whiteman off Wilson for 42. Sanders joined Spry and they put on 14 together until Spry capitulated to Wilson for 35. The score was 149 for 4 at lunch, Sanders and Duggan were together and England was 195 ahead.

It was clear after lunch that Hide had read the declaration book to her remaining bats for when she *did* declare, at 2.45 pm which meant an additional 29 minutes batting, a further 25 runs had been added. No matter that three wickets had fallen in the process. The end result was that Australia needed 221 runs to win in exactly 180 minutes. It was the kind of challenge that Dive could afford to refuse, being one up, even though she certainly had the supporting talent.

If the change in batting order was anything to go by, Mollie Dive had every intention of accepting the odds. Hudson the stickler was at 7, she herself was at 3 and Betty Wilson was brought from 7 to 4. Without doubt it was a tactician's batting order. But, the best laid plans . . .

In the first minute of the Australian innings the score was 0 for 1 and 16 balls later it was 3 for 2. Long before time the run-scorers Dive and Wilson were together. Mary Duggan was the menace and she struck again to make it 14 for 3, Dive going for 4. At that stage Duggan's tally was 3 for 2, two catches – Hide in the slips and wicketkeeper Morgan – and an lbw doing the damage. The two wickets that surely gave Duggan most pleasure and her side too, occurred with the demise of both Wilson and Paisley to identical inswingers. If the score, at 26 for 5, had the same unbelievable qualities for both captains it had to be tinged with different feelings and it was the Australian's who were on the run.

The run was halted temporarily when Batty and Hudson were together. They put on the highest partnership – 14 – before Batty was bowled by Hide and 40 for 6 marked the tea interval. Afterwards, Larter lasted 20 minutes making 4 runs before she was caught in the slips by Duggan off Hide. Whiteman and James made 3 between them but Jones offered stubborn resistance and she and Hudson looked set to play out time. With 15 minutes to go, however, McEvoy clean bowled Jones for 17, and with the redoubtable Hudson on 17 not out, England had won by 137 runs.

Summary of the Third Test 1951

England won by 137 runs

England: 238 and 174 for 7 dec
Australia: 192 and 83

Best Batting

	1st Innings	
England:	M E Hide	65
	M Maclagan	59
Australia:	N Whiteman	36 n o
	A Hudson	30

	2nd Innings	
England:	M E Hide	42
	M Spry	35
Australia:	A Hudson	17 n o
	M Jones	17

Best Bowling

	1st Innings	
Australia:	N Whiteman	4 – 56
	B Wilson	3 – 27
England:	M B Duggan	4 – 74
	M Maclagan	2 – 26

	2nd Innings	
Australia:	J James	2 – 33
	U Paisley	2 – 34
	B Wilson	2 – 44
England:	M B Duggan	5 – 30
	M E Hide	2 – 15

Highlights

Hide's return to captaincy was celebrated by winning the match and finishing with the highest batting average. This included her fourth 50 in 12 Tests. Maclagan registered her second half-century of the series. The bowling honours for England were undoubtedly Duggan's, whose 5 – 30 in the second innings was a match winning feat and came off 20 overs, 10 of which were maidens. For the second consecutive time she took 9 wickets, on this occasion for 11.56 each.

For Australia, Hudson's batting was admirable, but Whiteman's efforts with both bat and ball were good and included a match 5 – 82 in 46 overs.

NEW ZEALAND IN ENGLAND 1954

Not only was this the first time for a team of New Zealand cricketers to visit England, but for most of the fortunate players this tour was that dreamed of occasion come true. Experience there was in plenty, with six of the side having played against England when she toured in 1949, but there was also a galaxy of youngsters which had the makings of star quality.

Captained by Auckland all-rounder Rona McKenzie, it was a team that was, in the words of Dame Elizabeth M Knox Gilmer the then President of the New Zealand Women's Cricket Council: "Eagerly looking forward to meeting new and old friends, as well as playing the matches on grounds that till now have just been famous names to us."

And the first of those famous grounds was to be Headingley, the home of the Yorkshire County Cricket Club.

Leeds: Headingley Cricket Ground, June 12, 14 and 15

It was a rain-sodden pitch amply supplied with piles of sawdust that welcomed the New Zealanders when they elected to bat on the Saturday of the first Test. A pitch difficult for the bowlers it would be assumed, requiring much wiping of the ball between deliveries. And for a while so it seemed with Mary Duggan and Helene Hegarty getting little help from the soft wicket and making little impression on the defensive bats of openers Joan Hatcher and Joyce Clothier. When Duggan broke through in her ninth over and Hegarty had given way to leg-spinner Kay Green, however, only 18 runs were on the board and play had been under way for 40 minutes.

Hatcher had departed for 11 and when the first hour was up, off-spinner Hide had dismissed replacement Joy Lamason and Green had returned Clothier to the pavilion with a score of 11. Suddenly it was 26 for 3 and the wicket was perhaps not the quiescent pudding it looked.

Verna Coutts and Phyllis Blackler were together for a somewhat restorative 23 runs until Hegarty, finding life somewhere in the pitch, had Coutts caught behind for 6. But, with a determined Blackler now joined by her Captain, no more wickets went down before lunch and the 50 had been registered.

After the interval the partnership added a spirited 40 or so runs before Blackler offered an accepted spooner to Hazel Sanders at forward short leg off Hide. Her 42 runs had taken 109 minutes but included 5 boundaries and occurred at a crucial time in the match.

Eris Paton was the next bat and stayed with McKenzie for 15 minutes, scoring 3 runs in that time to take the New Zealand total to 102 for 6. Peg Batty joined McKenzie but was run out for a single and the tourists were again in trouble. A useful knock by the number 10, Mary Rouse, helped things along, but when McKenzie was out with the score at 137 for 9, only 7 more runs were added before the innings closed.

In the 45 minutes remaining for the day's play, England fared no better than had New Zealand at the same stage in her innings. In fact with a closing total of 18 for 3, the position was in New Zealand's favour.

An early breakthrough on the Monday, when Betty Birch was clean bowled by the pace of Joan Francis for a duck, must have added to the New Zealanders' elation. But this was soon to evaporate after Barbara Murrey joined Hide with the score at 24 for 4. In 67 refreshing minutes

Opener Joan Westbrook is deftly caught at silly mid-on by New Zealand's Eris Paton in the first Test at Headingley in 1954. A low scoring match saw England victorious by six wickets. The other fielders are Joan Francis, second slip, Peg Batty first slip, and the wicketkeeper is Joyce Clothier.

Murrey scored 56 runs, making some delightful strokes and even running a four, before she was bowled by McKenzie. Just one run later Hide was also bowled by McKenzie for 48.

With the score on 117 for 6, Duggan and Sanders were together – but not for long. Duggan became McKenzie's third scalp within 6 overs and at that stage the medium pace bowler had claimed 3 for 10. Finally, after a mini-stand with Mary Johnson, Sanders too succumbed to McKenzie caught with a left-handed interception by Batty at mid-off for 14.

England was 139 for 8 then Hegarty was at the crease 3 minutes before stepping on her wicket to leave the score at 139 with 9 wickets down, and the question was whether or not England would end with a deficit on the first innings. In the event, last player Green was not out 4 when the innings closed at 154. Johnson had made 11.

There were 2 hours 40 minutes of play remaining and during that time the New Zealanders gave almost a repeat performance of their first innings. They were 25 for 3 before once again Blackler came to the rescue, this time supported by a stubbornly patient Clothier. McKenzie, too, played a similar role taking up where Blackler left off when the latter was out for 35, bowled by Hide. Two more wickets fell before the close of play some 40 minutes later, by which time New Zealand had managed to acquire 93 runs.

Soon after play began on the third and last day, Batty put up a simple catch to Sanders off Hegarty and went for 11. McKenzie went next, clean bowled by Hegarty for 18 and the total was 103 for 8. Hegarty then had Betty Butler caught behind for a duck. Because an injured Francis was unable to bat, New Zealand ended with a score of 104 just 94 ahead.

McKenzie opened the bowling and with her second ball had wicket-keeper Joan Westbrook caught behind. Wilkie joined Jean Cummins and these two scored steadily and sensibly until Cummins was lbw to Paton for 14. The next two players Hide and Birch made only 9 between them. It took Murrey to restore the equilibrium with Wilkinson, and these two saw England through after lunch to the winning total of 95 runs by a 6 wicket margin.

Summary of the First Test 1954

England won by 6 wickets

New Zealand: 144 and 104
England: 154 and 95 for 4 wickets

Best Batting

1st Innings

New Zealand:	P Blackler	42
	R U McKenzie	29
	M Rouse	15 n o
England:	B Murrey	56
	M E Hide	48

2nd Innings

New Zealand:	P Blackler	35
	R U McKenzie	18
England:	J Wilkinson	51 n o
	B Murrey	20 n o

Best Bowling

1st Innings

England:	M E Hide	3 – 23
	K Green	2 – 26
	M B Duggan	2 – 47
New Zealand:	R U McKenzie	4 – 18
	J G Lamason	4 – 51
	J Francis	2 – 26

2nd Innings

England:	M B Duggan	3 – 29
	H Hegarty	3 – 30
	M E Hide	2 – 5
New Zealand:	E Paton	2 – 17

Highlights

Although no New Zealander managed a half-century in this low-scoring match, Blackler's batting formed the strength of both innings. It was remarkable that her second innings 35 contained 8 boundaries. The brunt of the bowling was taken by Lamason and McKenzie and both did well to achieve match analyses of 17.75 (off 41.1 overs) and 6.6 off a total of 28 overs respectively.

Murrey's 50 was the first of her career in 4 Tests and Wilkinson's was also her first in 6 Tests. Hide topped the match bowling with 5 wickets off 39 overs at 5.6 each, with Duggan a good second at 15.2 each off 47.5 overs. Both Green and Hegarty bowled well in their Test debut.

Ukulele lady Verna Coutts strums happily to teammates Betty Butler and Mary Rouse on arrival in England. She's keeping their pecker up and they hope to keep their end up. The New Zealand girl cricketers are to play three Tests — at Leeds, Worcester and the Oval —and 16 other matches in the next four months. Medium-

Eris Paton, a member of the New Zealand women's cricket team to tour England this year, has a batting average of 427.

New Zealand woman bats well in Test

The women cricketers of England and New Zealand were fortunate to have fine weather for their first Test match at Headingley, Leeds.

New Zealand won the toss, and on a pitch dead after the heavy rain of earlier in the week, scored 144, to which England replied with 18 for three.

One of the New Zealand openers, Hatcher, at 18, was leg before to Duggan, and eight runs later Lamason was caught at square-leg from a hefty pull. Without addition, Clothier left, and three wickets were down for 26.

Phyllis Blackler, who wears spectacles, quickly reached double figures, but her partner, Coutts, was less confident, and after batting 40 mins. for six was caught at the wicket. At lunch the tourists were 50 for 4.

Blackler continued to score freely, and was particularly severe on Duggan. With the total at 89, however, she gave an easy catch to forward short leg. She had then scored 42 out of 63 in 100 minutes.

An on-drive for four by McKenzie sent the score to 102, made in three hours, but at that total Paton left.

Six wickets were now down, but the total reached 144 before Duggan claimed the last wicket.

Molly Hide returned the best figures of the England bowlers with 3 for 23 in 30 overs.

England had a disastrous start to their innings, quickly losing their first three wickets to catches. At the close they were 18 for three, so still needed 127 for the lead.

Women's Test match at Headingley

ENGLAND BEAT N.Z.: WILKINSON IS 51 n.o.

Y.E. News Sports Reporter   Headingley, Tuesday.

ENGLAND defeated the New Zealand tourists by six wickets in the women's Test match here to-day, thanks principally to Joan Wilkinson, the Cheshire county player, who hit 51 not out in England's second innings total of 95 for four.

She had eight boundaries

wickeet when Batty hit a simple catch to Sanders fielding close-in. off Hegarty's bowling

BLACKLER HITS 42

Y.E. News Sports Reporter   Headingley, Saturday.

ENGLAND women claimed four wickets before the New Zealand score had reached 50 in the first women's Test with New Zealand in this country here to-day.

A fifth wicket stand, however, took the score past the 80 mark. P. Blackler knocked 42 before she was caught and bowled. The visitors took three hours to reach 100.

New Zealand won the toss. The sky was overcast and there was a fairly stiff breeze, but the sun fre-

Scoreboard

NEW ZEALAND WOMEN—First Innings

J Hatcher, lbw b Duggan ....: .. 11
J Clothier, c Wilkinson b Green ... 11
J Lamason, c Birch b Hide 4
V Coutts, c Westbrook b Hegarty ... 6
P Blackler, c Sanders b Hide 42
R McKenzie, not out 21

WOMEN'S CRICKET

THE SECOND TEST

At Worcester, July 3, 5 and 6. Drawn.

THE draw which resulted from the second Test match at Worcester is about the best thing that could have happened, both to enliven the interest for the final match at the Oval on July 24, 26 and 27, and to put heart and attack into the New Zealand batting.

England won at Leeds, and won well, by si~ so now we still stand one up in the rubber. is New Zealand are improving all they become more accustomed

I·verybody enjoys playin~ Cathedral and river b bringing memories of the Adelaide to bat, whe monoto the w of the match

It beca and the sp responsible playing in h point. She h wickets of our for 24. Birch a partnership impr of 112 was disapp wicket ; the New never seen the ball tu

Before the close o Zealanders had batted. A. Sanders, playing in three of the wickets. She, to the conditions to her liking

Monday morning found and before the luncheon interv who swings across to the le polished off the remaining 4 w only 18 runs. New Zealand we Coulston, a left-handed bat with had again distinguished herself b score.

England's second innings showed th could bat. Hide made 64, and Wilkinso with the crowd, scored 47 ; but the inn was made by Birch, who employed every fully executed, and almost dancing at the w 83 splendid runs, and also to carry her bat at day. I:ngland were now 288 runs for 7 wicke

The third day opened with England havi overnight. New Zealand needed 338 runs to policy would they adopt ?

From the onset it was apparent that they in close up the shutters and play for safety. A as this kills cricket, but knowing the capabiliti batsmen 338 runs would have been a difficult therefore they made the right decision, dull thoug to be.

As the daily press put it on the following d monumental patience of Clothier, who batted the five and a half hours' day for 37 not out, e Zealand to draw the second Test." To the I who must have felt very disappointed, I wo you want to win your matches you must hold and either go right out or right back to sp Now for the Oval . . . and England should wi

It's all eyes on the ball as J. Hatcher (New Zealand) puts one past the slips in the Women's Test Match at the Oval.

SPEEDY BETTY

Betty B·rch hammered an un- defeated 83 in quick time for Eng- land women in the second Test at Worcester

M. Duggan's 4 For 8 Spell

New Zealand 63 All Out

Worcester's Mary Duger Worcester's medium off bowling swingers, finished off swingers, cricket in Zealand's cricket in an hour's Test match today women's Test match today read ground In a spell all claimed at a overnight runs while and and England had in only 28 runs— had in with a dead was some rea ...stance out of a ·c fast between t to and were there 102 for four.

Rain delayed by which time game had dep

THE CRICKETER, JULY 24, 1954

FROM OUR SPECIAL CORRESPONDENT

The other third Test match, between the women of England and New Zealand at the Oval, was also left drawn yesterday. When the end of an interrupted day came at 6 o'clock New Zealand had scored 186 in reply to England's 281, on Saturday. Monday's play having been washed out by rain. England had won one and drawn the other in the series of three matches. A high one stage snapped off the Women's Cricket Associa- ...emed to be symptomatic intention to control the

Women's Cricket

The Editor, THE CRICKETER.

Dear Sir—A parson, as well as an old cricketer, I had sought the fullest advantage of questioning men, strangers as well as acquaintances, upon their opinion of women's cricket. The verdict is unanimous in spontaneous and serious admiration. It is remarkable what a large proportion of the attendances at Test matches were men glad to watch every hour.

It is regrettable that some Press reports have been super- cilious. Off-drives finding the fine-leg boundary are not unknown to Adam and he came before Eve.

One regular, long-experienced Ovalite said he found women's cricket more interesting than men's !

Yours faithfully,

F. G. FROST.

4 The Drive,
Buckhurst Hill, Essex.

---

was his mother. ----of the Doctor himself

NEITHER UNCERTAIN NOR COY

The day's play opened if not with a concerted before Du with a plea about whos slower ball. tainty nor c with a wicket-keep during a spe her pace, m luck. Couls timing a hoo Hide, in h spinners full as they resur only 28 runs— with a dead N was some rea

ENGLAND—Fir
Coulston 4 for

NEW ZE
J. Clothier, l-b-
J. M. Coulson
P. Hatcher, b. Jo
*R. Blackler, l-b-
V. U. McKenzie
J. Coutts, c. Du
P. M. Lamason, r
J. Batty, c. Murr
+V. Currie, c. Mur
Francis, b. Hea
Farrell, c. Hea
Extras (b. J.

Total
BOWLING—First I
Hexarty, 27—10—48
9—6—7—0 ; Hide. 10—6

	M	R	W
	27	26	1
	13	32	1
	18	16	1
	9	20	0

	/9	
	11	
	47	
	64	
	83	
	4·	
	20	
	12	
	4	
	4	
	288	

	R	W
	72	4
	33	1

Worcester: Worcestershire County Cricket Ground, July 3, 5 and 6

Flushed with success from their recent tour of the Western Counties, the confidence of the New Zealanders was high and the second Test eagerly awaited as the chance to square the series. On this occasion the eighteen-year-old Jean Coulston made her debut as a left-handed opening bat and right-handed pace bowler. Also included for this match was the experienced slow bowler and steady bat Ina Lamason, together with the number one wicketkeeper, Vi Farrell, now recovered from injury. England made just one change bringing in newcomer Anne Sanders whose off-spin replaced the leg-spin of Kay Green.

Hide won the toss and having decided to bat was prevented from so doing by rain. The very heavy rain not only delayed play by almost three hours but also flooded the original wicket. Considerately the groundsman provided another and the game eventually got under way with Westbrook and Cummins facing the pace of Francis and Joy Lamason. It quickly transpired that the drying wicket was likely to play tricks, with the ball both staying low and popping up disconcertingly, and, although it was Francis who struck the first blow in dismissing Cummins for 9, the spinners were soon brought into the attack.

It was 23 for 1 when Wilkinson joined Westbrook and they were looking to settle in when the latter was caught by Eris Paton to give Coulston her first Test wicket. But Coulston featured again quite soon when she took two difficult catches at point which helped Francis to gain the vital wicket of Hide and Ina Lamason to dismiss Wilkie, who was in good form for her 24.

At 63 for 4 Birch and Murrey were together. After a partnership of 24 runs, however, Birch was drawn out of her crease by one of Blackler's tantalising slows to be well stumped by Farrell. Shortly afterwards Murrey was caught behind off Ina Lamason and it was Hazel Sanders to play out the 14 minutes to tea with Duggan. The temptation of Blackler proved too much for Sanders though, and she succumbed to a catch by Francis having made 5. This meant that after the interval Duggan returned with number 9 Johnson who was promptly stumped by Farrell off the first ball she faced. The bowler, of course, was Blackler who, after Duggan was out lbw to Francis for 10, proceeded to tempt Hegarty. Finally the latter was also stumped having made 8 runs. The England innings closed at 4.59 pm with the total at 112.

The eleventh wicket of the day fell with New Zealand just 9 runs to the good, and thereafter the wicket treated the tourists despairingly. When at the close of play the scoreboard read 40 for 6, it was largely due to the spin of Anne Sanders: Her three wickets had cost just 6 runs.

The Monday morning saw both a dry wicket and an England team in the mood to finish things off. It was Eris Paton, on 6, and Ina Lamason with 2 to her credit who had to face the swing and pace of Duggan and Hegarty. After 45 minutes, though, both had gone to Duggan and New Zealand's resistance was virtually over. Duggan also claimed the next two wickets and with just on an hour to lunch New Zealand were all out for 63.

To show that, after all, the wicket was much more friendly than on Saturday, the England openers Westbrook and Cummins made their best stand – putting on 52 before Cummins was bowled by Paton for 31. Only two runs later Westbrook was caught by McKenzie off Blackler for 19 and Hide and Wilkinson were together. There then followed a sparkling partnership which displayed these two contrasting bats at their best. They lifted the scoring rate to beat the clock, bringing up the 100 partnership in 70 minutes. By the time Wilkinson was out for 47, caught by Coutts off Francis, England was 210 ahead.

The match was into the third session of the day when Birch replaced Wilkinson. Even though Hide soon departed for 64 Birch continued the run–getting spree in fine style. Murrey, Duggan and Sanders came and went while Birch flashed the bat effectively. At the day's end she was still there on 83 accompanied by Johnson with 4, and England were in the triumphant position of being 337 runs ahead with 3 wickets in hand.

With the scent of victory in the air and the weather friendly, Hide declared at the overnight total leaving New Zealand the daunting task of making 338 runs to win and herself the prospect of a full day's play to capture 10 wickets. To date, New Zealand had never exceeded 122 in the second innings of a Test against any country and the odds were very much in favour of an England victory.

Clothier and Coulston again opened for the visitors and, by lunch, a total of 105 minutes had produced some 40 runs and one wicket: Coulston had been caught by Duggan off occasional bowler Wilkinson for 9. Incredibly, also, opener Duggan had bowled 17 maidens in two spells. It was clear that New Zealand had their backs firmly to the wall with only a draw in mind.

The second wicket to fall was that of Joy Lamason, who was run out for 19 from a fine throw-in by Birch, ten minutes after lunch. At 45 for 2, Blackler joined Clothier, and with the latter totally untemptable, she made all the running taking 69 minutes to score a noble 46. When Blackler was out the score had reached 113 for 3, and with just under three hours left for play the odds looked to be evening up somewhat with the pressure on England to get wickets.

The next three wickets to fall did so with the addition of only 34 runs but it took far too long to get them. There were several missed chances but a final stand of 27 between Batty and Clothier saw New Zealand through to a draw. Clothier had batted 5½ hours for her tremendously patient not out 37, and Batty ended with 21 not out. New Zealand finished with a score of 174 for 6 and an enhanced reputation.

Summary of the Second Test 1954

Match Drawn

England:	112 and 288 for 7 dec
New Zealand:	63 and 174 for 6

Best Batting

1st Innings

England:	J Wilkinson	24
	B Murrey	19
	B D Birch	15
New Zealand:	J M Coulston	18
	E Paton	12

2nd Innings

England:	B D Birch	83 n o
	M E Hide	64
	J Wilkinson	47
New Zealand:	P Blackler	46
	J Clothier	37 n o
	P Batty	21 n o

Best Bowling

1st Innings

New Zealand:	P Blackler	4 – 22
	J Francis	3 – 30
	I M Lamason	2 – 23
England:	M B Duggan	4 – 15
	A Sanders	3 – 8

2nd Innings

New Zealand:	J Francis	4 – 72
England:	A Sanders	1 – 16
	M Johnson	1 – 20
	M B Duggan	1 – 26

Highlights

The spinner's wicket of the first day gave New Zealander Blackler four wickets off just 41 balls. Her match analysis was a good 5 for 66, but the bowler of the match was Francis who took her 7 match wickets off a total of 37 overs. Blackler, though, showed her all-round ability with the brave 46 in New Zealand's battle against certain defeat.

To find such a wicket on a debut as did Sanders must be a spin-bowler's dream, but Duggan once again came through with a match 5 for 41 off 48.5 overs, 35 of which were maidens. Hide's fifth Test 50 took only 60 minutes but Birch's first pipped it by just 2 minutes.

England's team for the final Test against New Zealand at The Oval in 1954 are: Standing L-R: Jo Batson (12th), Mary Johnson, Helene Hegarty, Jean Cummins, Joan Westbrook, Anne Sanders, Olive Marshall. Sitting: Barbara Murrey, Mary Duggan, Molly Hide (Capt.), Joan Wilkinson, Betty Birch.

Kennington, London: The Oval, July 24, 26 and 27

The third and final Test match between New Zealand and England held the prospect of a keenly fought game where the visitors needed a positive decision. A draw, however bravely executed, would be of no use to them here if England were not to end up victors in the series.

It is certain that Hide did not even contemplate defeat, nevertheless, the one change in the home side – Olive Marshall of Yorkshire for Surrey's Hazel Sanders – was a means of improving the outfielding and adding to the bowling power without depleting the batting strength.

The New Zealanders made two changes – one forced on them by injury to Eris Paton. It meant that the young pace bowler Joyce Currie made her Test debut and the other was a recall of Hatcher to the side instead of Joy Lamason.

A happy looking New Zealand team at The Oval for the final Test in 1954. They are (from L)
Captain Rona McKenzie, Ina Lamason (Vice-captain), Phyl Blackler, Vi Farrell, Joan
Hatcher, Joyce Clothier and Joyce Currie, Verna Coutts (partially obscured) with Peg Batty,
Jean Coulston and Joan Francis.

In bright sunshine with a hard, fast, but, as usual, placid wicket
promising plenty of runs, England's openers Westbrook and Cummins
faced the pace bowling of Francis and Currie. Within three overs the
bowling had been changed to Coulston and Batty, the former claiming
Westbrook's wicket with her first ball and rendering England 5 for 1.

Rapid changes of bowling seemed to be the McKenzie tactic, no
doubt in an attempt to unsettle the batsmen. This ploy made no
difference whatsoever to Wilkinson who survived all to bring up her
fifty and forge a second wicket partnership of 79 with Cummins before
the latter was caught in the slips by Clothier off McKenzie for 32. With
Hide and Wilkinson together at lunch, the England total had reached
88.

Not long after the interval Wilkie was well caught by wicketkeeper

Opener Jean Cummins is well caught in the slips by deputy wicketkeeper Joyce Clothier off the bowling of Rona McKenzie. Jean made 32 in England's only innings of 281. Rain restricted play and the match was drawn.

Farrell off Francis for 62. Then Hide swung at a straight ball from Coulston and was bowled for 17. This brought Murrey in to join Birch and these two produced some exhilarating cricket until Birch misjudged a call and was run out for 29.

At 174 for 5 Duggan joined Murrey who cruised on with her delightful leg-side play to a sparkling 50, reaching 62 before going lbw to Francis. Then Duggan took up the offensive, but was caught behind off Francis for 34, and the score was 246 for 7. After this Marshall went for 7, then Hegarty followed without adding to the score, leaving Johnson and Sanders to spend 24 minutes together making 33 runs. When Sanders was bowled by Batty she had made 9 and Johnson finished with 25 not out. England's innings ended after 4 hours 38 minutes batting with a score of 281.

New Zealand played out time with Clothier and Coulston looking full of confidence. At the day's end both were still there and 35 runs were on the board.

The weekend had given way to the threat of wet weather and the Monday was unrelenting in this respect. No play was possible until Tuesday 27th, and even then the skies were unfriendly. At 11.30, though, play *did* start and a minute later New Zealand was 35 for 1 when Clothier went lbw to Duggan for 11.

There was, of course, no hope of a decision in this match unless England could dismiss New Zealand twice in the day for 280 runs or less. After their showing at Worcester the likely capitulation of the New Zealanders in such a way was remote. Apart from any of these considerations it was the weather that had the upper hand and, in a day interfered with by rain, it was no surprise that the Tourists batted through to the close, finishing around 6 o'clock with 186. The Third Test was thus a disappointing draw and England had won the series.

Summary of the Third Test 1954

Match Drawn

England:	281
New Zealand:	186

Best Batting

		1st Innings
England:	J Wilkinson	62
	B Murrey	62
	M B Duggan	34
	J Cummins	32
	M Johnson	25 n o
New Zealand:	I M Lamason	37 n o
	J M Coulston	24
	P Batty	24

Best Bowling

		1st Innings
New Zealand:	J M Coulston	4 – 38
	J Francis	3 – 98
England:	H Hegarty	5 – 48
	M B Duggan	3 – 48

Highlights

Wilkinson's second 50 of the series and her career took 81 minutes and gave her a series average of 46.25 with which she topped the statistics. Murrey, second in the averages with 40.25, made her 50 in 60 minutes. The best bowler for New Zealand was Coulston who was also second highest scorer, but with her 3 wickets in this match Francis emphasised her outstanding contribution having taken 12 wickets in all Tests at 18.83 each off 80 overs.

For England there was little doubt that Duggan was most successful with her 13 wickets overall – off 126 overs – but here Hegarty took precedence. She bagged 5 wickets in an innings for the first time at 9.6 apiece off 27 overs, 10 of which were maidens.

ENGLAND IN NEW ZEALAND AND AUSTRALIA 1957-8

The third of the selected teams to tour abroad was accompanied by that most dogged destroyer of cricket – temperamental weather. It rained, and it rained a lot. The omen was there, unsuspectingly, when the New Zealand Shipping Company's passenger liner the RMS Rangitane suffered a mid-voyage collision with a freighter. At 12.55 pm on Thursday October 10, in a sudden blinding rainstorm typical of the tropics, the two vessels collided in the Panama Canal, holing the Rangitane in her bow and causing the much more extensively damaged Hawaian Tourist to run aground. The result for the liner was a hold-up of five days at Balboa, in heat so sweltering that the tar between the upper deck planking bubbled. Eventually, however, the ship again got under way and arrived in the Port of Wellington on November 2nd. Among its disembarking passengers were the undaunted representatives of the cream of England's women cricketers.

After nearly five weeks at sea, land-legs were to prove distinctly rubbery, and getting them into the action of the cricket field was to be another case of "delayed by rain". As might well be imagined, exercises on board ship had been pursued with varying degrees of enthusiasm by the team members. Some turned out to be very poor sailors indeed and the rocking motion of the ship did not go very well with the rigours of early morning keep fit routines before breakfast!

More enjoyable, and certainly more entertaining for the passengers, were the traditional deck cricket matches against the crew. So lusty were the attempts – also traditional it seems – to hit as many of the specially made sawdust and rope balls over the side, that the Rangitane's Captain had to beg a further supply from a passing ship. It was Hazel Sanders, one of the more diminutive members of the team who notched up the record on this occasion. But, despite the restrictions on space and an over-abundance of food, it was a pretty healthy bunch of cricketers who finally set foot on New Zealand soil.

Daily Practice Has Kept Women Cricketers Fit

Daily practice during their trip to New Zealand in the

Rain Foils English T
In Quest Of D

The unkind weather which has women cricketers in each of their five m the visitors of gaining a decision in th South Island.

Sporting Chance For N.Z. In Women's Cricket Match

NEW ZEALAND were well on the board shortly after the resumption of play in the third and last day of the women's cricket test against England this morning.

Clothier and E. Dickson were batting steadily and put up New Zealand's 50 just before noon. At this stage both batsmen were pushing the runs when any loose bowling of the English bowlers allowed them to take chances.

J. Clothier run out		8
E. Dickson c M. Duggan b J. Hawes		5
M. Speight b E. Barker		0
V. Coutts c H. Sanders b Hawes ..		2
R. McKenzie b McFarlane		14
G. Sutherland b Duggan		8
E. Paton not out		75
P. Blackler b Duggan		0
C. Sinton b Hawes		10
J. Currie b McFarlane		0
Extras		10
		—
Total for nine wickets		128

London liner in canal collision

PANAMA CITY, Thursc
..hips collided hea
..anama C
..the Ame
..aiian Tou
on Rangita
..rs bound
..s damaged
..ed under

..erican fr
..nd it took
er.
..en blinding
of the tropic
. vessels as t
he canal
one was
..es. ...nedin
no played a
g New Zea-
30 after four
..r 22 runs.
..inutes and
..against all
..ui rangiand s bowlers.

The day otherwise mostly belonged to England which now looks favoured to win the match on the third and final day tomorrow. England's first innings closed at 186, giving it an advantage of 56 and by stumps it had lost three wickets for 44 in its second knock. It thus has a lead of 100 runs with seven wickets to fall.

N.Z. Fight Back In Women's Cricket Test

AUCKLAND, Today.—England w: all out for 186 after 14 minutes' pl; when the second Test against the Ne Zealand women's team was continue at Eden Park today.

The England not out batsmen Hele Sharpe (6) and J. Hawes (0) beg: briskly but they had added only 11 ru to the overnight total of 166 for eig wickets before Jean Coulston clea bowled Miss Hawes (4).

Dorothy McFarlane had a life wh two fielders collided when going for catch and Miss Sharpe was similar fortunate next ball. Miss McFarla was finally caught by Joyce Caugh and the innings ended with 186 on t board.

New Zealand fared poorly and fo wickets were down for 22 runs befo the captain, Rona McKenzie, and t Otago all-rounder, Iris Paton, made stand. The pair took the total to 46 lunch.

New Zealand fought back after lun and scoring was slow. Then, after partnership of 33 with Miss Pat Miss McKenzie was clean bowled Miss McFarlane for 14. Gwen Su erland got to five before Miss Dugg claimed her wicket. New Zealand n had six wickets down for 74.—(PA)

ENGLAND.

First innings .. ..

During a tour notorious for extremely wet conditions, cloudless skies top the England team for the first Test against New Zealand in November 1957. Standing L-R: Jo Batson (12th), Edna Barker, Dorothy Macfarlane, Helene Hegarty, Ruth Westbrook (Wkt) Audrey Disbury. Sitting: Olive Marshall, Hazel Sanders, Cecilia Robinson (Vice-capt.), Mary Duggan (Capt.), Betty Birch, Joan Wilkinson.

Christchurch: Lancaster Park, November 29, 30 and December 2

Incredibly, for as yet the epithet "Rainmakers" had not inured the team to the monotonously depressing weather, the first practice session was delayed by rain. And rain continued to interfere with all the matches. It meant that the run up to the first Test in Christchurch was highlighted by only one win – and that against a weak "Country" side.

No-one was surprised, though everyone was dismayed, by the curtailment of pre-Test nets. Yes, because of rain. However, Friday November 29 goes on record as being a lovely, clear, and sunny morning. It was warm too, and the distant snow-capped peaks were not seen as indicators of past weather so ruefully suffered, but as the picturesque bonus to a perfect cricket setting.

Having lost the toss England opened with fast bowlers Dorothy Macfarlane and Helene Hegarty who made little headway on a very soft, wet wicket. Only when slow bowlers Edna Barker and Mary Duggan came on did prospects begin to look a little more hopeful. The first breakthrough was Duggan's when she bowled Evonne Dickson for 5 and the New Zealand score was then 18 after almost an hour's play. Mary Speight joined the number one, Joyce Clothier, and after getting settled against the containing spin, began to use her feet well. At lunch, no further wicket had fallen and the score had reached 62.

The interval had obviously produced a spur to Clothier and Speight when the latter, particularly, attempted to force the pace. In fact, against the renewed attack of Hegarty and Macfarlane immediately after lunch 20 runs were added in some 10 minutes. But just as the partnership was taking hold, Duggan changed the bowling bringing on off-spinners Disbury and Barker. It was the former who got Clothier caught behind while attempting a sweep to make the score 86 for 2, and then Speight played–on a ball from Barker. Three wickets were down for exactly the 100 and Captain Rona McKenzie joined Verna Coutts.

Although Coutts started well she was not confident against the spinners and soon lost her wicket, caught by Joan Wilkinson off Duggan for 10. This signalled a very good spell by Duggan who next broke up a promising partnership between McKenzie and Gwen Sutherland when she had the latter lbw for 13. At 146 for 5, Phyl

Smiling in the sunshine a group of New Zealanders waiting to resume play in the first Test at Christchurch, 1957. They are (L-R), Jean Coulston, Joyce Clothier, Evonne Dickson, Brenda Duncan, Mary Speight. Eris Paton is partly hidden behind Phyl Blackler (leaning forward), and standing, the Captain Rona McKenzie.

Blackler joined McKenzie whose forceful on-side driving and hooking had taken her into the mid-thirties. Equally powerful and never a laggard, Blackler hit two boundaries off Macfarlane in one over before going to left-armer Duggan for 24. When Duggan had McKenzie caught at silly-mid for a well-played 60, she had taken 4 wickets and New Zealand had reached 213 for 7.

The last four players, Betty Thorner, Joyce Currie, Jean Coulston and Brenda Duncan only managed to put on another 10 runs, with Duncan remaining not out 0. This left England some twenty minutes batting to end of play.

On the Saturday pitch conditions were much drier and Cecilia Robinson and Wilkie were untroubled by openers Coulston and Currie when they resumed the England innings at 11 for no wicket. When she'd added 8 to her overnight score, however, Wilkie was bowled by first change bowler Duncan and England were 30 for 1. Betty Birch joined Robbie and while she attempted to score, Robbie seemed bogged down. At lunch England had 59 on the board for 2 wickets, Birch had made 25 of them, with Duggan on 0 and Robbie on 18, having added just 15 runs in her two hours at the wicket.

The post-lunch session saw a Mary Duggan determined to retrieve England's attacking spirit and she set about the bowling with forceful verve. In the first half-hour after lunch 44 runs were added and Duggan soon brought up her 50. Although McKenzie rang the bowling changes the partnership went relentlessly on with Duggan scoring powerfully off well-placed drives. The last bowler tried, Thorner, achieved the breakthrough when she bowled Robbie in her second over for 65, and the partnership had realised 136 runs.

The attacking stance was taken up by Hazel Sanders who scored a quick 16 runs – 8 off one Thorner over. Her wicket eventually went to Coulston off a skier caught at slip by McKenzie. The fast bowler then got Marshall for 0, Duggan for 108 and Barker for 0. Ruth Westbrook and Audrey Disbury were not out 8 and 7 respectively when the England innings was declared at 255 for 7.

In the 55 minutes left for play, Clothier and Dickson had knocked off 27 of the 32 run deficit, but with two innings still to play and one day left, a likely draw was in the offing.

Of the 177 for 7 wickets declared that New Zealand made by the tea interval on the last day, Dickson was the top-scorer with 65. The England side bowled well and fielded brilliantly with Marshall exceptional at cover and square. She was responsible for two run-outs but it was Hegarty who threw down the wicket of stubborn opener Clothier who made 26.

In an attempt to go for the runs Duggan changed the batting order but Currie got among the wickets and at the close England were 48 for 4. The first Test was a salutary draw.

Summary of the First Test 1957-8

Match Drawn

New Zealand	223 and 177 for 7 dec.
England:	255 and 48 for 4

Best Batting

	1st Innings	
New Zealand:	R U McKenzie	60
	M Speight	42
	J Clothier	34
England:	M B Duggan	108
	M C Robinson	65

	2nd Innings	
New Zealand:	E Dickson	65
	J Clothier	26
England:	J Wilkinson	11

Best Bowling

	1st Innings	
England:	M B Duggan	6 – 55
	D Macfarlane	2 – 49
New Zealand:	J M Coulston	4 – 73

	2nd Innings	
England:	D Macfarlane	2 – 35
New Zealand:	J Currie	3 – 36

Highlights

With McKenzie's first Test 50 and the gallant support of Speight and Clothier, New Zealand registered their highest ever score against England in this 223. Nor had they ever been in a position to declare in the past. Coulston, ably supported by Currie, again showed her very good style of fast bowling.

The contrast of Duggan's 108, including the second fastest century in 135 minutes, and Robinson's 65, which included one of the slowest 50s on record, still left England running out of time and a decision impossible. Macfarlane bowled well and Duggan using spin for the first time in a Test achieved 5 wickets in an innings for the third time in her career.

The Main Stand at Eden Park, Auckland, before the start of the second Test Match, December 1957.

Auckland: Eden Park, December 27, 28 and 29

Between the Christchurch Test and this second one just on a month later, several factors – aside from the weather that is – augured well for the England tourists. One of these was a spirited win in a two-day match against Wellington at the Basin Reserve. It was a game which was particularly heartening since, having been left some 30 minutes to score 64 runs, the challenge was met in the face of the fierce attack of the New Zealand fast bowlers Coulston and Currie. Another positive factor was the possibility of including Shirley Driscoll in the side. After a six week lay-off because of a damaged hand, Shirley now had the chance to do what she'd travelled thousands of miles to accomplish and that was to open the innings for England. Thirdly, and most important-antly, the second Test had the advantage of fielding an England side never more united in the common purpose of going all-out to win.

Come the day and both sides had made team changes. New Zealand had strengthened her batting when forced to leave out injured medium-fast bowler Duncan, by bringing in Caroline Sinton. For England, Driscoll was duly in, fast bowler Hawes replaced Hegarty and Helen

Sharpe took over as wicketkeeper.

England won the toss and Duggan elected to bat on a rain-affected wicket. In fact play was delayed for 45 minutes but soon after the start England were in trouble. Driscoll went for two and the score was a disappointing 7 for 1 wicket. But then the stalwart Robbie, with Wilkie batting her customary number 3 once again, got down to the task of accumulating runs. Both players exhibited a range of strokeplay that was tempered with caution and aided by some smart running between the wickets. Wilkie, in particular, was hard on the over-pitched ball and in this fashion lunch arrived with England on 49.

Unfortunately a light drizzle set in after lunch which, although it gave the bowlers trouble in handling the ball, also gave them a second wicket. Robinson went lbw to Coulston for 40. Shortly after Duggan joined Wilkie, rain stopped play.

It was just on two hours before play recommenced – the tea interval having been taken during that time – but after another 30 minutes Duggan was out, bowled by Speight for 10. Fortunately for England, while wickets tumbled Wilkie continued to wield a provocative bat. When Helen Sharpe joined her the score was a moderate 132 for 6, soon to be 159 for 7 when Wilkie herself was bowled by the ever-tempting Blackler just 10 short of her century. Barker too went at the close and England had totalled 166 for 8 in some 200 minutes of playing time.

By noon on the second day England were all out for 186. In reply, New Zealand began poorly with the run out of opener Clothier for a duck and partner Dickson being caught by Duggan off Hawes for 5. Replacements Speight and Coutts did not hang around long either; the former being bowled by Barker for 10 and the latter going to Hawes for a duck, caught by close-fielder Sanders. At 22 for 4 things were looking doleful for New Zealand.

The next pair in, Paton and McKenzie, set about restoring the position in determined fashion and were still there at lunch with the score at 46 for 4. After the break they continued to go along well until a Macfarlane swinger clean bowled McKenzie for 14. The partnership had put on a vital 33 runs in good time.

As did England's Wilkinson, Eris Paton then played the sheet anchor role for her team while wickets fell regularly at the other end. In fact only two players managed to score, Sutherland making 4 and Sinton 10. Duggan and Hawes polished off the last four wickets between them, but no-one could shake Paton who finished with a well-fought 77 not out in New Zealand's total of 130.

With about 80 minutes left for play Duggan was forced into changing the batting order because Driscoll had pulled a muscle while fielding. Unfortunately, substitute Sharpe was at the crease just two minutes before being comprehensively bowled by Coulston, and 1 for 1 created little joy in the England dressing room. Wilkie and Robbie together restored order but at the day's end were nevertheless out with England on 44 for 3 wickets.

It was a dull and threatening third and final day that began with Birch and Duggan looking to add to the 94 lead in a style that would allow England plenty of time to bowl out the opposition. The first set-back occurred within ten minutes though, when Birch fell to a Speight off-spinner with just 1 to her name. At this stage Mary Speight had taken 3 of the wickets to fall for just 5 runs.

Now Driscoll joined Duggan and virtually in an opening role proceeded to make good going with her captain. Duggan brought up her 50 in 71 minutes and when out had scored a splendid 85 runs and mounted a 5th wicket partnership of 104 that took only 83 minutes. Within half-an-hour of her departure two more wickets had fallen but at lunch Driscoll was not out for 32 and England declared at 171 for 7.

Needing 228 to win in 210 minutes New Zealand, to their credit, made a valiant attempt at the target. In miserable drizzle from the start, which at times turned to quite heavy rain, they reached 100 for 3 and were putting England under pressure. Eris Paton produced a fine performance but when she went lbw to Duggan for 43, it signalled a Duggan breakthrough. The next three wickets all went to her spin and New Zealand were 187 for 7. Just 41 short of the target Mary Speight, who was having a grand match, made 24 before being run out. This left a situation where England needed one wicket with three balls to go. It was fast bowler Coulston who had to fce those three balls from Duggan and she had already taken 5 for 47. But the experienced Coulston, who at one time had opened the batting for her country, played them safely to achieve an honourable draw.

Summary of the Second Test 1957–8

Match Drawn

| England: | 186 and 171 for 7 dec |
| New Zealand: | 130 and 203 for 9 |

Best Batting

1st Innings

England:	J Wilkinson	90
	C Robinson	40
New Zealand:	E Paton	77 n o

2nd Innings

England:	M B Duggan	85
	S Driscoll	32 n o
	J Wilkinson	26
New Zealand:	E Paton	43
	E Dickson	39
	M Speight	24

Best Bowling

1st Innings

New Zealand:	J Coulston	3 – 30
	M Speight	3 – 34
England:	J Hawes	4 – 36
	M B Duggan	2 – 22

2nd Innings

| New Zealand: | M Speight | 3 – 32 |
| England: | M B Duggan | 5 – 47 |

Highlights

Wilkinson's 90 represented her highest score in Test cricket and the third 50 in her career. For Duggan to follow her previous Test century with 85 here, and to take 7 wickets overall for an average 9.57 apiece, was a premier performance. The fifth wicket partnership of 104 with Driscoll was a new record.

For New Zealand, Paton's 77 was not only a match saving innings but represented the highet Test score against England by a New Zealander. The most successful bowler, Speight, did extremely well to take 6 for 66 in the match.

AUSTRALIA IN 1958

Leaving Auckland on the s.s. *Monowai* was at the same time tinged with sadness and expectation. The New Zealanders had treated the team like royalty, and their farewell was no exception. It is the custom to hurl brightly coloured streamers between ship and quayside and to hang on to them until the inevitable tug of the moving vessel breaks the thin paper connection. As these then drift in the breeze and trail on the water, there is a symbolic poignancy that causes a catch in the throat as well as moistness in the eyes. Waving and last minute repartee all helps to heighten the emotional moment and both continue until distance makes intelligible sight and sound impossible. There were then three days of shipboard life in which to talk over memories and to guess at what lay ahead. And there was plenty of opportunity for catching up on letters home and sleep.

Crossing the Tasman Sea could be quite an experience it had been suggested by more than one seasoned New Zealand traveller. As the ship reached the open sea, however, all was calm, sunny and relaxing. The lull lasted only until nightfall. By breakfast-time the seas were so rough that of those who made it to the dining room, few indeed saw the meal through. Most of the journey continued in similar vein, only the stalwarts managing to stay on their feet. Among these was Mary Duggan, who, by every law of human frailty, should have been the one most in need of rest after her almost superhuman feats with bat and ball on New Zealand's *terra firma*.

And so it was with a large measure of relief mixed with an excited and buoyant air that the English tourists lined the deck to get first glimpse of the environs of Sydney Harbour. For those whose first view of that magnificent bridge this was, the sight was a thrilling one never to be forgotten. But before the welcome by hostesses and friends – the inevitable team photographs. Souvenirs to send home of course, and vital to publicise the game of cricket that everyone was keen to get on and play.

Sydney: The North Sydney Cricket Ground, February 7, 8 & 10

During the month that had passed between arrival at Sydney and returning for the first Test Match, England remained undefeated on the cricket field and had five wins in six matches. Among the wins was a significant victory by 10 wickets against an Australian XI at Brisbane, and another cheering 9 wicket result against the New South Wales State side. All systems were go for England riding the wave of success and eager to confirm their cricketing prowess by defeating the full Australia cohort. Yet again, however, it was rain that triumphed. On this occasion the most disappointingly cruel blow to English aspirations occurred when incessant and extremely heavy rain caused the match to be abandoned without a ball being bowled.

Melbourne: St Kilda Cricket Ground, February 21, 22 & 24

There came a stage when the entire England contingent began to believe that they would never play a Test Match in Australia. On the first day, it wasn't actually raining but the ground had been so saturated by the downpour on previous days that it was unfit for play. This was

Farewell to New Zealand – Auckland, January 1958.

Australia's team for the second Test (but the first played) at St Kilda, Melbourne in 1958. Standing (L-R): Barbara Orchard, Valerie Slater (12th), Val Batty, Faith Coulthard, Eileen Massey, Nell Massey (Wkt), Ruth Dow, Una Paisley (Capt.). Sitting: Betty Wilson, Joyce Dalton, Joyce Christ, Mary Allitt (Vice-capt.).

added to the disappointment of not being able to complete the match against the Victorian State XI which also had a delayed start. This, though, was not because of the weather but because some of the England team's luggage went astray on the road between Sydney and Melbourne. Unfortunately the luggage in transit contained most of the cricket gear. But when play in the Test Match began – on time – on the Saturday morning, events were sensational.

Duggan won the toss and elected to field. She obviously knew a thing or two about the state of the wicket because, of the thirteen overs bowled by the openers, Macfarlane and Hawes, nine were maidens. For the Australians, playing scoring shots seemed a difficult proposition and their situation didn't improve when spin bowlers Duggan and Barker took over. When Betty Wilson, the number 5, took guard at the wicket they were 11 for 3, every wicket going to a catch. Straight away, as becomes a class player, Wilson made her strokes and looked to have conquered both wicket and bowling until she was clean bowled by a perfect length ball from Barker which turned appreciably. After that, the demise of the Australians was rapid. Unable to cope with the accurate leg spin bowling of the indomitable Duggan, the next 6 wickets fell for only 14 runs. Almost unbelievably Australia were all out for 38 – the lowest score ever recorded by an Australian team anywere in the world. Mary Duggan's bag of wickets totalled 7, six of which were caught and one bowled, for only 6 runs. An amazing feat indeed in only 14.3 overs.

Much sooner than anyone could have imagined, then, England were at the crease. Having fielded first they knew the discomfitures of the wicket and with their own eyes had seen the devastation wrought by top class spin bowling. Fortunately, the Australian Captain, Una Paisley, did not open the bowling with the off breaks of Betty Wilson or the England score might have been even more reduced. Even so the bowling of medium pacer Joyce Christ and the medium-fast Eileen Massey had its rewards when England were 2 wickets down with only one run on the score-board. A very temporary stand by Birch and Wilkinson allowed another 12 runs to be added until Birch was bowled by Wilson for 8. Christ picked up another wicket when she had Wilkinson leg before. This brought number 4 Duggan in to bat.

If anyone was aware of what the wicket was really doing it must have been the England Captain, and for a while she proceeded to show her team-mates what it was possible to achieve. In moving down the wicket to a Wilson delivery, however, she failed to make contact and was stumped by 'keeper Nell Massey. This signalled a Wilson rout which had the rest of the England players prodding and poking at the deadly accurate bowling. The last 4 wickets went for 4 runs – all to Wilson – and included a hat-trick. England were all out for 35. In the space of some four hours an all-time record low score had been made and broken. It was a record that the English tourists could well have done without at such a time. In just 63 balls, Wilson took 7 wickets for 7 runs. With Duggan's 7 for 6, it meant that 14 wickets fell for just under a run apiece.

The result of such low scoring meant that Australia had to bat again that day. England opened with the fast bowlers, for by now the wicket showed signs of being firmer. Though success was not immediate, at the close of play Australia were 66 for 4, the wickets being shared by Duggan and Barker, and England were in an encouraging position. Every member of the team would have felt easier in her mind, however, if Betty Wilson had not still been there with 27 to her credit.

The second, but final day of play was bright and sunny and the wicket was hard. England opened with the fast bowlers and Hawes soon had Batty caught by Robinson at slip for 10. First change Barker trapped Christ lbw for 12 but Wilson went cruising on scoring freely all round the wicket. At lunch she was 88 and Australia 162 for 6. With partner Joyce Dalton batting spiritedly, Wilson went on after lunch in the same vein as before it and in ten minutes scored the twelve runs needed to complete her century. With the very next ball she missed the cut intended to celebrate the event and was bowled middle stump by Hawes. During her stay at the crease, Wilson saw Australia's score go from 27 for 3 to 176 for 7.

The next wicket to fall was Dalton's – run out as she had been in the first innings – for 26. The score was 184 for 8 and when the ninth wicket fell at 202 Australia declared, leaving England to amass 206 runs in 165 minutes.

Openers Robinson and Driscoll made a businesslike attack on the Australian bowling to bring up 25 runs in 25 minutes. Even when Driscoll was out and replaced by Birch the runs kept coming, and 50 were notched up in 56 minutes. But the second wicket went down for 52 and at this stage Duggan promoted herself in the batting order. She made 11 runs in 14 minutes but when she went, Robinson followed without adding to the total. England were 64 for 4 and there were now

Play in progress with Australia in the field at St Kilda in 1958. This was a match that Australia let slip from her grasp when England made the record lowest score of all time in her first innings 35.

only 54 minutes left in which to make 132 runs to win. At just over two runs a minute the task was not impossible – but that was ignoring the penetrating bowling of the spinners, Wilson and Dow. The England numbers 6, 7 and 8 went to Wilson for just 3 runs, and Dow was not giving runs away either. Now it was Australia striving to get the two wickets they needed for victory. Their frustration was in trying to remove Wilkie – who stonewalled for an incredible 86 minutes to be not out at close of play for 5 runs. England finished the day at 76 for 8 wickets, and the match was drawn. A moral victory to Australia perhaps but certainly a personal triumph for Betty Wilson. No Test player, female or male, has ever completed a hat-trick and a century in the same Test. To be top scorer in both, completely different innings, and to have taken 11 wickets at 1.45 runs apeice in 29.3 overs 18 of which were maidens, simply adds to the splendour of that achievement.

Summary of the Second Test 1957–8

Australia:	38 & 202 for 9 dec.
England:	35 & 76 for 8.

Best Batting

1st Innings

Australia:	B Wilson	12
England:	M B Duggan	12

2nd Innings

Australia:	B Wilson	100
England:	S Driscoll	24

Best Bowling

1st Innings

England:	M B Duggan	7 – 6
Australia:	B Wilson	7 – 7 inc. hat-trick

2nd Innings

England:	J Hawes	3 – 32
	E Barker	3 – 58
Australia:	B Wilson	4 – 9
	R Dow	4 – 21

Highlights

Six of Duggan's 7 first innings wickets were caught and one bowled. Three of the catches were made by Driscoll fielding at point. Another catch in the second innings gave Driscoll her fourth catch off the bowling of Duggan. Wilson's 7 – 7 included 4 wickets in 5 balls.

Adelaide: Adelaide Oval, March 8, 10 & 11

Between the drama at Melbourne and the official Third Test in Adelaide, only one two-day game was played. This was against the South Australian State team and the result was a convincing win for Engand by an innings and some 40 runs. It wasn't a result to assist the tourists' batting however, since the putting on of an exhibition for the sake of the spectators doesn't exactly simulate match play conditions. But at least for both cricket and royalty – the Queen Mother's visit to Adelaide coincided with that of the touring team – South Australia put on its most glorious wether.

It was very apparent that the bone hard wicket of the Adelaide Oval was a batsman's dream and, on the morning of Saturday, March 8, the toss of the coin favoured those of Australia. As before, Vice-Captain Allitt and wicketkeeper Massey opened, this time to face the hostile bowling of Macfarlane and Hegarty. Within one minute of starting play and off the second ball of the first over, Allitt was out for a duck. Caught Robinson bowled Macfarlane was a success which clearly sharpened the fielders' reflexes who were once again given the inspiration of Robbie's slip catching expertise. When Massey was run out 42 minutes later the score was 12 for 2. That it wasn't the wicket belying its looks, but probably the unaccustomed pace and accuracy of the slow attack was soon shown when at lunch, after 106 minutes play, Australia were 41 for 2. Dow and Paisley were then both looking comfortable but scoring remarkably slowly.

First to go after lunch was Ruth Dow to a catch by Disbury off Hegarty. Her 26 runs had taken 124 minutes to accumulate, and it was clear that a spurt was needed if the Australians were to make the running from a mediocre 56 for 3. Dow's going brought Betty Wilson to the wicket and, though looking confident, she too seemed pegged down by the bowling. Another wicket wasn't too long in coming, however, when Paisley played back to Macfarlane and stepped on her wicket. This made the score 66 for 4. It was now Val Batty who joined Wilson, and gradually they altered the pace of play. Batty made every effort to get on with it – her second, third and fourth scoring strokes all producing well run threes. And yet, when the 100 came up, it was at the rate of almost one run every two minutes. Tardy, considering the conditions. Then, though, runs began to flow from the bat. Both Wilson and Batty looked set for big scores when a run a minute became the norm. Ten minutes after tea saw Wilson's 50 and twenty minutes later Batty achieved hers.

Relief came for the England side when Batty was run out by a brilliant Marshall return, and Australia were 201 for 5. Christ joined Wilson who, three minutes before stumps, brought up her century to an ovation from an appreciative crowd. At the close she was 106 not out and Australia were 248 for 5.

The rest day was especially welcome for England because when play resumed on the Monday, another beautifully sunny day, Australia continued batting. Though Wilson again looked stylishly aggressive, England had the reward of her wicket when she was clean bowled by Hegarty after adding 21 runs to her total in almost even time. Dalton joined Christ and kept up the pace. A short time later two wickets fell in quick succession. First Christ was caught in the slips by Barker off Macfarlane and then number 9, Bath, was bowled by Hegarty; the score was 282 for 8. Time for a declaration one might have thought, but, no, Australia went on batting and finished with 292. Apart from the two run outs, Macfarlane and Hegarty shared the wickets between them.

As if to emphasise that the Adelaide Oval wicket was not the batsman's ideal it seemed, when Robinson and Driscoll opened for England against the pace attack of Massey and Test newcomer Marjorie Marvell, runs seemed equally hard to come by. The 39 minutes before lunch produced only 19 without loss, Driscoll accounting for 13 of them. After lunch spinner Dow, who had replaced Marvell, and Massey continued bowling and were patiently resisted. Two bowling changes later brought on Wilson who in her third over had Driscoll caught by the wicket-keeper for 29. England were then 43 for 1 wicket. Wilkinson was next in but stayed for only one run before going lbw to Wilson.

The inimitable Wilson who seemed instantly to find perfect length and flight, then had Duggan caught by Marvell for 2. With England's score at 51 for 3, the 50 having taken 112 minutes to achieve, the situation began to look like a repeat of the Australian innings. At a similar point they had scored 56 – but taken longer to bring up the 50.

While Robbie offered near passive resistance to everything sent down to her, Batson came in at number 5 and stayed 25 minutes for her two runs before being caught by Christ off Dow. Westbrook was next in and lifted the game and the scoring rate when she used her feet to the spin bowlers. Soon after Robinson made her 50 – in 238 minutes – Westbrook got hers, taking a comparatively speedy 99 minutes. At close of play the score was 154 for 4, with Westbrook on 59 and Robinson 60.

The third and final day dawned equally bright and sunny. For England, however, still 138 runs behind on the first innings, it was

Left-hander Jo Batson playing in the third Test at Adelaide in 1958, is out to a diving catch by Joyce Christ off spinner Ruth Dow for 2 runs. Nell Massey is the wicketkeeper and Mary Allitt is at square.

essential to get on with scoring or face the dismal prospect of a draw. Westbrook started confidently enough but, when Wilson came on to bowl was caught off the first ball of the over. Her going put England at 177 for 5, while the partnership with Robinson had contributed a valuable 119 runs.

Disbury got into the teens and her demise still left Robbie going stolidly on. At lunch she was 99 not out with number 8 Marshall on 3. Just 4 minutes after the interval Robinson was out for 102, caught at square leg by opening bowler Massey off her fast bowler colleague Marvell who had taken the new ball. Being still 65 runs behind the Australian total did not leave much room for declaration on such a wicket on the last day, but as if such a prospect was possible Barker's first scoring shot was a boundary. She and Marshall gathered runs mostly in twos and threes until the latter was caught behind off Wilson for 16. The total of 247 for 8 was soon 247 for 9 when Macfarlane failed

Coming off at the Adelaide Oval after their world record 10th wicket partnership of 78, in which Helene Hegarty (L) scored a record 34 and Edna Barker remained 50 not out. It was the third Test during the 1957-8 tour.

to score. Yet another victim for Wilson. Just as it began to look as though England would never make the Aussies total let alone pass it, Barker and Hegarty began to achieve the improbable. Some hard hitting and good running between the wickets soon had the 50 partnership up, and the exhilarating play gave the last hour of the England innings a spirited 78 runs. The fastest run-rate of either innings came to an end when Hegarty was caught by Dow off Wilson, leaving Barker 50 not out.

Though England had passed the Australian total by 33 runs, it was clear that no decision could be reached. Australia batted out time finishing with 78 for 2 wickets. With yet another drawn Test Match, England could only be left with the realisation of the *tour de force* that Betty Wilson represented, firstly in scoring 127, and then taking 6 for 71 on a supposed batsman's paradise. But, both teams must surely have continued to ponder the deception of a wicket on which it had proved so difficult to score.

Summary of the Third Test 1957-8

Australia: 292 & 78 for 2
England: 325

Best Batting

1st Innings

Australia: B Wilson   127
               V Batty   63

England: C Robinson   102
               R Westbrook   66
               E Barker   50 n o

2nd Innings

Australia: R Dow   30 n o
               M Allitt   25

Best Bowling

1st Innings

England: H Hegarty   4 – 70
               D Macfarlane   4 – 82

Australia: B Wilson   6 – 71

Highlights

Betty Wilson's 127 scored in 200 minutes was the highest Test score in an Australia v England series. Her 6 – 71 brought the tally of wickets in two tests to 17 for 87.

Cecilia Robinson's century took 365 minutes – the slowest on record.

Perth: The W.A.C.A. Ground, March 21, 22, 24

The experience of travelling the two gauge railway across the Nullarbor Plain brought the England tourists to the final Test Match in Perth. With an easy win over the Western Australian State team, a one day game, it meant that during the entire tour England had not lost a match. Was the last Test to maintain that record?

It would be supposing Cecilia Robinson less than human if such thoughts had not been present in her mind as she contemplated her first full Test captaincy in the absence of an unfit Mary Duggan. But at least the good omens were there when she won the toss for England and chose to bat on a plumb hard wicket. The weather was perfect.

Australia opened with Marvell and Massey, the Adelaide Test openers and due to some accurate bowling by Marvell, who started with seven maidens, Robinson and Driscoll had put on only 25 runs in the first hour's play. Gradually, however, the run rate picked up and at lunch the score was 72 for no wicket with Driscoll on 46 and Robinson on 24. When some 25 minutes after lunch Robbie was needlessly run out, the score of 95 was the highest opening partnership of all the Test Matches, both in Australia and New Zealand, that England had so far managed to produce. It was a good foundation from which to start to pile up runs when Wilkie came in at number three to join Driscoll who

England's team for the final Test at the WACA in Perth, March 1958. Standing from L: Betty Birch, Audrey Disbury, Helene Hegarty, Dorothy Macfarlane, Cecilia Robinson (Capt.), Edna Barker, Jo Batson (12th) Kneeling from L: Polly Marshall, Shirley Driscoll, Joan Hawes, Ruth Westbrook, Joan Wilkinson.

Cecilia Robinson, England's Captain for the final Test of the 1957-8 tour which took place at the WACA in Perth, just fails to hold on to what would have been a most magnificent catch. The bowler was Dorothy Macfarlane and the fortunate bat, opener Mary Allitt.

was now in full flow. But Wilkie was unlucky to be out for only 2 runs to a very good catch at mid-on by the newcomer McDonough, the West Australian Captain who had replaced the unavailable Ruth Dow.

101 for 2 saw the recalled Birch at the wicket. Her lack of match practice showed as she seemed bogged down by Wilson's bowling and couldn't make scoring shots of significance. The scoring rate was further affected dramatically when Driscoll was bowled by Paisley for 72. At the tea interval England were 169 for 5 having lost the wickets of Westbrook, stumped for 23, and Disbury, caught and bowled Wilson for 5.

The need to force the pace which invariably had fallen to the lot of the middle order bats throughout the tour, was theirs even to the last it seemed.

It was Barker who joined Birch at the wicket after tea and the two of them got on top of the bowling – with Birch looking a transformed player. Barker scored 16 runs in 23 minutes before being caught and bowled by Bath. She was replaced by Marshall who showed the same eagerness to set about the bowling. At 4.55 England declared with a total of 253 for 6 wickets, leaving Birch 72 not out and Marshall 20 not out.

The 25 minutes that Australia had to play out until stumps was not without incident. During the day the wicket had gained pace and off the final ball of Macfarlane's last over, which was also the last ball of play, Allitt made contact with an outswinger which went between second and third slip. Robinson at second slip dived to her right, took the catch, but in making contact with the ground the ball jerked out of her grasp. It was a brilliant attempt at the near impossible which could have meant a wicket down. In the event, the closing Australian score was 18 for no wicket.

Another good cricketing day on the Saturday with the wicket showing even more pace but absolutely no turn, had Australia batting confidently despite the loss of opener Allitt after 15 minutes play. She was bowled by Hegarty for 12, and the Australian score stood at 23 for 1 when Captain Una Paisley took her guard. Runs soon came from her bat with some good hooking and cutting. Meanwhile the other opener, Massey, continued cautiously. Two changes of bowling, Hawes for Hegarty and Barker for Macfarlane resulted in Paisley going when she attempted to hook a straight ball off Hawes which stayed lower than expected. At 71 for 2 it was Christ who came in at number four, with about 35 minutes to go before lunch. She and Massey were still there at the interval and the score was 91 for 2.

Soon after lunch, in Barker's second over, Christ was out to an excellent catch at mid-off by Wilkinson. Without adding to the score, Massey was out a few minutes later clean bowled by Hegarty. Now to join Wilson, whose appearance at number 5 had been greeted with suitable acclamation from the crowd as she walked to the wicket, was Val Batty. It was soon apparent that these two intended business when Wilson opened her innings with a well placed four. By now her powerful cutting had led the England Captain to arrange the off-side field accordingly. Nevertheless, she and Batty continued to elude the fielders with this delightful stroke.

When Batty has made 23 runs she had the misfortune to pull a leg muscle and thereafter needed the services of 12th man Betty Newman as a runner. This naturally slowed the scoring pace, yet, when Wilson was out for 43 caught Robinson off Hawes attempting to cut through slips, she and Batty had moved the total by 62 runs in even time.

At 158 for 5, Dalton joined Batty and the score moved steadily on to be 184 at tea. When the new ball was taken by Macfarlane just before 4 pm, the total was 200 without change. Still fifty or so behind the England first innings score, it was clearly not the time for Australia to lose a wicket nor for the fielding side to relax in concentration or to be wayward in bowling effort. But the new ball produced runs for the Aussies; chances were missed and though Dalton had a bit of luck in surviving a played-on which failed to remove a bail, Batty made her 50, and the England total was passed at around 5 pm.

Still no declaration from Paisley was how the England side probably saw it, for a couple of wickets would have put the former in a promising position for the third day. Instead, Dalton raised her 50 just 5 minutes before the end of play, Bath having come and gone for 1 after Batty had been caught in the deep by Marshall off Disbury. The day ended with Australia 280 for 7; Dalton was 59 not out and Eileen Massey 2 not out. Top scorer Batty had made 70 in 203 minutes.

The third day heralded a declaration by the Australian Captain and Robinson and Driscoll again opened England's innings knowing that quick scoring was essential if they were to declare and remove Australia in the one day. Against the usual fast bowlers Marvell and Massey, 11 runs came off the first 8 overs before Driscoll was caught hitting out at Marvell by substitute Newman fielding in the deep. Birch was next in and set the pace with some good batting and running between the wickets until backing up too eagerly she was run out from the crease; she made 17. With the run rate now slightly ahead of the clock, Westbrook joined Robinson and attempted to attack. She was tempted by one of Paisley's flighted balls and, as in the first innings, was stumped by wicketkeeper Massey. Disbury next in again fell victim to Betty Wilson who this time dismissed her caught and bowled for a duck. At 78 for 4, only 31 runs ahead and just 2 minutes to go to lunch, Barker could only play cautiously but still managed to score 2 runs in that time. After the interval Robbie brought up her 50 (which in 118 minutes was probably one of her fastest) and Barker opened out with some powerful drives. Her 26 contained four boundaries. These two had put on 51 for the fifth wicket but then Wilkinson, at number 7 made only 6 runs, Marshall also went for 6. The last three players, Hawes, Macfarlane and Hegarty, had a go, but it was Robbie who made the running. When the innings closed she was 96 not out and the England total 188.

Left to score 162 runs in 51 minutes to win, it was clear that the Australians were facing the improbable. Six England bowlers were tried, none of them having more than four overs. One wicket for 59 was the Australian closing total and that wicket a run out; it was Allitt's fate to be the last victim of a typically fine Marshall pick up and throw in.

Yet another drawn Test Match marked the tourists Antipodean adventure for 1957/8. Never a loss though, and that was some record to take back to England. For those with a chance to play the game against New Zealand and Australia in the future, next time was the time to win.

BETTY WILSON'S RARE TEST DOUBLE

By DOT DEBNAM

Victorian batswoman Betty Wilson made history today when, with a century for Australia against England in the second Test at St. Kilda, she completed a rare double. She took the hat-trick in the match on Saturday with her 7/7.

She is the first woman in Test cricket to get a century and a hat-trick in the same match. She has now made 36 centuries in all grades of cricket.

...e down for 27 ...t to the ...a's sec... ...rday.

Betty Wilson

SCOREBOARD

AUSTRALIA
First Innings, 38.
Second Innings

Allitt, b Barker		11
Massey, c Driscoll, b Duggan		5
Dow, c Hawes, b Duggan		1
Paisley, b Barker		11
Wilson, b Hawes		100
Batty, c Robinson, b Hawes		10
Christ, lbw, b Barker		12
Dalton, run out		26
Orchard, n.o.		17
E. Massey, c Robinson, b Hawes		4
Coulthard, n.o.		0
Extras		5
Nine (dec.) for 202		

Bowling: McFarlane 0 26.

nglish Women lose At 6-253

nglish women's cricket captain Cecilia ...nson made a bid to force a decision in the Test against Australia which started at the C.A. Ground yesterday.

...declared England's innings closed at ...or 253 in the hope ...king a wicket or ...during the 30 min... play before ...ps.

...was nearly reward...
...in ...he ...p. ...on. ...ll.

...the last ball before tea when Audrey Disbury was stumped by Miss Massey off the bowling of Miss Wilson for five.

After tea Betty Birch and Edna Barker added 29 runs in the first 20 minutes, and the 200 was posted in 255 minutes.

Miss Barker was caught and bowled by Joyce Bath for 16, and Olive Marshall and Miss Birch scored slowly until the innings was declared closed.

THEY CALLED HER 'BETTY O'NEILL'

A group of men were calling her "Betty O'Neill" at Adelaide Oval on Saturday.

English Leader Out Of Test

Mary Duggan, captain of the English women's cricket team, failed to pass a test of fitness yesterday and has been omitted from the side which will play against Australia in the last Test at the W.A.C.A. Ground today.

Miss Duggan has been suffering from fibrositis and has been undergoing special treatment in Adelaide. She batted at the nets at the W.A.C.A. G... ...terday.

The side w... vice-captain ...nson, who i...

This "Bradman" of women's cricket has scored 37 centuries in interstate and international matches. Miss Wilson also is one...

...mue its innings today. The highlight of the day was a brilliant catch ...t short mid-on by the West Australian player, Marie McDonough.

Miss McDonough dismissed Joan Wilkinson ...or two off the bowling of Betty Wilson when ...he fell full length and ...ook the ball inches ...rom the ground.

Miss Robinson won the ...oss and she opened the ...atting for England with ...hirley Driscoll.

Joyce Christ missed a ...ard chance at mid-off and the score mounted ...teadily until lunch. The ...eams left the field with ...t wicket down for...

ENGLAND
First Innings

ROBINSON, run out		35
DRISCOLL, b Paisley		72
WILKINSON, c McDonough b Wilson		2
BIRCH, not out		72
WESTBROOK, st Massey b Bath		23
DISBURY, st Massey b Wilson		5
BARKER, c and b Bath		16
MARSHALL, not out		29
SUNDRIES 2 w, 4 l b, 3 b		9

TOTAL, for 6 wickets decl. 253

FALL: 95, 101, 122, 154, 186, 190.

BOWLING: Marsh 28 14 45 0; E. Massey 10 2 37 0; Christ 4 2 3 0; Wilson 30 9 9 2; Paisley 19 3 46 1; Bath 24 6 41 2.

AUSTRALIA
First Innings

ALLITT, not out		10
MASSEY, N. not out		8
TOTAL, for no wicket		18

West Australian Test cricketer Marie McDonough dived full-length to hold this catch during the first day of the third women's Test match at the W.A.C.A. Ground yesterday.

The bowler, Victorian Betty Wilson appeals to the umpire as Eng... batsw... ...Wil... kinson waits for him to make his decision.

The other batswoman is Shirley Driscoll. The wicketkeeper is Victorian Nell Massey and the slips fieldswoman is Marj Mar... ...

PERTH, SATURDAY, MARCH 22, 1958.

...for 101.

At stumps, England had declared with six for 253 and Australia was none for 18 in reply. The match will continue today and on Monday.

(Details, Page 23.)

A Dive . . . And She's Out

Summary of the Fourth Test 1957–8

England: 253 for 6 dec. & 188
Australia: 280 for 7 dec. & 59 for 1

Best Batting

1st Innings

England: B D Birch   72 n o
            S Driscoll   72

Australia: V Batty   70
            J Dalton   59 n o

2nd Innings

England: C Robinson   96 n o
            E Barker   26

Australia: N Massey   40 n o

Best Bowling

1st Innings

Australia: J Bath   2 – 41
            B Wilson   2 – 83

England: J Hawes   2 – 54
            H Hegarty   2 – 57

2nd Innings

Australia   J Bath   3 – 11
            B Wilson   2 – 34
            J Christ   2 – 55

Highlights

In the first innings Driscoll made her highest Test match score and Batty achieved her second 50 of the series. Robinson's 96 n o totalled more than half the second innings score for England. Overall, the fielding of both teams was of high standard on a consistently fast outfield.

AUSTRALIA IN ENGLAND 1963

Before the arch rivals, in the shape of an Australian team, visited the 'home country' in the summer of 1963, England had made a triumphant first tour of South Africa in 1960/61. Under the captaincy of Helen Sharpe, an eager band of protagonists – whose eagerness to play for England was indicated by a willingness to pay their own way – won a four-match Test series. They were victorious in Durban, with an 8 wicket win, while the matches at Port Elizabeth, Johannesburg and Cape Town were all drawn. Seasoned campaigners like Helen herself, Polly Marshall, Ruth Westbrook and Anne Sanders, did well on a tour which also 'blooded' a few young hopefuls. Among these was the ebullient and talented Rachael Heyhoe, destined to become one of women's cricket's most charismatic and controversial characters. But before all that, the contest with the Australians.

Birmingham: Edgbaston Cricket Ground June 15, 17, 18th

The scene of the first Test for the Australian visitors was the pleasant Edgbaston ground on the outskirts of Birmingham in the Midlands. With nothing but wins or draws against county and territorial teams thus far on their tour, no doubt the England representatives were in the mood to see the Australians off right from the start. But if the plan included building up a good score, rapidly dismissing the Australians and ramming home the advantage – the usual optimistic dream on such occasions – that plan was defeated by the simple flip of a coin. It was Australia's fortune to win the toss and open proceedings on a beautiful sunny day with a firm, inviting wicket.

Australian captain, Mary Allitt, vastly experienced in the game and no stranger to the very different conditions of grounds in England, opened with newcomer Lyn Denholm. A boundary off the second ball of Macfarlane's opening over seemed to indicate that Allitt was set to attack whenever possible.

Four overs later, however, hers was the wicket to fall when a mistimed pull off the bowling of Mary Pilling led to a catch by Jackie

The official photograph of the 1963 Australian tourists. From L-R they are: Standing: Hazel Buck, Lyn Denholm, Patricia Thomson, Margaret Jude, Helen Lee, Norma Wilson, Shirley Banfield, Janice Wady, Coralie Towers, Elizabeth Amos, Lorraine Kutcher, Marjorie Marvell. Sitting: Joyce Goldsmith, Muriel Picton (Vice-capt.), Lorna Thomas (Manager), Mary Allitt (Captain), Miriam Knee.

Elledge; an encouraging start for two players making their England debut.

The Australian number three was another Test Match fledgeling – Janice Wady. She and Denholm survived the fast bowlers and saw the 25 come up in 28 minutes. The keen ground fielding combined with the off spin of Eileen Rump, also playing in her first Test, reduced the Australian pair to a string of singles until Duggan, the second change bowler, had Wady lbw. The score was then 41 for 2. This brought Hazel Buck, a powerfully aggressive bat, to join Denholm. Having opened her innings with a well struck four off Duggan, Buck continued in like vein until she too was to be content with scoring mostly in singles, contained by the accurate spin bowling.

With the score at 62, Denholm was caught by Robinson fielding at leg slip to Rump's bowling. Left-hander Liz Amos stayed with Buck until lunch and the score was then 73 for 3, with Buck on 21 and Amos on 7.

After the break Amos and Buck showed how to keep fielders on their toes by a good display of running between the wickets. Though the score mounted mostly in singles, these two looked comfortable, and it took a well held reflex catch by Rump off Macfarlane's bowling to break the budding partnership. Buck continued to bat soundly, and the century came up in 144 minutes. Wicketkeeper Norma Wilson was next to go caught behind by Westbrook off Pilling's bowling. The same bowler then had number 7, Miriam Knee, playing outside the off stump to offer a superbly taken catch to Duggan at slip.

At 116 for 6 the game seemed to be going England's way. When 20 runs later Hazel Buck was caught by Elledge off Duggan for 47, the position looked even better. Certainty of a quick end to the Australian innings was reinforced when Picton went for 12, and Marvell provided the second duck of the innings. Duggan took both wickets. It was then, however, that the Australian tail wagged effectively. Patricia Thomson, batting 9, and fast bowler Lorraine Kutcher, the number 11, stayed together until Thomson was lbw to Rump for 30. Kutcher was not out 7 and the Australian innings closed five minutes before the tea

Muriel Picton, caught Westbrook bowled Duggan for 12 in the first Test of the 1963 tour which took place at Edgbaston. The appealing fielders are slips Mary Pilling and Dorothy Macfarlane, with Cecilia Robinson at silly mid-on.

interval at 173.

The famed partnership of Robinson and Driscoll opened for England against fast bowlers Marvell and Kutcher. The scoring was slow with only 26 runs coming from 20 overs. It took an hour to bring up 25 runs and even when slow off break bowler Knee replaced Marvell the run rate was circumspect. It was Picton who, in the second over of her first spell, made the breakthrough for Australia by bowling Driscoll for 20.

With the total at 38 for 1 and with another 37 minutes to stumps, Rachael Heyhoe arrived at the crease. Three runs later she was out, caught by the wicketkeeper off the bowling of Knee. But England did not put up the shutters, the Vice-Captain and wicketkeeper Ruth Westbrook came in at number 4 and attacked the slow bowling. At close of play England were 59 for 2 wickets.

The weekend had not produced weather to change playing conditions in any way and the Monday morning saw a quick wicket for the Australians when Robbie was lbw to the left arm pace bowler Marvell. This seemed to be Marvell's day when she next clean bowled Westbrook just five balls later. At 89 for 5, and the experienced bats dismissed, it was a testing moment for the newcomers to the side.

The next in was Elledge, playing very cautiously indeed, but Sandra Brown opened her strike with a boundary. When Elledge was ought caught and bowled Picton, her 15 runs had taken 59 minutes to compile. With Brown at around a similar score, the situation was still in Australia's favour. June Bragger made 6 runs in her 8 minutes at the wicket, put Pilling managed to see through to lunch with a boundary to her credit.

When play resumed, pace bowler Kutcher opened the attack in her third over had Pilling lbw for 8. Experienced campaigner Macfarlane then joined Brown who was batting strongly. The two of them settled in well together and had put on 48 runs before Macfarlane succumbed to Knee for 17. Rump added a further 5 runs but became another Knee victim in a caught and bowled. The England innings thus ended 23 runs ahead of the Australians with Brown having scored a maiden half-century in a noble 57 not out.

In the eight overs bowled before tea, four each by Macfarlane and Pilling, openers Allitt and Denholm took advantage of Pilling's lack of direction by scoring 19 off her – including 4 boundaries – while Macfarlane conceded only one to the Australian bonanza of a run a minute. After tea, however, the run-rate was curbed and that, added to the threat of darkening skies, meant that when rain eventually stopped play half-an-hour before time and coincidentally with the fall of Denholm's wicket, Australia was 64 for 1. To achieve this state of affairs Duggan had used no fewer that eight bowlers, at least two of whom rarely bowled for their country.

On the final day it was Allitt and Wady who dictated the run of play and the scoring was steady but slow. When Allitt was out, caught by Heyhoe off Bragger for 43, she had taken 99 minutes to add 12 to her overnight score. Meanwhile Wady had scored 50 – in 93 minutes – and then went to a catch by Macfarlane, also off Bragger. At lunch, Hazel Buck and Liz Amos were batting carefully and the scoreboard registered 131 for 3.

With Australia still only 106 ahead of the England total an increase in the scoring rate was essential if a win was to be contemplated. That a draw was inevitable became clear when the new batsmen took time to play themselves in, and was confirmed when rain stopped play for five minutes at 3.25 and the Australians resumed batting after the stoppage. With around 190 for 5, some 170 runs ahead, obviously Captain Mary Allitt was not prepared to risk England getting the runs. Eventually a tea-time declaration with Australia 223 for 5 left England 105 minutes in which to get 200 runs. They ended the day with a drawn match at 91 for 3. Of these Jackie Elledge made a creditable 51 not out, deputising for an unwell Shirley Driscoll at number 2 in the order.

AUSTRALIAN WOMEN'S CRICKET TEAM SAILS IN

EDGBASTON WELCOMES THE LADIES!

Women Cricketers of Australia and England Face the First Test

LAST week the First Test—England v. West Indies; this week, the First Test—England v. Australia. It may seem confusing, but the latter is a match between women cricketers.

From JOHN THICKNESSE
EDGBASTON, Saturday.

ENGLAND'S women cricketers made a good start to their three-match series by getting Australia out for 173 by tea-time to-day, and making 60 for two wickets by close of play. A crowd of about 2,000 watched, but the cricket, though pleasant to watch, was uneventful.

In a five and a half hour even those notorious encounters between India and Pakistan have been known to produce more than 213 runs. Happily, we were compensated here by an over-rate which kept the action flowing—23 to the hour.

England's most successful bowler was the captain, Mary Duggan, who took four for 39 in 20 overs of orthodox slow left arm. Of the others, Eileen Rump, a tall off-spinner with an action reminiscent of Roy Tattersall's, deserved better than her two for 31.

Two fine catches were held. Many a county short leg would have been happy to clutch the one Cecilia Robinson took left-handed from a well-hit full toss, and one Miss Rump grasped low at silly-point that was little easier.

Before today I had never seen women playing cricket and was therefore able to watch with unprejudiced eye. On the whole it was a rewarding experience. They play a gentle, graceful game and enjoy themselves.

I had thought previously that there was something about the way a woman's shoulder was constructed that would make it difficult for her to bowl and, in particular, to throw properly. This is not so. With the exception of Dorothy MacFarlane (at about Shackleton's pace, the fastest) the England bowlers all deliver with a highish arm.

Throwing revelation

But the greatest surprise was the throwing. One or two of them buzzed the ball in at speed from below waist height, and, from up to 40 yards, few returns made the wicketkeeper hop about. On the debit side, running between wickets was distinctly bad.

What a man watching will have missed most, I think, was the air of physical conflict and muscle strength taken for granted in county cricket. Hazel —the Australian top-scorer— firmly, but took the —

A TEST MATCH against the Australians at Edgbaston is usually reckoned to be a near sell-out before a ball is bowled.

But the England-Australia Test starting there on Saturday is rather different—the teams are women cricketers. It remains to be seen how well Birmingham people support the match.

How did women raise their cricket to the level of Test

by W. G. WANKLYN

AUSTRALIA'S lost their captain wh— scored b—

match status? It all started 37 years ago, and the Midlands had a hand in it.

In 1926, 22 hockey players at Colwall a village in Herefordshire, decided to have a dab at cricket. In the same year the Women's Cricket Association, the governing body, was formed.

Women's cricket made steady but unspectacular progress through the 1930's and before the war Test matches were arranged with the Australians, games being played in both countries.

There was a hard struggle during the war years to keep going. It was kept alive, but since 1945 a steady flow of young recruits has helped women's cricket to —

— clubs have been formed in many towns and cities, and Association members do free coaching.

The popularity of cricket for —

Women's Test

AUSTRALIA OUT FOR 173

DUGGAN'S 4 WICKETS

By SIMON SMITH

England took the honours on the first day of the women's Test match at Edgbaston on Saturday by dismissing the formidable batting strength of the Australians for a modest 173.

The Australians were cleverly contained by naggingly accurate bowling and brilliant fielding. Only Hazel Buck, batting No. 4, threatened to reproduce the form in which she recently made 103 not out. She was caught by Elledge off the bowling of Duggan for 47.

Mary Duggan's bowling contribution, in addition to her shrewd captaincy, was four for 39, and the fast bowler, Mary Pilling, took three for 35.

England have scored 60 for two in reply and a lot now depends on the opening batswoman, Cecil Robinson, still there with 26.

Australia 173 (H. Buck 47; M. Duggan 4-39). England 60-2.

● *Setting the style—in head wear, too—is the Australian captain, Mary Allitt, as she plays forward to a ball from Pilling.*

INGLORIOUS FINISH TO ENGLAND'S INNINGS

SCARBOROUGH.—England women, with nine wickets standing, need 105 runs to avoid an innings defeat.

WOMEN'S CRICKET

RECORD STAND BY AUSTRALIA

A RECORD sixth wicket stand of 125 between the captain, Mary Allitt, and Miri took Australia out of a first innings lead in t women's Test match borough yesterday.

Allitt, who opened, was Knee with five wickets do and nine Knee was run o fine innings of 82 the were nine runs ahead of th total of 167.

The previous highest s stand in a Test in England 1937.

Australia were all out lead of 109, and at the clo had lost one wicket for 1c their second innings.

ENGLAND. — First Innings night 166-8)—M Pilling, b 1 MacFarlane, not out, 1: E. Run extras 4; Total 167. Ho 19.4-0-24-5, Knee 23-7-3 17-4-45-1.

AUSTRALIA—First Innings— MacFarlane, 76; L Denholm, lb 7; J Wady, lbw MacFarlane, 2 Westbrook b Pilling, 11; E. Am Duggan, 10; N. Wilson o and M Knee, run out, 82; P Thor Pilling, 23; M. Picton, run out not out, 25; L. Kutcher, run out Total 278. Bowling—MacFarla Pilling 30-6-71-2, Duggan 31-11 ENGLAND.—Second Innings— not out, 0; S. Driscoll, not out 0, Total (

Test pitch dryin

The Edgbaston pitch fo Test between England Indies on Thursday saturated, but by working the groundsmen brough great improvement.

Mr. Bert Flack, Warwick groundsman, said yester trouble really started when the county game wi hamshire was abandoned the Test pitch, but it is b basin and water seeped covers.

" There still will be son in the turf on Thursday, mean a difficult decisic captain who wins the toss

---

Fog and the last pair thwart Australia

THE loss of 2½ hours' play due to a thick swirling fog cost Australia victory on the last day of the second women's test match at North Marine Road yesterday. When play ended England had scored 93 runs for nine wickets and were still 16 short of the Australian innings lead of 109.

A crowd of more people stood on top popular bank to watch t tense 20 minutes as En last pair, Bragger and defied all Australian attem clinch the first-ever ini victory in a women's test m between the two countries.

AUSTRALIA—First Innings 278 all

ENGLAND—First Innings 167 all out.

Second Innings

C. Robinson c Wilson b Knee	11
S. Driscoll lbw b Kutcher	4
D. MacFarlane c Lee b Kutcher	4
R. Westbrook c Denholm b Lee	34
R. Heyhoe c Lee b Buck	20
M. Duggan c Denholm b Picton	12
J Elledge c Thomson b Buck	0
S. Brown c Wady b Knee	5
J. Bragger not out	2
M. Pilling c Wady b Knee	2
E. Rump not out	1
Extras	2

Total (9 wkts) 93

Bowling: Lee 1 for 15, Kutcher 2 for 23. Picton 1 for 17, Knee 3 for 22, Buck 2 for 3.

ENGLAND WIN SERIES IN LAST OVER

From Our Special Correspondent

THE OVAL.—England women beat Australian women by 49 runs.

England excitingly won the third Test match, and with it the series, thus regaining the Ashes which their opponent held since 1948-49. The promis keen finish was generously fulfille Australia set 210 to win at just dly, hesi again Miss B fter a stand ber 11 er of t dart c the a sh targe mural tely, i ha u th stur h.

Miss Rachel Heyhoe, of England, also provided some spectacle with a handsome six and a Truemanesque gesture of peering at the square leg boundary after completely missing a hook in that direction.

suffered the unusual fate of being stumped. And at 43 Miss Denholm, who had been attacking strongly, was out to Miss Bragger's second brilliant catch of the game.

Much might have been expected from ...ful combination of Miss Buck ...after some aggressive ...de catch to ...6 for four ...ick on the ...r, refused ...ing firmly, ...le ball with ...liss Hegarty ...auxhall end ...uck was out ...gully. Miss ...ght Australia ...the clock. ...aceful strokes, ...l runs, but at ...and it was left ...xuberant Miss ...positive stand, ...ager, when Miss ...lendid catch at ...Thomson out at ...the only policy, ...an had gone, it ...in the last over, ...ping round like ...tell and on the ...r of two excellent

Heyhoe for Six

WITH an entire series between England and Australia depending on the last day's play in the Final Test at the Oval yesterday, the stage seemed set for a major occasion. But women's cricket is not exactly a spectator sport, despite the graceful sidesteps and circuitous approach to the wicket of the slower Australian bowlers, and the fierce appeals to the umpire.

The tiny between The is in

d was evenly divided ls and elderly men. were not specially orm mistress had in two innings. urged on by

a demonstra- ...proportions Miss Mary

254 for 8 dec. (M. 59; Kutcher 5 for 59).

...nks			8
			20
			11
			12
			10
...e			12
...n out			37
...l, l-b 1)			3
			7

7 wkts dec.) 160
T.S.—1—24, 2—40, 3—69, 4—74

1, 12. 2—29 0, Kutcher, 14.3 8 -51 -3, Picton 9—4—28—1 INNINGS, 208 (E. Amos 55; ran 4 for 12

d INNINGS

...onk, b Duggan	13
...agger b Duggan	29
...scoll, b Hegarty	13
Brown, b Sanders	14
...ee run out	1
...ee, l-b-w, b Sanders	13
M. Picton, c Brown, b. Sanders	15
P. Thomson, l.b.w. b. Duggan	12
†M Jude, c. Westbrook, b Hegarty	10
L. Kutcher, not out	15
M. Marvell, l.b-w. b. Barker	15
Extras (b 1, l-b 6, n-b 2)	6

Total 160
FALL OF WICKETS.—1—40, 2—43, 3—64, 4—66, 5—90, 6—111, 7—128, 8—128, 9—113, 10—160. BOWLING—Hegarty, 16—4—12—2 Pilling, 6—2— 18- 0; Duggan, 27—15—40—1; Sanders, 33—14 ...—3 Brown 4—2—6—0; Elledge, 1—0—4—0; Barker, 2 2 1 8 4.

ENGLAND BEAT AUSTRALIA

Tense finish to a fine match

From TONY GOODRIDGE

THE OVAL, Tuesday.

IN the last over Miss Barker trapped Miss Marvell lbw and so brought England her first victory by 51 runs, in the women's Test match series against Australia since 1948-49

Australia always ... a fair objective ... Australians to ... h they set about ... gress was being ... llitt honourably

Summary of the First Test 1963

Match Drawn

Australia:	173 and 223 for 5 wickets dec
England:	196 and 91 for 3

Best Batting

1st Innings

Australia:	H Buck	47
	P Thomson	30
England:	S Brown	57 n o
	C Robinson	30

2nd Innings

Australia:	J Wady	50
	M Allitt	43
England:	J Elledge	51 n o

Best Bowling

1st Innings

England:	M Duggan	4 – 39
	M Pilling	3 – 35
Australia:	M Knee	4 – 49
	M Picton	2 – 40

2nd Innings

England:	J Bragger	2 – 21
	M Duggan	2 – 55
Australia:	J Wady	1 – 10
	M Picton	1 – 11

Highlights

There were three maiden half-centuries in the match and it was Australia's Jan Wady who made the fastest time of 90 minutes. England's Jackie Elledge completed hers in 100 minutes, but Sandra Brown's effort batting at number 7 in the first innings was a rallying one for her team. Her 57 not out, made in 150 minutes, included a 130 minute half century and a record 9th wicket stand of 48 with Dorothy Macfarlane who scored 17.

Scarborough: Scarborough Cricket Ground June 29, July 1 & 2

In coming to the famous seaside resort of Scarborough for the second confrontation with England, the Australians were following the path of the 1951 tourists, who had played their first Test there. And twelve years on saw yet another similarity in that Isabel Nowell-Smith who umpired on the earlier occasion was also standing in this Test.

Australia entered the second match of the series with convincing wins against Yorkshire and East Anglia behind them. There was only one change in the side which played at Edgbaston, and that was due to injury. Marjorie Marvell, the fast left arm opening bowler, who had damaged an ankle, was replaced by the youngest member of the team, Helen Lee, also a left arm pace bowler.

Unfortunately, the day before play was due to start was one of Scarborough's wet and windy ones. The dismal weather lasted all night long and Saturday morning was dull with constant drizzle. Expectations of the cricket ground being totally unplayable were not realised, however, though play had to be delayed until after lunch. This time, it was Duggan's turn to win the toss and at 2 pm England opened with Robinson and Driscoll against the bowling of Kutcher and Lee.

There were four maiden overs, one to Kutcher and three to Lee, no doubt a consequence of indifferent light and the weather conditions, before Robinson got off the mark with a cut for 3. An over later Driscoll opened her account with a 2 off Kutcher. The outfield was extremely slow and it was a matter of 24 overs before the first boundary got through. Meanwhile, Kutcher and Lee had been replaced by off spinners Knee and Picton. It was Picton who conceded the four to Robinson, but with only one more run added to her score Robbie was caught behind off Knee. England's first wicket was down for 53 runs after 79 minutes play.

Elledge was next in, obviously promoted in the batting order after her showing at Edgbaston, but stayed only 7 minutes before being clean bowled by a ball from Picton which turned considerably from the off. Heyhoe joined Driscoll only to see the latter fall to Knee in a replica of the Robinson dismissal. Only 13 minutes later Heyhoe attempted to pull a straight ball from the same bowler and was clean bowled. Duggan and Brown were now together and they saw through play to the tea interval when England was a far from secure 83 for 4. After the break, however, Duggan attacked the bowling in typical style, Brown followed her example and when the next wicket fell, Brown going for 26, the partnership had raised a useful 61 runs. But for the keen and well placed Australian fielders, the score would have been considerably more than its 137 for 5.

Wicketkeeper Ruth Westbrook was next at the crease but didn't play her usual attacking game. It wasn't long after Duggan became Knee's fifth victim of the match that she succumbed lbw to Lee for just 4 runs. Duggan made an invaluable 44.

June Bragger and Mary Pilling, batting at 8 and 9 respectively, looked all set to see England through to the close of play, but with six minutes to go Bragger was brilliantly run out by a fast pick up and return from Amos fielding at square leg. This left Macfarlane to play out time so that England could bat another day. With the score at 166 for 8 a few more runs would be more than useful.

But the Monday was another dull day and depressing for England when Pilling failed to add to her score and Rump was bowled by Lee for a duck. At 11.14 am Macfarlane and Pilling opened the attack for England against Allitt and Denholm. A cautious start was relieved by 3 leg byes off Pilling who was invariably wayward for the first few overs. It was Macfarlane who drew first blood by getting Denholm lbw to a ball which stayed low. Wady joined her captain at the wicket and seemed reluctant to score. After 20 minutes at the crease she too was lbw to Macfarlane for 2 runs. Australia were now 2 wickets down for 19 runs.

The Australians' over-cautious approach looked to be dispelled by the number 4, Hazel Buck, who went for runs as soon as she got in. Unfortunately after two successive boundaries off Pilling she was caught behind. At 34 for 3 it looked as though England were well and truly on top. Neither Amos nor Wilson got the better of the bowling, though, like Buck, Amos made her 10 runs relatively quickly. Sheet anchor Allitt who'd survived three dropped catches, was joined by Miriam Knee. These two ensured that no further wickets fell before lunch and at that time the score was 81 for 5.

After the break, Knee really got her head down and began to accumulate runs steadily, overtaking Allitt's score and doubling it by the time she was run out. Her partnership with Allitt brought Australia 9 runs ahead of England with 4 wickets in hand, and she made an inspiring 82 out of a total of 176 for 6. At the tea interval Allitt was on 58 with the new batsman, Thomson, 0 not out.

No doubt England were metaphorically and ruefully rubbing hands which had not only been exercised in fielding without reward for the two hours after lunch, but had also failed to hold catches which resulted in Allitt's continued presence at the wicket. Unfortunately for them, Thomson proceeded to don the mantle Knee had discarded and made 23 sparkling runs before being caught and bowled by Pilling. Next to go was Allitt for 76, bowled by Macfarlane.

Both Picton and Kutcher were run out leaving Lee not out 25. Picton had added 29 runs in her hour-long innings, however, and so at 6.21 pm, when the Australian innings closed at 276, they were 109 runs ahead of England and in a good position to force a win.

Because rain had delayed the first day's play considerably, the Monday not only started half-an-hour early but had been scheduled to end at 6.45 pm: thus England had to bat out 14 minutes. This was a trying time with Robinson needing a runner, and Driscoll sadly lost her wicket, lbw to Kutcher. Nightwatchman Macfarlane kept her end up for 7 minutes and England closed 4 for 1.

When the teams arrived at the ground the next morning it was to wonder at a Scarborough sea fret which completely blotted out the ground. After an early lunch play started at 1.15. Robinson opened proceedings with a boundary off Lee, but several maidens then followed. Macfarlane looked to be playing herself in but got an edge to Kutcher and was well caught at second slip by Lee. A juggling of the batting order brought Westbrook to the wicket and she began to strike the ball confidently. Once again, however, the mist returned, this time accompanied by a miserable drizzle, and it was not long before Robbie was caught behind bowled Knee for 11. At this stage, not even an hour of play had elapsed for England to be in the sorry plight of 27 for 3.

But now Heyhoe came to the wicket and after sensible restraint she too struck the ball with determination. The union between her and Westbrook was destined to be a temporary affair however, because a mishit to square caused Westbrook's downfall – caught Denholm bowled Picton for 24. At 52 for 4, Duggan, in at number 6, was in the front line to see to it that England cracked on with the run rate. But while Heyhoe pressed on, Duggan seemed unable to get the ball away.

A good tactical move by Allitt in bringing on the second-line bowling of Hazel Buck had the reward of Heyhoe's wicket just six minutes before tea. She was caught at square by Lee off a firmly hit pull. Elledge was next and stayed just two minutes for her duck, being caught at short fine leg by Thomson. Brown then joined her captain and the two of them survived to the tea break with England 79 for 6.

During tea the mist thickened and made play impossible. At 5 pm, however, it had cleared sufficiently for the match to resume. There was an hour and fifteen minutes left and though it was clear that England could not win, it was also very obvious that they could lose. Not too much action ensued and at 5.20 pm Duggan made her second appeal of the afternoon against bad light. This one was upheld and caused a delay of 23 minutes.

Duggan and Brown maintained stolid defence in a manner most contrary to their natural game, until at 6.10 Brown was caught at short mid-on off the bowling of Knee. Only 4 minutes later, Duggan pulled one to deep square leg straight into the safe hands of Denholm: 88 for 8. Pilling joined Bragger and stayed 7 minutes for her 2 runs. The number 11, Eileen Rump, was faced with the unenviable task of seeing England through with 19 minutes to go. She and Bragger had bowlers Knee and Picton, and very eager Australian fielders to contend with but not the mist which had miraculously cleared. It was contention without defeat as England ended the day with 93 for 9 wickets: A match drawn because of mist, but a moral victory to the Australians nevertheless.

Summary of the Second Test 1963

Match Drawn

England: 167 & 93 for 9
Australia: 276

Best Batting

1st Innings

England: M Duggan   44
                S Driscoll   33

Australia: M Knee   82
                M Allitt   76

2nd Innings

England: R Heyhoe   26
                R Westbrook   24

Best Bowling

1st Innings

Australia: M Knee   5 – 35
                H Lee   3 – 24

England: D Macfarlane   3 – 46
                M Duggan   2 – 63
                M Pilling   2 – 71

2nd Innings

Australia: M Knee   3 – 22
                H Buck   2 – 3
                L Kutcher   2 – 23

Highlights

Miriam Knee for Australia combined her second innings of 82, the fifty coming up in 91 minutes, with a record stand for the sixth wicket. This was for 125 with Allitt. The latter's 50 took 228 minutes. Knee's 5 – 35 in the first innings represents the best bowling analysis for the Scarborough ground.

The England team that won the final Test, the series and the "ashes" against the Australians at The Oval in 1963. Standing (L-R): Sandra Brown, Rachael Heyhoe, Jackie Elledge, Edna Barker, Helene Hegarty, Anne Sanders, Mary Pilling, Pamela Crain (12th). Sitting (L-R): Shirley Driscoll, Ruth Westbrook (Vice-capt. & Wkt), Mary Duggan (Capt.), Nora Bearsby (Manager), June Bragger.

Kennington, London: The Oval, July 20, 22 & 23

The third and final Test began at the famous home of the Surrey Cricket Club on a fine, sunny Saturday morning. In their wisdom, the England selectors had reinforced the side with more experienced spin bowling by bringing Anne Sanders and Edna Barker into the team, for Rump and opening bat Robinson. Helene Hegarty replaced Macfarlane as the front-line fast bowler. The Australians included Marvell, now restored to fitness, retained Lee, who had done so well at Scarborough, and brought in Margaret Jude to replace Norma Wilson behind the stumps.

Duggan won the toss and sent in openers Driscoll and Elledge to face Marvell and Kutcher on a hard but placid wicket. In the tenth over, of which six had been maidens, an unsettled Driscoll offered an easy catch to Buck at mid-off, and Kutcher had taken her first wicket. At 7 for 1

Westbrook joined Elledge but the slow scoring pace didn't alter appreciably: A mistake, perhaps, to send in a normally attacking number 5 at first wicket down. Shortly after Elledge scored her first boundary the spin bowler Knee and fast bowler Lee took over the offensive. After just two overs, however, Knee left the field and was replaced by Picton. This proved fortunate for the Australians because Westbrook, who loved to get after the slow bowling, did just that and was caught at slip by Marvell off Picton.

With the score at 31 for 2 Sandra Brown, the heroine of Edgbaston, took her stance at the crease; she played circumspectly but punished anything loose. The Australians, however, mostly maintained a consistent accuracy, and since the fielding too was good Elledge and Brown had to work hard for their runs.

After she had made 24, Elledge was lucky not to be out. Lee had the misfortune to see a slip catch put down. There were still not too many boundaries from either bat but Brown ran well between the wickets. In the 106 minutes of play before lunch, England totalled 85 for 2, Elledge having made her second 50 of the series.

Resuming after the interval, Brown and Elledge pushed the score along nicely until Elledge skied one off Kutcher to be caught behind by Jude. Shortly afterwards, Jude had another success when she stumped

Dame Anna Neagle meets members of the Australian team at The Oval in 1963. Here she is accompanied by the WCA Chairman Edith Stevenson and is shaking hands with Elizabeth Amos. To her left are Hazel Buck, Lyn Denholm, Marjorie Marvel, and Miriam Knee. On the right, Patricia Thomson, Margaret Jude and Coralie Towers.

Brown. Heyhoe was next to the wicket, where she joined Duggan who looked to be in good form. When these two came together the England score was 111 for 4. Exactly 100 runs later their attractive partnership, full of forceful play as well as the good taking of singles, ended with Heyhoe's dismissal for 36 runs. At this stage Duggan had made some 80 runs – her 50 taking only 71 minutes. She was not to get her century until three more wickets had fallen.

After Marvell had Heyhoe lbw, Kutcher followed suit in trapping Sanders for a duck. Barker batting nine made 4 before being bowled by Kutcher, and Kutcher then bowled Pilling for a duck. The combined pressures of Duggan's impending century, the need to score quick runs, if any at all, together with the accuracy of the bowling clearly led to the fall of those three quick wickets. It was Bragger who stabilised the situation keeping her end up with Duggan to be 8 not out when her captain declared at 254 for 8. Duggan herself made a triumphant 101 not out in an innings lasting 162 minutes.

Duggan's declaration provided just that right amount of time for the

Hazel Buck catches opener Shirley Driscoll after she'd made 2 during England's first innings at The Oval in 1963. The legs of pace bowler Lorraine Kutcher, who took 5 for 59 off 24 overs in that innings, are the ones visible at the top of the picture. The wicket-keeper is Margaret Jude and all-rounder Miriam Knee is at first slip.

fast bowlers to lick their lips in anticipation of a couple of quick wickets. The Australians, however, were having none of this and played to see the fast bowlers off. Sanders and Duggan then took on the task of removing the cautious pair, Allitt and Denholm. Success came on the second ball of Sanders first over when Denholm was lbw for 10 runs. At 20 for 1 and with 15 minutes to go, nightwatchman Lee saw Australia through to close of play without further mishap and a further two more runs on the scoreboard.

An equally fine day on Monday 22nd began with Lee and Allitt batting confidently against the bowling of Sanders and Hegarty. This slow-fast combination was a good tactical move on the wicket beginning to show signs of wear, but 57 runs were on the board before Bragger took a low left-handed catch at cover off Hegarty to dismiss Lee for 22. Buck joined Allitt and soon afterwards Duggan took over from Sanders. Not until Pilling had replaced Hegarty was there further success for England; and then it was Duggan who trapped opposing

Liz Amos leans beautifully into an off drive at The Oval in 1963. She was top-scorer in Australia's first innings with 55. The wicket-keeper is Ruth Westbrook and the head and shoulders are those of the bowler Mary Pilling.

Some of the 1963 Australian women cricketers doing the tourist thing among the pigeons in London's Trafalgar Square. From the left they are: Joyce Goldsmith, Hazel Buck, Norma Wilson, Lorraine Kutcher and Lyn Denholm.

captain Allitt leg before for 29 runs.

At 77 for 3 Amos joined Buck and these two, something of a dynamic duo, struck the ball hard. After lunch, when the score stood at 93 confidence and boundaries flowed. When eventually Duggan deceived Buck with a slower ball and she was stumped, the partnership had added 82 and the Australians were 159 for 4. It was then Knee who assisted Amos past her 50, which had been accumulated in 117 minutes, and who saw her partner run out from a good return to the wicket-keeper from Heyhoe. Soon afterwards Picton was lbw to Duggan but Knee and Thomson were still there at tea with the score on 190.

Much had come to be expected of the Australian 'tail-enders' but on this occasion they failed to live up to their reputation. After Knee went, caught and bowled Sanders for 10, both Thomson and number 9 Jude fell to her bowling. Kutcher was next out stumped by Westbrook off

Duggan, and with Marvell 0 not out the last four wickets went for only 8 runs. When the innings closed at 5.13 pm the Australians were 49 runs behind.

Throughout the match thus far Australia had a distinct edge on the England fielders. The first wicket to fall was a further tribute to this superiority when Driscoll, who appeared to be batting more forcefully than hitherto, was run out from a brilliant pick up and throw-in by Amos. It looked as though the home side would suffer only that loss at the day's end but with the fourth ball of the last over, Picton bowled Elledge. England's overnight total was 40 for 2.

The final day's play looked full of promise in the morning sunshine. Brown and Bragger kept up an even-time run-rate for the first half-hour and the prospect was looking good for a purposeful declaration. But then Bragger was caught behind off Knee and just five runs later Brown was stumped off the same bowler. Westbrook and Duggan were together and the latter thumped the ball, almost in a continuation of her first innings, scoring an impressive 32 in 24 minutes. At 74 for 4 and 123 ahead, Heyhoe joined Westbrook and continued the run spree. Shortly before 1 pm Westbrook was run out, but Heyhoe, having survived a dropped catch, was not out at lunch having struck 37 in 33 minutes. Sanders who was run out for 3 completed the England innings for Duggan then declared at 160 for 7, 209 ahead.

If England could make the going at almost a run a minute, who doubted the capability of the Australians in scoring 210 in 225 minutes? Certainly not they themselves because Allitt's first two scoring shots were boundaries and Denholm, after an opening single, followed suit. These two had 25 on the board in 22 minutes, and kept up the pace until Allitt was stumped. She had scored 13. As invariably happens on partnership occasions, Denholm was soon to follow being superbly caught by Bragger: Duggan's second victim. Within three runs of one another then it brought Buck and Amos together at the wicket. Was this where Australia was about to cruise along to victory?

Certainly both players hit the ball firmly, but after scoring only 13 Amos offered a dolly to Brown at silly mid-on, and she accepted it gratefully. Knee replaced Amos but scored just a single before being run out by a return from Heyhoe to the wicketkeeper. The total was now 66 for 4 and it began to look as though Australia was on the downslope. Buck was still going well and when Lee joined her at number 6 stability looked to be restored. It was then that the tide really turned in England's favour, for just 7 minutes before tea Buck was out to a superb diving catch in the gully by Driscoll off Hegarty. At the interval, then, Australia was 98 for 5.

The post-tea period saw Lee and Picton effect a mini-stand, adding 21 valuable runs but, at 111, Lee was lbw to Sanders. Thomson looked confident, however, and the score moved along nicely until a splendid catch by Brown at silly mid-on saw Picton's exit. 128 for 7 was soon 128 for 8 when Thomson was lbw to Duggan for 12. With Australia needing 82 in 50 minutes to win and England needing 2 more wickets, England had to be the favourite.

When Margaret Jude was caught behind off Hegarty with 35 minutes of play left, it looked as though England was home. Lorraine Kutcher and Marjorie Marvell obviously saw things differently and resisted well. Hegarty, Duggan, Elledge and Sanders had all fired at the two Australian fast bowlers to no avail. Then, was it inspiration or desperation that made Duggan bring on her off-spinning ally of the 1957-58 tour, Edna Barker? Barker, who had not bowled throughout the match, started with a maiden. In her second over she conceded a four and after Marvell took another four off the first ball of the third over, she stepped onto the back foot to play the second, missed and was plumb lbw. With three minutes to go, England had won the third and final Test of the 1963 tour and the series was theirs.

Summary of the Third Test 1963

England won by 49 runs

| England: | 254 for 8 dec. and 160 for 7 dec |
| Australia: | 205 and 160 |

Best Batting

1st Innings

England:	M B Duggan	101 n o
	J Elledge	59
Australia:	E Amos	55
	H Buck	47

2nd Innings

England:	R Heyhoe	37 n o
	M B Duggan	32
	S Brown	31
Australia:	L Denholm	29
	H Buck	29

Best Bowling

1st Innings

Australia:	L Kutcher	5 – 59
England:	A Sanders	4 – 29
	M Duggan	4 – 42

2nd Innings

Australia:	M Knee	3 – 53
England:	M B Duggan	3 – 40
	A Sanders	3 – 46

Highlights

Duggan's 101 not out, the century taking 148 minutes, was the first scored at The Oval. Elledge's second 50 of the series took 98 minutes. In the face of the England total, Kutcher's analysis of 5 – 59 represented a good effort on a wicket which notoriously favoured spin bowling. Amos's 50 took 117 minutes.

NEW ZEALAND IN ENGLAND 1966

One player, the veteran Phyllis Blackler, the Manager, Joy Lamason, and her sister-in-law assistant Ina Lamason, were the only three New Zealanders with experience of playing conditions in England to board the good ship *Rangitane* for the second ever tour of the United Kingdom. A very young side, with one of the youngest at age 24 their Captain Patricia (Trish) McKelvey, were on course to attempt what no New Zealand team had yet managed against England – to win a Test Match – and hopefully to win a Test Series. In a total of 7 tests so far, 3 had gone to England with 4 drawn games in four series. It was, perhaps, time for the pendulum to swing in New Zealand's direction.

If the progress of the tourists through the counties was to be something to go by, indications were that the Test arena would provide some closely fought contests. England too had a youngish look about her, though in Heyhoe, Barker, Disbury, Marshall and Plant there was no shortage of Test match experience combined with the talent to give at least as good as was got, and the first meeting in Scarborough was keenly anticipated.

Scarborough: Scarborough Cricket Ground, 18, 20 & 21 June

The last Test Match played at Scarborough was against the Australians in 1963 when fog descended and finally obliterated players from spectators – but also saved England from defeat. Whether or not play should have continued then is another matter but on Friday June 18, 1966, there was no doubt whatsover. Despite overnight rain, a wettish pitch and a slow outfield, the sun shone and that together with the sea breeze made speculations as to who would do what on winning the toss worth airing. As it was Rachael Heyhoe, captaining England for the first time, won the toss and decided to bat.

Sheila Plant and newcomer Jackie Whitney began the innings against the fast-medium bowlers, Jocelyn Burley and Jill Saulbrey. Early on each survived a possible catch off Burley, who was bowling accurately downwind, and only a change of bowling brought freer strokeplay.

After an hour, Whitney scored the first boundary of the day; the score was then around 24 runs and less than a run every two minutes seemed an unpromising start. She continued to gain confidence against the medium pace Betty Maker but when Jackie Lord replaced the latter, Whitney was bowled – disconcerted by the swing – having made 20.

With twenty minutes to go to lunch Heyhoe played circumspectly, content to let Plant, who was now going well, score the runs. At lunch England had 74 on the scoreboard, with just the one wicket down. Soon after the interval any thought of slow play became a distant memory as Heyhoe took the initiative and began to play expertly off the front foot; not, however, without surviving an lbw appeal when she'd scored only 10. The bowler was Burley whose consistently good attack was rewarded three overs later when she had Plant caught behind for 46. With the score on 96 for 2 Vice-captain Edna Barker joined her captain out in the middle. There then began a partnership which was always on the attack. After 28 minutes together Heyhoe reached her 50

A happy New Zealand touring party arrives on Anzac Day, in 1966, for a three Test series and 19 match tour. They are shown aboard the Rangitane docked at Tilbury.

The New Zealand team for the first Test at Scarborough in June 1966 comprises (L-R): Patricia McKelvey (Capt.), Beverley Brentnall (Vice-capt. & Wkt), Phyllis Blackler, Patricia Moore (12th), Janice Stead, Carol Oyler, Jacqueline Lord, Betty Maker, Jocelyn Burley, Judith Doull, Jill Saulbrey and Jean Stonell.

with a drive that split mid-on and mid-wicket. But Barker went four better and brought up hers with a beautifully timed six in the same direction – and that off fast bowler Burley who'd just had three maiden deliveries with the new ball. This, however, was not only after the hundred partnership had passed, but also signalled Barker's going. In the very next over she was clean bowled by Saulbrey for 54, to be replaced by Anne Sanders. At tea, 12 minutes later, the score was 228 for 3 Heyhoe on 97 and Sanders with a single to her credit.

It took two singles and a two off a cover drive to give Heyhoe her memorable century – particularly memorable because it was her first as Captain of England – and she went on to a total of 113. She was caught and bowled by Burley after an innings which had survived only one chance: A dropped catch from a full-blooded lofted drive over mid-on when she had scored 69. The luckless bowler then was the spinner Blackler who was doubly unfortunate in seeing Barker dropped in the same over when her score was 34.

Probably with the intention of getting quick runs, fast bowler Mary Pilling went in at number 6. She had failed to trouble the scorers, however, and was soon followed by medium pacer June Bragger who stayed 15 minutes for 5 runs. Finally, Olive Marshall entered the arena and when the innings was declared four minutes later she was not out 3 and Sanders not out 21.

England's total of 273 for 6 declared was assailed firstly by New Zealand openers Judi Doull and Jean Stonell, but with only 4 on the board Stonell was clean bowled by Pilling. She was replaced by Betty Maker who took 29 minutes to record a duck. At the close of play, which coincided with Maker's wicket, New Zealand had their backs very much to the wall with 8 for 2 and Pilling had the incredible analysis of 9 overs, 9 maidens and 1 wicket. Eileen Vigor also had a wicket with the second ball of her only over, and betwen them the other two bowlers used, June Moorhouse and Lesley Clifford, had totalled 7 maidens in 12 overs. It was an extraordinary final 48 minutes to a day which had otherwise been a feast of attractive run-getting.

A heavy atmosphere with good light, though no sunshine, presented a promising early spell for the faster bowlers and after Vigor completed the over outstanding from Saturday evening, Pilling and Moorhouse took up the attack. It was an attack the New Zealanders more parried than struck and the tally of maiden overs increased. After half-an-hour's play, however, Beverley Brentnall padded a ball from Pilling which struck the wicketkeeper below the eye and she had to retire from the field. The verstaile Heyhoe took up position behind the stumps and held on to a touch that Brentnall got to a Vigor ball. The third wicket was thus down for 21 runs, Brentnall making 6.

Carol Oyler then joined the opener Doull and these two saw New Zealand through to lunch without further loss and the addition of 27 runs. The 100 minutes of morning play had produced just 40 runs – one every 2½ minutes – and eight bowlers had been employed in the process.

In the afternoon session it was noticeable that the England fielding deteriorated while Doull and Oyler batted unenterprisingly on. In failing to hold their catches England laboured for nearly two hours to eventually capture the wicket of opener Doull. In a dour innings lasting 4 hours and 12 minutes, Doull scored 74 and was finally lbw to Pilling. Next to the crease was the Captain McKelvey, and she was still there at tea with Oyler to see 124 on the scoreboard with 6 wickets in hand, and still requiring 150 to lead England on the first innings.

As so often happens with established partnerships, just 14 minutes after tea, Oyler was caught by Bragger off the spin of Anne Sanders having added 6 runs to her score. With this at 35 it brought the New Zealand total to 130 for 5, and leg spinner Phyl Blackler joined her captain. Wickets then fell at 5 run intervals apart from the ninth wicket. When that fell just 15 minutes before close of play the score was 163 and remained at 166 over night, England's frustration including the failure to capture the last wicket.

A bright morning heralded the final day's play and in the 20 minutes it took to dismiss New Zealand, 12 runs were added to the score. When Marshall ran in from cover to catch Saulbrey off Barker's bowling for 9 it left Jackie Lord 6 not out and New Zealand 95 runs on the first innings.

With virtually two innings to complete in about 5 hours playing time it was obvious that England had to accrue runs quickly and declare. Once again Plant and Whitney opened soundly against Burley and Saulbrey. The latter bowled Plant for 7 and it was 25 for 1. Heyhoe joined Whitney whose was the next wicket to fall. At 60 for 2 Barker and Heyhoe were together but with five minutes to the lunch interval no risks were taken with the New Zealand bowlers. In the 35 minutes after lunch, however, the New Zealand players were shown that the wicket was full of runs if the batting spirit was applied. Heyhoe made 59 and Barker 28 in a third wicket partnership of 74 runs. England declared at 134 for 2 leaving New Zealand 180 minutes to score 230 to win.

Unfortunately for England rain stopped play just 11 minutes after the New Zealand innings opened, and cut short the available time by an hour. Clearly there was no hope of the batsmen going for the runs under these conditions and it was therefore a matter for England to bowl out a side already notorious for its sticking qualities. The inevitable draw, New Zealand finishing with 79 for 2, was remarkable only in the astonishing fact that all ten fielders bowled. Certainly a first in women's Test cricket.

Summary of the First Test 1966

Match Drawn

England:	273 for 6 dec. and 134 for 2 dec.
New Zealand:	178 and 79 for 2

Best Batting

	1st Innings	
England:	R Heyhoe	113
	E Barker	54
	S M Plant	46
New Zealand:	J Doull	74
	C Oyler	35

	2nd Innings	
England:	R Heyhoe	59
	J Whitney	40
New Zealand:	C Oyler	36 n o
	J Doull	33 n o

Best Bowling

	1st Innings	
New Zealand:	J Burley	3 – 68
	J Lord	1 – 16
England:	J Moorhouse	4 – 38
	E Vigor	3 – 29
	M Pilling	2 – 26

	2nd Innings	
New Zealand:	E Maker	1 – 31
	J Saulbrey	1 – 41
England:	E Vigor	2 – 7

Highlights

In her impressive debut as England's captain Heyhoe not only scored a century in the first innings and a not out half-century in the second, but also bowled and kept wicket. During the latter brief spell she took a catch. Ably supported by debut vice-captain Barker, whose first innings half-century in 65 minutes set the pace for a record 121 for the third wicket, Heyhoe's century took 142 minutes. But for somewhat mediocre fielding on the afternoon of New Zealand's first innings, England might have triumphed. Rain, as well as the cautious New Zealand batting, militated against a positive result. Doull's first innings 50 took over 200 minutes. Moorhouse making her Test debut for England did well with a bowling analysis of 38 – 20 – 38 – 4 an average of 8.5 conceding one run per over. With Pilling also bowling 38 – 27 – 26 – 2, between them the opening fast bowlers had 47 maidens in 76 overs.

Women's test

SOUND START BY ENGLAND

An opening partnership of 54 by the Surrey pair, Whitney and Plant, gave England a sound start to the first women's test match against New Zealand at North Marine Road today.

This was followed by gay, attacking batting by England captain Rachel Heyhoe, who scored 50 in 80 minutes to put the team in a commanding position.

Although the New Zealand attack was weakened by injuries — three of the front line bowlers were out of action — they were fortunate in getting a quick break through. England had won the toss and decided to bat.

Opening bat Jacqueline Whitney, playing in her first test, was twice missed in the slips, edging Burley before she had reached double figures, and Sheila Plant was let off when she snicked a ball from Saulburey.

With the New Zealand bowlers moving the ball in the air, the England pair were contained to 25 in a dull first hour's play. They began to look more lively against Maker and Lord, and had taken the score to 54 when Whitney misjudged a pitched ball from Lord.

Sweeping Blackler two leg boundary in the last over before lunch, Plant to 74 for one.

England
He
jou
lun
Sau
who
bat ... getting a touch.

Caught behind wicket

Plant, having added only six runs in 40 minutes, lofted a half-hit drive to silly mid-off where she was again missed, but in the same over from Burley, with her score 46, she was caught behind the wicket.

Getting off the mark with a single, Barker took England to 100.

Attacking every ball, Heyhoe cut Burley past point and pro-duced two elegant shots

ENGLAND.—First Innings 273-6 dec.
Second Innings
S. Plant b Saulbrey	7
J. Whitney c Stonell b Maker	40
R. Heyhoe not out	59
E. Barker not out	28

Total (2 wkts. dec.) 134
Fall of wickets: 1-25, 2-60.
Bowling: Saulbrey 1-41, B. Maker 1-31.
NEW ZEALAND.—First Innings 178.
Second Innings
J. Doull not out	33
J. Stonell lbw b Vigor	8
J. Stead lbw b Vigor	0
D. Oyler not out	36
Extras	2

Total (2 wkts.) 79
Fall of wickets: 1-11, 2-19.
Bowling: Vigor 2-7.
Match drawn.

New Zealanders fight back at Scarborough

A PATIENT, defensive half century by opening bat Judith Doull, which took three hours ten minutes, steered New Zealand out of serious difficulties, after England had taken three quick wickets in the women's test match, at North Marine Road, today. By mid-afternoon New Zealand were 86 for three in their first innings — still 187 behind.

New Zealand, having lost two wickets on Satur-day, began England 273 for six at the start of today's play, and the first nine overs, from fast-bowlers Pilling and Morehouse, were all maidens. The only incident in a first half-hour devoid of runs came when wicket-keeper Sheila Plant was hit in the face by a ball from Pilling and had to leave the field. Captain Rachael Heyhoe, who scored 113 on Saturday, took over behind the stumps. The deadlock was broken by the introduction of spinner

Scarborough Evening News
Saturday 18 June 1966

ENGLAND—First Innings 273 for 6 wkts. declared (Plant 46, Heyhoe 113, Barker 54; Burley 3-88).

NO HO-HUM BATTING BY HEYHOE IN 'OTHER' TEST

SPARKLING batting by Wolverhampton journalist Rachel Heyhoe, put New Zealand on the defensive at Scar-borough ..day.

Heyhoe, coming in after a sound opening partnership of 54 by the Surrey pair Sheila Plant and Jacqueline Whitney, scored 50 in

Birmingham: Warwickshire County Ground, Edgbaston
July 9, 11 & 12

The rain that spoiled the closing stages of the First Test at Scarborough followed the New Zealanders in their journey to all places south. With the exception of Devon and the West Country generally, rain interfered with play persistently. The representative game with a Midlands XI – one of the weaker sides – at the delightful club ground in Stratford-on-Avon resulted in an overwhelming victory for the visitors, but the more challenging territorial match against the West at Torquay had eventually to be abandoned. Somewhat short, perhaps, of concentrated match practice, the New Zealanders went into the second Test with just one team change: Reserve wicketkeeper and opening bat Janice Stead was replaced by pace bowler Wendy Coe. England also made one compensating change by reinforcing the batting. Their newcomer was

England's team for the second Test at Edgbaston in July 1966 is from L-R: Standing: Lynne Thomas, Lesley Clifford, Jacqueline Whitney, June Moorhouse, Mary Pilling, Olive Marshall, Sheila Plant (Wkt.). Sitting: June Bragger, Edna Barker (Vice-capt.), Rachael Heyhoe (Capt.), Eileen Vigor, Anne Sanders (12th).

the forceful Glamorgan bat and slow change bowler, Lynne Thomas.

Dawn on the first day was very unpromising indeed, providing, in fact, the most rain that Birmingham had suffered for many days. When play started at 11.30, however, the wicket could still be described as hard and dry and, on winning the toss, New Zealand's Captain Pat McKelvey chose to bat. The promise of a wicket full of runs was soon turned to dismay when, after playing out two maiden overs Judi Doull was clean bowled by Moorhouse for a duck with the last ball of the third. McKelvey joined Stonell and caution was again the New Zealand watchword. Twelve overs later Moorhouse struck again by bowling McKelvey for 11, at whoch stage New Zealand were 16 for 2 and Moorhouse had taken 2 for 7.

Betty Maker was next to the crease but scored only three singles before being run out. Carol Oyler who had been a rallying asset in the first Test, made no impression on the score and the situation was rapidly slipping out of New Zealand's grasp at 26 for 4 wickets. At lunch the situation was even more depressing for the tourists – on 40 for 5 – but at least the numbers 6 and 7 bats, Phyl Blackler and Bev Brentnall, were looking reasonably secure.

After the interval England persisted with Moorhouse's fast-medium deliveries and the off spin of Thomas. After a sequence of maidens, Thomas bowled Blackler who had been scoring freely off Moorhouse. Blackler's inspiring 32 runs included five boundaries and her 55 minutes at the crease in a crucial situation lifted the score to 66 for 6. Unfortunately Brentnall did not remain with an aggresive Joss Burley for long, but was caught at square leg by Barker off Vigor's lifting spin. With Burley and Coe together, it looked as though there might be something of a stand but Coe too went to Vigor – lbw for 9. The number 10 bat, Saulbrey, offered sound resistance and remained not out for 32 when firstly Burley was run out from an excellent return by Marshall, and then last bat Lord was bowled by Moorhouse for a single. Play finished at just after 4 pm with the score a creditable 131, considering the disastrous session before lunch.

Tea was taken concurrently with the close of New Zealand's innings and the home side had something of *déja vu* about it when, after just 7 overs, the score was 5 for 2: Whitney was first to go with a single, and Plant without scoring. Once again Heyhoe and Barker were together and the runs began to accumulate rapidly. The first change bowler was the left-arm pace bowler Saulbrey whose very first ball had Heyhoe offering a catch. This chance was not held, however, and the England captain and her deputy continued undaunted to bring up the 50 in 55 minutes. Barker too survived an lbw appeal by leg spinner Lord but soon succumbed to the same bowler for 31. But her going left a much healthier look to the scoreboard at 76 for 3. Marshall was next in but was the victim of smart fielding and without scoring was run out. Newcomer Thomas saw out the last 24 minutes of play with Heyhoe who ended the day with 54 runs to her credit, her fifty having taken 92 minutes.

After persistent rain on the intervening Sunday, Monday's wicket seemed little affected and both Thomas and Heyhoe found it to their liking. Runs were made freely and the partnership had put on 74 runs in 80 minutes before Thomas was run out for 58. The next player, Bragger, made 7 before being caught behind off Lord and she was succeeded by Moorhouse. At lunch the latter was going well with 9 to her credit and Heyhoe, who was caught at slip by Stonell with just 8 minutes to go, had been replaced by Clifford. England's score was then 202 for 7.

Clearly the aim was to pile on the runs as quickly as possible after lunch and Moorhouse and Clifford responded nobly to the demand. In just over the hour before Heyhoe declared, 70 runs were added in sparkling style for England to be ahead on the first innings by 144, with the two players not out on 50 and 31 respectively.

In the 50 minutes before tea England bowled 21 overs and took one wicket – that of Doull, who made 12 and was caught at square off Marshall. The other opener, Stonell, was well entrenched and had made 13. McKelvey, who'd replaced Doull, then assisted Stonell in resolutely resisting further loss of wickets to end the day on 27. With the former on 36 it left New Zealand with an overnight total of 80 for 1 and still 64 runs behind.

The third day found England fielding well and on the attack. After just 20 minutes play, the wicket of Stonell fell to Barker to a catch behind. Betty Maker managed only two runs before going lbw in the same Barker over and at 98 for 3 New Zealand looked to be in trouble. But McKelvey was still there and Oyler presented a safe bat. These two put on 19 runs before Barker clean bowled McKelvey who had taken 217 minutes over her slow but vital 37 runs. In the hour remaining before lunch, Blackler was run out for a relatively speedy 10 runs, and wicketkeeper Brentnall who replaced her, looked in solid form to help Oyler put New Zealand just two runs within meeting the first innings deficit. The total was then 142 for 5.

The England bowling after lunch continued with spin; Vigor's off breaks and Barker bowling mainly leg spin. Neither bowler had success, however, and were replaced by Bragger and Pilling. While the latter had an expensive five overs Bragger had Oyler caught in her first over by Vigor. With just four wickets to claim and with New Zealand only 43 runs ahead it began to look as though England would romp home. Instead it was New Zealand who made the running in the shape of Brentnall and Burley. Even the new ball had little effect on the confidence of these two who by the tea interval had put on some 80 runs. Just afterwards – with the addition of only three runs to her score, Burley was bowled by Barker for 46. Hopes that New Zealand might then declare were dashed by Coe's appearance at number nine. Leaving England 65 minutes to score 157 to win, New Zealand declared at 300 for 7.

All that England could do in answer to the challenge was to muster a bright 58 runs, with the loss of 4 wickets, to draw the match.

Summary of the Second Test 1966

Match Drawn

New Zealand:	131 and 300 for 7 dec
England:	275 for 7 dec and 58 for 4

Best Batting

1st Innings

New Zealand:	P Blackler	32
	J Saulbrey	32 n o
England:	R Heyhoe	85
	L Thomas	58
	J Moorhouse	50 n o

2nd Innings

New Zealand:	B Brentnall	84 n o
	J Stonell	47
	J Burley	46

Best Bowling

1st Innings

England:	E Vigor	3 – 24
	J Moorhouse	3 – 32
New Zealand:	J Lord	2 – 56

2nd Innings

England:	E Barker	4 – 94
New Zealand:	J Lord	2 – 17
	W Coe	2 – 30

Highlights

Poor scoring in New Zealand's first innings, where the run rate got more and more out of step with the clock, was compensated greatly by the record score of 300 in the second innings. Though Brentnall's 84 not out came at a run every two minutes, the 50 taking 118 minutes, it was a record highest score against England.

Three half centuries for England, including a maiden one by Thomas in 71 minutes, were part of a sound contribution from other scorers. Of the England bowlers, Vigor and Moorhouse were always containing, but Barker's analysis of 44 – 16 – 94 – 4 was an excellent performance. Five run outs in the match was a tribute to keen fielding on both sides.

London: The Kennington Oval, August 6, 8 & 9

For the third and final Test of the New Zealander's Tour, the home side made two changes and the visitors one. Audrey Disbury, the experienced England and Kent bat and slow bowler, replaced Bragger and pace bowler Rosemary Goodchild took over from Mary Pilling to make her first Test appearance. For New Zealand, Patricia Moore, the left-handed bat and medium pace bowler, replaced Wendy Coe.

Grey skies and the threat of worse to come did not deter Heyhoe from deciding to bat when, for the second time in the series, she won the toss. Once again though, the opening bowlers had the better of Plant and Whitney, for with just a boundary to her credit, Whitney was lbw to Maker and England were 4 for 1. Heyhoe, now getting accustomed to her 'opening role' at number 3, again stablised the situation and when Plant became Burley's victim in the latter's tenth over – of which seven were maidens – the score was 34 for 2. The 'old firm' of Heyhoe and Barker didn't make the usual impression on the scoreboard – Barker succumbing to the leg spin of Lord for the third consecutive Test innings and making only 7 runs – so that, at 49 for 3 England was not too buoyant.

Next to the wicket was Disbury who opened her account with a boundary – off Lord. She and Heyhoe then showed that the soft pitch

Rosemary Goodchild in action at The Oval against New Zealand in 1966. Rosemary celebrated her selection when an unintentional victory roll accompanied the second ball she bowled. Her match tally was 2 for 48 off 27 overs and she was England's most successful pace bowler. The Umpire in the picture is Sylvia Swinburne.

Opener Judi Doull made 29 before being run out by wicketkeeper Sheila Plant in the 3rd Test between England and New Zealand in July 1966. The series was drawn.

had plenty of available runs if shots were made, and the scoring pace quickened. Just on 1 o'clock, however, under increasingly threatening skies, Heyhoe offered a catch off Lord's bowling which was adroitly taken by the wicketkeeper. Marshall joined Disbury and played out time to lunch when England's score was 81 for 4. During lunch it rained.

Not long after the recommencement of play Marshall was bowled by Saulbrey for a duck. England still had 81 runs to their credit when Thomas assisted Disbury in the hunt for runs. In the 40 or so minutes before rain interrupted play, these two put on 33 runs. After the break Disbury scored just two singles before going to Saulbrey for 44, caught by Lord. At that stage, heavy rain again stopped play and eventually the game was abandoned for the day with the England score at 138 for 5.

It was a bright day for England to resume their innings on Monday, August 8, and Moorhouse and Thomas opened promptly at 11.30 am. After only 11 minutes with the addition of 2 runs, Moorhouse was

bowled by medium pacer Maker for a single. Clifford scored a
boundary before also going to Maker, this time caught by Blackler,
without adding to the score, Thomas was caught Maker bowled Burley
for 42. At 154 for 9 Heyhoe declared the innings closed.

New Zealand's usual number 1, Judi Doull, was this time accompanied by Jan Stead and the latter had the unusual experience of
seeing medium-fast bowler Rosemary Goodchild christen her debut
with a double somersault following the delivery of her second ball.
That unintentional victory roll was justified three overs later when
Stead was caught by Heyhoe for just 4 runs. McKelvey joined Doull
and for some fourteen overs the batting was very dull indeed, enlivened
only by four Doull boundaries. Just three minutes before lunch,
McKelvey, who'd seemed particularly bogged down, was lbw to
Vigor for 5. New Zealand was then 32 for 2.

Doull and Pat Moore opened the afternoon session to the continuing
spin of Vigor and Barker. After adding seven to her score, including
another boundary, Doull was comprehensively run out for 29. Carol
Oyler joining Moore began to look confidently set as the former was
driven on the back foot by Vigor and hit her wicket. When Phyl

*Joss Burley bowls Rachael Heyhoe for 31 in the second innings of the final Test at The Oval in
1966. New Zealand's wicketkeeper is Bev Brentnall, and Janice Stead is at slip.*

Blackler got to the crease New Zealand were not in a very promising position with four wickets down for 53 runs. But when, 81 minutes later she was spectacularly caught by Moorhouse off Barker, she had made a sparkling 68, and together with Oyler had effected a 93 run stand for the 5th wicket. Unfortunately for her country only Lord managed to give Oyler further backing, and she, at number 11, remained not out 25, with Oyler not out 67 when the innings was declared closed. At one minute after 6 o'clock, New Zealand was 70 runs ahead at 224 for 9 wickets.

The final 17 minutes of the day's play saw New Zealand's bowlers follow the spirited batting and the England batting emulate her weak fielding. At the close England had the dispiriting score of 5 for 3 wickets.

On the final day England opened with Disbury and Marshall, but within minutes of the start of play Marshall was bowled off stump by Burley without scoring. At 6 for 4 things were looking disastrous for the home team. Some semblance of resistance to the onslaught became reality when Disbury and Heyhoe got going, but all too soon Disbury went caught and bowled by Jill Saulbrey for 25. Barker joined Heyhoe and these two took the score along to lunch at 78 for 5. Whatever hope the England players may have had that their quick scoring leaders would lift England still further towards respectability were dashed when, with her first ball bowled after lunch, Burley had Barker lbw. This was Burley's fourth wicket, to be followed by a 5th when Heyhoe was bowled four overs later. At 85 for 7, only 15 runs ahead with 3 wickets remaining, New Zealand looked to have the game well under control.

It was the backs-to-the-wall play of Moorhouse and Clifford, and then rain which frustrated the New Zealanders. In all, play was held up some 50 minutes by rain though tea was taken during the first delay. In the course of play, however, the remaining three wickets were taken but not without stubborn resistance continued by Clifford and abetted by last player Vigor who remained not out 16. The situation left for the New Zealanders was to score 84 to win in 21 minutes. Undoubtedly robbed of victory, New Zealand at least scored 34 runs at the speediest rate yet managed in a Text except for the stirling first innings performance of veteran Phyllis Blackler.

Summary of the Third Test 1966

Match Drawn

England: 154 for 9 dec and 153
New Zealand: 224 for 9 dec and 34 for no wicket

Best Batting

1st Innings

England:	A Disbury	44
	R Heyhoe	42
	L Thomas	42

New Zealand:	P Blackler	68
	C Oyler	67 n o

2nd Innings

England:	L Clifford	32
	R Heyhoe	31
	A Disbury	25

New Zealand:	J Doull	20 n o
	J Stead	14 n o

Best Bowling

1st Innings

New Zealand:	E Maker	3 – 34
	J Saulbrey	2 – 24
	J Burley	2 – 28
	J Lord	2 – 37

England:	E Vigor	3 – 64
	R Goodchild	2 – 40
	E Barker	2 – 40

2nd Innings

New Zealand:	J Burley	7 – 41
	J Saulbrey	2 – 39

Highlights

With honours undoubtedly going to New Zealand in this match, three players were outstanding. Blackler's 68, with the 50 taking just 56 minutes, turned the whole flavour of the game. Her 93 stand with Oyler was a record for the fifth wicket. That Burley then capped the performance with a record 7 wickets for 41 runs in the figures 34.2 – 18 – 41 – 7 on the notoriously placid Oval wicket, was a magnificent achievement for a fast bowler.

Special mention must go to the wicketkeeper Brentnall who managed to concede only one 'bye' in the three Tests.

WOMEN'S TEST MATCH

New Zealand, 40 for five, make 131

ENGLAND women, unbeaten in the series against New Zealand, made a greta start in the second Test match at Edgbaston, capturing hal fthe tourists wickets for 30 runs.

Then veteran campaigner 46-year-old Phyllis Blackler whose first scoring shot was —the only boundary in the pre-lunch play, which saw New Zealand take for five at the interval—led a splendid recovery which produced another 101 runs to gives the visitors a total of 131.

Blackler, with lusty drives and pulls, twice hit June Moorhouse —who at the start had captured two for 7 in a fine opening spel —for two successive fours in an over.

Jul Saulbrey (four fours in an unbeaten 32) and Jocelyn urley, figured in the best stand the innings—38 for the ninth icket.

England's fielding was first class, two fine catches being made by England captain Rachael Heyhoe (Staffs.) at mid-off, and a brilliant left-handed catch was taken at square leg by Carole Qwler.

England used seven bowlers with June Moorhouse (Yorks.) playing in her second Test match, having three for 23, and

MISS HEYHOE FIGHTS BACK

New Zealand lost half their side for 30 runs and England their openers for five, on the first day of the women's second Test, at Edgbaston, but the tourists' first innings realised and England reached 94 for

Rachel Heyhoe (Staffordshire), the England captain, followed up her and 59 in the first Test with 54 out. She shared a third-wicket and of 70 in 65 minutes with Edna ker (Surrey).

NEW ZEALAND.—First Innings : 131 (J. all, b Moorhouse 0; J. Stonell, b Vigor P. McKelvey, b Moorhouse 11; a, run out 5; C. Owler, c Heyhoe lord 0, P. Blackler, b Thomas 52; R. rtnall, c Burker, b Vigor 7; J. Burley, out 22; W Cue, lbw b Vigor brey, not out 32; J. Lord, b Moor- se 1; extras 2). Fall of wickets : 1-0, 3-26, 4-36, 5-50, 6-60, 7-68, 9-124. Bowling: Moorhouse 18-9- 5; Pilluw 11-4-19-0 Clifford 11-4-15-1; mas 13-9- AND Saul R. 51: not 1-5 11-6- -0; res

England hold on for draw

THE OVAL. — Women's Test : England 154—9 dec. and 153. New Zealand 224—9 dec. and 35—0.

England fought back and helped by a rearguard action by Mrs. Lesley Clifford and a 40-minute break through rain, were able to draw the third of the women's tests at the Oval. All three matches in the series were drawn.

ENGLAND.—First Innings : 154—9 dec.

Second Innings
(Overnight : 5—3)

A Disbury b Burley	0
O Marshall c and b Saulbrey	25
R Heyhoe b Burley	0
E Barker lbw b Burley	18
J Moorhouse c Moore b Saulbrey	18
L Clifford c Moore b Burley	32
R. Goodchild c Doull b Burley	1
E Vigor not out	16
Extras (b 1, nb 5)	7

Total 153

Fall: 0, 1, 5, 6, 52, 78, 85, 103, 114.
Bowling: Burley 34—18—41—7;
Maker 23—13—26—1; Lord 26—11
—28—0; Saulbrey 23—12—39—2;
Blackler 8.3—12—0.

NEW ZEALAND. — First Innings :
224—9 dec. (Black er 68, C. Oyler
67 n.o.).

Second Innings

J Doull not out	20
J Stead not out	14
Extras (lb 1)	1

Total (no wkt) 35
Bowling : Moorhouse 1—0— ' 2—0

OVAL.—England drew with New Zealand.

England, at one time facing defeat, made fine recovery in the women's third Test match.

At luncheon England, with five second innings wickets down, were only eight runs on, and although R. Heyhoe, the captain, batted 130 minutes for 31 and J. Moorhouse stayed an hour for 18, nine wickets had fallen for 114 against good bowling by J. Burley.

After 40 minutes had been lost through rain, L. Clifford and E. Vigor, the last pair, defied all bowling changes for an hour while adding 41 before Clifford was caught off Burley. She had batted two hours and 40 minutes for 32.

Left to make 84 in 20 minutes, New Zealand had scored 35 without loss at the close.

ENGLAND WOMEN.—First Innings. 154 for 9 wkts. dec. (A. Disbury 44, R. Heyhoe 42, L. Thomas 42).

Second Innings

†S. Plant, b Burley		0
J. Whitney, c Moore, b Burley		0
*R. Heyhoe, b Burley		11
I. Barker, l-b-w, b Burley		18
A. Disbury, b Burley		0
O. Marshall, c and b Saulbrey		25
L. Thomas, c Brentnall, b Maker		4
J. Moorhouse, c Moore, b Saulbrey		18
I. Clifford, c Moore, b Burley		32
R. Goodchild, c Doull, b Burley		1
E. Vigor, not out		16
Extras (b. 1, l-b 1, n.-b. 5)		7

Total 153

FALL OF WICKETS—Second Innings—1—0, 2—1, 3—5, 4—6, 5—52, 6—78, 7—85, 8—103, 9—114, 10—153.
BOWLING.—Second Innings—Burley, 34—18—41—7; Maker, 23—13—26—1; Lord, 26—11—28—0; Saulbrey, 23—12—39—2; Blackler, 8—3—12—0.
NEW ZEALAND.—First Innings, 224 for 9 wkts. dec. (P. Blackler 68, C. Oyler not out 67).

Second Innings

D. J. Doull, not out	20
J. Stead, not out	14
Extra (l-b. 1)	1

Total (no wkt.) 35
Bowling : Moorhouse C. Oyler, P. Blackler, 1P.

England's fine recovery

By JOHN REASON

THE OVAL, Tuesday.

NEW Zealand's women cricketers have never won a Test match against anyone, so you can imagine the anguish here when England lost their seventh second innings wicket and were still only 15 ahead.

AL.—England drew with New nd.

land, at one time facing defeat, recovery in the women's third Test

luncheon England, with five second s wickets down, were only eight runs d although R. Heyhoe, the captain, t 130 minutes for 31 and J. Moor stayed an hour for 18, nine wickets allen for 114 against good bowling Burley.

er 40 minutes had been lost through . Clifford and E. Vigor, the last pair, all bowling changes for an hour adding 41 before Clifford was caught rley. She had batted two hours and nutes for 32.

Miss Burley claims seven

It is doubtful if England could have survived had 45 minutes' play not been lost through rain. At close of play New Zealand could surely be forgiven for thinking that God is an Englishwoman.

Their heroine was Joselyn Burley. She took seven wickets for 41 and bowled more than 30 overs at steady medium pace. Her most important victim was Rachael Heyhoe, England's capt. Miss Heyhoe plays forward as unfailingly as T. E. Bailey and her batting was easily the most accomplished in the match.

When Miss Burley bowled New Zealand must have felt that they had the match in their pockets. In fact that was as close as they ever came to winning.

ENGLAND—First Innings : 154-9 dec.

Second Innings

†S. Plant, b Burley	0
J. Whitney, c More, b Burley	1
L. Thomas, c Brentnall, b Maker	4
A. Disbury, b Burley	0
O. Marshall, c & b Saulbrey	25
*R. Heyhoe, b Burley	31
E. Barker, lbw b Burley	18
J. Moorhouse, c Moore, b Saulbrey	18
I. Clifford, c More, b Burley	32
R. Goodchild, c Doull, b Burley	1
E. Vigor, not out	16
Extras (b 1, lb 1, nb 5)	7

Total 153

Fall of wickets : 1-0, 2-1, 3-5, 4-6, 5-52, 6-78, 7-85, 8-103, 9-114.
Bowling : Burley 34-18-41-7; Maker 23-13-26-1; Lord 26-11-28-0; Saulbrey 23-12-39-2; Blackler 8-3-12-0.

NEW ZEALAND.—First Innings : 224-9 dec. (Black er 68, Oyler 67 not).

Second Innings

J. Doull, not out	2?
J. Stead, not out	14
Extras (lb 1)	1

Total (no wkt) 35
Bowling : Moorhouse 4-0-13-0; Goodchild 3-0-8-0; Barker 1-0-5-0; Heyhoe 1-0-8-0.
Umpires : Mrs. D. Coysh & Miss S Swinburne.

ENGLAND IN AUSTRALIA AND NEW ZEALAND 1968 – 1969

For the fourth occasion on which the cream of England's women cricketers did the double Australian Tour, the selectors chose a well-balanced team. Though some players were internationally experienced to the tune of more than a decade, such was the available talent that the average age of the sixteen-strong squad was just on twenty eight years.

Several innovations accompanied this team abroad. Firstly it was the 'new age' of flight, so this particular event marked the Women's Cricket Association's break with the tradition of sea travel 'Down Under'. Secondly, the team was sponsored not only by the Association's fund raising activities, but also by private donations from individuals, firms and industry. The Government, too, put money into this amateur endeavour, but even so, the players themselves needed to find some £200 as well as cash for personal expenses. The third innovation, which went a long way to defray personal cost to the players, was the generous kitting-out of 'on duty' uniform – to the tune of four separate outfits each – by the well known chain store of Marks and Spencer.

And so it was that a group of smartly dressed ambassadors of British sport excitedly boarded the 'plane at London's Heathrow Terminal, bound for Perth, Australia.

Adelaide: Thebarton Oval, December, 27, 28 and 30th, 1968

In the lead up to the first Test, four major two-day matches were played in Western and South Australian States, of which England won two and drew two. Although the 'possibles' for the match were all reasonably in practice, their complement was without Jill Cruwys, one of the pace bowlers, because she had broken a finger in the very first game against Western Australia and Lynne Thomas had also sustained a damaged hand. The 'probables' Heyhoe, Barker, Disbury and Bakewell were all fit, and in the end the latter made her Test début together with Jean Clark, Carol Evans and Chris Watmough. The

The England touring team to Australia and New Zealand in 1968-9. Back Row (L-R): Mary Pilling, Lynne Thomas, Audrey Disbury, Lesley Clifford. Standing: Shirley Hodges (Wkt), Heather Dewdney, Jill Cruwys, Anne Sanders, June Moorhouse, Carol Evans, Sheila Plant (Wkt). Sitting: Christine Watmough, Edna Barker (Vice-capt.), Rachael Heyhoe (Capt), Valerie Hesmondhalgh (Manager), Enid Bakewell, Jean Clark

Australians had six newcomers to the Test scene, but were bolstered by the experience of wicketkeeper Olive Smith, Lyn Denholm, Janice Parker (nee Wady), Vice-captain Miriam Knee, Captain Muriel Picton. The last four mentioned had toured England in 1963 on which occasion Picton was the team's Vice-captain.

Play started at 10.45 on the day after Boxing Day and it was England openers Bakewell and Disbury who took first strike on a hard wicket. In good weather conditions, left arm pace bowler Anne Gordon delivered an 8-ball over, from which Bakewell scored a single, and thus registered another first in the history of Tests between England and Australia. The eight-ball format was to be standard for the other two matches.

Runs came slowly but regularly in the first half-hour's play, giving a useful start, but when, after 63 minutes at the crease Disbury was bowled by Knee for 20, the first wicket total was 48. The off-spinner Knee was treated circumspectly by both Heyhoe and Bakewell for a few overs and was then seen off when she conceded twelve runs in her tenth over. Nevertheless, hers was the only success when at lunch the score had reached 97.

After the interval, the century was soon up and run-getting began to look easy. Within two minutes Bakewell achieved her maiden half-century and England looked set for a good score. Heyhoe's fifty was the next landmark – it having taken 76 minutes – and though each player was lucky not to be caught behind, their partnership went galloping on and reached its century. When Heyhoe was dismissed by Patsy May to a skier taken by Gordon at deep mid-wicket, the scoring rate was just ahead of the clock. At 175 for 2, Barker joined Bakewell but was clean bowled first ball by Knee.

Anne Sanders at number 5 stayed only 9 minutes for her 3 runs, going to a catch off the spin of Denholm – the sixth bowler to be used. June Moorhouse then joined Bakewell with the latter in her 70s, and the two were still together at tea. In a bright seventeen minutes after the break, Moorhouse lifted the run-rate, but then became Knee's third victim when she was lbw for 22. The score was then 220 for 5. Quick runs were clearly the order of a day rapidly drawing to its close, but the wicket was also showing signs of wear. The final five players managed another 25 between them, the rest being contributed by Bakewell and extras to make the final score a creditable 270. Bakewell's stalwart innings of 113 contained a maiden century in 238 minutes.

With 40 minutes left to close of play, Australia lost opener Elaine Bray to a misjudged run; Watmough at cover made the run out, and Australia were 10 for 1 wicket. The final score was 15 with opener Denholm on 12 and Janice Parker 0.

The second day's play started very slowly, it taking 37 minutes to add just 10 to the overnight total. Jan Parker was out for 3, yorked by medium pacer Clifford, and hers was the only wicket to fall during the morning session. At lunch Australia had made 73 runs, Denholm and Knee were togther, and England had summoned the services of seven bowlers to combat the dour batting.

Having established the cautious tempo of a run every two minutes, Denholm and Knee found it equally difficult to force the pace in the afternoon session. England had some cause for celebration at tea, however, because Clifford had run out Knee, who had scored 55 (in 145 minutes) and who had effected a 109 partnership for the third wicket with Denholm.

The News, Monday, Dec. 30, 1968

Century In Test Debut

By LOIS QUARRELL

A century in her first Test appearance by England opener Enid Bakewell and a brilliant second-wicket partnership of 127 between Bakewell and captain Rachael Heyhoe highlighted the first day of the women's cricket Test at Thebarton Oval yesterday.

England made 270 on a true wicket which took spin late in the day when Australian vice-captain Miriam Knee took 5/49 off 22 overs.

The match will resume at 10.45 a.m. today. Details.

Enid Bakewell . . . hit a splendid hundred.

PLAYERS in the first women's Test match between England and Australia, which continues at Thebarton Oval today, are shown swapping autographs on a bat. From left: Carole Evans (England), Lynn Denholm (Australia), Lesley Clifford (England), and Elaine Bray (Australia). A draw in the match seems likely.

By DOT MUMMERY

A great fighting sixth-wicket stand between Goldsmith and Miriam Knee saved a follow Australia in the Test at St. Kilda cricket ground

The pair added 88 in 118 minutes to lift tralia's score from 5-53 to 6-141.

England keep 'Ashes'

... nd of 59 by ... ng yesterday ... for England in the third women's cricket Test.

It was courageous, and never at any time dull, batting. The follow-on was 150 runs.

The dashing Joy Goldsmith joined Knee and the pair kept the game alive looking for runs.

They added 18 in 1. minutes, the highlight ing a glorious pull to the fence for Lesley Clifford

When 1. scored on-d. but betw. below women Any to have tu this strok had 75 on minutes.

Lefthander went to 21 wh. turned the ball to forward leg.

She brought . from a crowd c. 1500 with a delicate cut backward of point for two off Mary Pilling to take Australia's score to 5-85 with six minutes to play

tonic and Betty Wilson, ma- lians' dogged fight. In the 118 minute play in the pre-lur sion, only 62 run- ded but the never dull Off ti. bor.

lunch.

The unbroken sixth wicket partnership of 50 had been scored in 86 minutes.

Miriam Knee's .. were enjoying the Austra-
In the 118 minute ... experience in Eng-

9n3

... as 26 centuries ... at-tricks during career. Miriam .. wn as a med- .. wler having kets during .. r England. .. without .. ta Plant. .r little took a .. 'n the .. ctor-

.. cond .. Hodges .. mpetent job

.. enholm brought .. e 60 with a full- .. ded pull to the fence .. off Lesley Clifford. It was .. a beautifully timed stroke .. e leg and lifted Lyn to 28 and Australia to 4-51.

.e four, stood on the .. passed over the

.. ne injured her foot, to this stage were June Jill Cruwys came on as Bakewell 2-11 sub.

Taken wickets

Most successful bowlers her first Test series against Australia, played her early cricket for a boys' team at a junior school in England.

Fast bowler Moorhouse, to this stage were June Bakewell 2-11 and Moorhouse 2-19 and Enid

Mrs. Clifford and Miss Pilling held out for 79 minutes against the Australian attack after England had been in real trouble.

At stumps on the second day, Australia (213 and 2/50) still held the upper hand against England (193).

However, the match which ends at North Sydney today, seems almost certain to finish in a draw.

England needs only a draw to retain the "Ashes." The other two Tests were drawn.

The Australian bowlers let England off the hook yesterday after the visitors had collapsed against an accurate medium paced attack.

Lorraine Kutcher (5/49) and Anne Gordon (4/57) ripped through the early English batting.

Scoreboard

AUSTRALIA.
First Innings—213.
Second Innings.

L. Denholm, c Hodges, b Dewdney		
D. Newman, lbw, b Bakewell	30	
J. Parker, n.o.	8	
E. Bray, n.o.	7	
Sundries	4	
Total for two wickets	**50**	

BOWLING. — J. Moorhouse, 0/20; E. Bakewell, 1/10; L. Clifford, 0/14; H. Dewdney, 1/2.

ENGLAND.
First Innings.

E. Bakewell, lbw, b Gordon	12	
A. Disbury, c Wilson, b Kutcher	22	
S. Hodges, b Gordon	0	
J. Thomas, b Gordon	13	
R. Heyhoe, c Denholm, b Kutcher	59	
J. Moorhouse, c Kutcher, b Knee	0	
F. Barker, b Kutcher	8	
C. Watmough, st Smith, b Kutcher	15	
H. Dewdney, c Smith, b Gordon	42	
J. Clifford, b Kutcher	17	
M. Pilling, n.o.	3	
Sundries		
Total	**193**	

BOWLING. A. Gordon, 4/57; J. Goldsmith, 0/32; M. Ance, 1/27; L. Kutcher, 5/49; M. Wilson, 0/15; M. Picton, 0/8.

The Daily Telegraph, Saturday, January 11, 1969

Women's Cricket

Miss Barker's 100 rallies England

At 139 for 3, Dawn Newman joined Denholm and these two put on over 26 runs in the comparatively speedy time of 33 minutes before England had the reward of Denholm's wicket when she was well caught at extra cover by Bakewell off pace bowler Carol Evans. Denholm's 93 runs had certainly established a reasonable score for Australia, but at the time of her going the home team were still over 100 runs in deficit and had already batted as long. But Joyce Goldsmith was now at the crease with Newman and the two batted out time adding an extremely useful and encouraging 60 or so runs in the final 80 minutes play. They thus provided the best run rate of the Australian innings.

It took almost three quarters of an hour for the Australians to pass the England total of 270 on the final day's play, and shortly afterwards Dawn Newman was caught by Moorhouse off Clifford's bowling. Her 76 runs were made in attractive style and the number seven replacement, Anne Gordon, made every attempt to force the pace towards a declaration. Goldsmith, however, seemed bogged down in comparison. When Gordon was stumped off Sanders' bowling she'd made 26 in 38 minutes and the Australians had a lead of 45. No declaration was forthcoming, instead the Captain, Muriel Picton, took her place at the crease. Just on 3 minutes before lunch, Goldsmith was caught and bowled by Heyhoe for 58, and Jill Need joined her Captain. At the interval Australia declared with a total of 339 for 7 with Picton not out 11 and Need not out without scoring.

Since two innings were necessary for a result in about 210 minutes of playing time and England had a deficit of 69 to make up, a draw was inevitable. As a result the England side used the time for batting practice and at the close were 192 for 7. The first three players, Bakewell, Disbury and Heyhoe put on 130 between them, with Heyhoe making her second 50 in the match. The most successful bowler was once again Knee who in a spell of 17 consecutive overs bowled 10 maidens (her last five were all maidens) and took the wickets of the numbers 1, 2 and 4 bats. She was also the slip fielder who caught Heyhoe – off Parker's bowling. At the last, the wicket favoured the spin bowling though left arm pace bowler Gordon took two wickets for 35 runs.

Summary of the First Test 1968-9

Match Drawn

England: 270 and 192 for 7 wickets
Australia: 339 for 7 wickets dec.

Best Batting

	1st Innings	
England:	E Bakewell	113
	R Heyhoe	76
Australia:	L Denholm	93
	D Newman	76
	J Goldsmith	58
	M Knee	55

	2nd Innings	
England:	R Heyhoe	68
	E Bakewell	37
	A Disbury	25

Best Bowling

	1st Innings	
Australia:	M Knee	5 – 49
	P May	2 – 33
England:	L Clifford	2 – 55

	2nd Innings	
Australia:	M Knee	3 – 19
	J Parker	2 – 13
	A Gordon	2 – 25

Highlights

In this match the Australians had the bowling edge and England superior batting power overall, though their performance against the spin bowling left much to be desired. Unfortunately they could not retaliate in like vein to dismiss a dour Australia. The press coverage almost unanimously contrasted the 'lively' England attack to the 'painfully slow' Australian batting. Nevertheless four Australians made the 50, which for Newman and Goldsmith were maidens, and two century partnerships were forged. Denholm and Knee had a third wicket 109, while Newman and Goldsmith's fifth wicket stand was a more interesting 117. Knee's match analysis of 8 for 68 in 39 overs capped a good all-round performance. Bakewell's maiden century, and Heyhoe's two 50s were England's successes, and the side's fielding was first class.

Melbourne: St Kilda Cricket Ground January 10, 11 and 13

With an excellent win over the Victorian side on the very same ground just a few days earlier, England were in buoyant mood for the second Test. Shirley Hodges, who earned her place by helping to dismiss eight players in the Victorian match, was the only newcomer. Australia fielded an unchanged team.

On winning the toss England once again opened with Bakewell and Disbury against the attack of Gordon and Goldsmith. The wicket soon showed that it had a bit of bite in it when, after she had bowled three lively overs, Gordon had Bakewell caught by the wicketkeeper in her fourth. With the score on 6 for 1, worse was to follow. Disbury managed only 4 before being well caught and bowled by Goldsmith, bringing Captain Heyhoe, and Vice-captain Barker together.

Barker opened her account with a boundary off Goldsmith and looked well prepared to repeat the procedure, but took just a single off the second ball. It was now Heyhoe's turn at the same bowler, who when she finished an over in which a wicket fell, had conceded 6 runs. Such was the aggression now shown by this pair that first change, May, was given just three overs. At lunch the score was 106 for 2 with Heyhoe 32 and Barker 59. The 50 partnership had come up in 43 spectacular minutes.

When some 40 minutes after the interval Heyhoe was caught at backward point by Gordon off the spinner Knee, the third wicket had produced a partnership record of 137. Heyhoe had made 54, and Barker was therefore in her 80s when she was joined by Thomas.

There was no change in the run-rate until Barker, having brought up her century, was caught by Picton off Gordon with the very next ball. This heralded a good spell by the pace bowler for she next had Thomas caught by Parker for 16 and subsequently trapped Sanders lbw for the same score.

With the sixth wicket going down at 214 and the tea interval passed, England needed to score enough in good time to make a declaration. Just this circumstance was made possible by Hodges and Clifford in a spirited ninth wicket stand. Hodges finished with 21 not out and Clifford with 17 not out when the innings was declared at 254 for 8.

Australia had 32 minutes to play out. They did not manage to do so without losing a wicket – in fact three wickets. First to go was Bray caught by Clifford off Moorhouse for 7. Newman lasted only 11 minutes at the crease before she went to the off-spin of Anne Sanders, stumped by Hodges. Finally, night-watchman Smith was out for a duck on the last ball of the day, again stumped by Hodges but this time off the bowling of leg-spinner Bakewell. Australia's overnight score was 28 for 3. Denholm was 15 not out.

The second day started equally disastrously for Australia when, after receiving only three balls, the number 5 bat Parker was clean bowled by Moorhouse for 0. This brought Miriam Knee to join opener Denholm, whose was the next wicket to fall. At 53 for 5, Australia were still in trouble.

Having survived a possible run out early on, when Knee was joined by Goldsmith she went from strength to strength. At lunch the score had moved on to 90 for 5 with Knee on 29 and Goldsmith 17.

When Bakewell effected the next dismissal, Goldsmith being caught by substitute Cruwys at long on when she had made 36, Australia had been raised from the doldrums with a score of 141 for 6. But when Captain Picton joined Knee, she failed to add to the score. At 7 wickets down, Gordon started carefully, letting Knee continue solidly on her way to a century. After tea, at which the score was 145 for 7, she became Heyhoe's second Test victim when acting as wicketkeeper. The bowler was Clifford who had now captured two important wickets (Hodges had left the field after receiving a blow on the arm thus joining Barker on the injury list. The latter ran into the pickets attempting to save a boundary and badly damaged her knee).

The new bat, Need, took a boundary off Clifford before succumbing to pace bowler Moorhouse. It was then the turn of Patsy May to bolster the Australian innings. This she did to the tune of 12 not out while the stalwart Knee went to a Bakewell full toss which she hoisted into the

By Lyn Denholm's expressive gesture it looks as though June Moorhouse has been lucky in steering this one through the slips. An incident during the second Test at St Kilda, Melbourne, in January 1969. June was top scorer in the second innings with 39 not out. Elaine Bray is at slip.

safe hands of Thomas at mid-wicket. Knee finished just four runs short of a century and the final Australian score was 216.

England opened her innings 38 runs ahead with 15 minutes to play out. At the close the score was 20 for no wicket with Bakewell 5 and Disbury 14, taken off just 6 overs.

The first upset for England on the third and final day was the loss of Bakewell who didn't add to her score. Her going was the result of Gordon's accurate pace bowling. The same bowler then took the next two wickets, Disbury going for 33 and Heyhoe for 11. England was thus 54 for 3 and 92 runs ahead. But Sanders, batting 5, failed to score and became Gordon's fourth victim in this very fine spell.

Watmough joined number 4 Thomas (Barker, the usual 4 was still unfit), and stayed 19 minutes for her four, the bowler on this occasion being spinner Knee. The coming together of Thomas and Moorhouse proved of great benefit to England for they not only stabilised the situation but also put on some quick runs. At lunch they were together with the total at 87 for 5.

In some 35 minutes after lunch a further 22 runs were added before Thomas was stumped by Smith off Picton's bowling, having made 30. Clifford joined Moorhouse but after making 13 useful runs was lbw to Gordon. Hodges supported Moorhouse until at 11 minutes past 3 o'clock Heyhoe declared the innings closed. England's final score was 143 for 7, with Moorhouse not out 39 and Hodges not out 0.

Needing 182 to win in 119 minutes, Denholm and Bray made a gallant start with twenty-five on the board in 23 minutes. At the fall of the first wicket, Denholm being caught by Disbury off Clifford for 26, Picton changed the batting order. Parker, who had made a duck in the first innings, came in at number 3 instead of Newman. It was a strategy that had its effect for she remained not out on 35 at the close. As the wickets fell the Australians got more behind the necessary run rate though, paradoxically, scored at their best pace so far. The 75 came up in 73 minutes. Finally though it was the clock that beat them and the final total was 108 for 5 wickets. A draw, but a well played one.

Summary of the Second Test 1968-9

Match Drawn

England:	254 for 8 dec and 143 for 7 dec
Australia:	216 and 108 for 5

Best Batting

1st Innings

England:	E Barker	100
	R Heyhoe	54
Australia:	M Knee	96
	J Goldsmith	36

2nd Innings

England:	J Moorhouse	39
	A Disbury	33
	L Thomas	30
Australia:	J Parker	35 n o
	L Denholm	26
	E Bray	22

Best Bowling

1st Innings

Australia:	A Gordon	5 – 61
	J Goldsmith	2 – 44
England:	E Bakewell	4 – 49
	J Moorhouse	3 – 40

2nd Innings

Australia:	A Gordon	5 – 57

Highlights

The outstanding performances in the first innings of England's leaders Barker and Heyhoe gave the former her first ever Test century and Heyhoe her third consecutive 50 of the series. A record 3rd wicket partnership of 137, scored in 117 minutes, remains a world best.

For Australia, Knee's 96 was a possible match saver and gave her a second 50 in the series. The outstanding performance, however, was undoubtedly the bowling of Anne Gordon. She became only the second Australian to take ten wickets in a match (the other was Betty Wilson), and in the first innings had a run of five maidens in which she took three wickets.

An interesting feature of the match was the expert catching – some of it outstanding – which accounted for 20 out of the 30 wickets.

Left arm pace bowler Anne Gordon in action against England at the St Kilda Ground, Melbourne, in 1969. She took 10 match wickets on that occasion, 5 in each innings, for 61 and 57 respectively.

Sydney: North Sydney Oval, January 25, 27 and 28 1969

This match began 15 minutes late on the first day because of inadequate placing of the pitch. Rather unkindly, considering the mostly favourable comments in the Press to date, the women were given a wicket adjacent to a newly-planted waterlogged area of the field. After the Captains inspected the otherwise hard playing strip, the toss was won by Picton who elected to bat. Her team had just two changes in it – Lorraine Kutcher and all-rounder Margaret Wilson coming in for Jill Need and Patsy May. Wilson was making her Test début, as was leg spinner Heather Dewdney for England who replaced Anne Sanders.

Denholm and Newman opened for Australia against the pace attack of Moorhouse and Pilling. Progress was steady in the first half-hour which saw 25 runs on the scoreboard. It was not until the medium pace

Shirley Hodges survives a mistimed sweep during the third Test against Australia at North Sydney Oval in January 1969. She was, however, out for a duck having gone in as nightwatchman when England lost her first wicket for 16 runs in answer to Australia's first innings total of 213. The wicketkeeper is Olive Smith and the Captain, Muriel Picton, is in the slips.

bowler Clifford came on, after Moorhouse had bowled only four overs, that success came England's way. In her fifth over, Clifford deceived Denholm into playing early and had the reward of a caught and bowled. This brought Jan Parker to the wicket. She stayed just 14 minutes for her 3 runs before going to Clifford, well caught behind by Hodges.

At 55 for 2, Knee joined Newman. When she was caught backward of point by Dewdney off leg-spinner Bakewell however, it was without scoring. The capture of this vital wicket undoubtedly raised England's expectations but, when Bray joined Newman they set about restoring Australia's position with some controlled batting. These two were still together at lunch when the score was 92 for 3. Newman was on 44 and Bray had made 18.

Just on half-an-hour after lunch and having added 10 runs to her score, Newman was clean bowled by Moorhouse. At 111 for 4 Goldsmith joined Bray and played out the remaining 6 balls of that over. This had Bray facing Clifford who dismissed her lbw for 24. At this stage Clifford had taken 3 for 23. Australia lost no further wickets before tea but got behind the clock, having batted some 210 minutes for her 154.

After the interval Goldsmith was soon out – to a catch by Disbury off Thomas's slows. Kutcher, who had been going along well, completed her 50 but was the next to go after adding just 2 runs. The seventh wicket was thus down for 189. Dewdney bringing off a caught and bowled for her first Test wicket. The remaining wickets, of Gordon, Wilson and Smith went for 12 runs. The not out bat was Captain Muriel Picton who finished with 12. It was the pace bowlers Clifford and Pilling who completed the task and Australia finished with 213, leaving England to play out the remaining 25 minutes.

The established pair Bakewell and Disbury opened the innings and yet again Bakewell was the first to go – for the third consecutive time – to Gordon. Her 12 took only 20 minutes, though, and England was 16 for 1. Hodges acted as night watchman but did not remain long enough to see the night through because Gordon bowled her for a duck. When play finished it was Disbury and Thomas who were togther with the scoreboard registering 18 for 2.

With only eight wickets in hand and 195 runs behind, the England batting began cautiously on the second day. When Thomas was bowled by Gordon for 13 the total had reached 37 and 40 minutes had gone. That England recognised her vulnerability was shown when Captain Heyhoe deserted her quick-scoring reputaion to shore up a shaky innings. She saw wickets fall at 54, 57, 72, 119 and 128, until she herself was out at 134 for 9 having scored 59 important runs. But England was still not comfortable for runs. It took a tenth wicket stand of 49 by the pace bowlers Clifford and Pilling to give England a respectable first innings total of 193. Clifford finished with 42, and Pilling was not out 17. At the close of play both the Australian openers were out, Denholm for 30 and Newman for 8, leaving Australia's overnight score at 50 for 2, scored in just under the hour.

Parker and Bray opened on the third day with Australia needing to make a determined effort to put themselves in a position to declare and yet have sufficient time to remove England. The fifty partnership was brought up in 80 minutes and by lunch Parker had exceeded her 50 but just 6 minutes before lunch was out – stumped by Hodges off Watmough who was the seventh bowler to be brought into the attack. Parker made 60 while, at lunch, Bray was on 39 and number 5 Knee had scored 5.

Restarting at 151 for 3, these two produced some of the liveliest batting of the series enabling Australia to declare 36 minutes later with a total of 210. England were therefore left to make 231 to win in about 165 minutes.

Openers Disbury and Bakewell wasted no time against some containing bowling but, when Bakewell was stumped off the bowling of Knee, they were behind the clock. At 46 for 1 Heyhoe joined Disbury but was run out for just a single. Unfortunately the quick-scoring Barker was not well enough to bat and her place at number 4 was taken by Moorhouse. Disbury was the next one to go, clean bowled by Kutcher for 44, leaving England at 74 for 3 with about the same number of minutes left to play.

Thomas joined Moorhouse and the run rate beat the clock until Thomas was run out for 34. Eventually, however, it was the clock that triumphed after Watmough and Dewdney failed to add to the total. England finished with 155 for 6, with Moorhouse not out 59. The drawn match resulted in a drawn series in which England retained the mythical "ashes" that Duggan had regained in England in 1963.

Summary of the Third Test 1968-9

Match Drawn

Australia:	213 and 210 for 3 dec
England:	193 and 155 for 6

Best Batting

1st Innings

Australia:	D Newman	54
	L Kutcher	52
England:	R Heyhoe	59
	L Clifford	42

2nd Innings

Australia:	E Bray	69 n o
	J Parker	60
England:	J Moorhouse	59 n o
	A Disbury	44

Best Bowling

1st Innings

England:	L Clifford	5 – 51
Australia:	L Kutcher	5 – 49
	A Gordon	4 – 57

2nd Innings

England:	H Dewdney	1 – 22
	C Watmough	1 – 28
Australia:	M Knee	3 – 34
	L Kutcher	1 – 19

Highlights

In making a comeback to the Test arena Kutcher did Australia proud in scoring her first ever 50 and taking 5 wickets in an innings for the second time in her career. Newman's 54 made it her second 50 of the series. Parker also had her second career 50 in this match and this was Bray's first. Overall, Knee had an excellent series, coming second to Gordon in the bowling averages and heading the batting.

For England Heyhoe topped the series and in this match made her fourth 50. It was Clifford, however, who gave England her chance both by taking 5 wickets and for the probable match-saving 42 in the first innings.

The Basin Reserve Wellington, home of the first Test between England and New Zealand, February 15, 17 and 18, 1969.

ENGLAND IN NEW ZEALAND 1969

The W.C.A. team arrived in Auckland on 4 February where the welcome was very cordial but the weather threatening to be wet. In fact for the first match on New Zealand soil, the wicket was so similar to what would be expected in England early in the season that the tourists found it difficult to time the ball. But the fast Australian pitches were now behind them – though the reputations they had earned on them were very much in the present.

In the lead up to the first Test there were two matches scheduled: One against Auckland and the other against a stronger Wellington side. On both occasions the visitors were victorious and not only was the Wellington match an exciting one – the challenge to score 50 runs in 27 minutes leading to a nine wicket victory – but it included several likely New Zealand Test Players. It was also a game in which the two Test Captains were in opposition and, as such, this undoubtedly had repercussions for the first Test which took place a few days later.

Wellington: The Basin Reserve, February 15, 17 & 18

Each team had one player making her Test début. For England it was pace bowler Jill Cruwys, and for New Zealand Louise Clough – representing Otago Province – who was also a pace bowler. Nine of the New Zealanders were players who toured England in 1966, so it was a very experienced team that still had to record a first Test victory against England.

Captain 'Trish' McKelvey won the toss and chose to bat on a green wicket in overcast but warm conditions. Moorhouse and Pilling opened the bowling against Judi Doull and Janice Stead and a measure of the New Zealander's dour approach was evident when the first thirteen overs contained 8 maidens and produced just 12 runs. It wasn't until Enid Bakewell came on as second change that England had a success. Doull was the batsman to go – for 6 – out to a spectacular one-handed, overhead catch taken by Barker fielding at square leg.

At 17 for 1 McKelvey joined Stead and the scoring pace began to increase: it took 66 minutes to bring up 25 runs, but the 50 was registered in 85 minutes. When the lunch interval arrived these two were still together and the score was 86 for 1, with Stead on 40 and McKelvey 36.

Just 10 minutes after lunch Stead brought up her 50 runs but 4 runs later she was run out by a smart throw in from Cruwys. The second wicket had put on 86 runs and when Oyler joined her Captain she made every effort to score. The pace slowed, however, assisted by Oyler's dismissal just 10 minutes before tea was taken. Her wicket went to Clifford, off another brilliant catch by Barker at square leg, for 26 runs. At that stage New Zealand was 182 for 3. Vera Burt made her way to the wicket and safely played out the four remaining balls of the over.

Play resumed after tea with the scoreboard reading 188. When Burt was out, stumped by Hodges off Sanders' spin, it had moved on to 195. As firstly Coe, then Brentnall followed by Saulbrey and Lord, all went for a total of 21 runs, McKelvey remained steadfast. When Burley joined her at the fall of the eighth wicket her share of the 243 total was more than 120 runs. The England bowlers had no more success, however, and when bad light stopped play for the day, McKelvey had made 139 and Burley 16.

It took some 40 minutes for England to capture another wicket after play restarted on the Monday. Burley was bowled by Bakewell for 21. Clough was stumped by Hodges, giving Bakewell her fifth wicket of the innings, for a duck, leaving McKelvey not out 155. New Zealand's final total was 302.

In just under the hour remaining before lunch England's openers, Bakewell and Disbury put on 46, depsite the dismal light and drizzling rain. Indeed, after lunch play was interrupted for a few minutes but the opening pair surmounted the conditions until Disbury was caught at point by Saulbrey off Clough. She had made 31 and England had a solid start with 62 on the board.

As usual the number 3 bat was Heyhoe who, in typical style, opened her account with a boundary. Thereafter, conquering the clock as well as the bowling was what she had in mind. In her hour at the wicket she made just 23 runs but, when a ball from pace bowler Coe stayed low and beat the bat, England's total had moved on by 65 runs. As Barker was again injured (the result of a damaged hand), Sanders joined the indomitable Bakewell. At tea they were still together with Bakewell 84, Sanders 4 and the total 143 for 2.

Playing conditions were no better after the interval and Coe and leg-spinner Jackie Lord did a good containing job to slow down the run-rate. It was Burley, however, who made the breakthrough when Saulbrey took her second catch of the innings to dismiss Sanders for 10. At 157 for 3, Thomas joined Bakewell. Just half-an-hour later rain fell heavily and play stopped for the day at 5.05 pm, with the total at 179. Bakewell had passed the century mark at 106, and Thomas had made 7.

On the third and final day play was delayed for an hour and thus pointed to the game ending as a draw. England continued her innings, Heyhoe declaring with a total of 340 for 7 at 3.32 pm. Tea was taken and soon after the New Zealand second innings opened at 3.55, an appeal was made against the light. This was turned down but only 4 minutes later was allowed and the match was concluded as a draw.

Summary of the First Test 1968-9

Match Drawn

New Zealand:	302 and 4 for 0 wicket
England:	340 for 7 wickets dec

Best Batting

	1st Innings	
New Zealand:	P McKelvey	155 n o
	J Stead	54
	C Oyler	26
	J Burley	21
England:	E Bakewell	124
	L Thomas	47
	J Cruwys	40
	S A Hodges	34

Best Bowling

	1st Innings	
England:	E Bakewell	5 – 40
	L Clifford	2 – 73
	L Thomas	1 – 39
	A Sanders	1 – 47
New Zealand:	W Coe	2 – 44
	J Lord	2 – 74
	J Saulbrey	1 – 55
	L Clough	1 – 70
	J Burley	1 – 71

Highlights

New Zealand's 302 was her highest total to date and Captain McKelvey's 155 the best ever individual score. In a not out innings which lasted just over 5½ hours the century took 228 minutes. Stead's 54 was the first 50 of her career and also her highest score in Tests. England's century maker, Bakewell, capped this sterling performance by capturing 5 wickets in an excellent analysis of 41.5 – 24 – 40 – 5 giving away just 8 runs per wicket in three bowling spells.

Women's Cricket

DROPPED CATCHES

MISS CRUWYS' TEST DEBUT

LET ENGLAND AWAY TO GOOD START

IN 30 minutes, the New Zealand women's cricket team undid the work of a whole day, dropping four chances and letting England get away to a good start in their first innings of the first cricket Test at the Basin Reserve yesterday.

Both openers were dropped, and at the end of the day, 55 minutes early because of rain, opener Enid Bakewell was 106 not out and England were well on the way to leading on the first innings at 179 the ous iise en- ţive ept-

Jill the for iose

62. ried in- for irry) it :en- her irst uch ap-

only by tight bowling from Wendy Coe. Mrs Coe bowled extremely well for 20 overs, 10 of which were maidens, claiming one for 20.

Mrs Coe took the wicket of Rachel Heyhoe with an off-cutter that smashed into the England captain's stumps. She was then 23, and beginning to look set for a much bigger total.

But it was left almost completely to Mrs Bakewell, who is having a great match. In New Zealand's innings she polished off the tail

quicker than anything England had to offer, and Miss Coe much tighter.

Despite some good bowling from Jackie Lord the New Zealand spin attack did not measure up.

England cruised through until rain stopped play to be 179 for three, with Mrs Bakewell 106 and Lynne Thomas 7.

As rain swept over the ground, the two English girls took to their heels, scampering from the ground.

Regrettably, they had omitted to ask either the opposing captain, or the umpires. They were called back after about

Scoreboard

NEW ZEALAND

1st Innings				.. 302

ENGLAND

1st Innings

E Bakewell not out	.. .. ..	106
A Disbury c Soulbrey b Clough		31
R Heyhoe b Coe	.. ..	23
A Sanders c Soulbrey b Burley		10
L Thomas not out	.. .. ..	7
Extras (leg byes 2)	.. ..	2

Total for 3 wkts 179
Fall: 62 (Disbury) 130 (Heyhoe) 157 (Sanders).

Bowling

		O	M	R	W
J Burley	.. .. ..	22	4	40	1
L Clough	.. .. ..	15	2	47	1
J Soulbrey		14	3	28	0

Petite Enid dashes N.Z. hopes

ENID BAKEWELL, the petite England all-rounder with a penchant for instant success in test cricket, yesterday removed any hopes New Zealand had of winning its first women's cricket test.

... minutes with three singles, from 97 on.

Over-all, the New Zealand bowling appeared superior to England's, with Miss Clough

When rain stopped play at 5.5 p.m. England, chasing New Zealand's 302, was three wickets for 179.

On the Australian section of the tour Mrs. Bakewell also hit a century in her debut

McIlvey's great 155 not out.

...vey, the heroine the first day, added 16 to sh 155 not out.

Ier mammoth 322-minute innings gave her the distinction of the highest test score by a New Zealander, either man or woman, in a test on the Basin Reserve.

The previous best was Stew. Dempster's 136 against Eng-

Bowling: J. Burley, 22o, 4m, 40r, 1w; L. Clough, 15, 4, 2, 52, 1; J. Saulbrey, 11, 3, 23, 0; W. Coe, 20, 10, 20, 1; J. Lord, 15, 4, 42, 0.

ENGLAND

First Innings: E. Bakewell, not out, 106; A. Disbury, c Saulbrey, b Clough, 31; R. Heyhoe b Coe 23; A. Sanders

N.Z. Batsmen Falter After Record Stand

The New Zealand women's cricket team failed to take advantage of a record opening stand by Judi Doull and Janice Stead and scored 282 for nine wickets on the first day of the second test at Hagley Oval yesterday.

land's
How bowl
gave 27th birthday present by bowling Miss Heyhoe before the England captain had hit full stride.

In a morning interrupted by showers, New Zealand add-

Pilling bowls NZ out of test

New Zealand women's cricket captain, Pat Mc-Kelvey, going out to continue her record-breaking innings against England

Janice Stead on her way to a first innings 62 and a 128 partnership with Judi Doull in the second Test against England at Hagley Oval in 1969. The fielders are Lynne Thomas at point, June Moorhouse, slip, the wicketkeeper is Shirley Hodges and Mary Pilling is at leg slip.

Christchurch: The Hagley Oval, March 7, 8 and 10

Matches against the Provinces of Otago and Canterbury followed the first Test and these resulted in easy wins for the tourists. The third game against the Lady President's XI, which took place at Ashburton, was a draw that probably resulted from a piece of 'gamesmanship' by the New Zealand Captain. When she loaded the team with her Test bats she omitted the bowlers, Heyhoe responded by resting England's most successful all-rounders Bakewell and Moorhouse, together with Audrey Disbury. In that match, too, it was noticeable that England were not given the chance to pull one out of the bag as they had in Auckland.

For the warm sunshine that accompanied the first day of the second Test, however, England were at full strength – even to the restoration of pace bowler Carol Evans. There was just one change, Evans for Sanders, while New Zealand made three changes from the Wellington Test. All three were Canterbury players making their début in international cricket. Jennifer Olsen was a pace bowler, Patricia Carrick bowled slows and was a middle order bat, and Shirley Cowles batted higher in the order.

When McKelvey won the toss for the second time in the series Doull and Stead opened against fast bowlers Pilling and Evans. On the hard wicket Doull began more cautiously than her partner but the 25 was achieved in even time. Gradually both players came to dominate the bowling and it looked as though error on their part would be the only cause of a lost wicket. In fact the two hours play before lunch produced 88 runs, 35 of them to Doull and 48 to Stead, at which stage England had tried seven bowlers.

Nor did England fare much better after the interval, Stead's hooking and cutting nicely balancing the front-foot play of Doull. It was another forty runs on, after each player had achieved her 50, that England made the breakthrough. A fine pick-up and throw in by Barker when the opening pair thought a quick single was on, ended in Stead being run out for 62.

McKelvey joined Doull and they remained among the runs until tea. The score was then 200 with Doull 102 and McKelvey 26. Just 6 overs later and the complexion of the game had changed. Firstly Thomas took a catch off Moorhouse's bowling to dismiss McKelvey for 30, and secondly, Moorhouse took a slip catch off Pilling's bowling to get Doull's wicket when she had added only a single. At 205 for 3 it meant that newcomer Cowles and Carol Oyler were together.

Cowles attacked the bowling from the start, hitting two good boundaries in her total of 14, but then offered a simple catch which was taken by Disbury off Pilling. Brentnall replaced Cowles and for a while the pace of run-getting slowed. When Oyler went for 9, she'd been at the crease for 47 mins and there was just an hour of play remaining. Brentnall, having been joined by Carrick, and the total at 244 for 5, responded by more aggressive batting. But Carrick, coming down the wicket to Bakewell was stumped for 3. Lord was caught and bowled, also by Bakewell, for a duck, and it was Burley who joined Brentnall at 254 for 6. Evans bowled Burley, and finally Bakewell did the same to Brentnall who'd contributed a useful 38. Saulbrey was not out 5 and the close of play total 282 for 9.

New Zealand declared on the overnight total and so the second day began with Disbury and Bakewell facing up to Burley and Olsen. Conditions were still fine and warm, the wicket hard, and England's openers got off to a cracking start putting 25 runs on the board in 21 minutes. But then the promising outlook suffered a setback when Disbury got an edge to a Saulbrey delivery and was caught at first slip by Doull. At 34 for 1 Heyhoe joined Bakewell and the bright outlook was restored. When lunchtime arrived England's total was 127 for 1 with Heyhoe on 45, the two dropped catches she had survived early on ancient history, and Bakewell past the half-century with 58.

In the first 27 minutes after lunch a further 21 runs were added to make the partnership worth 114. Then Heyhoe attempted a lofted drive and was caught by the bowler, Burley, for 60. Barker was next in but edged one to second slip, and in a very fine spell Burley had taken her second wicket of the maiden over. At 148 for 3, Thomas assisted Bakewell in consolidating the innings to take the tea-time score to 223. Her own contribution was 23 and Bakewell had made 114.

In attempting to force the pace Bakewell was stumped off the first ball of the first over after tea. Leg–spinner Lord was the bowler who had another success when she had Cruwys caught by Stead for 1 in the same over. Moorhouse came in at number 7 and restored sensible batting until she was run out for 10. Clifford then added a bright 31 before being stumped by Brentnall of Carrick. Heyhoe subsequently declared the innings closed, leaving Thomas a patient 53 not out and England's total at 296 for 7 wickets.

With a deficit of just 14 runs to wipe off in the remaining 43 minutes of play, New Zealand was not concerned to do more than make a solid start to her innings. In an effort to take a vital wicket Heyhoe used six bowlers. Success came when the last of these, Thomas, bowled Doull with the third ball of her first over. It was the last ball of the day and New Zealand closed with 26 for 1 and 12 runs ahead.

For the third day the weather still held out and McKelvey and Stead began the task of putting New Zealand in a dominating position. Their scoring pace was steady and the 50 came up in just over the half-hour. When they had added the next 25, however, McKelvey was bowled by Evans. Cowles joined Stead and was forceful from the start, opening with two boundaries. With the score at 99 a promising partnership was ended when Stead was stumped off Bakewell's bowling for 34. The same combination saw the back of Oyler for 3 runs, and at lunch New Zealand had 117 on the scoreboard with 6 wickets in hand.

After the break Cowles, ably abetted by Vice-captain Brentnall, continued as to bat as though runs mattered. With strong pulls and good drives she appeared to be on top of the bowling. Just 4 short of her half-century, however, she played across a ball from Thomas and was bowled. Her most valuable 46 runs took 56 minutes to acquire.

Though time dictated otherwise, the rest of the New Zealand batting was relatively restrained and when Brentnall went lbw to Bakewell for 23, only Lord and Saulbrey offered effective resistance. Eventually Bakewell won through and the innings closed at 3.16 pm with the total on 186.

With England left to score 173 to win in 129 minutes, the odds were

The second innings of the 2nd Test at Hagley Oval, Christchurch, shows off-spinner Edna Barker bowling to New Zealand's Shirley Cowles who made a top-scoring 46. The non-striker is Bev Brentnall who made 23.

on a certain draw. From the first, however, it was clear that Disbury and Bakewell were on the attack. The 25 came up in 23 minutes; the 50 in 43 minutes and the 75 in 61 minutes – and yet the clock was still in front. At 84 Disbury snicked one to the wicketkeeper of Burley, having scored 41, which let Heyhoe in at number 3. It was clear that a win was in the Captain's mind as she laid about the bowling. Just 21 minutes later an attempted repeat of a hook shot which had earned her a six off Carrick, led instead to a catch at square leg. It was taken by Oyler off the pace bowler Saulbrey. Heyhoe's 37 runs included four boundaries and that six.

At 129 for 2, wickets didn't matter and runs most defnitely did. Thomas, who had replaced Heyhoe, was never a rapid scorer and couldn't get going. Having made 3 in 9 minutes she walked forward to a straight delivery from Saulbrey and was bowled. Barker joined the redoubtable Bakewell and the flow of runs was restored. When the 150 came up it was in 108 minutes. In a final 21 minutes most of the runs were taken in quick singles to defeat the defensive field placing. Finally it was Bakewell who scored the winning single. A fitting conclusion to a match in which she had contributed 180 runs and taken 8 wickets. England had won by 7 wickets the final score being 173 with Bakewell not out 66 and Barker not out 24.

Summary of the Second Test 1968-9

England won by 7 wickets

New Zealand:	282 for 9 dec and 186
England:	296 for 7 dec and 173 for 3

Best Batting

1st Innings

New Zealand:	J Doull	103
	J Stead	62
	B Brentnall	38
England:	E Bakewell	114
	R Heyhoe	60
	L Thomas	53 n o

2nd Innings

New Zealand:	S Cowles	46
	J Stead	34
England:	E Bakewell	66 n o
	A Disbury	41
	R Heyhoe	37
	E Barker	24 n o

Best Bowling

	1st Innings	
England:	E Bakewell	3 – 68
	M Pilling	2 – 44
New Zealand:	J Lord	2 – 30
	J Burley	2 – 87
	2nd Innings	
England:	E Bakewell	5 – 56
	L Thomas	3 – 33
	C Evans	2 – 28
New Zealand:	J Saulbrey	2 – 81
	J Burley	1 – 51

Highlights

Not only did Doull make her first ever century in this match but the first wicket stand of 128 with Stead was also a record. Two consecutive Test centuries for Bakewell placed the match on an even keel for the first innings but it was her 5 for 56 in the second that gave England the well-taken chance of a win. Without the ability of Hodges behind the stumps, though, things may have been different. She took 2 catches and made 3 stumpings in support of the England bowlers.

Auckland: Cornwall Park, March 28, 29 and 31

With England in the fortunate position of being one up in the series with one to go, it was no surprise when an unchanged team was fielded. For the opposition, Captain McKelvey went on record with the words:

"We are not disheartened by losing the second test. We are fighting fit and ready to go . . ."

But nevertheless New Zealand had the good sense to return pace bowler Wendy Coe to the side. Another change was the replacement of Carol Oyler by Ann McKenna who came in to strengthen the batting.

It looked a good wicket and when Heyhoe won the toss she chose to bat. Within the first half-hour, however, there might have been some regret over the decision because opener Disbury was out for 8, caught behind off the ever-threatening Burley. When Heyhoe took her place at 14 for 1 yet another throat-catching moment came for the England players. Off the very first ball she received their Captain was dropped at first slip. From then on, though, the old assurance was back and at lunch the score was 105 without further loss.

Resuming with Bakewell on 33 and Heyhoe 62, the accurate New Zealand attack kept the run-rate in check and this led to Bakewell's demise. Ever anxious to get on with it (one cheeky single almost leading to disaster before lunch) the keenness of Bakewell's backing up saw her out of the crease when a straight drive by Heyhoe was deflected onto the wicket by bowler Lord. At 150 for 2, Barker and Heyhoe were at the wicket together for the first time in a Test since Australia. The partnership didn't have time to develop, however, because just two runs later Heyhoe was caught in the deep by Cowles off Lord. Vice-captain Barker took on the free-scoring mantle and abetted by Thomas furthered England's position. Tea was taken when Barker was given out to a Brentnall stumping off Lord. The tea-time score was 224 for 4 wickets.

After the interval Thomas and Cruwys faced the pace bowling of Burley and the leg spin of Lord. Cruwys managed only 2 runs before the Brentnall-Burley combination was once again successful in a caught behind. Coe and Carrick took over the fast-slow combination and each was successful in obtaining a wicket. Coe removed Thomas caught behind for 42, and Coe had Moorhouse stumped for 18. At this stage Brentnall had featured in the fall of four successive wickets.

Clifford, Hodges and Pilling mustered 25 runs between them before Heyhoe declared the innings closed on a total of 293 for 9. This left New Zealand to play out the last 20 minutes. They did so without loss,

Doull and Stead opening as usual, and the overnight score was 12.

Play began at 10.30 in overcast and humid conditions. It was clear from the outset that Doull and Stead were prepared to graft their way to giving New Zealand a good start. The pair were shortly parted however, when Heyhoe set the fielding tone for the day by catching Stead off Evans for 9. McKelvey was next to the crease but didn't make much headway against some determined bowling. After 42 minutes she succumbed to Clifford in a caught and bowled, having made 11. At 44 for 2 newcomer McKenna joined Doull, but the runs still came very slowly. The partnership put on 21 at the rate of a run every two minutes until Bakewell, in her first spell of the morning, had Doull playing forward and missing. Hodges made the stumping, and Doull was gone for 38. Shirley Cowles, in at number 5, had to play out a few minutes before lunch and did so successfully leaving New Zealand at 65 for 3 and very much in need of runs.

After the interval Cowles did her best to make attacking shots and began to accumulate runs. The partnership was beginning to look useful when Evans broke through to see McKenna offer a catch to

Wicketkeeper Beverley Brentnall batting at Cornwall Park in the third Test against England in 1969. Shirley Hodges is the wicketkeeper. Remarkably, in a Test that England won to clinch the series by 2 - 0, both wicketkeepers featured in the fall of 6 wickets.

Clifford which was held. Her staunch 27 had taken 121 minutes, but the partnership had realised 54.

Wicketkeeper Brentnall joined Cowles and batted steadily. Having added nineteen runs to her lunchtime score though, Cowles became the first victim in a good spell of bowling by Pilling. Cowles was caught by Moorhouse for 41 and remained top scorer when Brentnall, Coe and Burley all went to Pilling's pace. Bakewell took the last two wickets, and Jill Saulbrey remained the not out bat on 19. The New Zealand run-rate was always well behind the clock and when the innings finished at 4.42 pm, it was with a deficit of 101.

The customary opening pair of Disbury and Bakewell had an uncustomary cushion of runs to support their sterling endeavours on this occasion but unfortunately hadn't suitable conditions for plumping up that advantage. Bad light intervened and in the thirty minutes of play that was possible, they did well to add 12 runs.

The final day after the weekend also started dull and play was held up a further ten minutes because of the light. Eventually, however, the England openers got going in fine style and though both were out by lunch, it was largely due to their efforts that the lead was a comfortable 223 runs.

Heyhoe's was the third wicket to go down and that was immediately after the break. She was replaced by Cruwys who scored a boundary and then holed out to Doull off Carrick. At that stage off-spinner Carrick had taken three of the four wickets down. Shortly after Moorhouse joined number 4 Thomas, Heyhoe declared the innings closed at 150 for 4. This left New Zealand a reasonable target of 252 runs in 213 minutes to win.

Things began to look England's way when, in almost a repeat of the first innings, Stead was caught behind off opening bowler Evans for 9. The outlook was even brighter when McKelvey was clean bowled by Evans for a single and the score became 19 for 2. This brought McKenna and the unshakeable Doull together, though, and from then on England were struggling to regain control.

Not only had the third wicket partnership taken the score along to 88 for 2 by tea, but the run-rate was looking bright. After the break it increased measurably and the prospect for a first ever New Zealand win was looking good. Even when Evans made the vital breakthrough to get Doull caught by Cruwys, Cowles and then Coe bolstered the innings. The balance tipped England's way, however, when Coe was stumped by Hodges off Bakewell. Her well-played 34 was the last score of substance that any subsequent New Zealander made. The devastating combination of Hodges and Bakewell virtually wrapped up the innings and presented the game to the England players. At the close, New Zealand had done extremely well to score 214 in 213 minutes in a courageous attempt to go for the win.

Summary of the Third Test 1968-9

England won by 37 runs

England:	293 for 9 dec and 150 for 4 dec
New Zealand:	192 and 214

Best Batting

	1st Innings	
England:	R Heyhoe	88
	E Bakewell	52
	E Barker	51
	L Thomas	42
New Zealand:	S Cowles	41
	J Doull	38
	A McKenna	27

	2nd Innings	
England:	E Bakewell	56
	A Disbury	47
New Zealand:	J Doull	75
	A McKenna	60
	W Coe	34

Best Bowling

1st Innings

New Zealand:	J Burley	4 – 62
	J Lord	2 – 85
England:	M Pilling	4 – 53
	E Bakewell	3 – 49
	C Evans	2 – 18

2nd Innings

New Zealand:	P Carrick	3 – 41
England:	C Evans	4 – 45
	E Bakewell	3 – 29
	M Pilling	2 – 60

Highlights

Three half-centuries in England's first innings brought Heyhoe to her thousand runs in Test cricket, Bakewell to her second of the series and Barker to her first. To add another half-century in the second innings and finish with 6 wickets for 78 runs in the match, were crowning achievements for Bakewell. Nor were the pace bowlers to be overshadowed on this occasion. Pilling's 6 for 113 and Evans' 6 for 63 remain the best match analyses of their Test career.

For New Zealand, Burley's 4 – 62 off 30.3 overs and Carrick's 3 – 41 off 14 overs kept the England bats in check. It was Doull's second innings 75 that inspired the will to win, however, and that forceful and fluent batting was her best of the series.

AUSTRALIA IN ENGLAND 1976

The Australians arrived in England on 22 May 1976 in response to an invitation to come and play cricket and make the year an even more memorable one in which to celebrate a Golden Jubilee. Starting in October 1926 with little more than pioneering spirit to back the enterprise, the Women's Cricket Association, supported 50 years on by Unigate Foods Limited, were able to mount another Three-Test Series against the most long-standing of its rivals. It was a generous sponsorship that not only made it possible to play on three world-famous cricket grounds, Old Trafford, Edgbaston and The Oval, but also found the teams contesting for the elegant St Ivel International Cricket Trophy.

Although this was a comparatively young Touring Team, it was one which contained a nucleus of players who had visited England before to play one-day World Cup Cricket. In addition, several of the players had represented Australia in Test matches in New Zealand. As for the England squad, the 'old hands', Heyhoe (now Heyhoe-Flint), Bakewell, Moorhouse (now Stephenson) and Hodges, were all included in the lucky thirteen, together with other veterans of the 1968/9 Test Series 'Down Under'.

It was the chairman of the W.C.A., Sylvia Swinburne O.B.E., who summed up the current situation and aspiration for the teams when she said:

"Both the England and Australian sides will be in a position to field well-established skilful players with Test experience and, as a result of their continuing training programmes for schoolgirls and juniors, each country also has a number of exciting young newcomers. The combination of maturity and youth should produce the kind of cricket which spectators want to watch."

Manchester: Old Trafford, June 19, 20 and 21

Manchester was living up to its national reputation as a great place for *rain*, when history was made by the Australians who were the first Test

The first Australian team ever to fly in to England arrive at Heathrow on May 22 1976. This was also the first home series to be sponsored, when the Women's Cricket Association had the generous support of St Ivel dairy products.

players to adorn the Lancashire County Cricket Ground. Not that it was the first time women had the pleasure of playing there – an England v The Rest trial match occurred as long ago as 1934. But on this occasion the Australians were put in by the England captain Rachael Heyhoe-Flint because the green wicket and the gloomy conditions indicated that rain was in the offing.

Just five overs into the match saw the decision appear to be vindicated as wicketkeeper Margaret Jennings fell to opposing wicketkeeper Hodges, caught behind off Pilling for 2. At 7 for 1, Wendy Hills, making her Test début, joined Lorraine Hill and the score began to climb steadily. When Hills, who was going well, lost her wicket to an excellent low catch at short mid-on taken by newcomer Janet Allen off Stephenson, she had made 36 and the second wicket had put on 73 runs. By then, though it was half-an-hour into the post-lunch session.

The next bat in, Jeanette Tredrea, was also making her début and seemed aware that the need for runs was pressing. Her second scoring shot was a boundary and from then on she gave a display of forceful batting which went a long way to brighten the darkening skies. She saw Hill replaced by another player making her début – Jannette Lumsden – and the two of them kept up the scoring rate. Only 3 minutes before tea, however, Tredrea moved down the wicket to a well-pitched up ball from spinner Bakewell and was stumped for 67. The Australian captain Anne Gordon joined Lumsden, scored a boundary off the last ball of pace bowler Julia Greenwood's final over before tea, and the Australians left the field in the more promising position of 186 for 4 wickets.

During the interval the rains descended and no further play was possible that day.

Since the second day of the Test was a Sunday, play did not start until 2 pm and was scheduled to finish at the normal time of 7 pm. This meant that the Australians had to chase runs to be in a position to put England in that day.

Lumsden, on an overnight score of 23, opened against Bakewell and scored just a single off the first over. Stephenson conceded 7 runs in her first over and it looked as though Australia had the upper hand. Immediately the new ball was taken by Pilling, however, Gordon supplied Allen's second catch of the innings and went for 11.

At 203 for 5, Sharon Tredrea joined Lumsden and opened her account with a boundary. Another lively partnership ensued and when Lumsden was bowled by Julia Greenwood, giving the latter her first wicket in Test cricket, the pair had put on 70 runs in 65 minutes. Lumsden's demise was the signal for the Australian declaration, leaving S. Tredrea on a 36 not out which included a six over the long-on boundary.

Enid Bakewell and Lynne Thomas opened England's innings facing up to the pace of S. Tredrea and Raelee Thompson. Whether or not the much heralded (in the Press) reputation of Australian women cricket's 'Thommo' had anything to do with it, the fact remains that both openers were out to Thompson within the hour and only 31 was on the scoreboard. Both players went to catches, Bakewell for 1 and Thomas for 12, so that it was an, albeit restrained, Heyhoe-Flint who had managed to double the opening score.

The left-hander Chris Watmough batting 4 managed only 14 runs in her 79 minutes at the crease, while Heyhoe-Flint put on another 40, but hers was a valuable supporting rôle at a difficult time. With only half-an-hour to the close, Allen joined her Captain. Time was successfully played out without further loss of wickets, and play ended for the day

The delectable Hills

PUT INTO BAT, Australia's women recovered from the loss of an early wicket to reach 186 for four before heavy rain during the tea interval put a premature end to the proceedings in the first of a three-Test series at Old Trafford yesterday.

Rachael Flint, the England skipper, was probably influenced by the poor light when she invited the tourists to bat. Her decision seemed justified when Mary Pilling, in her third over, had Margaret Jennings caught behind by Shirley Hodges with

spent two and three-quarter hours over 46 runs and Hills was at the wicket for two hours in gathering 36. Their kartnership produced 63 runs and prepared the way for Tredrea. Hills was first to go, caught brilliantly one-handed low down by Janet Allen at forward mid-on off June Stephenson, who also accounted for Hill. Then, at 107 for two, came Tredrea to brighten the afternoon with a delightful range of shots all round the wicket.

Flint switched her bowlers round but with Janet Lumsden

a third-wicket stand worth 73 runs.

Australian skipper Ann Gordon joined Lumsden and when the rains came Lumsden, was 23 and Gordon six.

Stephenson, with two wickets for 15 runs, came out best of the English bowlers. Pilling had one for 50 and Bakewell one for 25.

ENGLAND'S 15-year unbeaten reign as the queen of Test cricket faltered yesterday against an impudent young pretender in the shapely form of 19-year-old clerk Jeanette Tredrea from Victoria.

There was no sign of liberation when women's Test cricket made its first appearance at Old Trafford — Australia's scoring rate of 24 in the first hour was well in keeping with masculine tradition.

But after Braufard judo expert June Stephenson had ended a stubborn second wicket stand of 73 between Lorraine Hill (46) and Wendy Hill's (36) little Jeanette arrived at the wicket with the total on 80.

When she left 70 minutes later Australia were in command at 181 for four and Jeanette had hit eight 4's in her 67.

AUSTRALIA—First Innings

L. Hill c Warmough b Stephenson		46
†M. Jennings c Hodges b Pilling		2
W. Hills c Allen b Stephenson		36
J. Tredrea st Hodges b Bakewell		67
J. Lumsden not out		23
*A. Gordon not out		4
Extras (l-b 4, w 2, n-b 2)		8

Total (4 wkts) 186

Fall of wickets: 1-7, 2-80, 3-107.

Bowling to date: Pilling 14, 4, 50, 1; Greenwood 17, 5, 29, 0; Hullah 11, 2,

WITH one day's play remaining, Australia are in control of the first Test match in the St Ivel international women's cricket series at Old Trafford. England have lost three wickets for 111 runs in reply to a declared total of 273 for six.

Australia, 186 for four when rain stopped play on Saturday, added 87 in 85 minutes before declaring in mid-afternoon.

Jan Lumsden, a New South Wales teacher, hit eight fours in a splendid 65, and Sharon Tredrea, whose sister, Jeanette, had previously collected an exciting 67, struck the only six of the innings in her powerful supporting innings of 36 not out.

Stand of 54

Australia, who were put in to bat, lost their captain, Anne Gordon, to Mary Pilling at 205, but the sixth-wicket pair added 70 stylish runs before Pilling bowled Lumsden.

England, like their opponents, made a bad start by losing their first wicket, that of Enid Bakewell, for only seven runs.

The other opener, Lynne Thomas, was also dismissed 40 minutes later, with only 24 added, but Rachael Flint then played a true captain's innings.

With left-hander Chris ...nough taking a valu... ing role, 54 we... minutes bef... fell to ...

...ill re- ... the follow- ...as 66 not out, ...e fours and played ...rably-controlled innings. a ...Jan Allen was 11 not out in her first Test match.

AUSTRALIA—First Innings

L. Hill c Warmough b Stephenson		46
†M. Jennings c Hodges b Pilling		2
W. Hills c Allen b Stephenson		36
J. Tredrea st Hodges b Blakewell		67
J. Lumsden b Greenwood		65
*A. Gordon c Allen b Pilling		11
S. Tredrea not out		36

Total (6 wkts, dec) 273

Fall of wickets: 1-7, 2-80, 3-107. 4-181, 5-205 6-275.

Bowling: Pilling 19-5-72-2, Greenwood 22-15-49-1, Hullah 13-5-46-0, Bakewell 14-2-28-1, Stephenson 18-3-40-2, Thomas 6-0-28-0.

ENGLAND—First Innings

E. Bakewell c J. Tredrea b Thompson		1
L. Thomas c Jennings b Thompson		12
*R. Flint not out		66
C. Watmough st Jennings b Blunden		14
J. Allen not out		11
Extras (l-b 2, lb 4, w 1)		7

Total (3 wkts) 111

Fall of wickets: 1-7, 2-51 3-80.

England slip is showing

ENGLAND slipped up in the Women's Test against Australia at Old Trafford this afternoon. Skipper Rachel Flint won the toss and put in Australia to grab an early wicket on a greenish pitch.

But left-handed Lorraine Hill, from Victoria, and West Australia's W... able second-wi... ship befo... thro...

...ev...
aft...
gra...
wor...

...
T...
...ary O...

Hill took boundaries with successive shots against Pilling, who had a new ball spell of 9-3-27-1. At the Australians reached 60 without f loss from 9 8overs.

At 80 uperb cat Jan- t silly r ...ill to 36. ...and brought undary past ...illing, their most i sive bowler.

England save the follow-on

Unexpected

She was finally tempted out of her crease by a delivery from spinner Enid Bakewell, pitched so well up that t must have descended on her from the grim, grey Manchester sky. Shirley Hodges seized an unexpected stumping chance.

...e innings f Rachael moved of on a green

...s stayed despite a ...rmittent their star ...rist line shire-born for Kent. ...ent Janet ...her left ...catch at

(watermark: RACHAEL TAMES 'THOMMO')

with England 111 for 3. Heyhoe-Flint had made a vital 66, and Allen was on 11.

Though there seemed little chance of a definite result when the third day started on time at 11.30 am, both players acted as if there was. Attacking the pace bowling from the start 25 runs were added in almost even time, with newcomer Allen making all the running. When she was beaten by the pace of first change bowler Gordon for 32, the tally was 145. The experienced Stephenson now joined Heyhoe-Flint and together they consolidated England's position.

Soon after the new ball was taken, Heyhoe-Flint brought up her 100 and at lunch the score was 192 for 4. Not long afterwards, however, she was caught in the slips by Blunsden off Thompson for a true captain's innings of 110. Cruwys replaced her but soon went to S Tredrea for 4, and the score was 208 for 6. Still more than 60 runs behind England did not risk a declaration. Some 40 minutes later saw almost as many runs added and the declaration was made at 254 Stephenson an exemplary not out 60 and Hodges 8 not out.

With just on 2¼ hours of play remaining when tea was taken and with 50 on the board for the loss of one wicket, the prospect of a drawn game was inevitable. The Australians used the remaining time for batting practice and at the close were 128 for 6 wickets.

Summary of the First Test 1976

Match Drawn

Australia:	273 for 6 and 128 for 6
England:	254 for 6 dec

Best Batting

1st Innings

Australia:	J Tredrea	67
	J Lumsden	65
	L Hill	46
	W Hills	36
	S Tredrea	36 n o
England:	R Heyhoe-Flint	110
	J Stephenson	60 n o
	J Allen	32

2nd Innings

Australia:	M Jennings	52

Best Bowling

1st Innings

England:	J Stephenson	2 – 40
	M Pilling	2 – 72
Australia:	R Thompson	3 – 79

2nd Innings

England:	E Bakewell	3 – 11

Highlights

In this First Test spoiled by rain, the two teams looked evenly matched. The all-round batting performance by the Australians showed both power and potential, which the two maiden half-centuries by J Tredrea (in 81 minutes) and Lumsden (135 minutes) clearly emphasised.

For England, Heyhoe-Flint's century was her third in Tests but, remarkably, her first against Australia. It took 235 minutes. Stephenson's 50, in 118 minutes, was the third of her career. Both captains relied heavily on the pace bowling in this first contest and, taken together, pace accounted for some 80 percent of the overs bowled.

Birmingham: Edgbaston Cricket Ground, July 3, 4 and 5

Between the first and second Tests the Australians had just three matches: a two-day and two one-day fixtures which featured the West Country and the West Midlands as opposition. It couldn't be said that the visitors conquered the West exactly, but they certainly seemed to have had the best of the drawn games.

Perhaps because Heyhoe-Flint captained the Midlands team and the Australian medium pace bowler Betty McDonald took 4 for 32 in that game, she was the only change in the team and displaced Patsy May. The England XI also had one change, medium pace bowler and opening bat Megan Lear replaced Mary Pilling.

Heyhoe-Flint again won the toss and this time took first knock on a hard, fast wicket in bright sunshine. The scene was thus set for a good duel between evenly balanced sides. Had the Australians held on to their catches, both Bakewell and Thomas were dropped early on, and generally shown the reputation for sharp fielding that they'd earned,

England's line up for the second Test at Edgbaston in July 1976. Standing L-R: Janet Allen, Glynis Hullah, Julie Greenwood, Megan Lear, Jackie Court (12th), Jill Cruwys, Shirley Hodges (Wkt). Sitting L-R: Mary Pilling, June Stephenson, Rachael Heyhoe-Flint (Capt.), Barbara Pont (Manager), Enid Bakewell (Vice-capt.), Christine Watmough, Lynne Thomas.

the England total would not have reached 113 for no wicket at lunch. As it was, the Australians had little to relish but the continued prospect of chasing leather.

Play resumed at 2 pm with Bakewell on 59 and Thomas with 52. Calamity fell when, 3 runs later, Thomas was run out without adding to her score. This brought Heyhoe-Flint to the crease where, because of an ankle injury, her quick-scoring style was somewhat hampered. The Australian Captain subsequently put in a good spell of pace bowling which after a sequence of maidens captured the prize of Bakewell's wicket for 75. The England total was then 132. The next three bats, Watmough, Allen and Cruwys scored just 25 between them. Then, only seven minutes before tea, Heyhoe-Flint became wicketkeeper Jennings' third victim in four consecutive wickets, going to spin bowler Lutschini for 49.

In her second over after tea Sharon Tredrea bowled Stephenson for a single and Thompson had Lear lbw for 18 twenty minutes later. When Hodges also went to Thompson caught by J. Tredrea for a useful 13 runs, the last two bats Greenwood and Glynis Hullah were together. After just seven minutes in which no further runs were scored, England's innings was declared at 242 for 9.

Australia had about 70 minutes batting to the close, and openers Hill and Jennings both started with a boundary off each of the pace bowlers Greenwood and Stephenson. In fact Jennings began in fine style with three boundaries in her first four scoring shots. Success came to England after half-an-hour, though, when Greenwood bowled Hill for 9. Hills replaced her and was there at the finish with 14. Vice-captain Jennings had made 18 and the overnight score was 47.

Sunday play started at the usual 2 pm and runs accrued steadily. Within the hour, Hullah had claimed another wicket for England at the price of an added 49 runs. It was Lear who made a fine cover catch to dismiss Hills for 32. Jeanette Tredrea joined Jennings but stayed only 11 minutes before being lbw to Bakewell for 5.

The position at 82 for 3 looked quite encouraging for England but the next player, Lumsden, who had done well at Old Trafford offered a sound bat to all the bowling. She was finally stumped off occasional bowler Watmough for 34. By this time tea was in the past and Jennings appeared to have forgotten the art of scoring boundaries. At 144 for 4, Gordon joined her deputy and reminded her of the fast outfield with some fierce shots. The two of them kept pace with the clock until Gordon went lbw to Hullah for 26. When, 33 runs later, Jennings was stumped by Hodges off the indomitable Bakewell for a first ever century score of 104, the Australian innings was declared closed at 236 for 7 wickets. In the 20 minutes left for play, Bakewell and Thomas did well to register 17 on the scorebaord and remain not out 12 and 5 respectively.

So England began the last day 23 runs ahead and 10 wickets in hand. But that advantage could mean little if a drawn game was the only outcome. To remedy that outlook, the openers first settled in and then proceeded to dominate the bowling with some majestic strokes. Thomas, driving strongly, took 94 minutes for her 50, Bakewell 112 minutes for hers and at lunch, after 2 hours play, the score had moved on to 126 without loss.

When play re-started there was no relapse in the scoring rate – almost 2.5 runs per over – until with her score on 90, Thomas was run out. Her going recorded a first wicket partnership of 164. Watmough joined Bakewell (Heyhoe-Flint was unfit for batting) and, as a result of calling for a risky quick single, Bakewell, too was run out for 77. Allen joined Watmough and the declaration some 35 minutes later saw them both not out with the England total at 228 for 2. Watmough had made 36

Australia's Wendy Hills gets one away during her innings of 32 in the second Test at Edgbaston in July 1976. England's wicketkeeper is Shirley Hodges.

and Allen 18.

The challenge for the Australians was ot score 235 in 175 minutes which was not improbable on the hard batting wicket. Within 10 minutes, however, England had the psychological advantage of dismissing first innings century scorer Jennings for a single. Greenwood was also the bowler when, shortly after tea, Hills went for 18 after Heyhoe-Flint took a good one-handed catch at mid off. At 52 for 2, with just on 75 minutes left for play, J Tredrea joined stalwart opener Lorraine Hill. It was when Stephenson came into the attack for the 28th over that Hill went for 47, caught by Watmough. Her replacement, Lumsden, then had a rallying partnership of 36 with Tredrea before the latter was lbw to Stephenson for 28. With 6 wickets in hand, still 120 needed but with only 57 minutes to go, unless someone could throw the bat successfully another drawn game looked likely.

The Australian captain, batting number 6, certainly tried. For, when time ran out and Bakewell had claimed two more wickets, she remained 38 not out in a close of match total of 169 for 6.

Summary of the Second Test 1976

Match Drawn

England:	242 for 9 dec and 228 for 2 dec
Australia:	236 for 7 dec and 169 for 6

Best Batting

1st Innings

England;	E Bakewell	75
	L Thomas	52
	R Heyhoe-Flint	49
Australia:	M Jennings	104
	J Lumsden	34
	W Hills	32

2nd Innings

England:	L Thomas	90
	E Bakewell	77
	C Watmough	36
Australia:	L Hill	47
	A Gordon	38 n o

Best Bowling

1st Innings

Australia:	R Thompson	3 – 42
	M Lutschini	2 – 31
	S Tredrea	2 – 46
England:	G Hullah	2 – 32
	E Bakewell	2 – 48
	J Greenwood	2 – 58

2nd Innings

England:	J Stephenson	2 – 20
	E Bakewell	2 – 36
	J Greenwood	2 – 42

Highlights

Bakewell's two fifties in the match, her 4 wickets for 84 runs off a total of 43.4 overs, together with establishing a new record first wicket partnership of 164 with Thomas, was outstanding. Thomas's 90, made this her highest Test score to date with the two half-centuries her first against Australia.

Jennings notched up her century in 303 minutes which was Australia's all-time slowest. She also took 2 catches and made one stumping in a match which included three run outs.

The Australian tourists in an historic picture at Lords in 1976. Standing L-R: Sharon Tredrea, Jan Lumsden, Karen Price, Lorraine Hill, Wendy Hills, Jeanette Tredrea, Raelee Thompson, Patsy May, Julie Robinson. Sitting L-R: Marie Lutschini, Betty McDonald, Anne Gordon (Capt.), Lorna Thomas (Manager), Margaret Jennings (V-capt. & Wkt), Wendy Blunsden, Kerry Mortimer.

Kennington, London: The Oval, July 24, 26, 27 and 28

The home of the Surrey County Cricket Club provided the arena for the third and last Test Match in what, since the end of May, was proving to be a long, hot English summer of exceptional character. But there was another exception to this game in that it was the first to be played over four days.

As long ago as 1968 E.M. Wellings, a champion of women's cricket, had suggested that four days might provide the answer in deciding a series which had resulted in a sequence of drawn matches. At the time he was reporting the 1968/9 tour of Australia where, ordinarily, conditions were not dissimilar to the extraordinary dry spell in the Britain of 1976. So, the four-day Test had been mooted on more than one front when it became fact at the famous Kennington Oval.

To meet this innovation each side made one change, needless to say, was in aid of strengthening the batting without depleting the bowling support. For England, this meant that yet another player made her début when Jackie Court replaced Jill Cruwys, and for Australia it was all-rounder Karen Price who came in for Betty McDonald.

Once again Heyhoe-Flint won the toss and she elected to bat on a wicket that looked full of runs. But England was unable to take advantage of the toss and the conditions, giving one of the poorest first innings performances seen in a Test at The Oval. Such, it seems, can be the contrariness of providence when the game of cricket is in the balance.

It all began when Vice-captain Bakewell was caught behind off Thompson in the latter's second over for a single. Heyhoe-Flint, once again in the position of virtually opening the innings stayed for an uncomfortable 38 minutes and then poked at a ball from S. Tredrea

Australian jubilation contrasts with Janet Allen's disappointment as she is caught by Jan Lumsden off the spin bowling of Marie Lutschini, having made only 2 runs. This incident, at The Oval in 1976, was part of a low first innings score of 134. The other fielders are the Captain Anne Gordon at silly mid-off, and wicketkeeper Margaret Jennings.

which took her middle stump. At 25 for 2, Watmough joined Thomas but holed out to slip a catch by Lumsden off Thompson for a duck. Allen scored two runs before losing her wicket – again to Lumsden – off Lutschini's slows, and England was 42 for 4. It took Megan Lear's appearance at the crease to restore some semblance of judgement to the batting, but at lunch the tragedy of England's position was manifest in a score of some 21 overs to the hour almost half were maidens.

The afternoon session did something to boost England's pride when both Thomas and Lear showed a head-down solid front enlivened by the occasional cut and hook shot. Thomas in particular did well, bringing up her 50 with a boundary, an example which obviously inspired her partner.

A spate of boundaries was sufficient to see off Lutschini and ring changes in the pace attack until, in the 63rd over, slow bowler Price was brought on. Subsequently, the England pair were tamed and in a spell of six overs had succumbed. Thomas was the first to go caught by Blunsden for 73, and Lear was caught by Thompson for 21. At that stage Price had the notable figures of 2 wickets for 1 run off 32 balls.

The last four English wickets contributed just 19 runs to the final score of 134 in an innings that had lasted more than 4½ hours.

In the remaining 62 minutes of play, the Australian openers had no obvious problems with the bowling though Jennings offered a possible chance to Hodges when the Australian score was around 30. But at the close the Australian total had moved on to a creditable 59 for 0, with Hill on 29 and Jennings on 30.

When play started on the Monday the Australians were in the pleasant position of ahving more or less a day in hand and only 75 runs to make up. All systems were go for pressing home this advantage and winning their first Test series against England for 27 years.

Heyhoe-Flint opened the attack with Stephenson and Court but neither seemed to have the pace or penetration to worry Hill or Jennings. After seven overs Court was replaced by Bakewell, who always needed watching, but it was Stephenson who made the break-through getting Jennings lbw for 43. Seven balls later Bakewell had Jennings lbw without addition to the score and Australia was 92 for 2. The two new bats, Jeanette Tredrea and Jannette Lumsden, settled in well and at lunch the score had moved on to 138 for 2, with Australia now 4 runs ahead.

When Tredrea was caught by Bakewell off Court for 35, the partnership was worth 74 runs and Lumsden was batting forcefully. Gordon joined her and made 16 quick runs before she was bowled by Stephenson. By the tea interval, Lumsden had brought up her 50 – in

Jan Lumsden of Australia on her way to a forceful 123 at The Oval in 1976. Despite her contribution and England being dismissed on the first day for 134, this final Test – the first to take place over 4 days – was a draw. The wicketkeeper is Shirley Hodges, and June Stephenson fields at short leg.

102 minutes – and the score had moved on to 254 for 4, with Lumsden on 81 and Wendy Hills on 25.

The last session of the day saw England's fielders toiling away and the Australians having much the better of it with an additional 96 runs for the loss of two further wickets. The only cheer that England had to carry her overnight was the fall of century-maker Lumsden's wicket on the penultimate ball of the day. Caught behind off the bowling of Jackie Court, Lumsden had batted 278 minutes for her 123. It was an innings that reporter Henry Blofield at times likened to the batting of Australian Ian Chappell.

It was obvious that the third morning's batting conformed to the Australian captain's dictate of getting quick runs. Sharon Tredrea added 13 runs to her overnight score of 50 in 18 minutes before going to Greenwood, caught by Bakewell. There were two run outs that served only to add 15 runs, and when the innings closed at 379, there had been just 32 minutes of play. Australia was in the happy situation of being 245 runs ahead with the better part of two days in which to get England out. It was an apparently invincible position.

A tactical change in the batting order saw Thomas and Watmough open the England innings with Bakewell and Heyhoe-Flint following as 3 and 4. An immediate effect of the ploy was apparent when the first 4 overs that each of S. Tredrea and Thompson bowled were maidens: *caution* was the password of the day.

As so often happens on these dour occasions where the field is aggressively set, firm shots which penetrate the ring of fielders become boundaries, and there were four of such in the 22 runs scored by lunch. In that time – 63 minutes – 25 overs were bowled and four bowlers had been used.

The back-to-the-wall, not to say stonewall, batting of the two openers was only interrupted by the fall of Thomas in the forty-first over when Gordon took a catch off spinner Lutschini. At 48 for 1, Bakewell joined Watmough to outstay her when she was caught behind off co-spinner Price for 36. This brought England's leaders together but not for long. When Bakewell departed with just on an hour to go to tea, she had made 14 and the total was 76 for 3.

It was June Stephenson's turn to be promoted in the order and at the tea interval she and Heyhoe-Flint had taken the score past the innings defeat to 101. But 84 overs had been bowled and the new ball was due.

With Heyhoe-Flint on 26 and Stephenson on 4, this is how the score remained after an incredible sequence of 10 maidens from the pace bowlers, 8 of them bowled by Thompson with the new ball. This was defence, allied to the placid Oval wicket, on a purposeful scale. But for a lack of judgement by the England captain it would surely have been Stephenson who was there with her at the end of the day. As it was, the unfortunate run out brought in Megan Lear who was on 7 at the close with Heyhoe-Flint 63 not out. The England score was 151 for 4.

At the start of the final day it was clearly the Australians who had the advantage in needing 6 wickets with England still 94 runs behind. But Heyhoe-Flint was still there. Ably supported by Lear, she was still there at lunch 90 in credit with Lear on 32. The score was 209 for 4, and Thompson had bowled her 14th consecutive maiden in the innings.

Two things that could have changed the pattern of the game occurred after lunch. Lear was out to Thompson three overs after she had taken the new ball, caught by Lutschini in the slips for 39, and after just one more over Thompson left the field with a damaged finger and took no further part in the match. There were still 3½ hours of playing time to go.

LYNNE DEFIES PACE GIRLS

Women's Second Test

ENGLAND.—First Innings: 242 for 9 dec. (E. Bakewell 75, L. Thomas 52). AUSTRALIA.—First Innings: 236 for 3 dec. (M. A. Jennings 104).

Australia ignored a challenge to make 235 in 175 minutes on a good wicket at Edgbaston yesterday after Rachel Flint (who did not bat because of injury — an Achilles tendon) declared for England. Thus the second Women's Test limped to a draw illuminated by a superb one-handed catch at mid-off by England's captain which dismissed Wendy Hills at 52 for two and by the brief possibility around six o'clock of a decision either way.

The third and final Test at the Oval will extend to four days the hope of getting a result

Women's Test

BAKEWELL THE TOPS

and Australia ended in a draw with both sides revealing great batting strength.

Resuming at 17-0, the England opening pair, Lynne Thomas and Enid Bakewell bettered their innings partnership of 116 made to 164 before Miss Thomas run out with 90 to her credit

Australia play safe

By NANCY TOMKINS

whereas Australia apparently score freely only when defeat is out of the question.

A first-wicket stand of 164 by Enid Bakewell and Lynne Thomas broke the record 145 of Myrtle Maclagen and Betty Snowball made in Sydney 31 years ago. First Thomas, and then Mrs Bakewell was foolishly run out Thomas when within nine runs of a century and the adventurous ... when Chris Watmough

Jennings plods to earn draw for Australia

Mrs Flint bats for a day to deny Australia

The scoreboard

ENGLAND—First Innings: 242-9 dec. (E. Bakewell 75, L. Thomas 52).
Second Innings

E. Bakewell, run out		77
L. Thomas, run out		90
C. Watmough, not out		36
J. Allen, not out		18

in Miss Greenwood's second over, Miss Jennings having made 104 in the first innings.

England found runs hard to get at the start and were pegged to 24 in the first hour. Scoring shots came mainly from behind the wicket where a single to backward short leg by Enid Bakewell put up the 50 that had taken 93 minutes. Sharon Tredrea proved especially hostile and troubled Mrs Bakewell in a fine tenth over. When Ann Gordon and Wendy Blunsden replaced the fast

ENGLAND LET DOWN BY BATTING

By A Special Correspondent at the Oval

AUSTRALIA are in a strong position in the third and final women's test for the St Ivel Trophy at the Oval.

They dismissed England for 34, with a combination of accurate pace bowling and brilliant catching, Karen Price taking three for six in 14 overs, including 12 maidens in her Test début.

By the close, Lorraine Hill and Margaret Jennings, the Australian openers, had made 59 without loss.

Seven of England's wickets fell to catches in the slips and by the wicketkeeper Jan Lumsden and Miss Thompson each taking two.

Spectacular catch

The more important—and spectacular—of Miss Thompson's diving catches removed Megan Lear when her fifth-wicket partnership with Miss Thomas was beginning to flourish. Between them, they had added 64—the only bright spot in one of England's most dismal batting performances for many years.

England can thank Lynne Thomas, the Welsh hockey international, for saving them from total embarrassment. Her 73 in three hours—her third successive ... ry—was a mixture ... fence on powerful ... tting.

... was eventually fell to ... uged catch by Wendy ... at long-leg, off a ... ous full toss from Karen

England's opening attack against Australia posed little

JAN'S 123 HAS ENGLAND IN TROUBLE

By A Spec...

Australia ... eciding Tes... rophy at the ... t the close, they ... nnings lead of 216 w... ickets standing and two ...ay remaining.

Jan Lumsden, batting at No. 4, ...ok the dominating role and ...ored her first Test century and ...e first by an Australian woman ... the Oval. She was finally out ...r 123 in the last over of the day ... a fine diving catch on the leg-...de by Shirley Hodges, the ...ngland wicketkeeper.

Australia's openers, Lorraine ...ll and Margaret Jennings, laid ...e foundations with an opening ...and of 92. Both fell at that total, ...t Janette Tredrea gave Miss ...msden sensible support in a ...ird-wicket stand of 74.

ENGLAND.—First Innings: 154 (L. ...omas 73; Price 3-6, Thompson 3-31).

AUSTRALIA—First Innings

Hill, lbw, b Bakewell		49
...Jennings, lbw, b Stephenson		43
Tredrea, c Bakewell, b Court		35
Lumsden, c Hodges, b Court		123
Gordon, b Stephenson		16
Hills, c & b Bakewell		28
Tredrea, not out		50
Extras (b 9, lb 4)		6

Total (6 wkts) 350

Fall of wickets: 1-92, 2-92, 3-166, 4-... 91, 5-257, 6-350.

Bowling: Greenwood 17-3-48-0; ...phenson 39-12-58-2; Hullam 15-3-... -9-71-2; Court 20.5-2-64-2; Bakewell ...-0; Allen 4-1-12-0; Flint 6-0-...-0; Thomas 3-0-11-0.

Umpires: M. Howard & S. D. Hill.

Jan Allen was in at number 7 and stayed for 48 minutes without scoring before being caught by substitute Robinson off Blunsden. Meanwhile Heyhoe-Flint had passed the century mark (scored in 313 minutes) and at 3.25 pm England was in a position to make Australia bat.

Despite the loss of Jackie Court who went to Lutschini for 1 and held the fort for 28 minutes, and Shirley Hodges who stayed twice as long for twice as many runs, the Australians could not shake the tenacity of Heyhoe-Flint. She brought up her 150 and the 175 and was eventually out caught off the last ball bowled in the match for 179. England finished with a lead of 81 and, against all the odds, the final Test and the series was drawn.

Summary of the Third Test 1976

Match Drawn

England:	134 and 326
Australia:	379

Best Batting

1st Innings

England:	L Thomas	73
	M Lear	21
Australia:	J Lumsden	123
	S Tredrea	63
	L Hill	49
	M Jennings	43

2nd Innings

England:	R Heyhoe-Flint	179
	M Lear	39
	C Watmough	26

Best Bowling

1st Innings

Australia:	K Price	3 – 6
	R Thompson	3 – 31
	S Tredrea	2 – 31
England:	J Stephenson	2 – 58
	J Court	2 – 64
	E Bakewell	2 – 71

2nd Innings

Australia:	M Lutschini	3 – 70
	K Price	2 – 49
	R Thompson	1 – 23
	S Tredrea	1 – 46
	W Blunsden	1 – 54

Highlights

The first ever four day Test Match proved to be one of feats of endurance. Before considering England's second innings – replete with records as it was – Thomas's third consecutive half-century and Price's first innings analysis 14.2 – 12 – 6 – 3 were very worthy achievements. For Price to finish the match with 5 wickets at 11 runs apiece in a first Test against England was truly memorable.

The really astounding statistics to emerge, however, were those of England's second innings. This lasted 648 minutes to produce 326 runs when, of the 264 bowled, 157 overs were maidens. It is no wonder that Heyhoe-Flint's innings is the longest on record. For her fourth Test century though, she was outdone in patience by Robinson's (in 375 minutes) during the 1957-8 tour.

NEW ZEALAND IN ENGLAND 1984

Fifteen years had passed since a full Test series between England and New Zealand had occurred. When the third team of tourists arrived in June 1984, the seventh confrontation between the two countries was about to commence. Backed by the sponsorship of St George Assurance, the Women's Cricket Association had arranged three, three-day Test matches, three one-day internationals and an itinerary of fourteen other one or two-day matches against counties, territories and other similarly ranked teams. And all this was to be fitted into just ten weeks. In a climate of sponsorship, however, all things seem possible.

The fifteen strong New Zealand squad included among its members several teachers (not all PE specialists), civil servants, an accountant, a cricket coach and a groundswoman. The captain of this young team – which had an average age of 25 – was the youngest member of all. This responsibility fell on Debbie Hockley, then in her 22nd year, but she did have the guidance of manager Trish McKelvey to back her. Trish was a very experienced captain with tours of England, Australia and South Africa to her credit. Apart from her, however, only one member of the group had ever played in England.

With at least six newcomers to Test cricket among them, the tourists had to be the least fancied to come out victors in the series. As to the home country's first challenge, which was to be at Headingley, England was the definite favourite since she had won both the preceding one-day internationals with comfortable margins. It remained to be seen, therefore, what reserves of tenacity this particular group of New Zealanders could draw upon. If their cricketing history was anything to go by they would not be giving up easily.

Leeds: Headingley Cricket Ground, July 6,7 and 8

The New Zealanders came to Headingley with a county match triumph to boost their confidence, the county suffering defeat being local Yorkshire. Another plus was the fact that they could field a full team without injury dictating their choice, while England were without

Jackie Court – a leading all-rounder. It was the experienced Chris Watmough who stepped into an England side primed for success.

New Zealand elected to bat in humid conditions on a firm wicket. Opening with Nicki Turner and Ann McKenna, the visitors were soon in trouble when Turner was out to Cathy Mowat's third ball having scored a boundary off the second. England's jubilation was increased almost immediately when, after taking 3 off Mowat's next ball, replacement Jeanette Dunning was caught by wicketkeeper June Edney off the other pace bowler, Janet Aspinall. At 7 for 2, it was little wonder that the experienced McKenna, now joined by her Captain, applied caution above all else to the bowling which, though accurate, lacked fire or variation.

By the time both opening bowlers were changed, sixteen of the twenty-four overs bowled had been maidens. But against the further medium pace attack of Sue Metcalfe and Avril Starling, McKenna and Hockley kept up their digging-in efforts to recoup New Zealand's early misfortunes. At lunch they had taken the score to 46 for 2.

It was certainly slow stuff and when Hockley was out, caught behind off Metcalfe 15 minutes after play restarted, she had taken 124 minutes for her gallant 26. Incredibly, though, it had taken 35 overs to put 50 runs on the board, and 7 of those were extras.

Karen Plummer was next to the crease and played out the over safely. Hers was the next wicket to fall, however, when she was bowled by Starling who was in her thirteenth over and had conceded only 7 runs. Plummer had made 9, and at 67 for 4. Vice-captain Sue Rattray joined the ever-present McKenna.

After an initial settling in period Rattray got the left-arm spinner Gill McConway (a New Zealander by birth) away for a crisp boundary and proceeded to continue her innings in like vein. When she was out to a close catch off Starling just two minutes after tea, her bright 33 scored in 58 minutes contained 6 boundaries.

Unfortunately no capital was made out of this rallying position of 113 for 5 as the next wicket fell without addition to the score. Thus Rosemary Signal became yet another player to mark her Test début with a duck. It was Sue Brown who replaced her and who remained not out at the close with 9 runs in 96 minutes whilst Ann McKenna finally reached her 50. She did this in the last over of the day, which was the one and only bowled by Chris Watmough who then had the satisfaction of taking the opener's wicket. In her patient innings of 51, which took 337 minutes, there is little doubt that McKenna saved her team from an ignominious collapse. New Zealand ended the day with 147 runs for 7 wickets.

New Zealand declared first thing on Saturday morning and the very much in form Janette Brittin opened with Megan Lear. These two seemed totally unworried by the five bowlers captain Hockley summoned to the attack even though they could not be said to be on top of it, since the scoring rate was fairly sedate. Accurate line and length finally paid off for New Zealand when, just 4 minutes before lunch, opening bowler Brown had Lear caught in the slips by Elizabeth Signal (twin sister of Rosemary) for 31. The score stayed at 79 for 1 to lunch.

After the interval it was Carole Hodges who faced Brown and took a single off the first ball. With left-arm medium pacer Linda Fraser in support the scoring rate slowed somewhat, but Brittin brought up her 50 and then a change of bowling, off-spinner Rattray for Fraser, saw the fall of two wickets. Firstly Hodges was bowled by Brown for 8, and then Watmough was caught by Brown off Rattray for a single. With the score at 120 for 3, captain Jan Southgate joined Brittin who was now scoring more freely.

After Southgate had faced 6 balls she had scored 7 runs and this attacking batting at last saw the run-rate beating the clock and Brittin achieving her century. Again, though, it was she who remained behind when the wicket fell. But when Southgate departed, caught behind off Fraser, her 35 runs had taken just under an hour and the partnership had realised 70 runs.

Wicketkeeper Edney came in at number 6 and played out four balls to tea without scoring. Just on half-an-hour later she was another Fraser victim, going to E. Signal's second catch of the innings for 4. Janet Aspinall joined Brittin to score 19 and be not out with Brittin on 144 when England's innings was declared at 256 for 5.

In the final 25 minutes play, New Zealand openers Turner and McKenna resisted all temptations to score and closed on 0 and 2 respectively, with 2 byes giving the visitors 4 for 0 at stumps.

The last day began with the New Zealanders needing 106 to avoid an innings defeat, and the ball in England's hands to see that they did not make it. Starling and Metcalfe began but spinner McConway was soon in the attack. With 6 maidens in her seven over spell, however, it was clear that New Zealand were still not rushing things. Ironically though, the first wicket was a run out which meant that the 44 minutes of play thus far had produced 18 runs.

Dunning joined McKenna and managed to penetrate the attacking field to be 33 at lunch of which 32 came in boundaries. New Zealand then had a respectable 71 for 1 on the board, and England, having tried 7 bowlers, were looking hard pressed.

The breakthrough came just on half-an-hour after lunch when the

DEBUT FOR METCALFE

By RACHAEL FLINT

Sue Metcalfe, 19, the Yorkshire and Junior England fast bowler, makes her debut for England today in George Assurance

NEW ZEALAND STRUGGLE ON OPENING DAY

New Zealand at only two years after playing club cricket ton.

Metcalfe, a stude science at Alsag Crewe, has a holid: waitress in a small inn near Skipton; she impressed selectors with four for 12 against Kent in a county game at Doncaster two weeks ago.

England, two up in the three-match one-day series, have recalled Kent's opening bat Megan Lear and Middlesex pace-bowler Cathy Mowat.

Debbie Hockley, New Zealand's captain, is in good for took a century at Be

ENGLAND DENIED

The tourist include identi and Elizabeth has recovere a back injury which has kept her out of action for the last two weeks.

ENGLAND.—•J. Southgate (Sussex), J. Brittin (Surrey), J. Aspinall (Yorks), C. Watmough (Surrey), •J. Ed (Kent), M. Lear (Kent), A. Star

England battled hard for a v against New Zealand on the fi day of the First St Geor: Assurance Test at Headingl yesterday and, despite using ni bowlers, failed to prise out tl dogged New Zealanders.

The tourists started at fo for nought still needing 105 make England bat again, but match-saving innings came fro McKenna, who accumulated in 170 minutes. New Zealai finished on 194 for eight.

McKenna lasted until half hour after lunch, but then w excellently caught at slip l Lear off Hodges

Dunning, scored a positive 7 and Rattray contributed a har hitting 37, but New Zealand intention to play safe from th first day when they took 100 overs to achieve 147 for seve declared laid the foundatio

England v. New Zealand

HEADINGLEY.—Match drawn.
NEW ZEALAND.—First innings 147 for 4 dec.

ENGLAND.—First innings 256 for 5 dec (J. Brittan 144 no).

NEW ZEALAND — Second innings
(Overnight 4 for 0)

N. Turner run out	7
A. McKenna c M. Lear b J. Aspinall	29
J. Dunning c and b Aspinall	71
D. Hockley run out	7
K. Plummer lbw b S. Metcalfe	13
S. Rattray c Hodges b Aspinall	37
R. Signal not out	8
S. Brown c Lear b Hodges	3
E. Signal lbw b McConway	1
C. Jagersman not out	4
Extras (b 9, lb 2, w 1, nb 2)	14
Total (for 8)	**194**

Bowling: Starling 21—10—32—0; Mowat 11—6—16—0; Waatameugh 1—1—0—0; Metcalfe 9—3—20—1; Conway 25—17—28—1; Aspinall 11—4—33—2; Brittin 17—9—26—0; Hodges 28—17—25—2; Southgate 1—1—0—0.

NEW ZEALAND struggled to 147 for seven in a slow opening day of the St George Assurance first Test against England at Headingley

They owe much to the patience of Ann McKenna, their opener, who was dismissed with the final delivery making 51

ayer's resis: was bowled of Surrey, won the toss l conditions, he third ball (Middlesex)

In the next over Jan Aspinall, who plays for Warwickshire, had Jeannette Dunning caught behind for three with seven on the board.

Metcalfe strikes

New Zealand crept to 46 for two at lunch, with 51 overs completed bbie Hockley, their ime the second victim ey, the Kent wicket-runs later off Sue the Test newcomer re.

...ay, the tourists' vice-captain, hit a brisk 33 to brighten the day but fell immediately after tea to Aspinall.

Aspinall then got a ball to lift to Rosemary Signal, who top-edged it to Carole Hodges at

Cricketing twins Elizabeth (left) and Rosemary Signal, 22.

COURT GIVEN RECALL

England recall Jackie Court for the second St George Assurance Test against New Zealand at Worcester today. She replaces Chris Watmough (Surrey) who is unavailable because of teaching commitments.

Court missed England's one-day international win against New Zealand at Hastings because of injury and was then omitted after the second one-day win at Leicester end's drawn h Headingley.

New Zealand Jackie Clark, 22, a who scored an against the W.C.A. Presidents XI on Wednesday.

The last time n's Test cricket was staged cestershire county in 1951 when E defeated by Aust occasion on which women were defe cricket.

ENGLAND. — J. S cant), J. Court (Middle (Yorkshire), J. Brittin (S (Kent), M. Lear (Kei (Lancs & Cheshire), G. Anulian, S. Metcalfe Starling, C. Mowat (M NEW ZEALAND (from D. Caird, L. Fraser, R. Sig J. Clark, S. Gilchrist, K. Dunning, I. Jagersma, S. Brown. A. McKenna, N. T

Kiwis play on for pride

England h the St George the one-da series ag but tomo 55-over have m

BRITTIN IS HEROINE

ek is-ey the e drawn ion is to of their d win a England. e in the at Can-

glaring inability 1.8 runs Tests. esses a pen-ut New Zea-ked the more ak through be-bowl straighter and variation in attack, eth Signal's speed weapon.

stant thorn in New aland's side has been the England opener, Janette Brittin, who has dominated the series with scores of 101 and 88 no out in the one-day matches and 144 not out and 16 in the Tests.

With one eye on the 1985 tour to Australia, the England

JANETTE BRITTIN, England's prolific-scoring opener, narrowly failed to produce her third century in four innings against New Zealand at Worcester yesterday, when she was caught behind for 96. This lowered her average from 333 to 214·5.

England resumed at 15 without loss in reply to New Zealand's 225 for six declared. Brittin and Lear took the total to 84 before Lear fell to the leg-spinner Rattray.

Southgate and Brittin added

England v N. Zealand

45 in 29 minutes, but South-gate's bright innings ended when she spooned the ball back to Dunning.

dogged McKenna was caught by Lear off Hodges for a 29 that had taken 170 minutes. Hockley replaced her at 89 for 2 and when she departed 33 minutes later – to another run out – her team had passed the demarcation score that would require England to bat again. With only 3 wickets down, however, England still had much to do.

Hope was still alive when the fourth wicket fell at 127 to remove top scorer Dunning who had made 71. At that stage, however, just over 3 hours remained for play. The onus was still on England to make the bowling effort – and by that time 9 bowlers had been used.

That the game would end in a draw was virtually assured by the failure to remove Rattray who, as in the first innings, showed that she was an accomplished performer with the bat. She took 62 minutes to score 37 runs which included 8 boundaries before being caught by Hodges off Aspinall. Since only an hour was left for play when the number 8 bat reached the wicket and New Zealand was 179 for 6, England had lost her chance. New Zealand's final score at the close of play was 194 for 8. The visitors had certainly shown that only the very best of good bowling would remove them when their backs were to the stumps.

Summary of the First Test 1984

Match Drawn

New Zealand:	147 for 7 dec and 194 for 8
England:	256 for 5 dec

Best Batting

1st Innings

New Zealand:	A McKenna	51
	S Rattray	33
	D Hockley	26
England	J Brittin	144 n o
	J Southgate	35
	M Lear	31

2nd Innings

New Zealand:	J Dunning	71
	S Rattray	37
	A McKenna	29

Best Bowling

1st Innings

England:	J Aspinall	3 – 26
New Zealand:	L Fraser	2 – 61
	S Brown	2 – 71

2nd Innings

England:	C Hodges	2 – 25
	J Aspinall	2 – 33

Highlights

McKenna's half-century took 335 minutes but was a crucial prop for her team. Dunning's first 50 took 128 minutes and she and McKenna had a second wicket stand of 67 in the second innings. Rattray's match score of 70 was remarkable in that it contained 14 boundaries.

In the highest score of her Test career to date, Brittin's century took 213 minutes and included 8 boundaries. The total length of her innings was 5 hours. The 4th wicket partnership of 70 with Southgate took just 57 minutes.

England's most successful bowler in the match was Aspinall whose 5 – 59 came off only 24 overs.

Worcester: Worcestershire County Cricket Ground, July 14, 16 and 17

With only one representative game between the Headingley Test and the second meeting of the two teams at Worcester one week later, there was little opportunity for any radical change in the sides. New Zealand brought in Jackie Clark to strengthen the batting in the place of the injured Rosemary Signal and Shona Gilchrist replaced Karen Plummer. For England, an unavailable Chris Watmough allowed Jackie Court to regain her place in the side.

On this occasion Southgate won the toss and, probably with their resistance at Headingley so fresh in her mind, put the visitors in to bat. The tactic this time appeared to be ringing the bowling changes with the medium pace attack in an attempt to make New Zealand's openers Turner and McKenna play at the ball. In the two hours to lunch, however, 36 overs had been bowled and the score was 60 for no wicket

England take the field after lunch, and under threatening skies, at Worcester. Smiling pace bowler Cathy Mowat, the WCA's Chairman since 1985, is ahead of Jan Brittin and Avril Starling. Photo by courtesy of Mr Leslie Salmen.

and six bowlers had been tried.

It was not too long after the interval before the spin bowlers McConway and Hodges broke through the defensive barrier. When Hodges had Turner hitting against the spin and Aspinall took a cover catch, the more elegant of the openers was out for 45. McConway then gained the scalp of replacement Dunning for a duck and 20 minutes later the wicket of the resolute McKenna for 43. Both went to catches by Captain Southgate.

Hockley, coming in at second wicket down had taken a while to settle but Clark took even longer before scoring. When she was out after 27 minutes at the crease, caught and bowled by Brittin, she had scored just 3 runs and New Zealand was 113 for 4. At this stage Vice-captain Rattray, who had looked so good at Headingley, joined her captain and scored off the first ball. Caution tempered her natural attacking game, however, so that at tea she was on 14, Hockley had made 41, and the total was a moderate 152 for 4.

The next 25 runs of this promising partnership was slightly in advance of the clock with Rattray getting into her stride. It began to look as though England were going to have a tough time breaking this pair – the outfielding had begun to look ragged – when Brittin threw in from the covers to run out Hockley who had made 47. At 191 for 5, first Brown and then Jagersma supported Rattray through her 50 and at 209 for 6 wickets the innings was declared. Jagersma remained 12 not out and Rattray 57 not out.

With just over half-an-hour to stumps England openers Brittin and Lear managed 12 runs between them and England finished the day with 15 for no wicket.

Play started promptly on the Monday and Brittin soon got into scoring mode with 50 to her credit in just over the hour. Only 15 minutes later, though, and Rattray had broken through to get partner Lear caught in the slips by E. Signal for 26. This brought Southgate to the wicket.

The run rate was maintained slightly ahead of the clock when Southgate got going, but just as the partnership was gaining momentum, occasional slow bowler Dunning tempted Southgate who was caught and bowled for her 18 brisk runs. Court was next to the crease and managed to add 11 runs in the 14 minutes remaining to lunch.

Recommencing play on 146 for 2, it looked as though the hard, dry wicket was totally in favour of the strikers who were going at a run a minute until Brittin edged one to the wicketkeeper. Début bowler Gilchrist had the reward of this prize wicket and Brittin had the chagrin

Play in progress during the second Test at Worcester just before the non-striker, Nicki Turner, was out for 57. Left-hander Jackie Clark, driving a ball from Jan Brittin, went on to make the second innings top score of 79.

of going just 4 short of her century, but the pleasure of having given her team a solid foundation.

At 162 for 3, Edney joined Court and struck the ball firmly. When the latter was out just 4 minutes to tea, the partnership had realised a most useful 70 runs. Both Aspinall and Hodges made every effort to score quickly, with Hodges making a bright 20 in 13 minutes before being bowled by Gilchrist. Her going marked England's declaration at 271 for 6 leaving Edney at 51 not out.

In the remaining 69 minutes of play New Zealand made a steady start leaving an overnight score of 38 for no wicket with Turner and McKenna both on 18.

The last day's play began with Turner and Dunning (replacing an indisposed McKenna) facing medium pacers Aspinall and Starling, and New Zealand needing to knock off an eight run deficit before the business of the day could get under way in earnest. This was soon achieved, however, and things were going well for New Zealand when, in her 6th over, Starling had Dunning offering a catch to Lear. Hockley was next in, took some time to get going but was still there at lunch with Turner who was batting well. With every chance of increasing the scoring pace on a wicket that still favoured the batsmen, New Zealand had a good standpoint from 108 for 1.

Unfortunately for them, Hockley was run out for 29 soon after play restarted, and her replacement Clark was slow to get off the mark. Then, when Turner was out some 35 minutes later, caught by Aspinall off Court for 57, it was 129 for 3. Precious minutes were ticking by and New Zealand were only 83 ahead. Someone had to throw the bat and number 6 Rattray could be just the one to do it.

The score had moved on to 162, and 50 minutes had passed, when Rattray was run out for 16. With some 130 minutes of playing time left Captain Debbie Hockley had little choice but to go on batting. It was at this stage that McKenna resumed her innings but, having added a relatively speedy 7 runs in 22 minutes, was caught by Court off Hodges for 25.

Brown made just 8 runs in 18 minutes before going lbw to Starling, and then E. Signal joined Clark who had just passed the fifty mark. With the experience of the one-day defeats behind her, the New Zealand captain was in no position to risk England knocking off the 130 or so runs in the 75 minutes playing time that would be left at this stage. It was no surprise then that the remaining players used the time for batting practice, but it was a nice touch that Signal reached her first 50 in Test cricket with a six off compatriot Gill McConway in the last over of the day.

Summary of the Second Test 1984

Match Drawn

New Zealand:	225 for 6 dec and 311 for 7 wickets
England:	271 for 6 dec

Best Batting

	First Innings	
New Zealand:	S Rattray	57 n o
	D Hockley	47
	N Turner	45
	A McKenna	43

England:	J Brittin	96
	J Edney	51
	J Court	47
	M Lear	26

2nd Innings

New Zealand:	J Clark	79
	N Turner	57
	E Signal	55 n o
	D Hockley	29

Best Bowling

1st Innings

England:	G McConway	2 – 20
	C Hodges	1 – 24

New Zealand:	S Gilchrist	3 – 42
	J Dunning	1 – 27

2nd Innings

England:	A Starling	3 – 37
	C Hodges	1 – 37
	J Court	1 – 41

Highlights

With teams of all-rounders, as these seemed to be, the lack of a couple of top class penetrating bowlers showed. Had New Zealand attacked more in the first innings, the finish could have held more interest. However, for England, Brittin again demonstrated batting supremacy, bringing her average in the two Tests thus far to 230 in two innings. Wicketkeeper Edney made her first half-century in a full Test, and England's most successful bowler was Starling.

New Zealanders, Rattray, Turner, Clark and Signal all made first 50s and Gilchrist, on her début, was the most successful bowler with an average of 14.00 off 16.4 overs.

Canterbury, Kent: St Lawrence Cricket Ground, July 27, 28 and 29

New ground was being broken for Test cricket when the final match of the 1984 series between England and New Zealand was staged at Canterbury. And for the occasion, England made three bowling changes and strengthened the deep fielding department. Sarah Potter, Jill Stockdale and Helen Stother, pace bowlers all, replaced their like in Aspinall, Mowat and Metcalfe. Jane Powell displaced Megan Lear. Having won the third of the one-day matches in the interim, England again had the confidence edge. But New Zealand, who had been somewhat beleaguered by illness, had learned much and even now could be considered to have the better bowling attack. It remained to be seen whether the visitors could harness their undoubted batting talent to a more aggressive approach and at least occasion an England second innings.

When she won the toss this time, Southgate chose to bat and Brittin opened with a new partner in Hodges. Both players started with a

The England team for the third and final 4-day Test against New Zealand at the St Lawrence Ground, Canterbury. Standing L-R: June Edney (Wkt), Avril Starling, Angela Bainbridge (12th), Carole Hodges, Janette Brittin, Gill McConway, Jane Powell. Kneeling: Sarah Potter, Janet Southgate (Capt.), Jill Stockdale, Helen Stother, Jackie Court (Vice-capt.).

boundary and looked comfortable against the attack of Brown and Fraser. First change E. Signal had Hodges caught by Clark off her second ball, however, and England was 35 for 1, Hodges having contributed 15. Disaster followed as Southgate and then Court departed with 5 between them and the total at 44 for 3. This set-back brought newcomer Potter on the scene and normality was once again restored.

At lunch, though, Potter had departed, bowled by Brown for 21, but Brittin held the fort with replacement Powell and the score had reached a reasonable 89 but 4 wickets were down.

Consolidation formed the pattern of play after lunch and the 50 minutes after the restart was very satisfactory from England's viewpoint – the total having increased by a gratifying equivalent of runs – until Powell succumbed to slow bowler Dunning by being stumped for 37. Unfortunately Brittin outstayed her departure by only 6 minutes, a victim of the same bowler for 63 runs, and once again England was facing the fate of too few runs for too many fallen wickets.

But Edney, now joined by Stother, continued from where she had left off at Worcester making considerable headway after some suitably cautious opening play. She was still in command 67 minutes later when Stother was clean bowled by Gilchrist for 15, and had scored 49 very necessary runs in a seventh wicket partnership of 65. It was at this stage that Southgate, obviously with nothing but a win in mind, declared the innings closed at 4.16 pm on a total of 214.

Tea coincided with the declaration leaving New Zealand 105 minutes of batting time to the close and the occasion saw a new opener with McKenna in the left-hander Clark, who had ably demonstrated her staying powers at Worcester. The breakthrough came with just on a half-hour of play remaining when Stother had Clark for 39, caught by Starling at mid-off. At 62 for 1, captain Hockley joined McKenna and took the score comfortably through to 86 at stumps.

The morning's play on the Saturday went all New Zealand's way, resulting in a second wicket partnership of 83, until McKenna was bowled by Hodges for 48. Rattray, justifiably promoted to first wicket down, kept Hockley company until lunch but less than ten minutes after the interval had departed for 8, caught and bowled by Brittin.

It was Dunning's turn to aid and abet her captain, who had made some 80 or so runs of the 185 on the board, and she did so to good effect until she was run out for 27. At this stage, the score was 239 for 4 and Hockley declared the innings closed. She remained an admirable 107 not out in her team's first innings lead of 25.

The hard, dry wicket was still full of runs as England played out the

Members of the New Zealand Test side at Canterbury go for a pre-match jog. They are L-R: Karen Plummer, Elizabeth Signal, Ingrid Jagersma, Nicki Turner, Jeanette Dunning, Diana Caird, Jackie Clark, Shona Gilchrist and Ann McKenna.

50 minutes to tea and notched up 33 runs without loss. After the departure of Brittin who was lbw to pace bowler Brown for 35, Southgate too, on the batting mantle and England went cruising on to the close, finishing with 113 for just the one wicket. Hodges was on 48 and Southgate had made 28.

Play was cautious at the beginning of the final day and 20 minutes passed before Hodges scored the two runs for her half-century. Although two wickets fell before lunch. Southgate being caught behind off Gilchrist for 59 and Court falling similarly to Fraser for 9, the pace picked up and 100 had been added.

With Hodges going strongly and her well-deserved century behind her, runs were at a premium and caution a thing of the past. Potter displayed this view in her quickish 20 runs, and Powell did not waste much time in being run out for 8. At 3 minutes past 3 pm, England declared at 297 for 5 leaving Hodges with 158 not out and New Zealand requiring 273 to win in 110 minutes and an additional 20 overs.

New Zealand made no change to the opening pair of McKenna and Clark and lost the latter for 7 after 20 minutes when Stockdale took a catch off Starling. But Hockley restored confidence and attack to take the score to 51 at tea after 17 overs had been bowled. This virtually left the rate required at 2 runs per minute which was not the visitors habitual practice. They nevertheless continued to tilt at the windmills of fortune but were never up with the clock. Neither could any one of England's *eight* bowlers do better than gain a single wicket and, to the last, the lack of bowling penetration (on either side) dictated yet another draw. New Zealand finished with 145 for 4 wickets. Captain Debbie Hockley again finishing top-scorer with 62.

A happy incident at Canterbury in 1984 when Jackie Court at slip took a catch to give left-arm pace bowler Sarah Potter (L) her first Test wicket. June Edney joins in the celebration which dismissed Debbie Hockley for 62. In the first innings the New Zealand Captain had made a not out 107.

Summary of the Third Test 1984

Match Drawn

England:	214 for 7 dec and 297 for 5 dec
New Zealand:	239 for 4 dec and 145 for 4 wickets

Best Batting

1st Innings

England:	J Brittin	63
	J Edney	49 n o
	J Powell	37
New Zealand:	D Hockley	107 n o
	A McKenna	48
	J Clark	39

2nd Innings

England:	C Hodges	158 n o
	J Southgate	59
	J Brittin	35
New Zealand:	D Hockley	62
	A McKenna	33

Best Bowling

1st Innings

New Zealand:	E Signal	2 – 34
	J Dunning	2 – 36
England:	C Hodges	1 – 26

2nd Innings

New Zealand:	S Gilchrist	2 – 41
England:	J Brittin	1 – 15

Highlights

For England Brittin's match total of 98 led to an incredible 112.67 series average. The only player to approach this was wicketkeeper Edney who, in one less innings, averaged an excellent 104.00 for the series. Hodges made her highest Test score in this match, the century took 256 minutes and included 14 boundaries. She was also England's most successful bowler overall, with 6 wickets at an average 23.17 apiece. With her 107 not out, this first Test century taking 209 minutes, followed by a 62 in which the 50 took only 87 minutes. Hockley finished with a fine series average of 55.60. In only two innings E. Signal did well to top the averages with 56.00. The most successful bowler was Gilchrist with 6 wickets for 25.00 each. Wicketkeeper Jagersma supported her bowlers well with 5 catches and one stumping in the series.

HOORAY. Open a bottle Great news from the Test match. England's batting has knocked the opposition for six. Once again they are clearly the stronger side. No, not *that* Test, the other one.

Listen. England will never beat the West Indies at Old Trafford. I can't think who asked them to come here. No, I refer to the women's match - Canterbury, where the ~~tant High Com-~~ New Zeala~~~~ have ~~~~ ~~~~ against ~~~~ fine people. ~~~~ be asked again.

~~~~ Old Trafford they are wearing crash helmets and heart protection pads, bowling with intimidation and waving bats in triumphal egoism whenever they score 50. There, cricket is no longer a game for gentlemen. It is a game for men, which is quite different. But here in Kent the women's test match is like entering a time warp. This is how England must have been when it was still England. No jogging, no chat shows, no cholesterol and no Russell Grant, the unnecessarily bouncy astrologer on breakfast television. The pitch was "flat and true", a classic English virtue. All round the boundary were signs saying "St George". Suit-

run off again. "I'm June Edney, the wicket-keeper. I'm a house-wife and mum," said one. They are relentlessly pleasant, modest, non-posh young women who are patriotic, pay their own travel, never dissent from the umpire, Miss Hill, and m~~~~ century with only a~~~~
of the b~~~~
~~~~om the New ~~~~ dressing room, we ~~~~ strains of a Maori war song followed by a communal leap and a tremendous thud as the team landed. It is the sort of thing Prince Charles spends his life watching. As they came out, the players were greeted not by hooting and yelling, but by applause so arranged that each clap could be individually

THE SUNDAY TIMES, 29 JULY 1984

STEPHEN PILE

watches the other
Test match

and they'll take too long for

his bastion of new technology, as the women put up the score by hand.

At the start of play there was a crowd of 38. They included Mrs R. Bradley, Miss L. Cowden, Albert whose teeth whistled, Betty Bell, her sister-in-law Mrs Wapshott, the Tranter girls, Ann and Winnie, and Canon Hugh Pickle, who sat with his eyes glued to the game and the wireless commentary from Old Trafford pressed to his ear so that cricket assaulted virtually his every orifice.

"Although I live near the salubrious town of Didcot," he said, "I am actually the canon of Kobe in Japan. I represent the ~~~~ngland." His Pickle time ~~icket teams, ~~coa ~~iown is d ~~tter~~ s "(

my second religion. Some say my first. Oh, good shot!"

But all is not tranquility. Eighteen months ago the MCC turned down the women's application to play this match at Lords, even though it is the only chance the crowd there will have to see an England team triumph.

Unlike the men, the women's side is unbeaten in a Test match since 1951. Mind you, most of them have been draws. "I can't remember when there was last a result against New Zealand," said the England manager, Rachel Heyhoe Flint. They only play for three days, which is not long enough to fit in four innings, and so the games hardly ever finish.

The first two Tests have both been draws, but there has been no shortage of drama ~~with~~

Women of the willow wand

LANCASHIRE opener Carole Hodges scored a marvellous maiden Test century in England's second innings of the third St George Assurance Trophy match at Canterbury yesterday.

But the game ended in a draw and the cup for the series was shared.

Hodg~~~~ ~~~~ut when ~~~~ing her 139 with ~~~~e knock ~~~~e came

~~~~he hot ~~~~ added ~~~~oss of ~~~~(9)— ~~~~ersma.

ASPINALL IS LEFT OUT

Women's Cricket

HODGES CENTURY IN VAIN

By RACHAEL FLINT

Janette Brittin, the Engla~~~~ opener, scored her sixth si~~~~ cessive half-century against t~~~~ New Zealand tourists, on tl~~~~ first day of the third and fin~~~~ St George Assurance women~~~~ Test at Canterbury yesterday. England declared at 214 for seven at tea.

New ealand reached 76 for one after a bright opening stand of 62 in 22 overs between Ann McKenna and Jackie Clark, her new left-handed partner, who made 59.

Brittin, of Surrey, w~~~~ midway thro~~~~ at 149. ~~~~
~~~~ centuries ~~~~s this season. ~~~~ were 82 for four but ~~~~on and Powell added 66 for the fifth wicket in 44 minutes. Edney and Stother shared a seventh-wicket stand of 65 and Edney's 49 not out included seven fours.

Stother, out for 15, took 43 minutes to get off the mark as New Zealand fielded and bowled with great enthusiasm.

~~~~ New Zealand 110 minutes and 20 overs to score 273 for victory. The target was not sufficiently tempting and the early loss of Clark, excellently caught by Stockdale, set them back.

Hockley hit an aggressive 58 but the challenge was never ~~~~ on and they finished at 4.

English Butter Players of the Series awards went to England's Janette Brittin for overall average of 119·2 and New Zealand's Ingrid Jagersma for her outstanding wicket-keeping.

ENGLAND.—First innings 214-7 dec.

Second innings		
J. Brittin, lbw b Brown		55
C. Hodges, not out		158
J. Southgate, c Jagersma, b Gilchrist		59
J. Court, c Jagersma, b Gilchrist		20
S. Potter, c Dunning, b Gilchrist		20
J. Powell, run out		8
Extras (b 5, lb 1, nb 4)		10
Total (5 wkts dec.)		297

Fall of wickets: 1-70, 2-189, 3-207, 4-263, 5-297.

Bowling: Brown 36-12-92-1; Fraser 30-8-80-1; Signal 11-1-45-0; Rattray 5-0-20-0; Gilchrist 15-3-41-2; Dunning 4-1-11-0.

NEW ZEALAND.—First innings 239-4 dec.

Second innings		
A. McKenna, lbw, b Brittin		33
J. Clark, c Stockdale, b Starling		7
D. Hockley, c Court, b Potter		62
S. Rattray, c and b Hodges		10
N. Turner, not out		7
J. Dunning, not out		20
Extras (b 5, w 1)		6
Total (4 wkts)		145

Fall of wickets: 1-17, 2-95, 3-112, 4-118.

Bowling: Stother 5-3-8-0; Starling 6-1-23-1; McConway 8-1-25-0; Stockdale 7-1-21-0; Brittin 7-1-15-1; Hodges 7-0-18-1; Potter 8-4-17-1; Court 7-3-12-0.

Women's Cricket

BRITTIN KEEPS UP RECORD

CONCENTRATE, CONCENTRATE!
KEEP YOUR EYE ON THE —
THAT SOLITAIRE MUST HAVE
COST A FORTUNE!

GREAT BRITTIN'S GLORY

ENGLAND IN AUSTRALIA 1984–5

Although both New Zealand and Australia had made a practice of playing two Test series in the same year it was not usual for England to follow their example unless already abroad. In 1984, though, that unprecedented step was taken for a special reason: It was to share in the celebrations that the Australian Women's Cricket Council were putting on to mark the Golden Jubilee of Test match cricket between the two countries. So, on 4 December 1984, a fifteen-strong cohort of selected players, under the managership of Norma Izard, landed in Perth ready to show the Aussie's that Test matches could be won even if it took four days to do it. The gruelling schedule was for five four-day Tests, three one-day internationals and 10 other interstate matches to fit into as many weeks.

Practice and no fewer than three one-day games against Western Australia gave newcomers to Australian conditions time to acclimatise. It also gave England the fillip she needed to go into Test match contention because, after losing the first two games, the third was excitingly won. This showed, no doubt, that jet lag was well and truly over and the necessary adjustment to pace and light achieved.

Perth, Western Australia: The W.A.C.A. Ground, December 13, 14, 15 and 16

The psychological barrier was sufficiently breached for England's captain Jan Southgate to run the gauntlet of the world's fastest bowlers, Debbie Wilson, Denise Martin and Australia's captain Sharon Tredrea, when she won the toss and elected to bat. To mark the historic occasion England's first captain, Betty Archdale, had been invited to spin the coin. This she did, and so it was that fifty years on, the Jubilee series was under way.

True to expectation the ball flew, but England's openers Megan Lear and Carole Hodges weathered the initial attack of Wilson and Tredrea until the latter broke the wicket to return Lear to the pavilion for a score of 5 and an England total of 9 for 1. Jan Brittin came in at first wicket down and she and Hodges began to attack the bowling effectively. At lunch they were still together with the score a slow, but secure, 66 for 1.

Just over ten minutes after play restarted Brittin was caught at mid-off by Jill Kennare, a victim of spin bowler Lyn ('Lefty') Fullston, for 44. Not long after Southgate joined Hodges, the latter, on 34, edged one to wicketkeeper Chris Matthews off Wilson. Suddenly that comfortable position was a more ordinary 93 for 3. Vice-captain Jackie Court joined her skipper and the process of building runs was continued in fine style as she opened her account with a boundary off the 4th ball she received.

The partnership looked well set until just over the hour together when Southgate edged one to Verco at slip off medium-pacer Raelee Thompson and was out for 22. The pair had survived one or two chances but had done well to add a fine 55 and put England in the position of 4 for 148. At tea, veteran Chris Watmough had helped to improve the position to 181 for 4.

Before Court departed some 55 minutes after the interval, she had brought up her own 50 and shared in another sparkling 50 partnership –

The Australian Squad for the first Jubilee Test at Perth, December 13-16 1984. Standing L-R: Peta Verco, Karen Price, Jill Kennare, Denise Emerson, Denise Martin, Debbie Wilson, Jen Jacobs, Lyn Fullston, Trish Dawson. Sitting L-R: Chris Matthews (Wkt), Ann Mitchell (Manager), Sharon Tredrea (Capt.), Raelee Thompson (Vice-capt.), Annette Fellows.

The England Squad taken in Australia prior to the start of the Jubilee Series. Standing L-R: Janet Aspinall, Christine Watmough, Jane Powell, Avril Starling, Megan Lear, Carole Hodges, Sue Metcalfe, Joan Lee, Janette Brittin. Sitting L-R: Helen Stother, Gill McConway, Janet Southgate (Capt.), Norma Izard (Manager), Jackie Court (Vice-capt.), Jill Stockdale, June Edney (Wkt).

with Watmough – but justice was done when she was caught by Jen Jacobs in the gully off Wilson, having survived two chances off that bowler in her innings of 90.

At 226 for 5, wicketkeeper June Edney joined Watmough and was still there when play ended having seen the departure of the latter for a well struck 46. At stumps England was a well-earned 272 for 6 with Edney 18 and Janet Aspinall on 2.

Not half-an-hour after play started the next morning, Aspinall was brilliantly caught by Thompson off spinner Fullston for 11. This heralded a good spell by the spinner. With the pace of Denise Martin accounting for Gill McConway, who was clean bowled for a duck, the leg-break bowler took the other two wickets. Edney was caught by Verco for her 24 and Helen Stother went the same way for 3. The tourists' innings finished at 11.27 am with a total of 290, which had taken only some 6 hours to accumulate.

The 31 that openers Peta Verco and Denise Emerson put on in the remaining 54 minutes to lunch was just a taste of things to come. As play progressed so their confidence and batting strength indicated that England's bowlers were in for a trying time. The pair were beginning

Megan Lear is bowled for 5 in the first innings at Perth by Australia's captain Sharon Tredrea.

to look almost invincible when Verco was run out for 36 out of the 97 runs in which a new record partnership was established. It was a great start for Australia which Jill Kennare admirably built on with Emerson until the latter fell to Court. She missed the attempted pull shot and was bowled round her legs for 84.

At 157 for 2, Trish Dawson joined Kennare but was soon out, caught by Lear off McConway for 3, having faced just nine balls. Her replacement, Jacobs, fared only marginally better in scoring 5 before going leg before to Aspinall. The possibility of an England break-through was there with Australia tottering slightly to 174 for 4. But Fullston shored up the breach, saw Kennare to her half-century, and was herself on 10 at the close.

Starting at 196 for 4 and 94 runs behind, few doubted that Australia would soon make up the deficit. Only 25 minutes later, however, Kennare went to Aspinall caught by McConway for 56, and Tredrea was with Fullston. The latter went to another catch, this time by Court off Starling, and when Tredrea was caught by Lear off Helen Stother for 14, England were on top. Though Thompson stayed 70 minutes to make 5, there was little other resistance and Australia were all out for 251 with just 15 minutes to go to lunch.

In the happy position of being 39 ahead on the first innings, Lear and

Hodges were content to play out the two overs to lunch in sedate fashion. After the interval the pace of scoring was slow in response to the liveliness of Wilson and Martin, and with just 6 to her credit, Hodges edged one to Dawson off Wilson. Brittin joined Lear and the run-rate increased measurably. The next wicket to fall was Lear's, who played Thompson on for 23, and this left Brittin on 35 after some 40 minutes. It was Southgate who replaced Lear and then the run-rate really outran the clock. In this attacking period before tea, Brittin reached her 50 – it took 66 minutes – and 34 runs were added in 29 minutes.

Nor did the interval diminish the fierce aggression as Brittin cut, drove and pulled her way to one of the fastest centuries on record. Southgate, too, played her part in the 85 minute century partnership until bowled by left-armer Martin for 38. At 171 for 3, Court joined Brittin. She added a fiery 12 in short time before giving way to Watmough.

Now 227 ahead, the tourists continued attacking but, like Court, Watmough soon went to a catch off Thompson. The last wicket to fall that day was Brittin's. She was clean bowled by Thompson and her sparkling innings of 112, which had taken 175 minutes, had undoubtedly set the pace to put England in a winning position.

Starting at 207 for 6 – 242 ahead – on the last day, England spent 82 minutes acquiring a further 36 runs before declaring with 9 wickets down. Australia thus had some 270 minutes to make 282, and a very

England's Captain, Jan Southgate survives this diving attempt at a run-out by Australia's wicketkeeper Chris Matthews. Jan made 38 in the second innings.

sporting chance of a win.

A slowish start by the home side, whose openers Verco and Emerson had virtually to play their role twice as lunch intervened, was brought to an end when both were run out within 10 minutes of one another. Then Kennare, and a self-promoted Tredrea, had to restore the position of being just 38 for 2 before starting to make headway. They did both admirably, making a third wicket partnership of 94 in 91 minutes, before Tredrea was caught behind off Starling for 27.

Only 65 minutes remained for play when replacement Dawson was run out for 20 and Jacobs joined Kennare with Australia at 179 for 4. But Kennare, who had batted majestically, only survived another 20 minutes before being caught by Brittin off Stother for 103. After that, amid confusion (requiring three trips to the wicket to consult the Umpires!) as to whether it was time or overs that actually dictated the close of play, Australia lost two quick wickets for 7 runs. Eventually the finish of play was resolved at 5.30, by which time Australia had made 209 for 8 and the match was drawn.

Summary of the First Test 1984–5

Match Drawn

England: 290 and 242 for 9 dec
Australia: 251 and 209 for 8 wickets

Best Batting

	1st Innings	
England:	J Court	90
	C Watmough	46
	J Brittin	44
	C Hodges	34
Australia:	D Emerson	84
	J Kennare	56
	P Verco	36

	2nd Innings	
England:	J Brittin	112
	J Southgate	38
	J Aspinall	30 n o
Australia:	J Kennare	103
	S Tredrea	27

Best Bowling

1st Innings

Australia:	L Fullston	4 – 61
	R Thompson	2 – 50
	D Wilson	2 – 90
England	A Starling	3 – 40
	H Stother	2 – 43
	J Aspinall	2 – 48

2nd Innings

Australia:	R Thompson	4 – 47
	D Wilson	3 – 25
England:	H Stother	2 – 44
	A Starling	2 – 47

Highlights

Court's 50 in 73 minutes was just pipped by Brittin's in 66 minutes. The latter's second and fastest Test century took 135 minutes off an incredible 137 balls. England's most successful bowler, Starling, took her 5 match wickets off 53 overs, 28 of which were maidens.

Verco and Emerson's 97 first wicket partnership was a new record against England. Kennare's first century against England was the second in her Test career. Bowling honours for the match went to Thompson whose 6 for 97 came off 47 overs. In England's first innings 8 dismissals went to catches, the other two were bowled.

Adelaide, South Australia: The Adelaide Oval, December 21, 22, 23 and 24

Not since the 1957–8 tour had the privilege of playing at the Adelaide Oval been a pleasure in store for prospective Test players, for here was a ground that offered every encouragement to perform well in pleasant surroundings. The England side was unchanged from its thwarted victory at Perth, and Australia was forced into one change because of injury to the captain Sharon Tredrea and made another when South Australia's Annette Fellows, an upper order bat and useful right-arm slow bowler, was included. All rounder Karen Price came in for Tredrea, and it was the experienced Raelee Thompson who donned the mantle of captaincy for the occasion.

It was to be hoped that England's captain knew precisely the conditions of the final day's procedure when, on winning the toss for the second time, she put her side in to bat on a good looking wicket. Once again, Lear and Hodges opened the batting facing up to Wilson and Price.

In fiery mood, it took Price just 6 overs to trap Lear lbw for 7 and leave England on 20 for 1. Three overs later she bowled Hodges for 13 and just on the hour into play, England was 37 for 2 with Southgate on her way to join Brittin in the middle.

No doubt English expectations were high with this talented pair together but, although going well at the time, both were soon dismissed. It was Fullston who was the instrument of destruction by firstly making a brilliant catch at silly mid-off to see the back of Brittin for 22, and then doing it all by taking Southgate in a caught and bowled for 4. Suddenly, England were on a shaky 53 for 4.

Thompson was the bowler when Brittin went and she soon struck again by bowling Court, who had made 6. Then, 10 minutes before lunch she caught Edney off Wilson. It was a triumphant morning for the substitute Australian captain who had the added gratification of seeing England on the run with a total of 62 for 6.

Stalwart defence was Watmough's answer to the crisis when, for almost half-an-hour after the break, she withstood Wilson's pace and Jacob's spin. Eventually, however, she was rash enough to offer a chance to Emerson off Jacobs and realised a duck for her 68 minutes at the crease.

Meanwhile wickets had tumbled until McConway, the number 10, and Starling at 11 made some scoring strokes to boost the dying innings from 70 for 9 to 91 all out and thus record the highest partnership of the innings.

When Verco and Emerson faced Aspinall and Starling the myth that runs were hard to come by receded. The 8 overs to tea put 25 on the scoreboard at a run a minute, and England's bowlers toiled away for more than two hours before the breakthrough. At that stage it was 80 for 1, with Verco caught behind off spinner McConway for 29, and Emerson was batting very well. At the close she was on 53 and number 3 Fullston had a single in her account.

The start of the third day followed the pattern of the opening partnership the day before. When a wicket fell it was Fullston's, for 29, while Emerson went merrily on. Just over an hour into play and with the score at 147 for 2, it was Kennare who joined Emerson.

After facing just 6 balls, Kennare got her legs in the way of the seventh and Brittin got her second wicket. Kennare's duck was followed by Dawson's, and the picture was beginning to take on a different aspect with Australia now 148 for 4.

Jacobs offered a sound bat to the ball, but not for long. Hodges had her caught and bowled for 11, and then Fellows stayed to accompany Emerson in to lunch. The latter was on 95, Fellows had 5 and Australia was a much happier 177 for 5.

Having seen her century well past, Emerson's was the next wicket to fall when a diving catch by Brittin gave Starling her only wicket of the innings – the prize – and the opener went for 121. A mini-stand of 19 between Fellows and Price helped the score along but then Stother removed Fellows via a catch by McConway. Both Thompson and Matthews failed to score, going to McConway, and finally Stother bowled second top-scorer Price for 39. Australia finished with a total of 262.

With a deficit of 171 to make up and two days still to go, England's openers Lear and Hodges were in no hurry to make the running in the final session of play. The Australians, needing a wicket or two to capitalise on their advantage, were denied it because of a dropped catch which would have dismissed Hodges when she had scored 11. As it was, the latter finished on 34 and Lear was 20 not out at stumps, to make it 54 for no wicket.

Refreshed for the third day, opening bowler Price broke through Lear's defence after 45 minutes play and England were 61 for 1. Brittin joined Hodges but hers was the second wicket to go when caught and bowled by Fullston for 15

It was high noon when Southgate reached the middle and, having seen Hodges depart with only 3 added to the score, came through the difficult period to push the score along to 150 for 5 before she went lbw to Thompson for 25.

Court comes to England's rescue

ENGLAND'S vice-captain Jackie Court, 34, score a brilliant 90 to put he side in a commandir position on the first day the first women's Te against Australia in Per yesterday.

Court arrived when Engl: were in some trouble at 93 three but she took compl control, hammering the A tralian attack to all parts the arena.

She batted for 144 minu

Ton to Brittin puts England on top

A dazzling century from 25-year-old Jan Brittin placed the England women cricketers in a strong position on the third day of the First Test against Australia at the WACA Ground today.

Brittin completely changed the pace of the game as she cut, pullec and drove the Austra lian attack to all parts of the ground.

She brought up her half century in 66 min utes from 64 deliveries including eight bound aries, to take Englanc to 2.99 at tea and a

AUSTRALIA HOLD OUT

Despite a brilliant centur Jill Kennare, Australia could draw the first women's cr test with England in Perth terday.

England had set Austra target of 282

England 290 and 242-9 dec Britton 112, R. Thompson 4-44); tralia 251 (J. Emerson 84, P. 56) & 209-8 (J. Kennare 103).

TREDREA OI OF SERIES

ON the eve of today's sec women's Test aga England, Sharon Tredrea, Australian captain, has with drawn from the series follow ing the aggravation of an Achilles tendon injury in the first Test in Perth last week.

England batswoman June Edney scores runs with this hook shot during the Second Test at Ad———— 'ney, who scored 50, is watched by Karen Price (left), umpire Max ———ll and wicketkeeper Chris Matthews.

In Adelaide

ENGLAND

First innings		91
Second innings		
HODGES, c. Verco, b. Fullston		44
LEAR, l.b.w., b. Price		26
BRITTIN, c. and b. Fullston		15
SOUTHGATE, l.b.w., b. Thompson		25
COURT, c. Matthews, b. Wilson		28
WATMOUGH, c. and b. Wilson		70
EDNEY, b. Matthews, b. Fullston		14
ASPINALL, not out		14
STOTHER, b. Fullston		2
Extras (3 b, 1 lb, 1 w)		5

Total (for 8 wkts.) 279
Fall — 61, 83, 87, 135, 150, 233, 273, 279.

BOWLING	O.	M.	R.	W.
Wilson	24	9	39	1
Price	40.1	21	44	1
Thompson	20.5	9	19	
Fullston	50.3	20	87	
Jacobs	20	4	63	
Verco	8	3	13	
Fellows	3	—	10	

Wilson 1 w.

Innings: 473 min. Overs: 166.3

AUSTRALIA
First innings

VERCO, c. Edney, b. McConway
EMERSON, c. Brittin, b. Starling
FULLSTON, c. Hodges, b. Brittin
KENNARE, l.b.w., b. Brittin
DAWSON, c. Southgate, b. McConway
JACOBS, c. and b. Hodges
FELLOWS, c. McConway, b. Stother
PRICE, b. Stother
THOMPSON, st. Edney, b. McConway
MATTHEWS, b. McConway
WILSON, not out
Extras (1 b, 6 lb, 1 w)

1
Fol
242
BO
As
Sta
Mc
Ho
Co
Bri
Sto

ngland revives hopes in Test

By PAT MICKAN

ngland women's cricket vived its hopes in the Test yesterday, cemen-

England collapse as Price strikes

AUSTRALIA made a confident start on the first day of the second women's cricket Test by tumbling England out for 91 runs and replying with 84 for one at the Adelaide Oval yes-terday.

ing, colorful left arm off-

ying defen-

ward point short of her

Southgate, veral mid-ner Jackie ut lbw by swinging t Raelee

red into a aggressive ...almough, whose 'Mr Hyde' turnabout was quite remarkable considering she was out in the first innings for a duck after 69 minutes.

The Surrey physical education nine boundaries covers, despite nges by Thomp d Debbie Wilson aught and bowled

ssal followed a the Australians y chances in the

is still in a com l will want to take kets cheaply this ugh time to score as to win. ustralia's distinc spite a chipped

England win a thriller

ADELAIDE: England yesterday won the second women's cricket Test by five runs in a nerve-tingling finish at the Adelaide Oval – Australia failing to reach a target of 125 runs.

With the lunch interval well behind her, it was now that Watmough played the innings that not only restored the débacle of her first innings effort but gave England the chance to make a match of it. With wicketkeeper Edney, she played her natural game and increased the score in a partnership of 83 runs before being caught and bowled by Wilson for 70. Her 50 had taken 64 minutes. At this stage, with 233 for 6, England were 62 ahead.

Aided by Aspinall, Edney pursued the runs sedately and had helped to further England's score by another 40 before she was caught behind off Fullston for 50. The next wicket fell within one minute of stumps, and England lived to fight another day with a closing score of 279 for 8.

Only 26 minutes into play on the final day and England were all out for 296, leaving Australia to get 126 to win.

The ony disadvantage for Australia – who had 330 minutes in which to cruise along to victory – was the injury suffered by Denise Emerson who had made her 121 with a damaged hand. She nevertheless formed the customary opening partnership with Verco and faced up to the fast-slow combination of Starling and McConway. Within 21 minutes both openers had gone, an lbw and a Hodges catch giving Verco 2 and Emerson 1, and the delighted Starling two wickets.

In another 20 minutes the 3 and 4 bats, Kennare and Fellows, had fallen to McConway for ducks, Kennare having achieved the dreaded 'pair'. The extraordinary situation of 4 for 4 was soon bettered, from England's point of view, with 6 for 5 but then Karen Price put her bat firmly against the ball and stopped the rot.

At lunch it was 26 for 5 and thereafter, with Fullston, the score steadily mounted and Price reached her 50 in 97 minutes. Just one run later, however, she became Starling's fourth victim when caught by Hodges. Australia was 73 for 6 and was chasing 53 for victory.

With Fullston going nicely Dawson helped the score along to 96 for 7 but then Fullston was lbw to Aspinall for 28. Four minutes later, Dawson went for 4 and then Captain Thompson and Matthews were together. These two resisted well but runs were difficult to come by. After 34 minutes at the crease Thompson went to McConway caught by Lear for 13. With England needing just one wicket to Australia's 16 runs, Starling had Matthews caught behind for 9. England had won by 5 runs.

Summary of the Second Test 1984–5

England Won by 5 Runs

England:	91 and 296
Australia:	262 and 120

Best Batting

1st Innings

England:	J Brittin	22
Australia:	D Emerson	121
	K Price	39

2nd Innings

England:	C Watmough	70
	J Edney	50
Australia:	K Price	51
	L Fullston	28

Best Bowling

1st Innings

Australia:	K Price	4 – 22
	J Jacobs	2 – 6
	R Thompson	2 – 16
England:	G McConway	4 – 32
	J Brittin	2 – 15
	H Stother	2 – 43

2nd Innings

Australia:	L Fullston	4 – 96
	D Wilson	3 – 45
	R Thompson	2 – 19
England:	A Starling	5 – 36
	G McConway	3 – 35

Highlights

England's lowest Test score since Melbourne in 1958 was largely due to Price whose 4 wickets cost 5.50 apiece off 17 overs. With the first 50 of her career preventing Australia's second innings collapse, her recall was a triumph. Emerson's fighting century, which took some 4½ hours, put Australia in a winning position. But Watmough and Edney, whose 50 was a career second and took 159 minutes, gave England's bowlers a slim chance. Starling in particular bowled with pace and determination and her 5 wickets were a career best. McConway provided excellent support in the spin department and ended with overall best match figures of 7 for 67 off 48 overs, including 22 maidens.

Brisbane, Queensland: The GABBA, January, 1, 2, 3 and 4

Keeping faith with the team that won at Adelaide, Jan Southgate managed to christen the New Year by winning the toss for the third time in succession. In a slight change around, Brittin (1) and Lear (2) were sent out to face an Australian side which had included three newcomers. In an attempt to improve the outfielding and strengthen the batting. Dawson, Jacobs and Fellows were replaced by the right-handed opening bat Lindsay Reeler, the slow bowler Lyn Larsen, and another right-handed bat, Wendy Napier.

Against Wilson and Price, England's openers made only slow progress with the 25 up in just on an hour. When 50 was on the board, some 34 overs had been bowled but shortly afterwards, second change Verco bowled Brittin for 36 and the score was 53. But soon after lunch Lear was bowled by Wilson, and at 62 for 2 Hodges and Southgate were together.

With Hodges playing strongly on the leg-side and Southgate playing her normal aggressive game, Australia's bowlers were hard put to constrain the pace of run-getting and it took a spectacular piece of fielding by Wilson to produce the third wicket. It was Hodges who was run out for a useful 32, and England were 126. Replacement Court was only at the crease for 16 minutes before going to the spin of newcomer Larsen, caught by Emerson for 6.

Watmough faced up to 42 balls, off which she managed 17 runs before being caught and bowled by another of the newcomers, Reeler. At 166 for 5, and with just on 1½ hours left for play, Edney joined Southgate who had scored her first Test 50 of the tour. But it was Aspinall who was to see out the day with Edney when Southgate was caught by Larsen off Reeler for a well-played 74 which had included 10 boundaries. When stumps were drawn England had made 230 for 6 with Edney on 34 and Aspinall on 4.

Although towards the end of a very hot first day the Australian bowling had become somewhat frayed, the next morning they did an excellent containing job in taking the last four wickets for an additional 45 runs. Except for number 11 Starling who hit her wicket, all were bowled. Edney finished with 47, and her additional 13 runs took 66 minutes.

Lunch had been taken before Verco and Emerson began another opening partnership which blunted the edge of the England bowling and saw through 64 overs until Verco was caught by Lear off Starling for 42. Kennare joined Emerson and took 40 minutes to get off the mark. She weathered this period of good England fielding and field-placing though, to be there with Emerson at the close and a meagre 17. Of the 132 runs scored in the four hours of play, Emerson scored 69 with her 50 taking 195 minutes. Nevertheless, with two days to go, Australia were in the position to make a really big score.

Whatever overnight plans and hopes had been mooted, the Australians were given food for new thought when Kennare was lbw to Stother five minutes after play began without adding to her score. Reeler then joined Emerson and the pair managed 19 runs in 23 minutes before Emerson was bowled by Stother for 84. With Wendy Napier as her new partner at 152 for 3, Reeler took on the scoring role, and, when Napier was caught by Lear off Starling for 9, 26 runs had been added. Replacement Larsen coasted along comfortably to lunch when the score had reched 202 for 4.

Play resumed with Reeler on 31 and Larsen on 11. With the thought for the day still the one about scoring as many runs as possible, these two did their best to the tune of another 48 runs in some 74 minutes before Reeler was bowled by spinner McConway for a well-earned 59, and the partnership had realised 72 runs.

The game was going entirely Australia's way with the middle order batting proving the selectors' wisdom. When Fullston joined Larsen the latter took the responsibility of continuing the momentum and the 6th wicket had added 31 runs when Fullston was caught by Starling off Hodges for 13.

Just 105 minutes remained for play when Price took up the pursuit of runs with Larsen in her 40s. But 17 minutes later, Starling broke through to get Larsen caught by Hodges for 52. Thompson replaced her but took 36 minutes to score just 2 before becoming Stother's third victim, Price having been caught by Brittin off Starling for a relatively sprightly and useful 18 runs. The last two players, Matthews and Wilson, added 15 between them before Thompson declared at 326 for 9 wickets with Australia 51 runs ahead.

The timing of the declaration left England 17 minutes batting. Brittin and Lear opened again and Australia had the delight of the latter's wicket with the first ball of the second over. Thompson clean bowled her and thereby not only realised the point of such a declaration but acquired her 50th Test wicket in style. England finished the day on 13.

It was Brittin and Aspinall who faced up to the attack of Price and Thompson on the final day and, once again, Australia had the boost of a quick wicket when Aspinall played-on a ball from Thompson and went for 8, only 4 minutes into play. The responsibility of stopping the rot was now a Hodges – Brittin task and, by lunchtime, they had done it but also virtually assured a drawn match.

INCONSISTENT fielding by the Australians saw the English women's cricket team move to a handy position (6-230) after the first day of the Third Test at the Gabba yesterday.

The day saw both brilliant and atrocious work in the field with the Australians dropping six catches in all. Bowler Raelee Thompson was by far the worst offender putting down three difficult chances from gully.

She was not alone though — Verco, Brown and Reeler also dropped catches — and it was only some very tight bowling from Reeler _____ Larsen ____ _____

For t ___
won th ___
good ba ___

The n ___
one stag ___
runs scor ___
coming a ___

Opener ___
Lear put ___
tin was bo ___
from Peta ___

Lear wa ___
Carole Hod ___
that strayed ___
came at noo ___ _____ _____ ___
Lear on 18. ___

Lear didn't last long when sumed, falling for 22 to a conce

By TIMOTHY PIE

Southgate saw Jackie Court caught by Emerson off Larsen for six, and Chris Watmough, caught and bowled on 17 by a brilliant reflex catch by Lindsay Reeler — excusing her for the chance she put down — before she also fell to Reeler.

Southgate's 74 runs was the highest score of the day and included 10 well-controlled fours which came from 160 balls after 177 minutes.

At the close of play June Edney was on 34, after bein_ _ _ed twice, and _ _ _ _ur.

_ n were obvi-ared its end, ground tak-

rly that of the longest _y and sev-

_ground for _ht about

PLENTY OF LEG GLANCES OUT THERE!

AUSTRALIA ENGLAND 5 TEST

Dropsies plague Australia women clinch series

MELBOURNE: Australia won the women's Jubilee Test cricket series with a seven-wicket victory in the fifth and deciding match at the Queen Elizabeth Oval in Bendigo yesterday.

With Australia poised to win the fourth women's cricket Test at Grahame Park, the final Test at Bendigo later this month has taken on new dimensions.

At lunch on the final day's play. England were tottering on the brink of defeat, having lost 5-107 and still requiring 138 runs for victory.

Australia secured an important break, shortly after play resumed yesterday when England captain, Janet Southgate was caught brilliantly behind off the bowling of Lyn Fullston for 12.

Almost from the start of the play last Friday, Australia, through-determined batting and good class bowling, has pinned England down, thus thwarting their efforts of going to a two-nil lead in the best of five series.

Perhaps the only time that the tourists held the upper hand was on the opening day when they won the toss ___ _____

singly, elected to send their opponents into bat.

For Southgate, her gamble almost paid early dividends when Australia's star bat, opener Denise Emerson was dropped early in her innings of 58.

Emerson, the sister of Australian bowling hero, Terry Alderman, went on to figure in an opening partnership of 114, the best of the series.

However, England bounced back through breakthrough t stralia so des needed.

Her marathon included six maide times was virtu playable and ha glish bats in all trouble.

Giving her s port was Lyn Fr South Australia ___ _____ _

and 20 respectively.

Then came the crunch. An inspired spell from left arm medium pacer, Denise Martin from Western Australia, who finished with 4-24 in 19 overs, brought Englan knees and they v in the pavilion well short of A first innings tall

One of her vic Southgate, clear for seven with a delivery gain breakthrough t

set England a formidable chase for victory.

The best of the English bowling attack was Middlesex pace bowler, Avril Starling was captured 4-57 off 26, including 10

n in 59
_d had
t their
r 204,
_ got
than
_e and
_e for

nings,
_t, and
_ [play-
_ was
_ Jill

ga century-nnare slam-urs yesterday igs of 42.

:ling innings :tory for the n when the run rate had om the re-runs an over _e start of the

Peta Verco se Emerson :s quietly at f the innings 0 overs there _9 runs on the

_merson was y England's _her for 23 in over, Austra-had reached ns but it was nare came to that the for-the match und.

she had been field in the ecause of a vi-int which had _any members arms, she came afternoon de-to lead Austra-istoric win.

She faced only 49 balls for her 42 runs.

When she was run out, victory was in sight with 108 runs on the board and ample overs in reserve.

Verco again had a solid hand.

After her 40 in the first innings, she made another 40 yesterday and chipped in to take three vital English wickets.

The 2-1 Test series victory was Australia's first over England in women's cricket since 1949.

Scoreboard

WOMENS 4TH TEST

AUSTRALIA v ENGLAND
At Grahame Park, Gosford

AUSTRALIA — 1st Innings 9 (dec)-332
ENGLAND — 1st Innings 149
AUSTRALIA — 2nd Innings 9 (dec)-153

ENGLAND — 2nd Innings

J BRITTIN b Martin	....	65
M LEAR c Verco b Wilson	....	2
C HODGES b Martin	....	5
J SOUTHGATE c Thompson b Fullston		12
J COURT st Matthews b Fullston	....	27
C WATMOUGH c Fullston b Thompson		0
J EDNEY b Verco	....	0
J ASPINALL c Martin b Wilson	......	1
H STOTHER c Matthews b Fullston	....	4
G McCONWAY st Matthews b Fullston		5
A STARLING not out	....	1
Sundries (4B 1LB 1W)	....	6
Total		**128**

Fall: 7, 19, 48, 102, 107, 108, 111, 120, :7, 128.

BOWLING: D Wilson 22-8-29-2, D Martin 26-20-12-2 (1w), R Thompson 16-8-17-1, L Fullston 25-8-53-4, P Verco 17-8-12-1

Batting time: 339 mins. Overs: 108.

Australia won by 117 runs.

Scoreboard

ENGLAND
First Innings 196
Second Innings

LEAR b Verco	....	40
BRITTIN run out	....	35
HODGES run out	....	20
SOUTHGATE b Wilson	......	
POWELL c Wilson b Fullston	....	27
COURT b Wilson	....	41
EDNEY c Martin b Verco	....	17
ASPINALL b Wilson	....	
STOTHER lbw b Fullston	....	20
STARLING b Verco	....	6
SUNDRIES (8b, 2w)	....	6
TOTAL		**204**

FALL: 46, 64, 96, 93, 121, 158, 158, 190, 193, 204.
BOWLING: Wilson 20-9-40-3; Thompson 25-17-29-0; Fullston 38-17-37-2; Verco 24.4-12-30-3; Larsen 6-3-9-0; Reeler 1-0-7-0; Kemare 3-1-2-0.

AUSTRALIA
First Innings 9-265, decl.
Second Innings

EMERSON b Stother	....	23
VERCO b Brittin	....	40
KENNARE run out	....	42
READ not out	....	5
REELER not out	....	4
SUNDRIES (2nb, 1w)	......	2
TOTAL for 3 wkts		**118**

FALL: 47, 108, 109.
BOWLING: McConway 20-8-30-0; Starling 13.2-3-40-0 (3nb); Stother 11-2-22-1; Hodges 2-0-15-0; Brittin 3-1-11-1 (1w).

Batting time: 166min. Overs: 49.2.
Australia won by 7 wickets.
Player of the match: Jill Kennare (Aust.).

• FOURTH WOMEN'S CRICKET TEST:
33-year wait over
for women's team

Within 20 minutes of resumption after the break, and some 30 runs ahead, Brittin edged one to Larsen off Wilson and was out for 39. Southgate joined Hodges who was batting with authority. When their partnership ended, Hodges being bowled by Larsen for 95, all possibility of an Australian second innings had vanished. At the fall of that 4th wicket only 100 minutes remained and England was 128 runs ahead. With a draw now inevitable play was called off at 4.30, half-an-hour before scheduled, with the England total at 204 for 7 wickets.

Summary of the Third Test 1984–5

Match Drawn

England:	275 and 204 for 7 wickets
Australia:	326 for 9 wickets dec

Best Batting

	1st Innings	
England:	J Southgate	74
	J Edney	47
	J Brittin	36
	C Hodges	32
Australia:	D Emerson	84
	L Reeler	59
	L Larsen	52
	P Verco	42

	2nd Innings	
England:	C Hodges	95
	J Brittin	39
	J Southgate	39

Best Bowling

1st Innings

Australia:	L Larsen	4 – 33
	L Reeler	2 – 27
	D Wilson	2 – 55
England:	A Starling	4 – 50
	H Stother	3 – 58

2nd Innings

Australia:	R Thompson	2 – 25
	P Verco	2 – 32
	L Larsen	2 – 40

Highlights

With Southgate setting the pace with her first tour 50 (in 135 minutes) and a stirring partnership of 64 with Hodges, and some good captaincy during Australia's long innings, England certainly showed determination in this match. But with three Australians making a half-century in a situation where they had not to lose at any cost, the sensible tactics prevailed.

Though Larsen's 50 was slow – 166 minutes – she did very well overall to combine it with best match bowling figures of 50 – 25 – 73 – 6 and a brilliant catch which dismissed Brittin in the second innings. Reeler's 50 took 165 minutes and Emerson's 195. Hodges, top scorer in the match, hit three consecutive boundaries off Verco. Her first tour 50 took 154 minutes. The home side's fielding showed marked improvement.

Gosford, New South Wales: Graham Park C G, January 12, 13, 14 and 15

Only eight days after leaving Brisbane with an intervening two matches in the State of New South Wales, the Tourists found themselves breaking new ground for the 4th Test at Graham Park, Gosford. Nothing in those two games had served to dampen English spirits unduly, despite a close thing against the State team at Pratten Park in Sydney where England wrested a draw. But, the 'old team' was a fit team and unlike the Australians, unhampered by injury. It was, then, the same eleven that fielded first when, for the fourth time, Jan Southgate won the toss.

Back in the Australian side for the match was left-arm seam bowler Denise Martin, replacing Karen Price. There was no change in the opening pair though and, sharp on 10.30, Verco and Emerson had the usual experience of facing the pace of Aspinall and Starling.

They got off to a good start, putting 25 on the board in 35 minutes but then had a desperately slow period after Stother and McConway took over the bowling. The next 25 runs were acquired in 71 minutes. But this too was weathered, and the run-rate assumed something like the established norm for these 4-day games in the second session.

At one stage, when Emerson had passed her 50, the opening pair seemed absolutely in control and dictated to the bowlers to the tune of 25 in 16 minutes to bring up the 100 partnership. But then, in the fifty-ninth over, spinner Hodges had Verco caught behind just two short of her 50 to put Australia in the sound position of 114 for 1.

New bat Kennare had added 3 to the total when Hodges broke through again to get Emerson caught and bowled. She had made 58. Both Kennare and Reeler played confidently, though, and had taken the score along to 149 at tea to be on 25 and 10 respectively. When play resumed, Kennare faced a further 5 balls before Court held on to a catch off McConway to make it 3 wickets down for 149.

While replacement Napier stayed at the crease 34 minutes for 3 runs, Reeler pressed on, surviving the new ball to which Napier had succumbed, for a further 5 overs. Eventually, however, she was lbw to Starling for 34. With the score at 185 for 5, Larsen and Thompson came together.

The sixth wicket went – it was Thompson's, lbw to Court for 9. Then Matthews and Martin provided McConway with two more wickets, scoring 6 and 8 respectively and leaving Larsen not out 28 in the day's closing total of 232 for 8 wickets.

On the morning of the second day Thompson declared to take the initiative in the attempt to break England's one-up hold on the series. It was again Brittin and Lear who opened for the tourists and they had to struggle for 61 minutes to get 25 on the board against the pace and accuracy of Wilson and Martin. But they steered their team through to lunch when the score was 66 for no wicket, and the prospect beginning to look brighter.

Within ten minutes of the start of the afternoon session, however, the complexion of the game altered radically as first, Lear, and then Brittin was dismissed. Wilson bowled Lear for 20 and Verco trapped Brittin lbw for 45 without any addition to the score. Verco's spin then had Hodges beaten and, at 67 for 3, England's captain and vice-captain were up against it and needed all their experience to deal with the beginnings of a desperate situation.

Patience was just beginning to tell when Court was bowled by Wilson for 8. The ever adaptable Watmough joined in Southgate's stubborn resistance, but saw the latter bowled by Martin half-an-hour later for 7 runs. It was now Edney, well capable of anchoring an innings, who joined Watmough at 93 for 5. But only 10 were added before the left-handed Watmough was caught and bowled by leg-spinner Fullston for 16. Shortly afterwards Edney was bowled by Martin and it was 103 for 7.

It was Stother who replaced Edney and had to face the remaining three balls of the over. But she was bowled by the first of these and Martin was on a hat trick. McConway foiled that delivery though but succumbed to the next, and England were a sorry 103 for 9.

Australia's delight was magnificently tempered by a last wicket stand of 37 between pace bowlers Aspinall and Starling who frustrated the home side for 1 hour and 25 minutes before Fullston had Starling caught by Reeler for 9. Aspinall was 28 not out in the final total of 140.

In the comfortable position of being 92 ahead with 2 days and something over an hour to go, openers Verco and Emerson had nothing to rush for and yet managed to make the 25 one minute faster than in the first innings. This might have been because Southgate chose to open the attack with the slow-fast combination of McConway and Starling. But then, after 42 minutes, McConway captured the prize wicket of Emerson who was stumped for 19. When this was soon followed by the run out of Kennare who did not score, England had the right to some satisfaction at the Australian closing total of 46 for 2.

The start of the third day was again a boosting one for the visitors because after 5 minutes, Fullston was caught by Court off Starling for a meagre 8 runs. And Reeler only stayed 25 minutes before Starling got her too, this time caught by Hodges. It was 60 for 4, then 60 for 5 as

The last wicket falls in the fourth Test at Graham Park Gosford, when Gill McConway was stumped off the bowling of opposite number, left-arm spin bowler Lyn Fullston, for 5. The jubilant Australians have won their first Test match against England for 36 years!

Verco got her legs in the way of a Starling delivery to give the bowler her third wicket of the morning in only 7 overs. Napier and Larsen were then together for 49 minutes putting 19 on the board before Larsen was lbw to Stother for 10.

With the England bowlers definitely on top, it was a gallant Matthews who knocked up a useful 19 in 18 minutes and then holed out to Starling within 10 minutes of the post-lunch session. But Thompson, after Napier's going just 4 minutes later, put her bat in the way of the ball to some effect.

The Australian Captain and pace bowler Martin together withstood the attack for 79 minutes, putting on a tardy 30 runs in the process, before Martin was bowled by Stother for 17. Last player Wilson joined Thompson and when they had added a further 25, the innings was declared closed at 153 for 9.

England began her innings needing 246 to win and with plenty of time to make it. Except for the fact that two wickets were down at stumps, the target of 202 on the last day did not seem an impossible one. Though Lear and Hodges had gone, Brittin was still there with 23 and Southgate had made 10. Even when Southgate was caught soon after play began, having added only two to her score, Court's defence allowed the slow accumulation of runs. When she went, just on 15 minutes to lunch, her partnership with Brittin had produced 54 runs. At a tricky time, Watmough took over with the score on 102 for 4.

It all began to look somewhat different, however, when Watmough was caught by Fullston off Thompson for a duck just on 12.30pm. The break thus came with England 5 wickets down and still needing 139 to win. But Brittin was still there having notched up her first series 50.

On resuming after lunch number 7 Edney was only at the crease 10 minutes before being bowled by Verco for a duck. Aspinall who replaced her seemed transfixed by Verco's bowling and took 20 balls to score a single. Then, 13 balls later, she was caught in the slips by Martin off pace bowler Wilson without adding to her score. Stother then joined Brittin only to see the latter clean bowled by Martin half-an-hour later. The score was 120 for 8. Stother went to Fullston for 4, and McConway managed to improve on that by 1 before being stumped off the same bowler. England, with 128 on the board, had lost the fourth Test by 117 runs.

Summary of the Fourth Test 1984-5

Australia Won by 117 Runs
Australia: 232 for 8 dec and 153 for 9 dec
England: 140 and 128

Best Batting

	1st Innings	
Australia:	D Emerson	58
	P Verco	48
	L Reeler	34
England:	J Brittin	45
	J Aspinall	28 n o
	M Lear	20
	2nd Innings	
Australia:	R Thompson	24 n o
	P Verco	24
England:	J Brittin	65
	J Court	27

Best Bowling
   1st Innings
England:G McConway3 – 39
   C Hodges2 – 20

Australia:D Martin4 – 24
   P Verco2 – 23
   L Fullston2 – 30
   D Wilson2 – 32

   2nd Innings
EnglandA Starling4 – 57
   H Stother2 – 24

Australia:L Fullston4 – 53
   D Martin2 – 12
   D Wilson2 – 29

Highlights

The first wicket stand of 114 between Australia's Verco and Emerson established a new record against any country. Emerson's 50, in 158 minutes, was her third of the series. Both Martin and Fullston brought off a career best in taking 4 – 24 and 4 – 53 respectively, with Martin taking bowling honours in the match with an average 6.00 per wicket in an aggregate of 45 – 28 – 36 – 6. For England, McConway again did well, as did Starling. In the match, Brittin scored 41 percent of England's runs. Her second innings 50 took 229 minutes.

Bendigo, Victoria: Queen Elizabeth Oval, January 25, 26, 27 and 28

With honours even between the two countries, the fifth and last Test held the promise of an interesting tussle ahead as history was created with a new arena for the women's game. England selected a side that had just one change in it, Jane Powell, a deep-field specialist and middle order bat, who came in for Chris Watmough. The Australians also made one change bringing in right-handed bat Karen Read for Wendy Napier. Once again the laws of chance favoured England's captain who, when she won the toss for the fifth time in succession, elected to bat.

The Bendigo wicket had a reputation as a placid one not expected to give much help to the bowlers, but it was still Wilson and Martin who opened the attack for Australia, and it was Brittin who took first strike when again opening with Lear.

Although both players were untroubled by the bowling, it took over an hour to put 25 on the board and then, in her 4th over, first change Thompson struck a definitive blow for her team when she had Brittin caught by Reeler at silly-mid on for 16. It was then Hodges' turn to make up for her recent batting trough and with a lunchtime score of 11 in her 46 minutes at the crease, it looked as though she was going about it cautiously. Lear had made 25 at the interval and England were on 55 for 1 wicket.

After adding three to her score, Lear was lbw to Martin – and the afternoon session was just on 20 minutes old. When Southgate joined Hodges, at 71 for 2, the score mounted slowly but surely and things were looking comfortable for England. But Martin found another good one and clean blowed Hodges for 39. Court stayed only 16 minutes before being caught by Larsen off Thompson for 5, and it was 98 for 4 when Powell made her way to the middle to join Southgate. These two were still together at tea and the score had climbed to a secure 133.

After the interval, Fullston and Thompson took over from spinners Larsen and Verco and in her 4th over Fullston bowled Powell for 13. Edney replaced her and after a competent start hit consecutive fours off seamer Martin who had taken the new ball with Wilson. This saw Thompson back in the attack and the demise of Southgate who was caught and bowled by her opposite number for 59.

Another 13 overs were left for play, and they were 13 that proved unlucky for the tourists. Australia's Captain had taken the ballast out of England and when she had bowled Edney for 19, the tail collapsed.

Only 12 runs were added for the last three wickets and the tourists finished the day with a total of 196 having batted for 6 hours.

The start of the second day saw no threat in the wicket for openers Verco and Emerson who cruised along to 25 and then slowly crawled to 50 under the attack of change bowlers McConway, Stother and Hodges. In the two hours to lunch they had taken 61 off 38 overs, but in the 40 minutes they were together afterwards, another 29 was added.

Emerson was the first to go, lbw to medium-pacer Stother for 43, and then partner Verco was caught by Starling off Hodges for 40 without adding to the total. Thus, at 90 for 2, Kennare and Reeler were together.

When Reeler lost her wicket, caught behind off Aspinall for 17, Kennare was still cautiously playing herself in with 8 against her name. When Read joined her, at 116 for 3, they went along very cautiously together, put on a spurt at one stage when 25 was scored in 35 minutes, and had put on 65 in a 4th wicket stand before Read was caught behind off Starling for 21.

Larsen joined Kennare and was still with her at the close of play. The last hour produced some 60 runs so that Australia finished with 228 and were in the very good position of being 32 ahead with 6 wickets in hand.

Play on the third day started promptly with Kennare on 81 and Larsen with 12. Within half-an-hour the score had moved on to 263 but 2 wickets had gone. Firstly Larsen was lbw to McConway for 25, and

Denise Emerson, Australia's most prolific scorer in the Jubilee series, on her way to 43 in the first innings of the final Test at Bendigo.

then Thompson was run out without scoring when a return from Starling hit the stumps. The next to go was Kennare who had scored 104 when she also was run out – this time from a direct throw-in by Brittin. When Fullston was caught by Hodges off McConway having made 15, Thompson declared Australia's innings closed at 285 for 8 wickets.

With the first 50 minutes of play having produced 57 runs, it was clear that there were runs to be had for an England needing to clear a deficit of 89. Unfortunately, however, England's players also emulated the Australian's in losing two wickets to run-outs. This meant that the tourists found themselves with only 54 on the board and their leading bats Brittin, who made 35, and Hodges, who did not score, foolishly and unnecessarily out.

Southgate steadied the position when she joined Lear but only 12 runs were added before the latter was bowled by Verco for 18. Powell was next to the crease and she and Southgate saw England in the position to make Australia bat again – but only just. With the score on 94, the 4th wicket to go was Southgate's. She was beaten by the pace of Wilson in the immediate post-tea session having made 26.

Powell, now joined by Court, went along steadily and a new period of consolidation began. The next 1¼ hours produced some 38 runs before Powell was caught at backward square by Wilson off Fullston for 27. At 131 for 5, it was Edney who played safely through to stumps with Court, the England score having moved on to 140.

The inevitability of a draw if England could hold out for a reasonable lead was probably the biggest non-gamble of the fourth and final day at Bendigo. There was no change in conditions when the tourists resumed just 51 ahead with 5 wickets in hand and Court, on 28, in the mood for a good performance.

One piece of ill-fortune that had afflicted both sides for this final day, however, was illness. England's Janet Aspinall (yet to bat) and Jane Powell, and Australia's Karen Read, Lyn Fullston and Jill Kennare, had all succumbed to a prevalent gastro-enteritis virus the previous day and night. The Australian trio did not take the field and were replaced by the official 12th man Wendy Napier, and two substitute Victorian players Jane Howard and Kerry Saunders. So England pursued her task until a further unfortunate circumstance had its effect on the match.

With the morning just 37 minutes under way, Jackie Court attempted to hook a rising ball from Debbie Wilson and was struck on the cheek. She subsequently left the field, with her score on 41, but returned when replacement Aspinall stayed just one minute for her duck. Wilson, who had bowled Aspinall, then clean bowled Court

England's Captain shows that the tourists have their backs to the wall in the fifth and decisive Test at Bendigo. The last pair Gill McConway (L) and Avril Starling put up stirling resistance but Australia had England all-out for 204. She won the series with a convincing 7 wicket win.

with the first ball of her next over, when the latter had already played out the last two balls of Wilson's prior over quite comfortably.

At 158 for 7, Stother joined Edney and began one of those encouraging rallies that showed England had both the spirit and the batting to meet the occasion. These two put on 32 for the eighth wicket before Edney was caught by Martin off Verco for 17. The last two wickets added 14, with McConway not out 8, and this left England with 204 and Australia requiring 116 to win and ample time in which to do it.

For a while it looked as though Australia was making heavy weather of the task, but Verco with 40 and Kennare with a gallant 42 saw them safely through to a seven wicket victory. The last time the Australians had won a Test series against England was in 1948-9. On that occasion it was a by the single win in the first Test at Adelaide. Raelee Thompson did magnificently to triumph against the odds by winning two Tests in a row and so create cricket history at Bendigo.

Summary of the Fifth Test 1984–5

Australia Won By 7 Wickets

England: 196 and 204
Australia: 285 and 118 for 3 wickets

Best Batting

1st Innings

England:	J Southgate	59
	C Hodges	39
	M Lear	28
Australia:	J Kennare	104
	D Emerson	43
	P Verco	40

2nd Innings

England:	J Court	41
	J Brittin	35
	J Powell	27
	J Southgate	26
Australia:	P Verco	40
	J Kennare	42

Best Bowling

1st Innings

Australia:	R Thompson	5 – 33
	L Fullston	2 – 31
	D Martin	2 – 37
England:	G McConway	2 – 52

2nd Innings

Australia:	P Verco	3 – 30
	D Wilson	3 – 40
	L Fullston	2 – 57
England:	J Brittin	1 – 11

Highlights

Another match 50 gave Southgate 306 runs in the series and put her second to Brittin who made 429 with an overall average of 42.90. Starling took one wicket in the match to bring her series total to 21, which cost her 20.52 each.

Emerson averaged a splendid 50.33 in 9 innings to head Australia's batting. Kennare's excellent century made her runner-up to Emerson with 38.55. All of the Australian bowlers played their part in this victory with Thompson's 5 – 33 off 28 overs, 12 of which were maidens, being a career best. She topped the averages with 18 wickets at 15.72 apiece, but both Wilson and Fullston did very well indeed to take 19 wickets at an average of 22.31 and 26.68 respectively.

BETTY ARCHDALE

No finer leader than the shy-looking scholar who was England's first captain could have been chosen to pioneer women's cricket abroad. In her own right Betty Archdale was a capable middle order bat and good close field but, to put her in the same category as Mike Brearley several decades later would mean that she, too, had charge of a young team – the average age was 24 – whose talents needed nurturing and controlling. It was a task she accomplished with consummate ease, taking England to victory in the two Tests againt Australia at Brisbane and Sydney, and drawing the one at Melbourne. In the one Test against New Zealand at Christchurch, in which England made the mammoth total of 503 for 5 declared – an all-time record – the margin of victory was by an innings and 337 runs.

Betty's cricketing days started when very young since she had two older brothers, but she also played at Bedales, the well known co-educational public school in Hampshire. Later she went to St Leonards, an all-girls school at St Andrews in Scotland, where her Vice-captain Betty Snowball was also a distinguished pupil.

The Second World War intervened in Betty's life in two ways.

Australian Captain Margaret Peden (L) and England Captain Betty Archdale create history at the Exhibition Ground Brisbane on December 28 1934. Australia won the toss but Betty led England to a nine wicket victory in the first Women's Test Match played.

Firstly she was prevented from captaining a second scheduled tour 'Down Under', which had to be abandoned when war was declared in 1939, and secondly she served her country by joining the WRNS. Her leadership qualities came for the fore in that role too, when she led a group of Navy women away from the Japanese threat to Singapore, and from there to Sri Lanka and Mombasa. For her wartime services she was awarded the MBE.

It was on August 15th 1946 that Betty finally sailed for Australia, not to play cricket now, but to take up an appointment as Principal of a Women's College at Sydney University. She has been in Australia ever since, becoming well known as a broadcaster and lecturer, on education topics particularly, and still lives in Sydney. For the occasion of the Golden Jubilee Test, which took place on the WACA ground in Perth from December 13 - 16, 1984, it was Betty who tossed the coin for proceedings to begin. It was a most fitting tribute in this, the Margaret Peden Memorial Test, that the first England captain should take such a part in celebrating the memory of an outstanding and famous Australian sportswoman. Besides being a personal friend, Margaret Peden was also her opposing captain for the inaugural Test in Brisbane in 1934 and throughout the Test series.

ARCHDALE, Elizabeth
Kent, East and England
Batting and Fielding

	Tests	Inns	No	Runs	highest	average	Ct
1934-5 v A	3	4	1	77	32*	25.66	1
1934-5 v NZ	1	1	–	27	27	27.00	–
1937 v A	1	1	–	29	29	29.00	–
All Tests Average: **26.00**							

MOLLY HIDE

To be the youngest, most fluently talented player in any England team must be trial enough, but to be its Captain too has to take on formidable proportions. In recent times lesser mortals have buckled under the strain, but Molly Hide was made of sterner stuff. It was not without a qualm or two, however, that she took on the captaincy for the 1937 series which marked the occasion of Australia's return visit, and their first tour abroad.

The three day, three match series opened at Northampton where

Margaret Peden led her side to a narrow 31 run victory after a first innings total of 300 gained a 204 reply by England now caught on a spinner's wicket. The upshot of the game for Molly was that her off-spinners reaped five wickets in the match but she failed with the bat. Was this captain's nerves? Fortunately not, as the equally tight-finishing second Test at Blackpool showed when England won by 25 runs. The final Test at The Oval was very much spoiled by rain which meant both a drawn game and a drawn series.

The aborted 1939 tour of Australia would not have had Molly Hide in it either as player or captain. She had been appointed vice-captain to Betty Archdale but her parents refused to let her go 'gallivanting' yet again. In the end the war prevented anyone from so frivolous a pasttime as cricket, and for Molly, as for most, the war effort took precedence. She worked on her father's farm putting her agricultural qualifications to good use.

After the war, however, it was a different matter. The old order may have changed somewhat, but it was Molly Hide who captained the 1948-9 touring team for its six-month trip to Australia and New Zealand. And this time it was a Molly who, with great confidence, led from the front. Her reputation as the finest all-rounder in England was undiminished, if not enhanced, and this perhaps had its disadvantages. There were members of the team, young, not so poised, and definitely in awe of so personable a leader.

It has been said of Molly that she demanded a lot of her players,

expecting them to live up to her standards and, perhaps, not sufficiently encouraging. On the other hand there are those who found her captaincy inspiring, and her expectations as a challenge; indeed a sign of respect for a colleague who knows what she is doing. There is a story of Molly

The classic driving style of Molly Hide. Her two centuries in Test Cricket, the finest a 124 not out at Sydney C G in 1949, were accompanied by four century stands including the record 235 for the second wicket with Betty Snowball.

and a certain England fast bowler who was getting nowhere bowling to a field fairly remote from the one they had set. Eventually Molly offered a suggestion which was: "If you bowl on middle and leg you should get her to pop one up!"

The luckless bowler replied: "I've been trying to do that for the last six overs."

"Oh," said Molly, and promptly took her off.

On the 1948-9 tour, Molly came up against Australia's Mollie Dive as captain and relished the challenge the latter's sporting approach gave to the matches. The first one at the Adelaide Oval resulted in her most resounding defeat – by 186 runs. The others, at the famous Melbourne and Sydney Grounds, were both drawn with rain interfering in the Sydney match. It was here, though, that Molly followed her 63 in the first innings with a not out 124 in the second. After that – fame – when she had the unique honour of having her portrait hung in the Sydney Pavilion. The pity of it is that few women cricketers get to see it, or Sydney, as the women have not played there since that heroic time.

With Australia having won the mythical "ashes" for the first time, it was New Zealand who had to bear the vengeful force of an England bent on winning. Only the one Test was played and England won it handsomely by 185 runs.

Australia returned again in 1951 with Molly Dive as captain. Though Mollie Hide was appointed for the three match series, injury kept her out of the first two Tests which were taken over by vice-captain Myrtle Maclagan. The Scarborough Test was drawn; on a tricky wicket, the Worcester Test went to the Australians by two wickets and England desperately needed a win at The Oval to restore the balance as well as pride. Fortunately Molly was fit enough, though not 100 percent, to play and captain the side. It was a triumphant return where she finished with the best match average of 48.5, took three wickets for 13.00 each, and led the team to victory by 137 runs. A very significant mark of captaincy in that match was to bring on fast bowler McEvoy, who had only bowled one over all the innings because Duggan was doing so well, for a final fling at the stubborn tail-ender Mavis Jones. McEvoy bowled her 4th ball and the strategy of keeping her waiting – and no doubt fuming – thoroughly vindicated.

In 1954 it was the New Zealanders who made their first sortie to the British Isles for, and this was also a first for them and declared their cricket maturity, three, three-day Tests. England's appointed captain for the series was Molly Hide who declared her own maturity by announcing it as her last season of representative cricket.

The series was won by England; the first Test, which England won by 6 wickets, proving the decider. Worcester provided another exacting wicket and New Zealand did well, under the captaincy of Rona McKenzie, to wrest a draw. The match at The Oval was again affected by rain and a draw was the almost inevitable outcome. Molly's personal achievement was by no means her best, but in a career that had spanned nearly 20 years, who would complain at a series average of 27.80 in five innings, and 6 wickets at 12.33 apiece off 72 overs, 46 of which were maidens? Perhaps only a Molly Hide.

HIDE, Molly E
Surrey, South and England
Batting and Fielding

	Tests	Inns	No	Runs	highest	100	50	average	Ct
1934-5 v A	3	6	2	83	34	—	—	20.75	3
1934-5 v NZ	1	1	—	110	110	1	—	110.00	—
1937 v NZ	3	5	—	133	64	—	1	26.00	4
1948-9 v A	3	6	1	285	124★	1	2	57.00	2
1948-9 v NZ	1	2	—	15	13	—	—	7.50	—
1951 v A	1	2	—	107	65	—	1	53.50	1
1954 v NZ	3	5	—	139	64	—	1	27.80	—

All Tests Average: **36.33**

Bowling

	Overs	Balls	Mdns	Runs	Wkts	average	5/I
1934-5 v A	88	528	47	88	4	22.00	—
1934-5 v NZ	4	24	1	11	0	—	—
1937 v A	97.2	584	33	177	14	12.64	1
1948-9 v A	54.1	325	10	132	6	22.00	—
1948-9 v NZ	9.3	57	2	28	3	9.33	—
1951 v A	19	114	6	39	3	13.00	—
1954 v NZ	72	432	46	74	6	12.33	—

All Tests Average: **15.25**

MARY DUGGAN

By the time Mary Duggan was appointed captain of the 1957–8 Touring Team, her bowling style had changed from medium-fast opening bowler to that of an orthodox left-arm spinner. It was a change which was to prove of crucial value to the team as well as to reflect a personal philosophy that did not always utilise the full resources of the players she took with her.

Anyone was going to have a difficult task replacing Molly Hide whose physical strength, toughness of spirit and experience contrasted markedly with Mary's more reserved, and rather gentle approach. These characteristics are of themselves admirable in many people but as a leader in a sporting context where corporate unity must join with sense of purpose for the best results, she seemed often to be imperceptive and too open to conflicting influences. In view of the illness that overtook her on the tour, and from the consequences of which she died in 1973, many apparently inexplicable crises can be understood in retrospect, and all that remains here is to record the match outcomes.

The two Tests in New Zealand, under Rona McKenzie's captaincy, were both drawn. In the first at Christchurch the home country made her highest Test score of 223 in the first innings to which England replied with 255 but too slowly. Slowly, that is, apart from Mary's century – one of the fastest on record – which was part of a storm of an innings of 108. Added to her 6 – 55 in the first innings, the match was a personal triumph but a team disappointment. The match in Auckland was stopped by rain on the first day and interrupted because of the weather on the others. It led, however, to a gripping match which was mostly in England's favour. A New Zealand rally in the second innings to produce her highest such total of 203 for 9 left England needing 1 wicket in 3 balls for the win. Duggan was responsible for 5 of the wickets that fell, taking them all in an unbroken spell of 21 overs, and it was she who was bowling the vital last over. Still, 5 for 47 combined with a second innings knock of 85 was another quality achievement.

Australia became a venue for four Test matches simply because the first was com-

Mary Duggan in action as a spin bowler. Her 7 wickets for 6 runs against Australia in 1958 is an all-time world record. The Umpire in the picture is Barbara Wood, an opening bowler, who toured Australia and New Zealand with Mary in 1948-9.

pletely washed out by rain. The extraordinary circumstances of the game with lost luggage and weather combined made the St Kilda ground in Melbourne something of a legend in the annals of women's cricket. Each country recorded her lowest ever total in an innings: Australia 38 with Duggan 7 for 6, and England 35, with Betty Wilson taking 7 for 7. Extraordinary as that game was, England escaped defeat only narrowly.

It was in Adelaide that Mary had to retire from the field, leaving Vice-captain Cecilia Robinson in charge. That game was a different kind of draw with quite large first innings totals by each team leaving little time for a second innings. England batted second and only once. The final Test in Perth was captained by Robbie from the outset. It too was drawn – time again running out though on this occasion England did start the second innings.

With all Tests drawn in 1957-8, when the Australians made their return visit in 1963 Mary had her chance to regain the "ashes". She was appointed captain for all three Tests scheduled to take place at Edgbaston, Scarborough and The Oval. It was a year in which there were some glaring omissions from the England team which could not quite be resolved along the lines of "bringing along the youngsters". Selectors – and captains too, of course – have their idiosyncrasies, but there was at least one shrewd commentator who was moved to write after the 2nd drawn Test:

"But jolly hard lines for the Australians. It was their game and only the Scarborough mist cheated them out of an innings win. If only England had had a sheet anchor like Allitt, or a forcing bat like Knee, or a few pairs of hands which hung on to the ball instead of letting it drop (was it eight that were grounded?). I know our team played like Trojans, but it was not good enough. Have we anything better?"

Women's Cricket 28 No. 6 1963, 102.

And we did have better! At the Oval there were three changes (there could well have been more) and in a tense finish, Mary Duggan had the conclusion to her Test career that many would have wished and probably she herself least expected. England won by 49 runs, Mary scoring a not out 101, with a match average of 133. She also took a total of 7 wickets for 82 runs in 61 overs, 31 of which were maidens.

DUGGAN, Mary B
Yorkshire and North, Middlesex and South
Batting and Fielding

	Tests	Inns	No	Runs	highest	100	50	average	Ct
1948-9 v A	3	6	1	33	24	—	—	6.60	2
1948-9 v NZ	1	2	—	21	18	—	—	10.50	—
1951 v A	3	6	1	102	23	—	—	20.40	2
1954 v NZ	3	4	—	66	34	—	—	16.50	2
1957-8 v NZ	2	4	—	210	108	1	1	52.50	1
1957-8 v A	2	3	—	25	12	—	—	8.33	—
1963 v A	3	6	2	205	101★	1	—	51.25	2

All Tests Average: **24.51**

Bowling

	Overs	Balls	Mdns	Runs	Wkts	average	5/I
1948-9 v A	41	246	7	117	3	39.00	—
1948-9 v NZ	22	132	9	21	3	7.00	—
1951 v A	119.2	716	37	239	20	11.95	2
1954 v NZ	126.1	757	67	165	13	12.69	—
1957-8 v NZ	126	756	37	159	14	11.35	2
1957-8 v A	71.5	431	31	99	11	11.00	1
1963 v A	136	816	57	239	15	15.93	—

All Tests Average: **13.49**

RACHAEL HEYHOE-FLINT

The successor to Mary Duggan was not only different from her in character, temperament and outlook, but was different from any past England captain or any likely future one. Unique, it would be supposed, could be the term applied to Rachael and cavalier, or other less flattering epithets, have also had their airing on occasion. But joy in the playing of cricket, and an exuberance that transmits itself to others, was always an attribute of her captaincy.

The year 1966, when the New Zealanders made their second trip to the United Kingdom for a three match series, marked the first appearance of Rachael as England's leader. It was a position she was to occupy for a decade and thus become the second longest-serving of England's captains – Molly Hide being the other. Like her predecessor, Rachael had a natural gift for attacking batting but that is where the comparison has to stop. For though Rachael was a useful County bowler she was not of Test standard. As to the art of captaincy, in the tactical sense, that was something that grew with her own stature as a player, and there are some remarkable instances that reflect on her maturity in both respects.

All three Tests against New Zealand, which took place at Scarborough, Edgbaston and The Oval, were drawn. In the first, Rachael made a century and *every player on the England side bowled* – except Sheila Plant the wicketkeeper, Sheila was slightly injured and had to leave the field whereupon Rachael took over to later effect the dismissal of Beverley Brentnall, the opposing wicketkeeper, who had been the one to cause Sheila's departure in the first place. Never a dull moment! At the end of that series Rachael's batting average was an outstanding 71.20.

The flamboyant Rachael Heyhoe-Flint whose captaincy of England from 1966 to 1976 finished in unprecedented controversy. Always an attacker of the ball and usually rapid scorer of runs, she prevented England losing the ashes in 1976 by frustrating Australia for 8 hours and 41 minutes in scoring 179.

That informed sources have spontaneously reported the 1968-9 Tour to Australia and New Zealand as one of the happiest six months of their lives owes more than a little to the 'top brass' trio of Valerie Hesmondhalgh (Manager), Rachael Heyhoe (Captain) and Edna Barker (Vice-captain). The squad was a united one, on and off the field, and it made for enjoyable, attacking cricket.

Though all three Tests in Australia were drawn, partly because the teams were evenly matched but also because the Australians were giving nothing away under the captaincy of Muriel Picton, the matches were fought out in a good spirit. Injuries seemed to bedevil England and, once again, Rachael's wicket-keeping skills came in useful. This time she took two catches behind the stumps. She also scored four half-centuries, two of them in the first match at Thebarton Oval, Adelaide, with a highest score at 76.

In New Zealand, Rachael met up with her old adversary of 1966 in captain Trish McKelvey. For the first Test at Wellington's Basin Reserve, and for the first time on the Tour, she could field a full team – no-one was injured. The result, though a draw, was an innings by both sides that exceeded the 300 mark. The other two games at the Hagley Oval Christchurch, not the most inspiring of pitches for a Test match and where the cloth sightscreen blew down, were both won.

It was the second of these that produced the most exciting tussle and finish and also showed how Rachael's captaincy had improved. The story goes that to tempt New Zealand into going for the win she kept on pace bowler Moorhouse who was not getting anywhere at all. In fact she was hit for 35 in 8 overs. The canny Yorkshire lass asked her captain later: "Why did you keep me on?"

"I knew," was the reply, "that if they got within sight of victory, they'd have a go at the other bowling."

And that other bowling was Enid Bakewell's, which had already accounted for 16 New Zealand scalps on the tour so far. The result was, that with her devasting leg-spin and the aid of Shirley Hodges behind the stumps, she took three more wickets and England won by 37 runs.

Between that Australasian tour and her last Test captaincy against the visiting Australian side of 1976, Rachael clocked up two firsts. One was to captain England against the recently formed Jamaican Women's Cricket Association, with the result that England won one and drew two of the three matches which took place on Jamaica in 1971. The other was to receive the honour of the MBE, which was awarded to her in 1972 as a general recognition of her services to women's cricket.

As for the 1976 series against Australia, it provided an extraordinary, almost unbelievable, cricket phenomenon which was all the more incredible since Rachael was the perpetrator.

The first two Tests at Old Trafford and Edgbaston were drawn. Rain affected the match at Old Trafford but Rachael scored a century in England's only innings. It was clear that the sides were evenly matched but Anne Gordon was proving to be a shrewd captain for Australia. The final Test at The Oval was an innovatory one in that it was scheduled to take place over four days if the other two Tests had resulted in a draw. And so it was.

On the first day England collapsed making their lowest total of the series at 134. Australia, seeking to take advantage of the unexpected, batted from 5.28 pm on the Saturday through to 12.02 on the Tuesday, amassing a total of 379. This left them virtually 1½ days to get England out and England requiring 254 runs to avoid an innings defeat. Given that England had not scored more than that in an innings so far, it looked to be Australia's game. Rachael, though, reorganised the batting so that her renowned 'stayers', such as Bakewell and Stephenson (Moorhouse) were suitably positioned to shore up any Australian breakthrough. In the event, however, neither of these players did so and it was Rachael herself, that equally renowned striker of the ball with many feats of rapid scoring to her credit, who stayed at the crease for 521 minutes to score 179 and see England through to another draw and a drawn series.

During her period of captaincy Rachael did not lose a Test and her team beat New Zealand for the first time in a decade. In her first Test as captain she scored one of the fastest centuries – 142 minutes – and in her last, one of the slowest at 313 minutes. To cap it all, she was out on the last ball of that final match. Cavalier, as ever.

HEYHOE-FLINT, Rachael
Staffordshire, Midlands and England
Batting and Fielding

	Tests	Inns	No	Runs	highest	100	50	average	Ct/S
1960-1 v SA	4	6	—	102	51	—	1	17.00	1
1963 v A	3	6	1	121	37*	—	—	24.20	1
1966 v NZ	3	6	1	356	113	1	2	71.20	3
1968-9 v A	3	6	—	269	76	—	4	44.83	3
1968-9 v NZ	3	5	—	234	88	—	2	46.80	2
1971 v J	3	4	2	220	107*	1	1	110.00	1
1976 v A	3	5	—	350	179	2	2	70.00	1
1979 v WI	3	5	1	162	62	—	1	40.50	2

All Tests Average: **47.74**

Bowling

	Overs	Balls	Mdns	Runs	Wkts	average
1960-1 v SA	30	180	7	59	1	59.00
1963 v A	3	18	0	13	1	13.00
1966 v NZ	8	48	1	44	0	—
1968-9 v A	12	96	2	44	1	44.00
1968-9 v NZ	—	—	—	—	—	—
1971 v J	8	48	2	19	0	—
1976 v A	10	60	0	44	0	—

All Tests Average: **74.33**

JANET SOUTHGATE

It was in 1976 that natural cricketer Jan (then Allen) played her first Test against the touring Australians, and it is doubtful that she ever considered her destiny to be that of captaining England on the historic occasion celebrating the Golden Jubilee of Tests between the two countries. Before that though there was an aborted tour of the West Indies in 1983, which she would have captained but for its last minute cancellation, and the actual captaincy on home ground against New Zealand a year later.

Getting back to that début, however, there are not too many players who have taken a wicket with the first ball bowled and also taken four catches in a very first Test match. Especially because the dismissed player was an opening bat and Jan was the fourth bowler to be brought on, the achievement has something of the unbelievable about it. In fact, Jan only bowled 9 overs and all of them in the second innings! No doubt her success in that match – she scored 32 at number 5 in England's only innings – assured her of a place in the other two Tests.

The first and last Golden Jubilee Captains of England, Jan Southgate (L) with Betty Archdale, taken at Perth in 1984.

It was a somewhat out-of-form Jan Southgate who, after totalling just 10 in three innings against the touring West Indies side in 1979, was omitted from the final Test at Edgbaston. She came through this set-back, however, to lead England against New Zealand in a three-day, three-Test series in 1984.

Now 29 years of age, Jan had as her opposing captain the youngest New Zealand had ever had in the 21-year-old Debbie Hockley. In other ways the teams were more evenly matched it seemed, for every game in the series was drawn. In personal terms it was Jan's best series so far since her 4 innings realised an average of 28.75 and she made a first Test 50. Included with that fine 59 in the third Test at Canterbury was a home record against New Zealand of 119 for the 2nd wicket. Her partner was Carole Hodges, who went on to make her highest Test score in a not out 158.

That 119 partnership between Jan and Carole was the pointer to further co-operation on the Australian tour later in the year. In the third Test on the famous Gabba in Brisbane, a fourth wicket stand of 85 with Carole superseded the 60 made with Rachael Heyhoe-Flint way back in 1976. This time though Jan had already had an effective third wicket partnership of 64 with Carole in the first innings when the 50 was brought up in 65 minutes. Jan's average for the match, her most successful, was an excellant 56.50 and clearly reflected her determin-ation to win: The match, though, was a draw.

After the close win by 5 runs in the second Test, a win at Brisbane would have cushioned England against her eventual defeat by two games to one with two drawn. Had the series been of the more usual three-Test form it would have been England's day. Whatever Jan herself may remember of that strenuous tour however, there is certainly another feature which marks the first ever four-day five-Test series and that is her winning of the toss on all five occasions.

SOUTHGATE (Allen), Janet
Sussex and England
Batting and Fielding

		Tests	Inns	No	Runs	highest	100	50	average	Ct
1976	v A	3	5	1	59	32	—	—	14.75	4
1979	v WI	2	3	—	10	7	—	—	3.33	1
1984	v NZ	3	4	—	115	59	—	1	28.75	2
1984-5	v A	5	10	—	306	74	—	2	30.60	2

All Tests Average: **28.09**

Bowling

		Overs	Balls	Mdns	Runs	Wkts	average
1976	v A	30.4	184	7	75	2	37.50
1979	v WI	6	36	3	17	0	—
1984	v NZ	3	18	1	9	0	—

All Tests Average: **49.50**

THE CAPTAINS

ENGLAND

	Tests	E	A	NZ	SA	J	WI	I	W	L	D
				Opponents						Results	
Betty Archdale	4	3	1						3	0	1
Molly Hide	11	7	4						4	2	5
Myrtle Maclagan	2	2							0	1	1
Mary Duggan	7	5	2						1	0	6
Cecilia Robinson	1	1							0	0	1
Helen Sharpe	4				4				1	0	3
Rachael Heyhoe-Flint	15	6	6			3			3	0	12
Susan Goatman	3						3		2	0	1
Janet Southgate	8	5	3						1	2	5

AUSTRALIA

	Tests	E	A	NZ	SA	J	WI	I	W	L	D
Margaret Peden	6	6							1	3	2
Mollie Dive	7	6		1					3	1	3
Una Paisley	4	3		1					1	0	3
Mary Allitt	3	3							0	1	2
Muriel Picton	4	3		1					0	0	4
Miriam Knee	1			1					0	0	1
Wendy Blunsden	1			1					0	0	1
Anne Gordon	5	3					2		0	0	5
Margaret Jennings	1							1	1	0	0
Sharon Tredrea	4	1		3					1	0	3
Jillian Kennare	4							4	0	0	4
Raelee Thompson	4	4							2	1	1

NEW ZEALAND

	Tests	E	A	NZ	SA	J	WI	I	W	L	D
Ruth Symons	1	1							0	1	0
Ina Lamason	2	1	1						0	2	0
Rona McKenzie	7	5	2						0	2	5
Patricia McKelvey	15	6	5		3			1	2	3	10
Deborah Hockley	6	3						3	0	0	6

ENGLAND'S RECORD HOLDERS

ENID BAKEWELL

Enid was relatively late in being called to play for her country for the first time on the Tour of 1968-9. By then she had abandoned her career as a PE teacher and was a contented wife and mother. Whatever it may have cost in leaving the family behind, however, must have been compensated for by the triumph that was her wonderment and must be a continuing source of pride for her family.

An orthodox left-arm spinner who modelled herself on Surrey's Tony Lock, Enid really came into her own on the softer wickets of

Enid Bakewell England all-round cricketer extraordinary. She is unique in scoring a century and taking ten wickets in the same Test. She is seen here batting at Lords in 1976 with partner Lynne Thomas with whom she shares the world record opening stand of 164.

AND, the bowling action responsible for 50 Test match wickets with 10 for 75 the pinnacle of her achievement. This was against the West Indies side at Edgbaston in 1979.

New Zealand. As an opening bat, however, she made her mark in the first Test against Australia in Adelaide with a maiden century. She did the same thing in the first Test against New Zealand at Wellington but, on that occasion, she also took 5 first innings wickets for 40 runs when New Zealand had accured their highest ever total of 302.

The second Test at  Christchurch provided another century and a not out 66 which resulted in a match average of 180. It also saw further success with the ball in a second innings 5 for 56 which was the vital factor in England's win. Fittingly, it was she who hit the winning run in the match. It was an occurrence, she reports, which was engineered by Vice-captain Edna Barker who was determined that it should be so.

It is no surprise that Enid, who notched up 1000 runs on that tour as well as taking 100 wickets, finished at the top of both bowling and batting averages in New Zealand. Her batting average was a remarkable 103.00. and she took 19 wickets at 12.73 apiece.

In the home series against Australia in 1976 she was the Vice-captain. Her best effort with the bat then was in the second Test at Edgbaston where a match average of 76 led the way and there was a century partnership with opener Lynne Thomas in both innings. This achievement is a unique one in international cricket and the scores were 116 and 164.

Enid played her last Test series against the West Indies when they visited England in 1979. It was a series in which England won two and drew the other of three Tests under the fine leadership of Sue Goatman. After the overwhelming 9 wicket defeat at Canterbury which indicated, perhaps, the relative inexperience of the West Indian players, their evident improvement came in leaps and bounds. By their enthusiasm and through keenness on the field their efforts were rewarded. The fast bowling was the liveliest that Enid says she has ever faced. Fortunately, though, the mainly short-pitched deliveries were all outside the off-stump otherwise the umpires might have found themselves dealing with a bumper crisis. Even so, when the opportunity presented itself, Bob Willis and Alan C. Smith were invited to help out by bowling to some of the England team in the nets. Enid recalls being petrified as Willis came in to bowl but was determined not to show it!

A century and two fifties marked another occasion for Enid to top the batting averages, but her crowning success was with the ball. In the final Test at Edgbaston, which England won by only 24 runs, she took 10 match wickets for 75 runs and had a second innings tally of 7 for 61 off 28.4 overs. Although this was not the first time that a woman cricketer had performed the tremendous feat of taking ten wickets and scoring a century in the same match – Betty Wilson did it in 1958 and included a hat-trick – it was the first time an England Test cricketer, *female or male*, had done so.

BAKEWELL, Enid
Nottinghamshire, Midlands and England
Batting and Fielding

	Tests	Inns	No	Runs	highest	100	50	average	Ct
1968-9 v A	3	6	—	189	113	1	—	31.50	1
1968-9 v NZ	3	5	1	412	124	2	3	103.00	2
1976 v A	3	5	—	168	77	—	2	33.60	5
1979 v WI	3	6	3	309	112★	1	2	103.00	1

All Tests Average: **59.88**

Bowling

	Overs	Balls	Mdns	Runs	Wkts	average	10/M	5/I
1968-9 v A	90.5	725	20	235	7	33.57	—	—
1968-9 v NZ	145	870	58	242	19	12.73	—	2
1976 v A	96.4	580	34	194	10	19.40	—	—
1979 v WI	87	522	38	160	14	11.42	1	1

All Tests Average: **16.22**

EDNA BARKER

Undoubtedly selected for the quality of her deep fielding as well as her all-round abilities with bat and ball, Edna, at the age of 20, was the youngest member of the touring party to visit New Zealand and Australia in 1957-8. Though batting a usual number 9 in the order, her selection for every Test match was indisputable for the economy of her bowling as well as for runs saved in the field. Her proficiency and adaptability in any fielding position was a great asset to the bowlers and Mary Duggan, in particular, made good use of the fact.

Edna's bowling strength was in playing a containing rôle. The accuracy and variation of her spin could subdue a bat and keep one end tight, while the wickets often went to her bowling partner. This useful skill did not lead to many wickets but it is reflected in a marathon performance in her first ever Test against New Zealand at Lancaster Park, Christchurch. She took 1 for 50 off 38 overs, 19 of which were maidens, and in one spell she bowled 20 overs unchanged to give away just 19 runs.

It was in Australia that Edna entered the record books for her batting. The Adelaide Test saw England make her highest total of the tour, in a 325 replying to Australia's 292, and going in at her usual number 9 Edna was not out for 50. This, her first Test 50, resulted in a last wicket partnership of 78 with Helene Hegarty who made 34. It was a partnership which remains an international record.

When selected to play at The Oval for the last Test against the touring Australians in 1963, Edna had the distinction of taking the last wicket which gave England the "ashes" for the first time in 15

An excellent fielder in the deep or at slip, a more than useful off-spinner in her early career and strong driver of the ball, Edna Barker is shown batting towards 50 not out at Adelaide in 1958. It was an innings watched and praised by Sir Donald Bradman.

years. The extraordinary part of this feat, however, was that in the entire match Edna only bowled 14 balls and she was brought on for the last 15 or so minutes of the game.

By the time Edna became Rachael Heyhoe's Vice-captain, against the touring New Zealanders in 1966, her rôle as a Test bowler was declining to give way to reliable and powerful all round the wicket batting. Ironically, however, she also returned her best series bowling average of 25.57. Now at number 4 or 5 in the line–up, she made her first century partnership – a 3rd wicket 121 with Rachael (113) in the first Test at Scarborough. Edna made 54 on that occasion and registered her second Test 50.

That 121 remained a record until Captain and Vice-captain did it again when touring Australia and New Zealand in 1968-9. Not only was their 137 an international record for the 3rd wicket, made at the St Kilda ground in Melbourne, but it also marked Edna's only Test century with exactly 100 scored in a rapid 138 minutes.

BARKER, Edna R
Surrey, South and England

Batting and Fielding

	Tests	Inns	No	Runs	highest	100	50	average	Ct
1957-8 v NZ	2	3	1	8	6*	—	—	4.00	1
1957-8 v A	3	5	1	93	50*	—	1	23.25	2
1963 v A	1	1	—	4	4	—	—	4.00	—
1966 v NZ	3	6	1	142	54	—	1	28.40	1
1968-9 v A	3	3	—	104	100	1	—	34.66	—
1968-9 v NZ	3	3	1	75	51	—	1	37.50	2

All Tests average: **25.05**

Bowling

	Overs	Balls	Mdns	Runs	Wkts	average
1957-8 v NZ	84	504	33	153	3	51.00
1957-8 v A	119	714	45	215	5	43.00
1963 v A	2.2	14	1	8	1	8.00
1966 v NZ	92.4	556	32	179	7	25.57
1968-9 v A	4	32	—	18	0	—
1968-9 v NZ	11	66	3	27	0	—

All Tests Average: **37.50**

BETTY BIRCH

During the Australians' 1951 Tour of England what seemed to stun many of the male spectators at Test matches was the ability of their outfielders to throw the ball in with great accuracy. Certainly this was a feature in which England were outshone – until, that is, Betty Birch was brought into the side for the final Test at The Oval.

Of her quick anticipation for the pick-up and her fine wristy returns the Press was more than appreciative. Undoubtedly in that Oval match she was a recognised part of England's eventual 137 run win. For whereas bowler "Duggan was both accurate and unsettling by reason of her liveliness," it was Birch "who stopped and returned the fiercest

The deep fielding of Betty Birch always met with crowd appreciation. Another who favoured the drive she here scores a boundary at The Oval in 1954 with a well-timed hook. The New Zealand Wicketkeeper is Vi Farrell.

hits without hesitation." The combination not only "gave England an advantage" but, of the play as a whole *The Times* reported:

"The high standard of the batting, bowling, and fielding clearly showed the advance in technique made by the women players, and the crowd of nearly 10,000 gave them deserved encouragement."

Not too many players on début have made a maiden duck – but with the not out 14 in the second innings and runs saved in the field Betty certainly made up for that. Extraordinarily enough, when she was making another first appearance in playing against the visiting New Zealanders in 1954 she also made a first innings duck! In the second Test at Worcester, though, it was a different story. Her 83 not out in the second innings included the fastest England Test 50 on record – taking just 58 minutes – and her 6th wicket partnership of 71 with Mary Duggan (20) took only 54 minutes. Previously, the fastest partnership for the 6th wicket against New Zealand was made in 1935 by Mollie Child (86★) and Mary 'Dick' Richards (28★). Strangely enough, theirs was also a 71 and it took 47 minutes.

As her "wristiness" was so much part of Betty's fielding, so it was with her batting and it led to a very full follow through. And what people tend to remember most about Betty's technique is the flourish accompanying the power of her driving. It was a style that obviously impressed itself on the selectors' minds too, because she was a certainty for the 1957-58 touring team – even though by that time she had taken up a job teaching PE in Melbourne, Australia.

Betty played in both the New Zealand Tests and two of the three matches in Australia, only missing out on Adelaide because of illness. It was the final one in Perth that was most memorable for her though. Going in at number 4 in the first innings instead of her usual number 5, she made a 72 not out which had the character of two different innings about it. Before the tea interval, at which time England was 169 for 5, Betty made 27 of which 15 were singles. After the interval though, the rest – 45 – took some 15 minutes less and contained eight boundaries. During that period there was a 6th wicket partnership of 27 with Edna Barker (16) which took 23 minutes, and a not out 57 partnership with Polly Marshall (20★) for the 7th wicket that took a remarkable 42 minutes. The latter is an England-Australia record and certainly an international fastest.

BIRCH, Betty D
Middlesex, South of England
Batting and Fielding

	Tests	Inns	No	Runs	highest	100	50	average	Ct
1951 v A	1	2	1	14	14★	—	—	14.00	—
1954 v NZ	3	5	1	130	83★	—	1	32.50	1
1957-8 v NZ	2	4	—	38	25	—	—	9.50	1
1957-8 v A	2	4	1	104	72★	—	1	34.66	—

All Tests Average: **23.83**

Bowling

	Overs	Balls	Mdns	Runs	Wkts	average
1954 v NZ	3	18	1	10	0	—

JANETTE BRITTIN

It was when the West Indies toured the United Kingdom in 1979 that Jan Brittin entered the arena of Test cricket. Like many an eventual opener before her, the first Test at Canterbury saw her batting a lowly number 7 where she made 28 in her only innings. On that occasion England won by 9 wickets so Jan did not get the chance to improve on her score. By the final Test she was up at number 3, where, unfortunately, she managed a match average of only two runs. Quite obviously though, her batting ability had shone through as had the signs that here was a fine all-round talent.

Some five years on saw the maturity of Jan's development as an opening bat when, with distinctive flair, she scored her first century against the touring New Zealanders. In the first Test at Headingley, Leeds, she made a not out 144 in England's 256 for 5 declared, which was her only innings of a drawn match. In the subsequent two Tests Jan's scores were: 96 (one innings only), 63 and 35 which led to an astounding overall series average of 112.67. That average remains the highest achieved by any woman opener in a full series of 3-day Test cricket.

Now well into her fluent batting stride, Jan did comparatively little bowling but could usually be relied upon for economy with her spin and often obtained the vital wicket. This was true on several occasions but no more so than on the 1984-5 Golden Jubilee series in Australia. Among the 4 wickets that she took, for 34 apiece, were those of Lyn Fullston and Jill Kennare in the crucial second test at Adelaide. That was the match that England won by 5 runs in a thrilling finish, and Lyn and Jill were batting 3 and 4 in Australia's 1st innings. In successive

The free flowing style of opener Jan Brittin. Against New Zealand in 1984 she topped the averages with 112.67 and on the five Test Jubilee tour of Australia in 1984/5 did likewise with a woman of the series average of 42.90.

overs Lyn went for 29, Jill for a duck and, at that stage, Jan had taken 2 wickets for 9 runs. She finished that unbroken spell of 15 overs before lunch with a very creditable 2 for 15.

Jan ended the tour as the player of the series and it was the quality of her batting performances which undoubtedly deserved that accolade. Her scores in that five Test series of four days duration (which some might say was too many for too long) were: 44 and 112, 22 and 15 (batting at number 3 on both occasions), 36 and 39, 45 and 65 and 16 and 35 – the last three sets being obtained in the number 1 slot. Always aiming to better her own high standards, Jan would probably criticise the variation in these scores. It is always worth remembering however, that it is both the situation in which scores are achieved and the style in which the lead is given that are the true indicators of performance.

BRITTIN, Janette
Surrey and England
Batting and Fielding

	Tests	Inns	No	Runs	highest	100	50	average	Ct
1979 v WI	3	5	2	34	28	—	—	11.33	3
1984 v NZ	3	4	1	338	144★	1	2	112.67	2
1984-5 v A	5	10	—	429	112	1	1	42.90	3

All Tests Average: **50.06**

Bowling

	Overs	Balls	Mdns	Runs	Wkts	average
1979 v WI	25	150	7	61	2	30.50
1984 v NZ	74	444	26	153	3	51.00
1984-5 v A	70	420	22	136	4	34.00

All Tests Average: **38.89**

AUDREY DISBURY

In Audrey Disbury women's cricket found its complement of those serving King or, in her case, Queen and Country when first playing for England. Since 'Dis' was in the Women's Royal Naval Service – the WRNS – all the services were now on the cricketing map.

An all-rounder who occasionally bowled her high-flighted off-breaks at Test level, Dis was more particularly known as a forceful bat who liked to get on with things, and a very good close field whose sharp reactions were best suited to a silly-mid position.

On the Tour of 1957-58, Dis's appearance on the cricket field was somewhat delayed by suspected glandular fever but she soon recovered to play in the first New Zealand Test at Christchurch. In the second at Auckland, however, she was ousted by opener Shirley Driscoll, now recovered from hand injury. This could perhaps account for the fact that later on in her Test career she decided to become an opening batsman too – but there is no authentic statement to back that hypothesis! In fact, she played in two Tests in Australia and Shirley was in the side both times – perhaps showing her the way? Dis managed to score only 25 runs in those three Tests.

Small beginnings perhaps, but when selected to play in the final Test against the visiting New Zealanders at The Oval in 1966, she had got nearer the top position to bat at number 4 in the order. She was runner-up (69) to Rachael Heyhoe (73) in best match figures but was top scorer in the first innings with 44. It was an occasion when England struggled a bit and this sensible batting helped England through to a drawn match and a drawn series.

It was on the second Tour of Australasia in 1968-69 that Dis finally made it and made it very well. Though there were no earth-shaking scores, it was her ability to force the pace that, allied to Enid Bakewell's steady effort, hardly ever failed to give England a solid start. Though her top score was 47, only four times in eleven innings was the first wicket down for under 30. The highest partnership was a 95 scored in second innings of the

The wristy power of Audrey Disbury rarely failed to bring runs. A keen close field in the silly-mid position and occasional off-spinner, Audrey's all-round ability saw her to a 13 year Test career.

final Test at Cornwall Park in Auckland, where England clinched the series in winning by 37 runs.

It was Jamaica that saw Dis capitalise on the experience gained over 15 years in producing her first Test 50. The first match at Jarrett Park started well with a century partnership for the first wicket in which both she and Lynne Thomas scored 56. Though this was one of Dis's slowest innings, the 105 partnership took just 131 minutes. It remains a unique record since no further matches were played against Jamaica after the Caribbean Federation was formed.

DISBURY, Audrey
Kent, East and England
Batting and Fielding

	Tests	Inns	No	Runs	highest	100	50	average	Ct
1957-8 v NZ	1	1	1	7	7*	—	—	—	—
1957-8 v A	2	3	—	18	13	—	—	6.00	1
1966　v NZ	1	2	—	69	44	—	—	34.50	—
1968-9 v A	3	6	—	148	44	—	—	24.66	2
1968-9 v NZ	3	5	—	149	47	—	—	29.80	1
1970-1 v J	2	3	—	68	56	—	1	22.66	2

All Tests Average: **24.16**

Bowling

	Overs	Balls	Mdns	Runs	Wkts	average
1957-8 v NZ	25	150	8	48	1	48.00
1957-8 v A	23	138	5	51	1	51.00
1968-9 v A	5	40	0	24	—	—
1968-9 v NZ	2	12	0	7	—	—
1970-1 v J	2	12	0	4	—	—

All Tests Average: **67.00**

SHIRLEY DRISCOLL

Shirley Driscoll (now Dixon) was selected to tour New Zealand and Australia in 1957-58 as an opening bat and close field whose favourite position was at point. Unfortunately, while batting against North Island at the Basin Reserve, Wellington, she got a blow on her hand which broke the metacarpel bone and put her out of the game for some six weeks. This was a particularly tragic occurrence as it happened in the very first match of the tour. After a day's fielding in one of the most bitter of Wellington's notorious winds, Shirley and Robbie had about 10 minutes of batting time to play out. The resulting incident was the team's loss and Shirley's frustration, which fortunately ended when she was passed fit to play in the second Test in Auckland. Even then, after a first innings score of 2, she could not get down to her motivating desire to open for England since a pulled muscle caused her to go in at number 6 in the second innings. But nothing if not versatile, Shirley made the second highest score of 32 not out to help England declare at 171 for 7, and featured in establishing a fifth wicket partnership of 104 with Mary Duggan who made 85. This is a record for England in New Zealand.

Still further delay on the Test scene because rain prevented any play at all in the first match against the Australians at Sydney, it was Melbourne, with its extraordinary outcome that saw Shirley in her rightful slot at number 2 – and she made a duck! But so did three others and the top score was 12. In the second innings, however, when near normality was resumed, Shirley made the top score of 24. Her *piece de resistance*, though, was in taking 4 catches in the match of which 3 were

Shirley Driscoll, making a superb off-drive, bats during the 1957-8 tour down under. Fielding at point, also Shirley's favourite position, is the Australian vice-captain Mary Allitt.

in the first innings. All the catches were off Duggan's bowling and, though a few have a similar catches total, none have the record of the same match with the same bowler. It is a record all the more poignant because of Shirley's earlier hand injury.

It was not until the final Test at Perth that Shirley scored a half-century, which took 112 minutes, in a first innings 72 that gave full range to her eloquent and forceful driving.

In all, her Test career spanned six years and, but for illness, would surely have continued and contained many more fine innings.

DRISCOLL (Dixon), Shirley
Surrey, South and England
Batting and Fielding

	Tests	Inns	No	Runs	highest	100	50	average	Ct
1957-8 v NZ	1	2	1	34	32*	—	—	34.00	—
1957-8 v A	3	5	—	134	72	—	1	26.80	5
1963 v A	3	5	—	67	33	—	—	13.40	2

All Tests Average: **21.36**

MARY DUGGAN [See also under: 'ENGLAND'S CAPTAINS DOWN UNDER']

When Mary was selected to tour Australia and New Zealand in 1948-9 it was as medium-fast swing bowler and forceful middle-order bat. With best performances of 24 against Australia in the first Test at the Adelaide Oval, and 3 for 21 off 22 overs in the only Test against New Zealand in Auckland, her success with both bat and ball could only be described as moderate for that series. When Australia visited England in 1951 and the New Zealanders followed three years later, however, Mary's excellent bowling had a very different effect.

Most players have difficulty in countering the well flighted, good length ball that comes across the body and when such are accompanied by variation in pace and turn off the wicket, it takes a very good player indeed to score effectively. That Australian side of 1951 was probably the most individually talented of any, having as it did the like of Betty Wilson batting at number 7, but on two occasions Mary took 9 match wickets with her natural left-arm deliveries. Her 9 for 107 at Worcester included a first innings 5 for 40 and in the third Test at The Oval her 9 for 104 included 5 for 30 in the second innings. That Test was won by England to square the series.

Against the New Zealanders in 1954 Mary bowled a total of 126 overs and took 13 wickets in the series at 12.69 apiece, with a best performance of 5 match wickets for 41 runs at Worcester.

In all, Mary took more than 5 wickets in a match nine times in a career which spanned 15 years. During that time she changed to spin bowling and that seemed to spark a change in her batting also. Subsequently she scored two centuries, her 108 at Christchurch, New Zealand being the second fastest on record at 135 minutes. By that time she was England's Captain.

HELENE HEGARTY

At the time Helene Hegarty entered the cricket scene, Surrey was the strongest of the counties and had little room for an aspiring young fast bowler. She played for a Middlesex club and, having qualifications for that county, was urged by some to try there because with Surrey she would surely not get a bowl. But to Surrey she went, got selected, did bowl, and in 1954 played for England against the visiting New Zealanders. It was this kind of battling with the odds and tenacity of purpose that epitomised Helene's bowling and made her the women's cricket equivalent of 'Fiery' Fred Trueman.

It was in that 1954 début that Helene took most wickets in a three Test series ending top of the averages with 11 wickets for 138 runs at 12.54 apiece. This excellent achievement included her best performance of 5 for 48 at The Oval. It was a match in which the visitors batted second on a

Mary Duggan, captaining her last Test at The Oval in 1963, celebrated her finale with a memorable first innings 101 not out. She led England to victory, wresting the "ashes" from Australia, who had held them since 1949. The wicketkeeper is Margaret Jude.

Helene Hegarty's lively pace always earned the respect of the opposition. Her best performance was 5 for 48 against New Zealand at The Oval in 1954 on a rain-affected pitch. At the other Oval – Adelaide – she had two batting triumphs: a 10th wicket partnership of 78 with Edna Barker, and an individual performance of 34. Both of these are world records.

rain affected pitch and needed to be dismissed twice for 280 of England was to win. The match ended in a draw, but it looked as though she was still going all out for a result.

Although Helene played very little in the preceding season because of a rib injury, together with six other Surrey players, she was chosen for the 1957-8 Tour of New Zealand and Australia. On that tour she played in just three of the five Tests to take 7 wickets for a total of 183 runs, all seven on the fast Australian pitches. It was in Australia, too, that Helene put herself in the batting records. In the drawn match at the Adelaide Oval, she made a 10th wicket score of 34 and, with Edna Barker, established a 10th wicket partnership of 78 made in 62 minutes. Both of these are world records.

Helen's last appearance for England was against the visiting Australians in 1963. Selected for the final Test at The Oval which England won having drawn the other two, she took three wickets to conclude her career with 21 wickets in only 7 Tests.

HEGARTY, Helene
Surrey, South of England
Batting and Fielding

	Tests	Inns	No	Runs	highest	average	Ct
1954 v NZ	3	3	—	8	8	2.66	1
1957-8 v NZ	1	—	—	—	—	—	—
1957-8 v A	2	2	—	38	34	19.00	—
1963 v A	1	—	—	—	—	—	—

All Tests Average: **9.20**

Bowling

	Overs	Balls	Mdns	Runs	Wkts	average	5/I
1954 v NZ	102	612	45	138	11	12.54	1
1957-8 v NZ	31	186	17	32	0	—	—
1957-8 v A	87.3	525	30	151	7	21.57	—
1963 v A	43	258	14	94	3	31.33	—

All Tests Average: **19.76**

RACHAEL HEYHOE-FLINT [See also under: 'ENGLAND'S CAPTAINS DOWN UNDER']

Rachael first played Test cricket on the tour of South Africa in 1961 under the captaincy of Helen Sharpe. Thereafter she was selected for every Test series at home and abroad to finish her career in 1979 by playing against the West Indies, in England, when the home side was then captained by Sue Goatman. In between times, Rachael led England and in so doing always played positive cricket. Although in actual span of years Molly Hide holds the captain's record, in the number of Tests played Rachael has more captaincy appearances than anyone except New Zealand's Trish McKelvey.

On her début Rachael's attacking style of batting did not realise a great average – a mere 17.00 – but she registered the fastest 50 of the tour with the 51 she scored at Johannesburg: It took 66 minutes. Playing against the Australians in 1963 her average was better but the highest score was a 37 not out at The Oval. A remarkable feature of that innings however, was not only that it took just 33 minutes, but

With more half-centuries than anyone in Test cricket, 13, Rachael Heyhoe-Flint is seen on-driving at The Oval in 1966. In 1963 in the final Test against the Australians she became the only woman to score a 6 at this formidable venue. With Edna Barker, her partner in this picture, Rachael holds the world record 137 for the 3rd wicket which was made at Melbourne on the 1968-9 tour.

that in the process she became the only woman ever to hit a six on that formidable ground – and she did not take the shortest route either!

In a record 25 appearances for England, Rachael scored 4 centuries, including a not out 107 and the highest ever score against the Australians in a marathon 179 which contained a record 28 boundaries. Against the Jamaicans abroad in 1971, she registered her highest average of 110, and in two other series reached the 70 mark. Only Enid Bakewell has equalled the number of centuries scored, but when it came to 50s Rachael is way out on her own with 13.

With Enid, however, Rachael, who normally batted at number 3 in the order, made three second wicket century partnerships of 136 in Auckland, 127 in Adelaide and 114 in Christchurch. It was with Edna Barker that she made two third wicket century partnerships. They were 121 against New Zealand at Scarborough in 1966, and an international record 137 against Australia in Melbourne in 1968-9.

To end such a career with an overall Test average of 47.74 is a truly staggering performance.

MOLLY HIDE [See also under: 'ENGLAND'S CAPTAINS DOWN UNDER']

On the first ever tour of Australia and New Zealand in 1934-5, Molly made only one Test century and that was against a raw New Zealand side which was overwhelmed by the might of England's batting. In reply to New Zealand's 1st innings 44, in which only one player managed a score greater than 5, England made the huge total 503 for 5 declared and thus provided a source of records which have been hard to beat. Even

Molly Hide who captained England from 1937 to 1954 was a talented all-rounder. It is said that she underrated her off-spin bowling. Her most successful bag of Test wickets was, the second Test at Blackpool in June 1937. She took 5 for 20 off 74 balls, in Australia's second innings, England won by just 25 runs.

with today's practice of 4-day Tests, with their related over-lengthy innings, the second wicket partnership between Molly and Betty Snowball is unlikely to be surpassed. Their 235 remains an international record. It was made in 142 minutes during which time Molly made 110. Betty, therefore, already had notched up her century (in 115 minutes) and she went on to make a career highest 189.

On three occasions Molly featured in century partnerships. They were all for the 3rd wicket: 134 with Betty Snowball (99) – Molly made 64 – at The Oval in 1937; 108 with Myrtle Maclagan (115) – Molly made 34 – at Blackpool in 1937; 107 with Joan Wilkinson (47) – Molly made 64 – at Worcester in 1954.

The renowned spin bowler Myrtle Maclagan has said that Molly, also a spin bowler but of different style – not so flighted and quicker off the pitch – never bowled herself enough as captain. Nevertheless there are three occasions on which she took five wickets in a match, with a best tally of 8 for 58, and in her first season as captain against the Australians – 1937 – she topped them all with 14 wickets taken in the series.

CAROLE HODGES

Full Test representation for 24-year-old Carole came with the visit of the New Zealanders in 1984. It was a début that was highlighted by a century and showed, with good off-spin bowling and keen fielding, that England had the services of a talented all-rounder for many years to come.

Batting in place of the usual number 3 in the first Test at Headingley, Carole made a modest 8 runs in England's only innings. Solid and unadventurous New Zealand batting dictated that the game ended in a draw. The second match at Worcester saw Carole at her expected number 7 in the batting order – where she made 20 runs in 13 minutes. Once again New Zealand played two innings to England's one, and the inevitable draw followed. In the final Test at Canterbury Carole opened with Jan Brittin, made a moderate 15 runs in her first innings but had the pleasure of removing opening bat Ann McKenna who, in making her 48, had frustrated the efforts of five bowlers before Carole got a chance at her. The second innings then saw Carole make the highest Test score of any player against New Zealand on home soil, a not out 158, and forge a home record second wicket partnership of 119 with Jan Southgate who made 59.

All-rounder Carole Hodges, England's Captain against the Indian tourists in 1986, shows the style in which she reached her highest score of 158 not out. This was against the touring New Zealanders at Canterbury, Kent, in 1984. A fine fielder to her own bowling, Carole also holds the record of Test catches.

Later in the year Carole was selected for the Golden Jubilee Series tour to Australia. Though going in mostly at number 2 and 3 in the order, her performance with the bat was variable giving to rise to scores of 34 and 6, 13 and 44, 32 and 95, 1 and 5 and 0 and 39. Her success with the ball was a modest 5 wickets but she excelled in fielding taking 12 catches of which two were off her own bowling. Usually fielding at point, and by preference a close field, Carole reports that her most memorable catch was in taking Karen Price at square, off the pace bowler Avril Starling in the second Test at Adelaide. It was not a spectacular but a vital catch which frustrated the power of Karen who liked to hook. Since she was well capable of making a century, getting her out was an important feature in England's 5-run win.

With the three catches she took in the New Zealand series, Carole shared the record of 15 Test catches with Hazel Sanders who established that feat in 1958.

HODGES, Carole A
Lancashire & Cheshire, England
Batting and Fielding

	Tests	Inns	No	Runs	highest	100	50	average	Ct
1984 v NZ	3	4	1	201	158*	1	—	67.00	3
1984-5 v A	5	10	—	269	95	—	1	26.90	12

All Tests Average: **36.15**

Bowling

	Overs	Balls	Mdns	Runs	Wkts	average
1984 v NZ	107	642	38	139	6	23.17
1984-5 v A	132	792	39	281	5	56.22
All Tests Average: **38.18**						

SHIRLEY HODGES

Selected as England's second-string wicketkeeper to tour Australasia in 1968-9, Shirley won her full place in the team for the second Test at the St Kilda ground in Melbourne. Thereafter she kept her place with some inspired keeping and sound, perceptive batting at a usual number 9 in the order.

Undoubtedly the highlight of the whole tour was the third Test in New Zealand where the home side's second innings was crucial in deciding whether the series was to be won or drawn. Shirley caught two of the upper order bats off the fast bowling of Carole Evans and then combined with Enid Bakewell to stump numbers 6,7 and 9. In the match overall she had 4 stumpings and this put her top of the league for England versus New Zealand. Internationally only Australia's Alice Wegemund and New Zealand's Edna Ryan went one better. No-one, however, has exceeded her record of 16 dismissals in a 3 Test Rubber which also occurred on that occasion. New Zealand, too, provided Shirley with an infinite batting average. In her two innings she was twice not out with a total of 45, the 34 scored in 36 minutes at the Basin Reserve in the 1st Test being her highest score.

As wicketkeeper in all the 1971 Tests in Jamaica Shirley had 5 stumpings in the three match series. Her final Test match series was also against the West Indians when they toured England in 1979. She took 10 catches and led the field with 5 of the catches being taken in the first Test at Canterbury.

In the interim the Australians had toured England in 1976 and, for Shirley, it meant obtaining leave of absence from her job as a PE teacher to represent her country yet again. She made 3 stumpings and took 2 catches in that series. Probably the most memorable of those catches would be the one which dismissed Jannette Lumsden in the final Test at The Oval. Lumsden had made 123 in a chanceless innings which had the England team toiling away most of the day and wondering if they were going to do the same on the next. Jackie Court was bowling and it was the last but one ball before close of play. Jan pushed at it, it popped up on the leg-side and Shirley dived managing to keep her glove underneath to take the difficult catch.

In the 14 Tests included in the decade in which Shirley was England's top wicketkeeper, she took 19 catches and made 22 stumpings. An incredible 53 victims in 15 matches played on the 1968-69 Tour overall, of which 37 wickets went to stumpings, makes these achievements unlikely to be bettered either for England or internationally.

In only 8 Tests against the chief rivals, Australia and New Zealand, taking a total of 9 catches and making 17 stumpings is a superlative performance.

No-one has more Test match victims than Shirley Hodges. Here she shows that fierce concentration which put her in that top spot. With her in the picture is Australia's Sharon Tredrea with a fine hook that helped her on the way to a half-century in the first ever one-day game at Lords in 1976.

HODGES, Shirley A
Sussex, South and England
Batting and Fielding

	Tests	Inns	No	Runs	highest	average	Ct /	S
1968-9 v A	2	3	2	21	21*	21.00	2	3
1968-9 v NZ	3	2	2	45	34*	—	5	11
1971 v J	3	1	—	2	2	2.00	—	5
1976 v A	3	4	1	27	13	9.00	2	3
1979 v WI	3	1	—	5	5	5.00	10	—

All Tests Average: **16.67**

Wicketkeeping:	against Australia	against New Zealand
Catches:	4	5
Stumpings:	6	11

MYRTLE MACLAGAN

Until Mary Duggan and Betty Wilson each took 7 wickets in an innings at Melbourne's St Kilda Ground in 1958, Myrtle Maclagan's 7 for 10 at the Exhibition Ground in Brisbane was a record good enough to be supposed unbeatable. But Myrtle's triumph has in no way lost its singular aura because of a very particular circumstance: It was the first ever women's Test to take place anywhere in the world and the date was 28 December 1934. A maiden 50 in a total of 72 in the first innings capped this bowling feat and made the occasion one of the most memorable in a career which spanned 17 very memorable years indeed.

Although an all-round sportswoman who had the opportunity to indulge her ability at tennis and squash as well as cricket while serving as an officer in the WRAC, Myrtle was a self-taught cricketer. This was reflected in her batting style which owed its somewhat tight look to a very individual grip. Myrtle admits that when this was changed years later by Arthur Coysh, who was one of those rare coaches of women able to exploit a successful talent without imposing copybook style, she felt a much freer flow to her batting.

It was both batting style and personal character, though, that made Myrtle a first-class opener who saw her rôle as one of staying there until the scoreboard registered fifty. In this she was aided for many years by the ideal partner, whose technique was the perfect foil to her own, in Betty Snowball. Often referred to as the 'Hobbs and Sutcliffe' of women's cricket, these two opened together nine times in eleven innings for seven Tests in the series of 1934-5 and 1937. Their highest stand was 145 in the second Test at Sydney Cricket Ground in 1935.

In the post-war years Myrtle's partner was Cecilia Robinson and,

though more alike in batting temperament, they too formed a successful opening pair registering a highest stand of 95 in the first Test at
Scarborough in 1951 against the Australians. On this occasion Myrtle
captained the England side in the absence of an injured Molly Hide as
indeed she did in the second Test at Worcester. The result of the
matches was a draw and a win to Australia by two wickets respectively.
About this elevation to the captaincy Myrtle had one reflection and one
regret. The first was a self-knowing comment that, while a happy
captain of County, Territorial and particularly Services teams, she did
not feel completely at ease when captaining England: The regret was
that she did not give the Middlesex player Winnie Leech more of a
bowl in that second Test.

Myrtle is one of just three players who have scored over a thousand
runs in Test cricket. In 25 innings she scored 1007 runs which included
two centuries and six fifties. Her most successful season with the bat
was in 1937 when she topped the batting averages with 78.75. This
magnificent achievement has never been bettered in Tests against
Australia at home or abroad. But as an all-rounder — her favourite
fielding position was a close cover — who reckoned that her strength
was in her off-spin bowling, it was the Tour of 1934-5 that marked out
her potential as a Test player of stature. In that series she headed the
bowling with 20 wickets at 8.45 apiece, came second to Snowball in the
batting averages but had one less innings, and was the only player to
score a century. In this, she has the unique record of being the first
woman scorer of a Test century.

To those whose chief recollection of
Myrtle is as a stayer at the crease
who was very difficult to remove, it is
worth reflecting that among the more
recent players who have had the
privilege of opening an innings for

*Here Myrtle Maclagan shows the bowling style that
devastated the Australians on the first tour of 1934-5.
With 20 wickets and 253 runs in that series against
Australia, Myrtle leads the field. Against Australia
in England in 1937 she led again with 315 runs and
11 wickets. Her staying power as an opener is
legendary. She has two Test centuries, the highest a
119, and two century partnerships to her credit, with
a notable 6 half-centuries.*

England, none can beat the run-rate of 1.19 per minute set up for the first wicket by Maclagan and Snowball in 1935. That day not just 50 but 145 – a record for England in Australia – was registered on the scoreboard, with the 100 partnership having taken just 89 minutes. And that was also the occasion on which Myrtle made 119 and brought up her century with a majestic four through the covers.

To achieve a batting average of 41.95 and combine this with bowling figures of 15.58 in a total of 14 Tests during which she also took 12 catches, points to Myrtle as a player of outstanding all-round ability.

MACLAGAN, Myrtle E
Surrey, South of England
Batting and Fielding

	Tests	Inns	No	Runs	highest	100	50	average	Ct
1934-5 v A	3	5	—	253	119	1	2	50.60	4
1934-5 v NZ	1	1	—	26	26	—	—	26.00	—
1937 v A	3	5	1	315	115	1	1	78.75	1
1948-9 v A	3	6	—	153	77	—	1	25.50	3
1948-9 v NZ	1	2	—	62	47	—	—	31.00	1
1951 v A	3	6	—	198	59	—	2	33.00	3

All Tests Average: **41.95**

Bowling

	Overs	Balls	Mdns	Runs	Wkts	average	5/I
1934-5 v A	165.3	993	93	169	20	8.45	1
1934-5 v NZ	38.4	232	14	57	6	9.50	1
1937 v A	141	846	47	283	11	25.72	—
1948-9 v A	110	660	30	254	9	28.22	—
1948-9 v NZ	22	132	12	16	3	5.33	—
1951 v A	94.5	569	35	156	11	14.18	1

All Tests Average: **15.58**

OLIVE MARSHALL

Known to everyone as 'Polly', Olive Marshall was that epitome of Yorkshire grit and tenacity that enabled her to overcome a debilitating typhoid illness and go on playing cricket for England. As such she became the pride of Pickering, the town in North Yorkshire where she lives and runs an 'Open All Hours' shop. That her renown was not confined only to Pickering though, was brought home at a match where Polly was out supporting the local men's club of which she is one of the Vice-presidents. The usual raffle tickets came round and on

Polly Marshall turns one to leg with slip fielder June Bragger looking on. A useful change bowler, an attacking bat with a highest average of 52.50 and a deep fielder with whom only the foolhardy would risk a run, Polly's all-round ability saw her playing for England from 1954 to 1966.

buying hers, the seller (himself a useful Yorkshire league cricketer whose pride was to have scored 48 off Fred Trueman) naturally asked for a name. When told it was Polly Marshall he replied: "Not *the* Polly Marshall, the cricketer?"

"Of course," Polly's friends delightedly told him. "The very same" and were especially pleased because this was some 18 years after she had last played for England. That was a match, her last Test at The Oval in 1966, that Polly is not likely to forget. It certainly gave her a record first though – because it is the only occasion on which a "pair" has been collected on a last appearance.

Polly's first appearance for England against New Zealand in 1954 fortunately did not begin that way, nor did it begin in a blaze of batting glory: She scored a modest 7 runs batting at number 8 in the order. One day of that match – also at The Oval – was completely washed out giving each side one innings in a drawn game. But that début was impressive enough to ensure this talented all-rounder, whose deep fielding was particularly memorable for its accuracy of return, a Test career which spanned twelve years.

In 1957-8, Polly toured New Zealand and Australia where again it was her fielding ability that was most prominent, and which, in Auckland, accounted for a record three run-outs in an innings. It was at Perth, though, in the final Test match of the series that she aided Betty Birch in establishing a record seventh wicket stand of 57 runs in 42 minutes for England against Australia, which still holds. Her not out 20 with Betty's not out 72 helped England to declare her first innings at 253 for 6.

She toured South Africa in 1960-61 and this is where her batting and bowling came into its own. Now in her preferred position of opening the innings, she was the only one to score more than 300 in the 4 Test series, and holds the record 1st wicket stand of 147 with Helen Sharpe (now Griffiths) made at Newlands, Cape Town. Her scores of 56 and 63 in consecutive innings on that occasion was the first such feat, and only Molly Hide had done better with her 63 and 124 not out at Sydney in 1948. But in scoring that 63, Polly also played what she feels to be her finest innings. It was a chanceless one in which the South African bowlers were on form and she was completely on top of the bowling. Since the century partnership came up in the two hours before lunch, it looks as though it was indeed one of those dreamed-of days. The 147 took just 152 minutes.

It was this tour that also showed her true qualities as a useful medium-pace change bowler. Although she puts her success down to a somewhat unorthodox round-arm style, there was no doubt of its effectiveness when she finished by taking 8 wickets at 11.12 apiece to top the bowling averages.

MARSHALL, Olive
Yorkshire, North and England
Batting and Fielding

	Tests	Inns	No	Runs	highest	100	50	average	Ct
1954 v NZ	1	1	—	7	7	—	—	7.00	—
1957-8 v NZ	2	3	—	7	5	—	—	2.33	—
1957-8 v A	3	5	1	44	20★	—	—	11.00	1
1960-1 v SA	4	7	1	315	81	—	3	52.50	—
1966 v NZ	3	5	2	5	3★	—	—	1.66	1

All Tests Average: **22.23**

Bowling

	Overs	Balls	Mdns	Runs	Wkts	average
1957-8 v NZ	27	162	7	59	1	59.00
1957-8 v A	43	258	20	76	1	76.00
1960-1 v SA	85	510	45	89	8	11.12
1966 v NZ	21	126	12	20	1	20.00

All Tests Average: **22.16**

GILLIAN McCONWAY

A resident of the United Kingdom since 1973 and subsequently a Naturalised Citizen, nevertheless, New Zealand born Gill McConway made a unique entrance on the England Test scene by playing her first series against her own countrywomen when the latter toured England in 1984. Now a Sports Centre administrator, Gill was a very experienced cricketer whose left-arm spin bowling was a boon to the England side both at that time and when she toured Australia in 1984-5.

The sort of results that Gill made a habit of, and which showed the containing nature of her bowling, was such as 2 for 20 from 15 overs in the second Test at Worcester and 1 for 28 off 25 overs, which included 17 maidens, in the previous test at Headingley. In total, she bowled more overs than any other of her colleagues despite the fact that she took only those 3 wickets for an average of 65.00 apiece. *In the entire series Gill did not bat.* In fact that was a series remarkable for the number of players on either side who "Did Not Bat."

On the harder Australian wickets Gill had greater success in terms of wickets taken – coming second to Avril Starling with 16 tour wickets overall at an average of 22.06 each. In the only Test that England won, at the Adelaide Oval, Gill took 7 match wickets for 67 runs and her 4 for 32 off 27 overs in the first innings represented a best performance. Once again she bowled more overs than any other England bowler, and it is interesting that her Australian counterpart, Lyn Fullston, did the same for her team.

McCONWAY, Gillian
East Anglia and England
Batting and Fielding

	Tests	Inns	No	Runs	highest	average	Ct
1984 v NZ	3	—	—	—	—	—	—
1984-5 v A	5	10	4	47	13★	7.83	2

All Tests Average: **7.83**

A player of the recent era leg-spinner Gill McConway has gone from strength to strength. In the Jubilee series 1984-5, she had a best innings performance of 4 for 32 off 27 overs with 12 maidens. This was the Test that England narrowly won at Adelaide. She took a total of 7 wickets in the match overall and bowled more overs than anyone else in the five Test series.

Bowling

	Overs	Balls	Mdns	Runs	Wkts	average
1984 v NZ	115	690	55	195	3	65.00
1984-5 v A	229.1	1375	99	353	16	22.06
All Tests Average: **28.84**						

DOROTHY McEVOY

It is not every fast bowler that can boast to the fact that England felt the need to recall her at the age of 41 – but this is exactly what happened to Dorothy McEvoy. Having 'retired' from the game the year after her return from a personally successful, but injury-prone, tour of Australia and New Zealand in 1948-9, this strong-hearted opening bowler of lively pace and classic action, responded to her country's call in 1951 in the best possible way: She ensured that England did not lose the series.

After England's defeat in the tour 'Down Under', which meant that Australia gained the mythical "ashes" for the first time in three encounters bridging 15 years, Dorothy Mac has not been the only member of that visiting team to pay tribute to the outstanding quality of Australia's women cricketers in the era of Mollie Dive's captaincy from 1948 to 1951. But the fact that it was virtually those same players who came to England in 1951, makes her achievement a lasting memory and one to savour.

The story has been told before – it figures in the Third Test at the Oval which took place from July 28-31, and elsewhere – but this time we'll let the words of the celebrated author of *Maiden Over*, Nancy Joy (now Wansborough), garnish those final tense moments. Remembering that England needed to win the Third Test to draw the series, the following is what she wrote in her match report when, with about two hours to go, England looked home and dry with Australia on 5 for 5, the damage having been done by the swing bowling of left-armer Mary Duggan.

"This was at quarter to four, and brought in Amy Hudson, and, though her partners came and went, there stayed the joker – two hours for 17 runs, presenting a spirit as imperturbable as any that can have been shown at the Oval. And such was her defiance that it communicated itself to the mercurial Mavis Jones, whom nobody expected would remain five minutes. Hide, Maclagan, even the tempting Sanders, tried their best, and the clock was now beginning to race on. Hudson and Jones had been together 35 minutes, and only 15 now remained when Hide tossed the ball to McEvoy. With all the fury and determination in the world the fast bowler thundered to the wicket. Two to the off and one to the leg – and never a touch from Jones. The fourth ball shattered the middle stump – and England were home by 137 runs."

Adding the fact that this was the second time McEvoy bowled during the second innings, having been taken off after just one previous over, completes the picture. It is made more graphic by Mac's own words, which were always nothing if not direct. They go something like this: "Two went whistling past her bosom, the third shaved her bottom and the fourth knocked back the stumps." And all that on the renowned placid – in those days – Oval wicket.

A memorable way to finally depart the game of games there is no doubt, together with the fact that The Oval was also the venue for the first six (the first of just two), ever hit into the stands by a woman when Mac did it during a representative match. But had war not intervened –

she was one of those selected for the aborted tour of Australia and New Zealand in 1939 – there is little doubt that other feats of bowling courage and determination would have accompanied her performances. As it was, she has another highlight to cherish. She achieved the best bowling figures of her Test career in New Zealand in 1949. With a match analysis of 6 for 53 off 43.2 overs, it was Mac's 5 for 23 in the first innings that assured England of victory.

An exuberant character and fast bowler of real pace and determination, Mac has a best performance of 5 for 23 off 19.2 overs in the only Test against New Zealand in 1949.

McEVOY, Dorothy E
Surrey, South and England
Batting and Fielding

	Tests	Inns	No	Runs	highest	average	Ct
1948-9 v A	2	3	1	13	9	6.50	1
1948-9 v NZ	1	1	1	4	4*	—	2
1951 v A	2	3	1	16	16	8.00	1

All Tests Average: **8.25**

Bowling

	Overs	Balls	Mdns	Runs	Wkts	average	10/M	5/I
1948-9 v A	63	378	17	123	3	41.00	—	—
1948-9 v NZ	43.2	260	20	53	6	8.83	—	1
1951 v A	48.4	292	17	73	4	18.25	—	—

All Tests Average: **19.15**

JUNE MOORHOUSE

When she came into England's side against New Zealand at Scarborough in 1966, Yorkshire's June Moorhouse (now Stephenson) did so principally as a pace bowler. She rewarded her selection by taking most wickets – 4 for 38 in the first innings of a drawn match. On

that occasion she did not bat in either innings and so it was at Edgbaston that June showed her willow-wielding capabilities. There, she not only scored a maiden not out 50 but also established a unique not out partnership 76 for the 8th wicket with fellow Yorkshire player Lesley Clifford who contributed a not out 31. That remains a world record for a partnership which took only 64 minutes.

The Yorkshire all-rounder, June Stephenson, is unique in that her three half-centuries were all not out. Her swing bowling and fine close fielding were instrumental in a career that spanned 10 years and 12 Tests.

Gradually, as June's batting came to be appreciated for its solid defensive qualities, she was used at crucial phases of an innings and rarely fell short of what was expected of her. The same could be said of her bowling. She swung the ball effectively at medium pace and it was not often that she failed to take a wicket, although that 4 for 38 in 38 overs of which 20 were maidens on her first appearance for England remained her best performance.

In every series in which she played, and she was selected to tour Australia and New Zealand in 1968-69 and played against the visiting Australians in 1976, June made a 50. Although one obviously never forgets the first, which took 71 minutes, probably her 59 not out at the North Sydney Oval in 1969 would be more memorable. It was made in the second innings, with England batting last and needing 231 to win. June was promoted from 6 to 4 at a time when England was 74 for 3. She and Lynne Thomas (34) put on a 4th wicket stand of 75 in 54 minutes – going for the runs. After Lynne's departure, however, numbers 6 and 7 made ducks until number 8 – Lesley Clifford – came in to stop the rot with her old ally. It appears that England just survived to make that draw on an occasion when June's second half-century took 76 minutes.

It was at Old Trafford in 1976 that June scored her third half-century. Although it was her slowest, taking 118 minutes, it also occurred in her highest ever score of 60. The incredible thing about it though was that it was yet another not out. Assuredly, to score three not out 50s as an all-rounder, one of which was a maiden 50 when batting at number 8, is an outstanding achievement.

MOORHOUSE (Stephenson), June
Yorkshire, North and England
Batting and Fielding

	Tests	Inns	No	Runs	highest	100	50	average	Ct
1966 v NZ	3	4	1	76	50★	—	1	25.33	1
1968-9 v A	3	6	2	142	59★	—	1	35.50	3
1968-9 v NZ	3	4	1	53	25	—	—	17.66	4
1976 v A	3	4	1	74	60★	—	1	24.66	—

All Tests Average: **26.53**

Bowling

	Overs	Balls	Mdns	Runs	Wkts	average
1966 v NZ	102	612	50	156	7	22.28
1968-9 v A	64	512	22	139	4	34.75
1968-9 v NZ	59	354	16	130	1	130.00
1976 v A	75	450	20	128	6	21.33
All Tests Average: **30.72**						

CECILIA ROBINSON

During the period of 15 years for which 'Robbie' was an England opening bat, her name was primarily linked with just two partners: Myrtle Maclagan and Shirley Driscoll. With both of these it was touring abroad that established the association and, but for a back injury which put her out of cricket altogether in the 1954 season when New Zealand toured England, there might well have been a third. For, just as Maclagan was an undisputed choice for the number 1 slot, so it was when her retirement left Robbie in charge.

The fairly humble beginnings on the 1948-49 tour 'Down Under', where she averaged a combined 20.50 in 8 innings which produced a highest score of 41, were soon faint memories among the triumphs that followed. Two centuries, 105 in 1951 and 102 in 1958 against the Australians, put her in a select group with Myrtle and Rachael Heyhoe-Flint who have done likewise. Both Myrtle and Robbie, however, accomplished the feat with one at home and the other abroad.

At Scarborough in 1951 it was a faultless performance of elegant strokeplay, the hallmark of her batting, that gave Robbie a century in just under 5 hours. In typically modest way she gave the credit to Sussex veterans John and James Langridge. It was their coaching in winter nets that put the sheen on a style that was fashioned by regular attendance at the Alf Gover Cricket School in Wandsworth in earlier years. Of Alf Gover himself Robbie has said that it was not only his coaching but his interest and support that always meant such a lot, and they gave her that essential basis for progress. As a PE teacher at the famous Roedean school for girls, she would certainly know what she was talking about.

In Australia the venue was the attractive Adelaide Oval where England scored their highest innings total of the tour – 325 – and several other records were established. One was Robbie's century, which is the slowest ever recorded by an England player at 375 minutes, but which also produced an England record fifth wicket stand of 119 with Ruth Westbrook in 162 minutes. Ruth scored 66.

Cecilia Robinson, one of England's longest serving vice-captains. The other was Betty Snowball who Robbie replaced as Myrtle Maclagan's opening partner on the tour of 1948-9. Robbie scored two centuries and nearly made it a third when she carried her bat for 96 in the second innings of the only Test match she captained – that in Perth on the 1957-8 tour. Here she pulls a ball to the boundary at The Oval in 1951. The Australian wicketkeeper is Lorna Larter.

It was at Adelaide that Robbie had to take over the captaincy when Mary Duggan retired from the field unwell. She took the entire responsibility for the final Test at Perth and played a fully-fledged Captain's rôle when she scored 96 not out in the second innings and carried her bat through to an England total of 188. With the 35 she scored in the first innings her match average was 131. At both Adelaide and Perth the matches were drawn, resulting in a drawn series.

During the course of the tour, Robbie – always a very good fielder – was requested to desert her usual position at silly or mid-on to become a slip. Largely in that position she took 5 catches in the 3 Test Rubber to finish joint first with Shirley Driscoll. This excellent effort, together with her many good scores made her a leading player on the tour as a whole and put her top of the batting averages in Australia with a splendid 64.00.

ROBINSON, M Cecilia
Kent, East and England
Batting and Fielding

	Tests	Inns	No	Runs	highest	100	50	average	Ct
1948-9 v A	3	6	—	138	41	—	—	23.00	—
1948-9 v NZ	1	2	—	26	25	—	—	13.00	1
1951 v A	3	6	—	201	105	1	—	33.50	1
1957-8 v NZ	2	4	1	131	65	—	1	43.66	—
1957-8 v A	3	5	1	256	102	1	1	64.00	5
1963 v A	2	4	—	77	30	—	—	19.25	2

All Tests Average: **33.16**

ANNE SANDERS

In her first Test match, played against the visiting New Zealanders at Worcester in 1954, Anne came in as bowler to replace Kay Green's leg-spin and was fortunate to find a wicket that suited her off-spin variety beautifully. The result was that she helped reduce the tourists first innings score to a meagre 63 runs – and what is more, did it in style. She did it by taking out the numbers 3, 4 and 6 bats – in a spell of 3 for 8 off 10 overs, 6 of which were maidens. Although that match was drawn, Anne's 4 for 24 total wickets was a very promising start to a career that spanned fifteen years.

A solid bat, whose favourite shot – the leg-glance – could help tot up more runs than appearances indicated, her best performances were on the South African Tour in 1960-61. During that series she went in at a usual 6 or 7 and batting in 5 innings was twice not out with a highest score of 40. It was on this tour too, that Anne turned in her best bowling figures and took most Tour wickets. On the occasion of England's 8 wickets win at Durban, she took 7 match wickets for 69 runs in a total of 56.1 overs with 24 maidens. It was the best match performance of her career and helped to clinch victory in the series. Always a good backer-up to her own bowling, Anne was also a safe close field. She excelled in South Africa by making 8 catches to head the list.

When the Australians toured in 1963, Anne was called up for the final Test at The Oval. In England's first win against the "old adversary" in 5 Tests, she magnificently took 7 match wickets for 75 runs off 53.2 overs, and thus, with her Middlesex colleague and captain Mary

Anne Sanders began her Test career well in taking 4 wickets for 31 runs against New Zealand at The Oval in 1954. Her all-round qualities came to the fore in South Africa in 1960-1. There she forged a record 6th wicket partnership of 77 with Alison Ratcliffe but it was in Jamaica in 1971 that her off-spinners reaped a best match total of 6 for 80. Here, in a Middlesex versus Surrey match, the fielder is Jean Cummins.

Duggan, was responsible for 14 of the 18 wickets that went to the bowlers.

Again, when New Zealand visited in 1966, Anne played in one Test. She made a useful fourth wicket stand of 32 with Edna Barker in her only innings of 21 not out. Her experience of matches against both Australia and New Zealand stood her in good stead for selection to tour 'Down Under' in 1968-69. There she played in 3 of the 6 Tests. This tour was undoubtedly Enid Bakewell's spinning success but when put on to bowl, Anne rarely failed to meet expectations, and could be relied upon to do her utmost to remove the stubborn opponent and hold the crucial catches.

Anne's final appearance for England was at Monymusk against Jamaica in 1971 where she was responsible for 7 wickets in the match with one catch and 6 for 80. That was the only match England won in that three-Test series.

SANDERS, Anne
Middlesex, South and England
Batting and Fielding

	Tests	Inns	No	Runs	highest	average	Ct
1954 v NZ	2	2	1	9	9	9.00	2
1960-1 v SA	4	5	2	85	40★	28.33	8
1963 v A	1	2	—	3	3	1.50	1
1966 v NZ	1	1	1	21	21★	—	1
1968-9 v A	2	4	—	22	16	5.50	—
1968-9 v NZ	1	1	—	10	10	10.00	—
1971 v J	1	0	—	—	—	—	1

All Tests Average: **13.63**

Bowling

	Overs	Balls	Mdns	Runs	Wkts	average
1954 v NZ	42	252	30	31	4	7.76
1960-1 v SA	164.3	987	60	252	17	14.82
1963 v A	53.2	320	23	75	7	10.71
1966 v NZ	25	150	9	26	0	—
1968-9 v A	42	336	8	101	3	33.66
1968-9 v NZ	13	78	1	47	1	47.00
1971 v J	56	336	21	80	6	16.66

All Tests Average: **16.11**

HAZEL SANDERS

Hazel Sanders was one of those individuals who always seemed to pose problems to the bowler and yet was often looked upon by her colleagues – and friends – as one who scored her runs luckily. Now why was this? It was probably because her dreamy personality belied her attacking play and, on deeper analysis, her bat was never close enough to her body for really effective contact to be made with the ball. It meant, of course, that she had a style uniquely her own. It meant, too, that more often than not she stepped away from the ball before crunching it through the covers or lofting it over mid-wicket. Whatever she did though, it was usually quick and effective, or it was fatal.

Her speed of reaction in her favourite fielding position at silly mid-on was also fatal – this time to her opponents. In a career spanning 10 years she shares the record of 15 catches (taken in 12 Tests) which, apart from the wicketkeeping record of Shirley Hodges, is a world best.

As to her batting, in 22 innings she scored two 50s, the first of which showed her total awareness of the cricketing situation and state of the

The sweep and the cut were Hazel Sanders' characteristic shots. Here, in 1951, she plays spinner Betty Wilson effectively and with elegance.

game. In 1949, when playing against New Zealand at Eden Park, she went in at number 7 when England was 73 for 5 and scored an exemplary 54 in 109 minutes. This helped to restore stability to a first innings which eventually reached 204 and ensured victory to England in this only Test by 185 runs. Her second innings not out 26 gave her the leading average of 80.00 for the match. Wicketkeeper Grace Morgan was the runner-up with 22.00, and she and Hazel shared a sixth wicket stand of 75 in that important first innings.

Scarborough in 1951 was the venue for Hazel's second 50 which, though unrecorded, has to be one of the fastest against Australia. Going in at her usual number 6 in the order in the first innings, Hazel joined Cecilia Robinson who was well on her way to a century. When Robbie (105) was out, the fifth wicket partnership had realised 70 runs in 52 minutes. Ten runs and one wicket later, Hazel was run out by Betty Wilson for her 53.

SANDERS, Hazel
Surrey, South and England
Batting and Fielding

	Tests	Inns	No	Runs	highest	100	50	average	Ct
1948-9 v A	3	5	—	40	20	—	—	8.00	1
1948-9 v NZ	1	2	1	80	54	—	1	80.00	2
1951 v A	3	6	—	141	53	—	1	23.50	3
1954 v NZ	2	3	—	31	14	—	—	10.33	4
1957-8 v NZ	2	4	—	23	16	—	—	5.75	4
1957-8 v A	1	2	—	3	2	—	—	1.50	1

All Tests Average: **15.14**

Bowling

	Overs	Balls	Mdns	Runs	Wkts	average
1951 v A	5	30	2	13	0	—

BETTY SNOWBALL

In the realm of men's cricket it appears that no finer tribute can be made to a wicketkeeper than to be likened to the great Australian, W.A.S ('Bert') Oldfield. If this comparison is one where neatness of style and an economy of movement almost undetectable because of an innate sense of anticipation is encapsulated, then it was justly deserved of the women's cricket equivalent in Betty Snowball. And it was none other than the Australian Press which, when she toured with the very first team in 1934-5, gave unstintingly of such praise.

Betty, though, outdid 'Bert' in one respect – her batting. At the height of her career she was a prolific opener and she established the world record for the highest Test score of 189, which took 222 minutes and was made against New Zealand in 1935. Her batting average overall – spanning a period from 1934 to 1948 – was an incredible 40.86 in just 18 innings. Her style, which was not without a flourish or two, she owed to the coaching of the inimitable Learie Constantine who saw to it that she moved her feet to the ball. This made her execution of the cut, one of her favourite shots, a particularly effective stroke at a time when few women had it in their repertoire.

Petite of frame and stature, under Sir Learie's guidance, Betty had her bats specially made by the firm of Lambert's at Nelson in Lancashire. There is an interesting story relating to one of these which recently came to light. A gentleman living not far from her home in Herefordshire telephoned to ask if her father played cricket because he had come across a bat that had both the signature of Learie Constantine and a certain E.A. Snowball on it. Naturally Betty was able to surprise him by saying that *she* was the cricketer and the bat an old friend dating from 1929.

A batting record which has about it the touch of poignancy is her 99

Betty Snowball, a natural when it came to wicketkeeping, makes no mistake in running out Barbara Peden (later Munro) during the first tour of 1934-5.

scored against the Australians at The Oval in 1937. It was the final Test – which England drew to level the series, largely thanks to her batting and the bowling of Joan Davis who took 8 for 86 in the match – and the 99 was a run-out.

But it was no ordinary run-out for her partner who called for the run, anxious that Betty should get her first century against the Australians, was Betty Archdale; and it was Betty A who captained England abroad when Betty S was the Vice-captain and Betty G (Green) was the manager. That – the three Bettys – was itself a unique record for a trio who assured that the Tour of 1934-5 was both a successful and a happy one.

As England's longest-serving Vice-captain, Betty was also deputy to Molly Hide in 1937, at home, and 1948-9 abroad, though on the latter occasion her work as a PE teacher only allowed her to play in the Australian part of the

The spearhead of England's narrow victory by 5 runs in the second Test at Adelaide Oval in 1985, opening bowler Avril Starling took 5 for 36 off 16.5 overs in the second innings. She finished the tour top of the averages with 21 wickets at 20.52 apiece.

tour. She was not, therefore, able to return to the place of her early triumph – that 189 which included 23 boundaries – and celebrate again, with Molly, the memory of their world record second wicket stand of 235 at Lancaster Park in Christchurch, New Zealand.

For all of her Test career in which she opened the innings it was as number 2 to Myrtle Maclagan, and they formed the perfect partnership with Betty's nimble aggression and Myrtle's solid reliability. They were perfectly attuned, too, as wicketkeeper and spin bowler. Betty's admiration for Myrtle's bowling is no more aptly summed up than by the fact that she always felt guilty when she let through 4 byes, but was absolutely devastated when she let through one. And this was because she knew that Myrtle had planned that particular ball, and that now she would have lost the attack against the player of it and would have to start scheming all over again.

Any bowler of worth will know that the wicketkeeper who appreciates her as a tactician is nothing less than a godsend. Very few have the insight allied to the ability to carry it out, but Betty was certainly prime among them. In her 10 Test appearances she claimed 21 victims of which 13 were caught and 8 stumped. Even today, no-one has beaten her record of four stumpings in an innings. This was against Australia at Sydney in 1935, when three of the stumpings were to slow bowler Joy Partridge and the other to pace bowler Mary Spear.

SNOWBALL, Elizabeth A
Lancashire and North, Hampshire and West, and England
Batting and Fielding

	Tests	Inns	No	Runs	highest	100	50	average	Ct / S
1934-5 v A	3	6	3	192	83*	—	2	64.00	4 4
1934-5 v NZ	1	1	—	189	189	1	—	189.00	2 2
1937 v A	3	5	—	191	99	—	1	38.20	6 2
1948 v A	3	6	—	41	22	—	—	6.83	1 —

All Tests Average: **40.86**

Wicketkeeping:	against Australia	against New Zealand
Catches:	11	2
Stumpings:	6	2

AVRIL STARLING

Avril crowned a successful cricketing career when she was chosen for the Test series against the visiting New Zealanders in 1984. A medium-fast bowler with a free high action, Avril did well enough in that series to be selected for the ensuing Golden Jubilee Tour to Australia.

One of the extraordinary features of the New Zealand matches was the number of players on each side who never batted. As a usual number 9 or 10, Avril was inevitably one of those. She certainly bowled though, even opening the bowling with Sarah Potter in the final Test at Canterbury, and her best performance was in the second Test at Worcester where she took 3 for 37 off 20 overs. An overall 6 wickets at 30.33 apiece made Avril the most successful of the faster bowlers.

The livelier Australian wickets seemed to bring out Avril's very best bowling and with a series total of 21 wickets she topped the averages with a fine 20.52. Included among these wickets was the 5 match wickets for 87 in the first test at Perth taken with 53 overs, and the 5 for 100 in the fourth Test at Gosford, off 55 overs. Entirely her supreme performance though was the 6 for 84 off 36.5 overs in the second Test at Adelaide. Not only was this so because the match figures included her best average of 5 for 36, but because it occurred in the second innings of the Test which England won by the very tight margin of 5 runs and Australia was batting last. Altogether a triumphant series for Avril. She even got to bat and made the most of it by being not out more times than any other player!

STARLING, Avril
Lancashire & Cheshire, England
Batting and Fielding

	Tests	Inns	No	Runs	highest	average	Ct
1984 v NZ	3	—	—	—	—	—	1
1984-5 v A	5	9	5	30	9	7.50	2

All Tests Average: **7.50**

Bowling

	Overs	Balls	Mdns	Runs	Wkts	5/I	average
1984 v NZ	107.3	645	51	182	6	—	30.33
1984-5 v A	217.5	1305	88	431	21	1	20.52

All Tests Average: **22.70**

LYNNE THOMAS

Carmarthenshire born Lynne Thomas came into the England side in the second Test against the visiting New Zealand team in 1966 as a replacement spinner and steady number 6 or 7 bat. Her success on that occasion, she scored a maiden half-century in a score of 58, ensured her appearance in the third match and her selection for the 1968-9 Tour to Australia and New Zealand. On that tour she established her usefulness as a bowler, and enhanced her batting reputation with an overall average of 35.71 in 9 innings.

With the self-elected absence of Enid Bakewell from the team which toured Jamaica in 1971, Lynne found her chance to open the innings and did so very effectively creating a first wicket record of 105 with Audrey Disbury and a second wicket record of 154 with Rachael Heyhoe. She excelled in her bowling taking 20 wickets overall at 9.65 apiece to top the averages. Her 5 wickets for 51 in Jamaica's second innings at Sabina Park, was bettered by the 6 for 44 she took in the 2nd innings at Monymusk. In that match, Lynne helped England to her one win – by 10 wickets – of the tour. Lynne's total cull in that occasion was 9 wickets for 61 runs off 61 overs.

Again opening the innings, this time *with* Enid, when Australia toured England in 1976, Lynne added three more half-centuries to

All rounder Lynne Thomas, her off-spin produced 9 for 63 against Jamaica in 1971, is better known as an opening bat. She holds the world record 1st wicket partnership of 164 with Enid Bakewell but never scored a century in her 10 year career.

bring her tally to 7, but still the magic century eluded her. She has, though, the unique distinction of holding, with Enid, the world record highest score of 164 for the first wicket. It was made at Edgbaston in the second innings when Lynne was run out for 90 and Enid went on to be run out for 77. That of itself is a record and, with the first innings partnership of 116 between the pair – in which Lynne was again run out but for 52 and Enid went on to score 75 – making it a century partnership in both innings, it is a record which is unlikely ever to be matched.

THOMAS, Lynne
Glamorgan, West and England
Batting and Fielding

	Tests	Inns	No	Runs	highest	100	50	average	Ct
1966 v NZ	2	4	1	115	58	—	1	38.33	—
1968-9 v A	2	4	—	93	34	—	—	23.25	2
1968-9 v NZ	3	5	2	157	53★	—	1	52.33	2
1971 v J	3	3	—	175	74	—	2	58.33	1
1976 v A	3	5	—	245	90	—	3	49.00	—

All Tests Average: **43.61**

Bowling

	Overs	Balls	Mdns	Runs	Wkts	average	5/I
1966 v NZ	43	258	23	63	1	63.00	—
1968-9 v A	11	88	1	33	1	33.00	—
1968-9 v NZ	64	384	16	135	5	27.00	—
1971 v J	148.4	892	66	193	20	9.65	2
1976 v A	25	150	3	79	0	—	—

All Tests Average: **18.63**

JOAN WILKINSON

When Sergeant Joan Wilkinson ('Wilkie') first played for England she was given leave to do so by the WAAF. She had seen wartime service with them and by the time she had retired that branch of the women's forces had changed its designation to the Women's Royal Air Force (WRAF) and her Test career was long past.

What everyone remembers about Wilkie's cricket is the way she seemed to dance around the popping crease, playing forward to kill spin or drive the ball and, particularly, skipping back to cut the ball anywhere between the slip and cover point. She rarely got bogged down and always gave the bowler something to think about. Herself a tantalising leg-spinner who liked to give the ball plenty of air, she was very effective at breaking up a stubborn partnership and in Test cricket this was her occasional rôle. As a fielder in the silly-mid positions she was extremely difficult to pass. Wherever she played, she was adopted by the crowd and on occasion has been known to offer her bat to any persistent heckler who thought he could do better – much to the amusement of everyone.

On the 1948-9 Tour of Australia and New Zealand she did not bowl at all and her success with the bat was only modest with a highest score of 27 in 6 innings. This pattern was more or less repeated in 1951 against the Australians in England. Against the New Zealanders in 1954

Lancashire lass, Joan Wilkinson's Test career spanned the years 1948 to 1958. She hooked, swept, cut and drove her way to a career best 90 runs in the second Test in Auckland, New Zealand, during the 1957-8 tour. Here she is shown sweeping one to the boundary at The Oval in 1957. The author is at slip.

she wielded her bat very effectively at number 4 or 5 in the order, scoring two 50s in the three match series and finishing top of the batting averages with a very good 46.25 in just 5 innings. Her 51 not out in the second innings at Headingley was instrumental to England's 6 wicket victory.

Her last appearance for her country was on the 1957-8 Tour of New Zealand and Australia where it was against the former that she again produced her best batting and the highest score of her career: A 90 in the second Test at Auckland which gave her the best match average of 58.00.

WILKINSON, Joan
Lancashire, North and England
Batting and Fielding

	Tests	Inns	No	Runs	highest	100	50	average	Ct
1948-9 v A	2	4	—	40	27	—	—	10.00	2
1948-9 v NZ	1	2	—	14	13	—	—	7.00	—
1951 v A	2	4	—	35	20	—	—	8.75	—
1954 v NZ	3	5	1	185	62	—	2	46.25	2
1957-8 v NZ	2	4	—	143	90	—	1	35.75	2
1957-8 v A	3	5	1	19	6	—	—	4.75	1

All Tests Average: **19.81**

Bowling

	Overs	Balls	Mdns	Runs	Wkts	average
1951 v A	13	78	2	50	—	—
1954 v NZ	30	180	9	61	2	30.50
1957-8 v NZ	3	18	0	11	1	11.00
1957-8 v A	14	84	1	53	1	53.00

All Tests Average: **43.75**

AUSTRALIA'S RECORD HOLDERS

MARY ALLITT

One of the remarkable features of Mary Allitt's (now Loy) Test career, which spanned 12 years, was that on her début she lost her wicket to Mary Duggan and on her last appearance she was also out to Duggan. Neither, in 1951, probably had any inkling of the fact that they would end up as opposing captains for the series which closed both Test careers.

From Scarborough in 1951 to Kennington in 1963 saw Mary progress from Vice-captain – she was Una Paisley's deputy when England toured New Zealand and Australia in 1957-58 – to captain but never to change her position in the batting order. Just as she always preferred to field at point, so she was wedded to the opening slot and her solid style was well suited to the position. It was rare for her to fail to score, her strength being a powerful wristy cut through the gully area, but neither did she bring off the spectacular. In fact, it was not until her last Test series that she made a half-century. That, though, was a crucial one which put Australia in a winning position. Indeed they should have won but were

An opening bat whose favoured shot was the cut, Mary Allitt captained Australia on the tour of England in 1963. This was also her most successful series giving her only Test 50 and establishing a world record 6th wicket stand of 125 with Miriam Knee.

robbed of well-deserved victory by a typical Scarborough sea fret.

Although Mary's 76 in that second Test took 281 minutes, until Miriam Knee joined her Australia were desperate for runs at 51 for 5. But her patient defence had its reward and put her in the international records with a sixth wicket partnership of 125 that took 193 minutes. Miriam's eventual score was 82. Certainly her most successful series with the bat, Mary had also forged a first wicket partnership 64 in the first Test at Edgbaston when she made 43 and Lyn Denholm 31. This is still a record for Australia in England.

ALLITT (Loy), Mary
New South Wales and Australia
Batting and Fielding

		Tests	Inns	No	Runs	highest	100	50	average	Ct
1951	v E	3	6	—	79	30	—	—	13.16	—
1957	v NZ	1	1	—	1	1	—	—	1.00	1
1957-8	v E	3	6	—	68	25	—	—	11.33	2
1961	v NZ	1	2	—	33	31	—	—	16.50	—
1963	v E	3	5	—	167	76	—	1	33.40	—

All Tests Average: **17.40**

PEGGY ANTONIO and ANN PALMER

Peggy Antonio and Ann Palmer were together the scourge of England's batting might on the very first tour in 1934-5. They were Australia's bowling counterpart to Myrtle Maclagan. Well Palmer was, for she was the off-spinner in this duo who were Victoria's pride and joy: Antonio was the leg-spinner who could turn the ball both ways.

In the first Test at the Exhibition Ground in Brisbane, Australia elected to bat first and were soon devastated – to the tune of 47 runs – by Myrtle who took 7 for 10 off 17 overs. In reply, England made 154 with Ann taking 7 for 18 off 13.2 overs including Myrtle's wicket when the latter had made 72. Thereafter, except for one occasion, it was Peggy who broke through Myrtle's batting armour.

Although England won the series convincingly, and truly out-batted Australia, the third Test was drawn with Ann taking 3 wickets and Peggy 8 wickets in the match. Between them they were responsible for 22 of England's 34 dismissals overall. It was a very remarkable achievement and seemed to set the standard for Australia's future spin bowling. Only Betty Wilson – another Victorian – has a better analysis than Ann's 7 for 18, and who knows what Ann might have achieved if she had gone on playing. It is nice to know that she was in good form at the Golden Jubilee Dinner held at the Melbourne Cricket Club in January 1985. According to the diary entry, written by tour member Helen Stother for that occasion:

"The speech by ex-player Ann Palmer had to us all in stitches – how moving it was to see them so proudly renewing friendships of 50 years ago."

Peggy went on to tour England in 1937 and in the first Test at Northampton, which Australia won by 31 runs, she took 9 wickets in the match, with a first innings 6 for 51. In the second match, which England won by 25 runs, Peggy had an 8 wicket tally with 5 for 31 in the second innings. In an exciting drawn series Australia showed that they were now a real force on the Test scene.

World War II and marriage saw the end of Peggy's Test career – but not of her interest in cricket. She was on the scene to play against old friends when they toured in 1948-9.

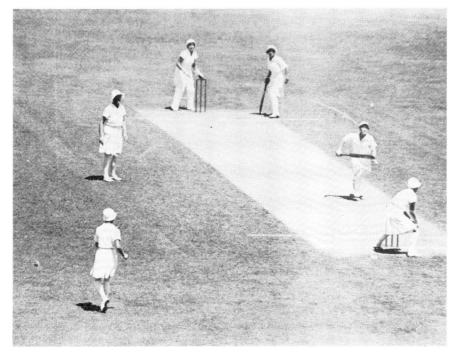

Touch and go for Peggy Antonio who, with Ann Palmer at the other end, put on a spirited 33 in a last wicket stand in the first innings of the second Test at the famous Sydney Cricket Ground in 1935. England's Captain Betty Archdale, and Vice-captain Betty Snowball look expectantly on, but Antonio survived.

ANTONIO (Howard), Peggy
Victoria and Australia
Batting and Fielding

	Tests	Inns	No	Runs	highest	average	Ct
1934-5 v E	3	6	1	61	18★	12.20	—
1937 v E	3	6	—	67	37	11.16	—

All Tests Average: **11.63**

Bowling

	Overs	Balls	Mdns	Runs	Wkts	average	10/M	5/I
1934-5 v E	75.4	454	15	219	12	18.25	—	1
1937 v E	89.2	536	24	212	19	11.15	—	2

All Tests Average: **13.90**

PALMER, Ann
Victoria and Australia
Batting and Fielding

	Tests	Inns	No	Runs	highest	average	Ct
1934-5 v E	3	6	—	92	39	15.33	1

All Tests Average: **15.33**

Bowling

	Overs	Balls	Mdns	Runs	Wkts	average	10/M	5/I
1934-5 v E	46.2	370	9	120	10	12.00	—	1

All Tests Average: **12.00**

MOLLIE DIVE

It was Mollie Dive who, in 1948, became Australia's second captain against a visiting England Touring Team. But she did not enter the Test forum completely new to the game because earlier in that year she had led a very strong side to an overwhelming defeat of New Zealand by an innings and 102 runs. In so doing she not only became the first to beat New Zealand on their home ground, it was at the Basin Reserve in Wellington, but also featured in a second wicket partnership of 96 with opener Amy Hudson.

From those promising beginnings Mollie's sporting and attacking cricket philosophy saw her victorious against Molly Hide's touring side of 1948-9 by a win in the first Test at Adelaide. It was during that three match series that she and Betty Wilson established an Australian record against England. That 123 for the third wicket, in which Mollie scored 51 and Betty made 74, took only 85 minutes, and it gave Mollie her

Mollie Dive, Australia's captain who won and retained the "ashes" in her two-series term.

BELOW . . . batting against England at the Sydney C G in 1949, she turns one to leg. The slips are Joan Wilkinson and Mary Duggan. With Betty Wilson, Mollie holds the record for a 3rd wicket stand of 123.

second Test 50.

When Australia toured England in 1951, Mollie had two captains against whom to deploy her tactical skills: Myrtle Maclagan for the first two and Molly Hide the third. On a tricky wicket at Worcester, it was she and Betty Wilson who stabilised the second innings situation to help Australia to a narrow victory by two wickets. In the final match at The Oval, however, England won by a comfortable margin of 137 runs which, nevertheless, left Australia holding the "ashes". Until Raelee Thompson won the Jubilee Series against England, Mollie was the only Australian captain to have done so, but she remains the only one to have won them and held them in consecutive series.

As a steadfast supporter and actively encouraging communicator on the Australian women's cricketing scene, who is also a devotee of men's Australian Rules Football, it is a delight to know that her rôle as a sportswoman has been recognised. In the rebuilding programme for part of the North Sydney Oval, there is to be a "Mollie Dive Stand".

DIVE, Mollie
New South Wales and Australia
Batting and Fielding

	Tests	Inns	No	Runs	highest	100	50	average	Ct
1948 v NZ	1	1	—	59	59	—	1	59.00	—
1948-9 v E	3	5	—	74	51	—	1	14.80	1
1951 v E	3	5	—	44	33	—	—	8.80	—

All Tests Average: **16.09**

Bowling

	Overs	Balls	Mdns	Runs	Wkts	average
1948-9 v E	16	96	4	22	1	22.00

All Tests Average: **22.00**

DENISE EMERSON

In her first ever Test series, that played against England when they toured Australia in 1984-5. Denise played in all five matches, scored a century with a 121 in the second Test at the Adelaide Oval, made three half-centuries with scores of 84, 84 and 58, and took three catches. This extremely impressive performance by an opening bat whose only representative appearance was in the 1982 World Cup, put her top of the series averages and registered a new Australian first wicket partnership record. Of the 114 made in the fourth test at Gosford, New South

Wales, Peta Verco (Cook) scored 48 and Denise finished with 58.

EMERSON, Denise
Western Australia, New South Wales and Australia
Batting and Fielding

	Tests	Inns	No	Runs	highest	100	50	average	Ct
1984-5 v	5	9	—	453	121	1	3	50.33	3

All Tests Average: **50.33**

LYN FULLSTON

The South Australian spin bowler who, because of her orthodox left handedness has become known, in the typically Australian way of bonhomie as 'Lefty', made her Test début on the tour of India in 1984. Her impact was immediate, as taking 7 match wickets for 95 runs off 52 overs in the first Test at Delhi, showed. No slouch with the bat either, Lyn also made 16 not out batting number 8 in Australia's only innings while numbers 9, 10 and 11 all made ducks.

In the subsequent two Tests Lyn took 3 wickets, added another not out in three fairly modest innings but then finished with a fourth Test flourish. As in the beginning she took 7 match wickets, this time for

161 off a staggering 112.5 overs with 57 maidens, and also ended with two not out scores of 31 in each innings. She thus finished high in the batting averages for that tour with a 63.50.

This excellent run-up to the England tour of Australia later in the year meant certain selection for Lyn and, indeed she played in all five Tests. Together with fast

Denise Emerson, sister of the Australian Cricketer Terry Alderman, is a stylish opening bat. She played her first Test against England in the 1984-5 Jubilee series. She was impressive in scoring a century, three half centuries, and making a record opening partnership of 114 with Peta Verco.

bowler Debbie Wilson she took 19 wickets for the series, giving a best performance of 4 for 53 off 25 overs in the fourth Test at Gosford which Australia won by 117 runs.

Clearly her leg-spin bowling was a continual threat to the England players and, in the fact that she bowled some 90 overs more than any of her colleagues, her Captain saw it the same way. There is no doubt however that, by finishing with a batting average in the middle of the order and taking 5 catches in the series, Lyn is an all-rounder of quality.

FULLSTON, Lyn
South Australia and Australia
Batting and Fielding

	Tests	Inns	No	Runs	highest	average	Ct
1984 v I	4	6	4	127	31★	63.50	5
1984-5 v E	5	7	—	117	29	16.71	5

All Tests Average: **27.11**

Bowling

	Overs	Balls	Mdns	Runs	Wkts	average
1984 v I	240.1	1441	102	395	20	19.75
1984-5 v E	290.3	1743	109	507	19	26.68

All Tests Average: **23.13**

ANNE GORDON

The great force for Australia when England toured under Rachael Heyhoe in 1968-9 was the fast bowling of Victorian Anne Gordon. In the three Test series she bowled exactly 1000 balls - that series had agreed to the old Aussie custom of eight ball overs – took 16 wickets at 16.68 apiece and besides being only the second Australian to take 10 wickets in a match was the first fast bowler so to do.

As well as that magnificent match 10 for 118 at the St Kilda Ground in Melbourne – it was the second Test – Anne also made 19 runs towards an Australian record eighth wicket partnership of 37 with Miriam Knee (96) in her only innings. Needless to say, Anne topped the averages for the number of wickets taken in that series and if further testament to her bowling skill is required, it can be seen in the fact that most of her wickets were those of the upper order bats and most prolific of England's run-getters.

Although she did not play in the Test against New Zealand in 1975, Anne was the obvious choice to captain the side against England when

Left-arm pace bowler and attacking right-hand bat Anne Gordon is seen practising her defence in the Lords net under the discerning eye of Ted Dexter. Anne captained Australia on their tour of England in 1976 and is one of only two fast bowlers ever to take 10 wickets in a match. She did it, 10 for 118, against England at the St Kilda Ground, Melbourne in 1969.

the Australians toured in 1976. By this time a previous injury restricted her own bowling activity and she was second in line to the pace attack of Sharon Tredrea and Raelee Thompson, both of whom were to follow her as captains.

Three records that Anne uniquely holds are: She remains the only Australian captain to take 10 wickets in a match, she was the first to captain a 4-day Test against England, that was at The Oval in 1976, and she was the first to captain Australia against the West Indies. That two Test series preceded the England tour in 1976 and, like the latter, was drawn.

Her final appearance for Australia was in an only Test against India which took place at the WACA in Perth in 1977 and which Australia won by 147 runs. On that occasion Anne stood down from the captaincy in favour of Margaret Jennings.

GORDON, Anne
Victoria and Australia
Batting and Fielding

	Tests	Inns	No	Runs	highest	average	Ct
1968-9 v E	3	3	—	53	26	17.66	3
1976 v WI	2	2	—	27	15	13.50	—
1976 v E	3	5	1	91	38★	22.75	1
1977 v I	1	1	—	24	24	24.00	—

All Tests Average: **19.50**

Bowling

	Overs	Balls	Mdns	Runs	Wkts	10/M	5/I	average
1968-9 v E	125	1000	33	267	16	1	2	16.68
1976 v WI	16	96	5	29	1	—	—	29.00
1976 v E	85	510	33	164	2	—	—	82.00
1977 v I	20	120	7	30	1	—	—	30.00

All Tests Average: **24.50**

AMY HUDSON

In an interesting Test career that began in 1935 and ended in 1951, Amy Hudson's successes seemed to flourish with time. She came in as an opening bat in the final match at Melbourne, the only one that was drawn in the three-game series, and was run out for 16 when batting with her captain Margaret Peden. At that time she was a medium pace bowler who, in the same match, took 1 for 7 until the leg-spinner

Antonio got among the wickets. She came to England in 1937 and once again played in the final Test only. This time her batting position was in the middle of the order (Antonio opened) and she had become a leg-spin bowler who gave the ball plenty of air. When England toured in 1948-9, however, Amy played in all three Tests as the regular opener with Joan Schmidt but bowled little. At that time, Betty Wilson and Myrtle Craddock (later Bayliss) formed the spearhead of the spin attack, and Amy was well down the bowling list. She nevertheless culled a match 5 for 46 at Melbourne (including 3 for 9 off 19 balls) and took some useful wickets at other times: The 3 for 11 off 5 overs in the final Test at Adelaide being followed by her second half-century of the series. It took a Betty Wilson to oust Amy to second place in the batting averages for that series, and that can be no matter for disappointment with a 46.25.

Amy's last trip abroad was in 1951 and the veteran of the party did herself proudly. Perhaps less inclined to the risky shots than hitherto, Australia had cause to be grateful for her staying powers both in the first and last Test: The former for a draw and the latter for respectability in England's 137 run win.

Although she took few wickets in 1951 she did not buy them with runs. In the first Test she got both of England's openers Maclagan (56) and Robinson (105) and then, batting at number 3 made 70 – her highest score of the series. The highest score in her three half centuries, 81 not out, was made at Adelaide Oval in 1949.

With Una Paisley, Amy holds a record 90 for the second wicket scored by Australians on their home ground. This was at Sydney Cricket Ground in 1949.

All-rounder Amy Hudson first played against England in 1934-5. She had a career lasting through five series, never made a century but scored three 50s. Her bowling style changed from medium pace to leg-spin and she could be relied on to take a vital wicket. She is shown playing for New South Wales against Queensland.

HUDSON, Amy
New South Wales and Australia
Batting and Fielding

	Tests	Inns	No	Runs	highest	100	50	average	Ct
1934-5 v E	1	2	—	24	16	—	—	12.00	1
1937 v E	1	2	—	21	11	—	—	10.25	—
1948 v NZ	1	1	—	46	46	—	—	46.00	1
1948-9 v E	3	5	1	185	81*	—	2	46.25	1
1951 v E	3	6	1	172	70	—	1	35.00	—

All Tests Average: **32.21**

Bowling

	Overs	Balls	Mdns	Runs	Wkts	average
1934-5 v E	23	138	11	20	1	20.00
1937 v E	6	36	0	42	0	—
1948 v NZ	14	84	3	38	2	19.00
1948-9 v E	35.1	211	9	78	8	9.75
1951 v E	23.3	141	2	82	5	16.40

All Tests Average: **16.25**

MARGARET JENNINGS

To play in only eight Tests, score a century and two half-centuries and be a partner in 24 dismissals, is an outstanding achievement. In a Test career which lasted just five years, wicketkeeper Margaret Jennings holds this unique record for Australia.

A notable feature of her début in 1972 is that it marked the first time Australia had been beaten by New Zealand in 34 years. Although Margaret's part of things with the bat was not spectacular – she managed only 4 runs in two innings – there was obviously sufficient promise in her wicketkeeping to keep her in the side for the return match at the Basin Reserve in Wellington in 1975. It was an occasion when she added 4 to her previous highest score and maintained her wicketkeeping skills by taking three catches and making one stumping. At the end of this drawn game, Margaret had a tally of 6 catches and 2 stumpings in two Tests.

It was on the tour of England in 1976 that her batting not only matured but gave her an average of 40.40 in 5 innings. Immediately prior to that, though, two Tests in the West Indies (the third was cancelled because of political unrest) saw an average of 28.5 in only two innings, and her place now at number 2 in the order. Margaret also captured another 6 stumpings to aid Marie Lutschini with 4 wickets and Wendy Blunsden with two. Both those Tests were drawn.

In the three Tests in England – all of which were drawn – Margaret scored a 52 and a 104, the 104 being the only century recorded by an Australian wicketkeeper. Once again her keeping was exemplary, she conceded no byes in England's first innings of 134 at The Oval, and resulted in her finishing the series with another 6 catches and 2 stumpings in credit.

Her final Test match against India at Perth in January 1977 was one that she also captained. It provided a win for Australia by 147 runs, a half-century for Margaret, and two more catches behind the stumps.

Margaret Jennings, the only Australian wicketkeeper to have scored a century. Here she has England's Shirley Hodges scrambling for the ball during the second Test at Edgbaston in 1976 when that 104 was made.

JENNINGS, Margaret
Victoria and Australia
Batting and Fielding

	Tests	Inns	No	Runs	highest	100	50	average	Ct / S
1972 v NZ	1	2	—	4	2	—	—	2.00	3 1
1975 v NZ	1	1	—	6	6	—	—	6.00	3 1
1976 v WI	2	2	—	57	30	—	—	28.50	— 6
1976 v E	3	5	—	202	104	1	1	40.40	6 2
1977 v I	1	2	—	72	57	—	1	36.00	2 —

All Tests Average: **28.42**

Wicketkeeping:	against New Zealand	against England
Catches:	6	6
Stumpings:	2	2

JILLIAN KENNARE

The only South Australian ever to captain her country, Jill has more than that cricketing achievement to her credit. This right-handed upper order bat and occasional swing bowler played her first Test against New Zealand in the series of 1979. Her average of 19.25 in 4 innings was not particularly impressive though in the match that Australia won by an innings and 74 runs, the second Test at the Unley Oval, Jill was the second top-scorer with 42.

When Australia toured India in 1984 Jill captained the side and although all four Tests were drawn, the third one at the Gujarat Stadium in Ahmedabad led to a few records. For Jill personally it provided her first century and the score, 131, represents the highest by an Australian to date. Two others in the team also made centuries, opener Peta Verco (was Cook) being run out for 105 and Karen Price not out 104. This was the first time in Test history that three players scored a century in the same, and only, innings. Apart from that the total of 525 is the highest recorded in a three-day Test, the previous highest being in 1935 when England made 503 for 5 declared against New Zealand in Christchurch.

There was not any doubt of Jill's importance in the Australian batting line-up during England's most recent tour of 1984-5. She played in all five matches even though she delivered a "pair" in the second Test at the famous Adelaide Oval. Such wisdom of decision at a time when several changes were made in the Australian side consequent on their losing that Adelaide Test was probably based on the fact that Jill had performed the admirable feat of a century (103) and half-century (56) in the first Test at Perth. The selectors' faith in her ability was rewarded

South Australian Jill Kennare plays a favourite hook shot. She made a pair in the second Test at the Adelaide Oval during England's tour in 1984-5, but maintained her place in the Test side and justified it with a 104 in the ashes-winning match at Bendigo.

when yet another century (104) in the final Test at Bendigo, and a second innings 42, clinched the match and the series in Australia's favour. Despite that "pair", Jill was second only to Denise Emerson in the Australian averages and was the only player on either side to score two centuries.

KENNARE, Jillian
South Australia and Australia
Batting and Fielding

	Tests	Inns	No	Runs	highest	100	50	average	Ct
1979 v NZ	3	4	—	77	42	—	—	19.25	—
1984 v I	4	6	—	278	131	1	1	46.33	1
1984-5 v E	5	9	—	347	104	2	1	38.55	2

All Tests Average: **36.95**

Bowling

	Overs	Balls	Mdns	Runs	Wkts	average
1984 v I	4	24	2	9	1	9.00
1984-5 v E	5	30	6	14	0	—

All Tests Average: **23.00**

MIRIAM KNEE

On her first appearance for Australia, which was against New Zealand in 1961, Miriam had the salutary experience of being lowered in the batting order – from number 8 to 9 – but also had the satisfaction of taking most wickets for her team. This beginning may have indicated that bowling, she was a right arm off-spinner, was to be her strength, or it may have spurred her to improve her batting. Whether or not that was so, however, the fact remains that Miriam became one of Australia's outstanding all-rounders.

When she first played against England, touring in 1963, it was to make a duck in the first innings, but she compensated for it with 25 not out in the second and was again the leading wicket taker. Thereafter, she did not look back and her batting position in the middle of the order was assured.

It was in the fateful second Test at Scarborough, where firstly rain and then mist interfered with play, that Miriam made her highest score of the series. She also had a match analysis of 8 for 57 off 52 overs, which included a 5 for 35 in the first innings. In this match, too, Miriam (82) and captain Mary Allitt, who went on to make 76, established Australia's sixth wicket record partnership of 125. Australia had only one innings in this drawn Test and it was a match she was unlucky not to win.

It was undoubtedly the series against the England Touring Team of 1968-9 that saw Miriam at her best. She scored two more half-centuries, missing out on a century by just 4 runs, and had another 8 wicket match in the first Test with a 5 for 49 in the first innings. As in England in 1963, she finished top of the bowling averages, but on this occasion also topped the batting and registered another partnership record. It was 37 for the eighth wicket during her 96 at Melbourne, and her partner was Anne Gordon who made 19.

Having been Australia's Vice-captain in 1968-9, Miriam was the obvious choice to captain the team chosen to play against New Zealand at Melbourne in 1972. It was Miriam's last appearance for her country and the team contained eight newcomers to Test cricket. After dismissing New Zealand cheaply in the first innings (89), the visitors rallied in the second (335) and beat the home side by 143 runs. It was the first time Australia had lost to New Zealand and it was the first ever 4 day Test.

Miriam is fourth in the league of Australia's wicket-takers with 35 to her credit but has played in fewer Tests than those above her. Her matches against England resulted in very good figures, with a batting average of 37.88 and a bowling average of 14.83.

KNEE, Miriam
Victoria and Australia
Batting and Fielding

	Tests	Inns	No	Runs	highest	100	50	average	Ct
1961 v NZ	1	2	—	14	10	—	—	7.00	—
1963 v E	3	5	1	118	82	—	1	29.50	2
1968-9 v E	3	5	1	185	96	—	2	46.25	2
1972 v NZ	1	2	—	2	2	—	—	1.00	—

All Tests Average: **26.58**

Bowling

	Overs	Balls	Mdns	Runs	Wkts	average	10/M	5/I
1961 v NZ	55	330	16	81	4	20.25	—	—
1963 v E	126.4	760	45	228	16	14.25	—	1
1968-9 v E	121	968	46	217	14	15.50	—	1
1972 v NZ	27	216	9	44	1	44.00	—	—

All Tests Average: **16.28**

JANNETTE LUMSDEN

The New South Wales strong upper order bat Jan Lumsden made her Test début for Australia in the 1976 season during which an exacting two-tour programme took in the West Indies and England. While her two innings in the drawn Tests against the West Indians brought her an encouraging 34.50 average, it was her performance in England which produced a memorable century and put her among the top class of Australia's batting élite.

The first Test at Old Trafford saw a maiden half-century (65) against the home side and a match average of 37.00, and at Edgbaston two solid scores keeping her average in the 30s helped to frustrate England's attempts at a decision. The ensuing stalemate led to the historic Oval Test in which 4 days were scheduled for play. England, having gone cheaply on the first day faced a 240 run deficit – to which Jan contributed more than her fair share with an innings of 123 in a total of 379 which included 6 extras.

During her 258 minute innings, Jan had a fifth wicket partnership of 66 with Wendy Hills (28) and a sixth wicket stand of 93 with Sharon Tredrea, who went on to make 63. The former remains a record for Australia in England. It is unlikely that Jan will forget her dismissal by bowler Jackie Court, to a tricky catch on the leg-side by wicketkeeper Shirley Hodges, with the penultimate ball on Monday, 26 July, 1976. Her consolation was to head the batting averages for that series with a noble 52.00.

Jannette Lumsden batting against England in 1976. This was the best season of Jan's short career and saw a fine 123 scored in the final test at The Oval. Having dismissed England cheaply – for 134 – on the first day, Australia replied with a splendid 379. The wicketkeeper is Shirley Hodges and June Stephenson is at short leg.

The batting and off-spin bowling of Miriam Knee reached the record books boths abroad and at home. Though she didn't make a century – her highest was 96, she shares a record century partnership with Mary Allitt. She twice took 5 wickets in an innings and has a best match analysis of 8 for 57 against England at Scarborough in 1963. She again took 8 match wickets against England at Thebarton Oval, Adelaide, in 1968-9. On that occasion she also scored a half-century.

LUMSDEN, Jannette
New South Wales and Australia
Batting and Fielding

	Tests	Inns	No	Runs	highest	100	50	average	Ct
1976 v WI	2	2	—	69	42	—	—	34.50	—
1976 v E	3	5	—	260	123	1	1	52.00	3
1977 v I	1	1	—	16	16	—	—	16.00	1

All Tests Average: **43.13**

Bowling

	Overs	Balls	Mdns	Runs	Wkts	average
1976 v E	11	66	7	19	0	—
1977 v I	5	30	2	4	0	—

UNA PAISLEY

In her first Test for Australia, in New Zealand in 1948, Una scored a century and in her first Test as captain, against New Zealand in 1957, she did it again. In a career spanning 13 years and 12 tests, however, making a century against England was to elude her. But her success in the 9 Tests she played against the 'Old Country' came in other ways. She did not lose the three she captained, and she still – since Adelaide in 1949 – holds Australia's record fourth wicket partnership of 115 with Betty Wilson. Her share of the partnership was 46, having gone in when Australia was 19 for 3 in the first innings.

No mean bowler who could flight and spin the ball, Una was very successful in breaking up stubborn partnerships and taking that crucial wicket. In the drawn second Test against England at Melbourne in 1949, she took 3 first innings wickets for 10 runs off 8 overs, 5 of which were maidens. This was her finest performance, but in her last appearance for Australia against New Zealand at Dunedin in 1961, Una finished with the best analysis of 3 for 43 off 29 overs. It included the dismissal of opening bat Joyce Powell (was Clothier) who was top scorer with 63.

Though short and stocky in physique, Una was an alert and safe fielder who moved quickly to the ball and had a good accurate throw. She finished well up in the order of number of catches held, and a particularly memorbale one was that off Hudson's spin to dismiss century-maker Cecilia Robinson in the Scarborough Test of 1951.

During her period of captaincy she proved to be a good tactician and her opposing captains were New Zealand's Rona McKenzie and England's Mary Duggan. She remains the only home captain in

Una Paisley (R) padding up for net practice at Lords with fellow tourist Joan Schmidt during the Australian visit to England in 1951. Although Una scored two centuries neither was against England. With Betty Wilson, she holds the international record of 163 for the fourth wicket made at Wellington against New Zealand in 1948.

women's cricket to have a Test match completely washed out by rain. This occurred against England at Sydney in February 1958.

PAISLEY, Una
Victoria and Australia
Batting and Fielding

	Tests	Inns	No	Runs	highest	100	50	average	Ct
1948 v NZ	1	1	—	108	108	1	—	108.00	1
1948-9 v E	3	4	—	143	46	—	—	35.75	2
1951 v E	3	5	—	33	15	—	—	6.60	2
1957 v NZ	1	1	—	101	101	1	—	101.00	—
1957-8 v E	3	4	—	66	29	—	—	16.50	2
1961 v NZ	1	2	—	20	15	—	—	10.00	—

All Tests Average: **27.70**

Bowling

	Overs	Balls	Mdns	Runs	Wkts	average
1948 v NZ	10	60	4	11	1	11.00
1948-9 v E	53.3	321	16	108	6	18.00
1951 v E	70	420	10	165	6	27.75
1957 v NZ	2	12	0	9	0	—
1957-8 v E	63	378	21	100	3	33.33
1961 v NZ	29	174	11	43	3	14.33
All Tests Average: **22.94**						

MARGARET PEDEN

Once Australia's first captain realised how much her team was out-classed by the all-round superior technique of the visiting England players at Brisbane, what a task to instil courage and a sense of purpose in her side for the remaining two Tests. Some of lesser inner strength might well have quailed at the challenge but not so Margaret Peden. Her testament of success showed itself in the fact that after two heavy defeats by 9 and 8 wickets, the third Test in Melbourne was a well fought draw. Not only that but when, in 1937, she captained the first Australian side to tour England her win by 31 runs in the first Test at Northampton was a vindication of mutual faith between herself and her team: Apart from herself, five of that victorious team played against England in 1934–5.

Margaret was a steady bat whose preferred position was as opener, though she would adapt it to suit both the situation and the talents of her players. Thus, her record in twelve innings reads: 7, 7, 8, 10, 2, 10, 2, 2, 1, 1, 9, 1, 1, where the lower order positions were often match saving ones.

Though she has no remarkable scores to her name, the highest being a 34 scored at Northampton where she opened with Peggy Antonio who scored a duck and left Australia 0 for 1, that consolidating innings led to an all-time record. Hazel Pritchard, one of the pioneer players was the number 3 and when Margaret went, lbw to opposing captain Molly Hide, 127 was on the scoreboard. It formed the first ever century partnership for Australia in an innings which, at 300, was the highest.

Another triple century innings (302) was made by her team at Blackpool in a tight match that England won by 25 runs. The final Test at The Oval was thus crucial. Unfortunately after making 10 in the first, Margaret made a duck in her second, and last, Test innings. But, according to England's wicketkeeper Betty Snowball, it was a duck that never should have been. Betty maintains that Margaret did not

Australia's first cricket captain and lifetime supporter of women's sport, Margaret Peden (L) tosses with Molly Hide at Blackpool in 1937. Having led Australia to a first ever victory at Northampton by 31 runs, this second Test levelled the series when England had an equally exciting win by 25 runs. With Hazel Pritchard, Mrs Peden still holds Australia's 2nd wicket record of 127.

touch the ball she caught and for which it seemed that all the team except herself appealed. The Umpire gave it out and what would anyone of Margaret Peden's sporting calibre do? Why, accept it of course. A memorable Captain and lady, to whom Australia's women cricketers owe much.

PEDEN, Margaret
New South Wales and Australia
Batting and Fielding

	Tests	Inns	No	Runs	highest	average	Ct
1934-5 v E	3	6	2	32	11	8.00	—
1937 v E	3	6	—	55	34	9.16	—
All Tests Average: **8.70**							

MURIEL PICTON

Slow bowler and useful lower order bat Muriel Picton first captained Australia against New Zealand in that country in 1961, was then Vice-captain to Mary Allitt in England in 1963 and finally was her successor to lead the side against the touring England squad of 1968-69. A unique feature of her career was that all Tests she captained were drawn, as were all seven of the matches in which she played.

A quiet and unassuming person, it was when England toured in 1968-9 that Muriel's underlying determination to play positive but sensible cricket came to the fore. She was, perhaps, the ideal choice for

This picture of off-spinner Muriel Picton ended in success when Ruth Westbrook was caught at slip by Marjorie Marvel. It was taken at The Oval in 1963 when Muriel was Australia's Vice-captain. She led Australia when England toured in 1968–9.

Karen Price, the first part-time professional Development Officer with the Australian Women's Cricket Council, is one of the few Australian's to take 10 wickets in a match and to have scored a century. Both were achieved when, as Australia's Vice captain, she toured India in 1984.

Australia as opposite number to the effervescent Rachael Heyhoe on her first captaincy abroad.

In drawing that series Australia were a team that provided several unusual records. Fast bowler Anne Gordon took ten wickets in the second Test at Melbourne and pace bowler Lorraine Kutcher, batting at number 7 in the third test at North Sydney, scored the only half-century of her career and followed it with 5 wickets for 49 in England's first innings. Lyn Denholm, Miriam Knee and Dawn Newman scored two half-centuries apiece and Jan Parker (Wady), Elaine Bray and Joyce Goldsmith made one each. Clearly Muriel had the capacity to bring the best out of her team.

In a career that ended with that satisfactory series, Muriel herself had a best match bowling performance of 3 for 51 off 23 overs in the first Test at Edgbaston in 1963. Her highest score was a 29 in the Second Test at the ill-fated Scarborough match of 1963, and to that occasion she owes her Australian record 53 for the ninth wicket when her partner Helen Lee ended with a not out 25.

PICTON, Muriel
New South Wales and Australia
Batting and Fielding

	Tests	Inns	No	Runs	highest	average	Ct
1961 v NZ	1	2	1	31	19★	31.00	1
1963 v E	3	5	—	57	29	11.40	1
1968-9 v E	3	4	3	23	12★	23.00	3

All Tests Average: **15.85**

Bowling

	Overs	Balls	Mdns	Runs	Wickets	average
1961 v NZ	35	210	11	49	0	—
1963 v E	68	408	20	160	7	22.85
1968-9 v E	25	200	2	96	1	96.00

All Tests Average: **38.12**

KAREN PRICE

An extraordinary mark of Karen Price's début Test, against New Zealand at the Basin Reserve, Wellington, in 1975, was that she made the lowest score in her team's highest ever innings total of 362. On an occasion when nearly everybody on both sides made a few – it was a 4-day Test – and the average Australian score was about 35, Karen contributed just the two. Whether her reputation of being unpredict-able stemmed from that time or not, it is a fact that she had the knack of mixing the very good with the indifferent. She was a pace bowler too, however, and so always had the chance to "come good" during a match. In her first Test though, this talented all-rounder was not asked to bowl.

Karen's chance to realise that latent potential came in 1976 with the touring side that took in the West Indies on the way to England. Even then, Karen had to wait because she was not included in either of the two Tests in Jamaica nor the first two Tests in England. It was The Oval wicket that first felt her impact – she took 5 match wickets for 55 after a first innings 3 for 6 – but little contact was made with the ball. In that respect Karen halved her previous highest score in being run out for 1.

Perhaps it began to seem that Karen's Test career was to be short-lived, though in actual playing experience it stemmed from Junior representation in 1970. She was not called when India visited Australia in 1977, nor did she play against New Zealand in 1979. Her chance finally came when Australia went to India for a three-day, four-Test series in 1984.

In the first Test she batted 10 and 2 and made a "pair". In India's first innings though she opened the bowling and took 4 for 52. The second Test at Lucknow was a bowling triumph in which Karen became only the third Australian to take 10 wickets in a match. She followed a first innings 6 for 72 with 4 for 35. In the final Test at Ahmedabad Karen made a not out 104 in Australia's only innings which totalled 525 and in which two others also made centuries. Since all the matches to that time were drawn the final Test was played over 4 days. It too was drawn.

England toured Australia for the Jubilee Series of 1984-5 and when the captain and opening bowler Sharon Tredrea was injured after the first Test, Karen replaced her for two matches and was then dropped. She took a total of 5 wickets at 23.60 apiece and had three innings in which she averaged 36.00 and scored an half-century 51.

In what can only be described as a uniquely chequered Test career, Karen did well to achieve the two pinnacles aimed at by any all-rounder: Ten match wickets and a century.

PRICE, Karen
New South Wales and Australia
Batting and Fielding

	Tests	Inns	No	Runs	highest	100	50	average	Ct
1975 v NZ	1	1	—	2	2	—	—	2.00	—
1976 v E	1	1	—	1	1	—	—	1.00	—
1984 v I	4	7	1	167	104*	1	—	27.83	1
1984-5 v E	2	3	—	108	51	—	1	36.00	2

All Tests Average: **25.27**

Bowling

	Overs	Balls	Mdns	Runs	Wkts	10/M	5/I	average
1976 v E	50.2	302	29	55	5	—	—	11.00
1984 v I	151	906	44	365	16	1	—	22.81
1984-5 v E	86	516	38	118	5	—	—	23.60

All Tests Average: **20.69**

HAZEL PRITCHARD

Hazel Pritchard was a pioneering Test player and opening bat whose obvious batting quality was somewhat inhibited by Myrtle Maclagan's devastating spin on the very first Tour of 1934-5. In those three Tests, which were virtually three half-days of play, her six innings read: 4, 20, 0, 0, 5 and 5. Four times she was out to Maclagan, who was also responsible for the notorious "pair" in the second Test at Sydney. But undaunted by all this, Hazel came through to be included in Australia's team making its first tour of England in 1937.

That things were very different on this occasion has been recorded by the gallant Major, one C.H.B. Pridham who, after the final Test at The Oval wrote in the July issue of *The Cricketer* that: Miss H. Pritchard ". . . has earned the title of the Australian lady Bradman. This is no idle complement. She attacks the bowling all the time she is at the wicket, and drove the first ball she received past extra-cover for 4. About the same height as Miss Snowball, she has a most pleasing personality. The sight of Miss Pritchard at the wicket with Miss Snowball behind the stumps, is a delightful picture of feminine grace; comparable with the lawn tennis memory of Senorita Lili d'Alvarez, when the latter was in her prime. Miss Pritchard takes obvious pleasure in her cricket and bats with joyous abandon."

That day Hazel made 66 runs in 70 minutes which included ten boundaries and, for the only time in the series, was bowled by Maclagan! It was a fine conclusion to a tour which produced three half-

Between 1934 and 1937, Hazel Pritchard became a transformed player. She never made a century, her highest score was 87 against England at Northampton in 1937, but was hailed in the Press as "The Woman Bradman".

centuries, the nearest she came to the full century was an 87 in the first Test at Northampton, and a top tour average of 51.00. To this day she holds the second wicket parnership record of 127 with Margaret Peden.

PRITCHARD, Hazel
New South Wales and Australia
Batting and Fielding

	Tests	Inns	No	Runs	highest	100	50	average	Ct
1934-5 v E	3	6	—	34	20	—	—	5.66	—
1937 v E	3	6	—	306	87	—	3	51.00	1

All Tests Average: **28.33**

KATHLEEN SMITH

It was home ground for the Queensland Captain Kath Smith when she played in the very first Test against England, which began on 28 December 1934. For this left-arm opening bowler who batted right-

Redoubtable left arm pace bowler and forceful right-hand bat, Queensland's Kath Smith, kept Australia's batting respectable in the 1934-5 series. Here she is seen batting at Northampton in 1937 when she made a first innings top score of 88. The bowler is Eileen Whelan next to Umpire Kathleen Doman, Joyce Haddelsey is in the gully, Betty Belton at slip and the wicketkeeper is Betty Snowball. Kath's partner is fast bowler Nell McLarty.

handed, it was a début that indictaed what an asset Australia had in its Vice-captain when she made a forceful top-scoring 25 runs out of a first innings total of 47. What is more, out of only 5 boundaries scored in the match as a whole, Kath scored three: The others were scored by England's Myrtle Maclagan and Molly Hide.

England won the series comfortably but the Australians improved with every game and Kath was unlucky not to make a half-century, falling just three short of that target in the second Test at Sydney. Even on that occasion, however, she scored over half her runs in boundaries. In fact, only Essie Shevill managed to pass the 50 mark, and that was in the second innings at Brisbane where she made a not out 63. Though this feat put Essie top of the averages at 22.00, Kath was a close second with 20.16 from her 6 innings. Considering, too, that England totted up over 800 runs (play was a three-afternoon affair in those days) and that England only lost 30 wickets overall, her 7 wickets for 25.00 apiece was a fine effort.

No wonder then that Kath was a certainty for the tour to England in 1937. And, in the very first Test at Northampton she not only made the top first-innings score, but she achieved that elusive half-century in a magnificent 88. She also, in a line-up which included the renowned fast bowlers Nell McLarty and Mollie Flaherty, took 4 wickets for 50 runs in the second innings – her best average – to help Australia to her 31 run victory.

Another half-century 63 at Blackpool and a near-miss 45 at The Oval once again saw this powerful all-rounder well up in the batting averages for the series.

SMITH, Kathleen
Queensland and Australia
Batting and Fielding

	Tests	Inns	No	Runs	highest	100	50	average	Ct
1934-5 v E	3	6	—	121	47	—	—	20.16	1
1937 v E	3	6	—	214	88	—	2	35.66	1

All Tests Average: **27.91**

Bowling

	Overs	Balls	Mdns	Runs	Wkts	average
1934-5 v E	66	396	11	175	7	25.00
1937 v E	109	654	28	235	6	39.16

All Tests Average: **31.53**

RAELEE THOMPSON

The most fascinating aspect of Raelee's Test career is that her major triumph arose out of another's misfortune. It was bad luck that Sharon Tredrea, Raelee's Victorian team-mate and co-opening bowler on many an occasion, wrenched her Achilles tendon in the first Test of the Jubilee Series at Perth. The match was drawn and the chance to go on to win was denied Sharon who remained unfit for selection in the other four Tests. Her deputy did her proud, however. Raelee not only won the Test series but also registered an all-time first in winning the last two of them to make it a 2-1 result with two Tests drawn.

1984-5 was the era of the innovative marathon 5-Test series, with each match of four-day duration, and the climax of Raelee's career. Interestingly enough, at the Melbourne St Kilda ground in 1972, it was also a four-day game that marked her début. Another first then gave victory to a New Zealand team led by Trish McKelvey, and Raelee's part in the opening attack with Tina McPherson of New South Wales, was to take one match wicket for 65 runs. She was top scorer in Australia's second innings with 25, though, and accomplished that batting feat at a lowly number 8.

The "return" match with New Zealand at the Basin Reserve in Wellington took place in 1975. With newcomer Sharon Tredrea, Raelee was responsible for 12 of the 16 wickets that went to the bowlers, and for the first time she had taken 5 wickets in a Test. They cost her 24.8 apiece off a total of 77.4 overs. In all, though the match was drawn, this Test was something of a success story for the Victorians with Lorraine Hill scoring a maiden not out century in her 118.

The big tour for the Australians in the 70s was that to England in 1976 which included a two-Test sortie in the West Indies. Both matches, a return to the three-day variety, were drawn on wickets that favoured spin bowling, and Marie Lutschini in particular made good use of the fact.

The extremely hot English summer of 1976 gave rise to wickets that were as near to their Australian counterparts as it is likely to get, but apparently without the accompanying pace. Not the first Test though. That took place at Manchester's Old Trafford, where rain and gloomy conditions assisted the Thomspon swing to a best innings analysis of 3 for 79 off 36 overs. At Edgbaston, Raelee notched up another first innings 3, this time for 42, to end with a match total of 3 for 99. In both of Australia's innings she was not out, accumulating 10 runs. It was the final Test at The Oval that gave Raelee her best analysis overall with 4 match wickets for 54 runs and she finished as Australia's

Fast bowler Raelee Thompson played for her country from 1972 to 1984 and captained the side for four of the five Jubilee Tests. The latter provided a triple triumph when she took 5 wickets in an innings for the first time, topped the bowling averages and won the ashes for Australia after a gap of 35 years.

chief wicket-taker for the series.

An intervening only Test against India at the WACA ground in Perth in 1977, which Australia won by 147 runs and which gave Raelee 6 match wickets for 66 runs, made this outstanding Australian medium-fast bowler the most internationally represented player. Two years later, her career continued with appearances against New Zealand for the third time. In a full three match series, each of four days duration, which took place in Australia, Raelee was runner-up to Sharon in the wicket-taking stakes: Against Sharon's 16, Raelee took 14. In the second Test at the Unley Oval in Adelaide, which Australia won by an innings and 74 runs, Raelee took 8 match wickets for 31 in 31 overs. But even yet, the coveted bag of five wickets in an innings eluded her.

All this changed against the visiting England tourists in 1984-5. In what was to prove her most triumphant hour, this Melbourne police-woman did it at a time when it was most needed. She took 5 for 33 in the first innings in the final Test at Bendigo off 28 overs, and she removed her opposing top-scoring captain Jan Southgate with a caught and bowled for 59. This undoubtedly paved the way for the clinching of that historic series in Australia's favour.

THOMPSON, Raelee
Victoria and Australia
Batting and Fielding

	Tests	Inns	No	Runs	highest	average	Ct
1972 v NZ	1	2	—	33	25	16.50	—
1975 v NZ	1	1	1	13	13	13.00	1
1976 v WI	2	2	1	12	9*	12.00	—
1976 v E	3	4	3	26	14	26.00	3
1977 v I	1	1	—	7	7	7.00	4
1979 v NZ	3	4	2	14	5	7.00	—
1984-5 v E	5	8	2	57	24	9.50	4

All Tests Average: **12.46**

Bowling

	Overs	Balls	Mdns	Runs	Wkts	average	10/M	5/I
1972 v NZ	33	264	10	65	1	65.00	—	—
1975 v NZ	77.4	466	31	124	5	24.80	—	—
1976 v WI	41	246	13	108	3	36.00	—	—
1976 v E	140	840	62	232	10	23.20	—	—
1977 v I	38	228	9	66	6	11.00	—	—
1979 v NZ	132	1056	65	162	14	11.57	—	—
1984-5 v E	188	1128	86	238	18	15.72	—	1

All Tests Average: **17.46**

SHARON TREDREA

Billed as the fastest bowler in women's cricket when at the age of 22 she toured England in 1976, Sharon's opening partner was Raelee Thompson who, at the same time, appealed to the Press because of the similarity in name to the famous Australian Jeff Thomson. Of the two, however, there was no doubt that Sharon was pacier and when eight years later Raelee took over the captaincy because Sharon was injured, she took on the rôle of change bowler. Even without Sharon, Australia was fortunate in having a choice among several quality players to open the bowling.

In England Sharon reinforced the all-round qualities that she had already shown in her first Test against New Zealand the year before. On that occasion, with 7 match wickets for 171 and a score of 45 in her one innings, her potential was evident. The three-Test series in England provided an average of 38.33, which included a 63 in the final match at The Oval. Her success with the ball was only moderate, however, despite that fact that, more than many a season, the wickets were almost akin to those of Australia in that excessively hot, dry summer.

Her second Test series against New Zealand, when for the first time a full three matches were arranged of 4-day duration, saw Sharon as Australia's captain. It was marked by a team which contained six new players for the first Test and by the fact that every player had a bowl. Very satisfactorily for her, Australia won the series – with a win by an innings and 74 runs at the Unley Oval in Adelaide – and Sharon had her best season with the ball taking 16 wickets at 13.56 apiece to be the leading wicket-

Deprived of the full-captaincy in 1984-5 by an ankle injury, all-rounder Sharon Tredrea had a ten-year playing span for Australia. This bowler of real pace in her prime has a best series average of 13.56, against New Zealand in 1979, and a best innings performance of 4 for 22. Her one half-century was scored against England at The Oval in 1976. The Umpire in the picture taken at Lords in 1976 is Isabel Nowell-Smith.

taker.

It was unfortunate that injury prevented this fine player from leading her country in more than one Test of the Jubilee Series in 1984-5. At least she could rejoice that Raelee, her Victorian colleague and erstwhile opening partner, carried on the winning tradition.

TREDREA, Sharon
Victoria and Australia
Batting and Fielding

		Tests	Inns	No	Runs	highest	100	50	average	Ct
1975	v NZ	1	1	—	45	45	—	—	45.00	2
1976	v WI	2	2	—	56	34	—	—	28.00	—
1976	v E	3	5	2	115	63	—	1	38.33	1
1979	v NZ	3	4	—	89	36	—	—	22.25	4
1984-5	v E	1	2	—	41	27	—	—	20.50	2

All Tests Average: **28.83**

Bowling

		Overs	Balls	Mdns	Runs	Wkts	average
1975	v NZ	66	396	17	171	7	24.42
1976	v WI	33	198	8	105	0	—
1976	v E	149	894	68	247	6	41.46
1979	v NZ	106.6	854	36	217	16	13.56
1984-5	v E	19	114	4	44	1	44.00

All Tests Average: **26.13**

PETA VERCO

Not too many Western Australians have reached the pinnacle of representing their country as has Peta Verco (was Cook), and her successes should provide the inspiration for many to follow. This right-handed opening bat and good medium-slow bowler has achieved much in a Test career that started with the one match against India in her home State, at the WACA ground in Perth, in 1977.

As her bowling was of the medium pace variety and her main rôle was to open the bowling, Peta's first innings was at a lowly number 9 in the order. Her success with the ball was moderate – 2 wickets for 31 runs off 17 overs in the match – but combined with her 26 not out there was much obvious potential.

In 1979 Peta opened the batting in all three Tests against the touring New Zealanders but, except for a 68 in the second innings at Melbourne's Albert Ground – the venue of the last Test – she made

One century, four half-centuries, 12 catches and a total of 21 Test wickets mark the achievement of this talented all-rounder who played in 13 Tests from 1977 to 1984-5. With Denise Emerson, she has two century partnerships, the 114 at Gosford in 1985 proving an Australian record.

relatively few runs. That experience heralded real achievement nevertheless, and her talent positively matured in 1984. Firstly against India, and then England, Peta was an established opener and a *tour de force* for her team.

Successive scores of 81, 67, 34 and 105, 78 and 2 resulted in an astounding series against India. Her selection for all 5 Tests against England saw equally impressive batting which led to an average of 30.00. Two century partnerships with Denise Emerson led to an outright first wicket record of 114 at Gosford. Peta made 48 and Denise 56 of those runs.

In the bowling department her off-spin variety led to 9 wickets at 21.00 apiece and she held a record 6 catches to match the feat of wicketkeeper Chris Matthews.

VERCO, Peta
Western Australia and Australia
Batting and Fielding

		Tests	Inns	No	Runs	highest	100	50	average	Ct
1977	v I	1	1	1	26	26*	—	—	—	—
1979	v NZ	3	4	—	102	68	—	1	25.50	3
1984	v I	4	6	—	286	105	1	3	47.67	3
1984-5	v E	5	9	—	270	48	—	—	30.00	6

All Tests Average: **36.00**

Bowling

	Overs	Balls	Mdns	Runs	Wkts	average
1977 v I	17	102	6	31	2	15.50
1979 v NZ	71	568	30	132	7	18.85
1984 v I	93	558	36	140	3	46.67
1984-5 v E	132.4	796	57	189	9	21.00
All Tests Average: **23.43**						

NORMA WHITEMAN

The eighteen-year-old fast bowler Norma Whiteman made her début for Australia in 1948 when one Test was played against New Zealand in Wellington. Although scoring just 2 runs and taking one wicket on that occasion – it was that of top scorer Joan Hatcher (23) – there were better things to come. But, that she was not a mere opening bowler who could bat a bit was highlighted by the three catches she took in the match. In fact Norma was a bowler of real pace who could move the ball in the air and had a beautifully free action. She was also a good striker of the ball and a very fine fielder whose usual position was mid-on.

When England toured in 1948-9, Norma was a certainty for selection, pairing up with Alma Vogt in the first, and Mollie Flaherty in the other two Tests. It was the first Test at Adelaide, which Australia won by 186 runs, that produced her best performance on the field. She took 5 wickets in the match for 50 runs off 31 overs and, in the second innings, had a hand in 6 wickets – bowling four and catching two.

In the drawn second Test at Melbourne Norma shared an eighth wicket first innings partnership of 34 with Joyce Christ (44) in 17 minutes, and went on to score a 30 that contained four boundaries. Hers was the last wicket to fall in Australia's total of 265. That score saw her promoted to number 6 in the second innings and she responded with 14 not out. An overall average of 35.00 was no mean feat to accompany her 9 wickets and 4 catches in the three match series.

Norma's last season of Test cricket was the 1951 tour of England where, once again, her all round cricketing qualities were of great value to her country. In the drawn match at Scarborough it was she who managed to stay 23 minutes with Betty Wilson (81) and establish an eighth wicket record partnership of 28 for Australia in England in that time. Her own contribution was 10 runs, but they were a vital ten in a spell when England looked to be doing better than finishing with a first innings lead of 35.

When Australia won by two wickets at Worcester, Norma's rôle was

Norma Whiteman was not only the fast bowler of the era, 1948-1951, but a fine all-rounder. In just seven tests she took 22 wickets, 12 catches and had a batting average of 25.16. Here she is bowling at The Oval in 1951, with Umpire Edith Stevenson just in view.

one where she took 5 match wickets for 82 off 42 overs, scored 25 not out batting at her usual number 9 in the order and took 4 catches of which 3 were in the first innings.

England won at The Oval by 137 runs to square the series. But it was there that Norma made 36 not out and was thus Australia's first innings top scorer. She also took 5 match wickets for 82 off 46 overs and brought off two catches. The former gave her 12 wickets in the series and a career tally of 21 wickets against England. Her total of 5 catches in the series and 12 catches overall makes her the top Australian fielder for just 7 Tests played.

WHITEMAN, Norma
New South Wales and Australia
Batting and Fielding

	Tests	Inns	No	Runs	highest	average	Ct
1948 v NZ	1	1	—	2	2	2.00	3
1948-9 v E	3	4	2	70	30	35.00	4
1951 v E	3	5	2	79	36*	26.33	5

All Tests Average: **25.16**

Bowling

	Overs	Balls	Mdns	Runs	Wkts	average
1948 v NZ	27	162	15	20	1	20.00
1948-9 v E	104	624	42	169	9	18.77
1951 v E	141.3	849	45	263	12	21.91

All Tests Average: **20.54**

BETTY WILSON

Undoubtedly Australia's greatest all-rounder, and probably the finest woman cricketer of any era, words cannot do justice to the artistry of Betty Wilson. She had to be seen to be believed.

When she came on the Test scene in 1948, playing in the first international between Australia and New Zealand at the Basin Reserve Wellington, her impact was immediate. In Australia's only innings she scored 90 and then took 10 wickets in the match for 6.5 runs each. Her tally in the second innings was an astounding 6 for 28 off 14 overs, in which she cut a swathe through the middle order batting. Australia won that only Test by an innings and 102 runs.

Rumour has it that Betty, in the spare time that she had after office hours, used to practise her spin bowling at a solitary stump. Did she also emulate the great Don Bradman by practising with a single stump as a cricket bat one wonders? Well, whatever secrets lay behind being able to flight the ball and turn it both ways at will, or to cut a fast, perfectly good length ball off the middle stump, her successes certainly proved the worth of dedicated practice.

England, under Molly Hide, first met with Betty later on in 1948 and in the first Test suffered the onslaught of both bat and ball: The former providing a first innings 111, the latter a first innings 6 for 23. In the match overall, Betty took 9 for 62 and her efforts were crucial in Australia's defeat of England by 186 runs.

The second Test too, was a near thing for England. Betty took 6 match wickets for 62, and had a match batting average of 55.00, but the last Test in Sydney was ruined by rain and Australia had only one innings. Nevertheless Betty, whose usual batting position was 5 or 6, topped both averages: A batting 53.60, and a bag of 16 wickets at 12.62 each.

The team that toured England in 1951 was a very strong one; it must have been to have Betty mostly at number 7 in the order. An exciting series again resulted in her topping the batting with 43.75 and the bowling with 16 wickets at 16.68 apiece. There was no centuries, though, and it is possible that her finest hour was the 41 not out she scored on a dire wicket at Worcester to stave off an Australian first innings collapse.

There are good times and there are glorious times, for some, on the cricket field. The glory was Betty's during England's Tour of 1957-8, at Melbourne's St Kilda ground. Mary Duggan won the toss and put Australia in to bat on a wicket that had been deluged by rain. The tactic worked and Australia were all out for 38, Betty being the top-scorer with 12. It was Duggan's leg-spin

The active batting style of the complete all-rounder, Betty Wilson. In just 14 Tests she made 3 centuries, 3 half-centuries, took 68 wickets and held 10 catches.

The supreme player of her and any other era, Betty Wilson has the unique world record of scoring a century and taking 11 wickets in a match. The eleven wickets included a hat trick.

that did the damage to the tune of 7 wickets for 6 runs.

After 96 minutes, England were all out for 35, Mary being the top-scorer with 12. It was Wilson's spin that did the damage to the tune of 7 wickets for 7 runs, which included a hat-trick and four wickets in 5 balls. That hat-trick, *which is the only one in women's Test cricket*, had Edna Barker (bowled), Joan Hawes (stumped) and Dorothy Macfarlane (lbw) as the victims. At least two of those unfortunates had some cause to remember the occasion slightly more positively, however, because it was Edna who bowled Betty in the first innings and Joan who got her in the second. Unhappily, though, by the time the latter occurred, Betty had scored exactly 100.

Another century at Adelaide and 6 wickets for 71 in England's only innings, secured yet another, which was also her last, Test series in which Betty led both the batting and bowling averages for Australia. In her career overall, 16 innings resulted in 3 centuries and 3 half-centuries and she took a wicket every 42 balls. Betty also featured in three century stands with Mollie Dive (123), Una Paisley (163) and Val Batty (135). She also holds Australia's record for the tenth wicket (39) with Mavis Jones.

It is gratifying to know that this Victoria-born sportswoman, now living in Perth, has, in 1985, been recognised as the superlative cricketer she was by being placed firmly among her compatriots in Australia's 'Sports Hall of Fame'.

WILSON, Betty
Victoria and Australia
Batting and Fielding

	Tests	Inns	No	Runs	highest	100	50	average	Ct
1948 v NZ	1	1	—	90	90	—	1	90.00	1
1948-9 v E	3	5	—	268	111	1	1	53.60	2
1951 v E	3	5	1	175	81	—	1	43.75	2
1957 v NZ	1	1	—	47	47	—	—	47.00	2
1957-8 v E	3	4	—	282	127	2	—	70.50	3

All Tests Average: **57.46**

Bowling

	Overs	Balls	Mdns	Runs	Wkts	average	10/M	5/I
1948 v NZ	40	240	14	65	10	6.50	1	1
1948-9 v E	147	882	70	202	16	12.62	—	1
1951 v E	118.3	711	24	267	16	16.68	—	—
1957 v NZ	38	228	14	65	5	13.00	—	—
1957-8 v E	137.2	824	50	204	21	9.71	1	2

All Tests Average: **11.80**

Debbie Wilson Australia's emergent fast bowler of the 1984-5 Jubilee Series who took most wickets at 22.31 apiece. Here she is bowling to England's captain Jan Southgate.

DEBORAH WILSON

With her only previous experience of representative cricket one season with the Under 25 team in 1983, right-arm fast bowler Debbie Wilson was elected to the full Test side the following year aged 23. In the 4-day 5 match series against the touring England team in 1984-5 Debbie came through admirably. She played in all the Tests taking a total of 19 wickets and thus, with Lyn Fullston, headed the list for the number of wickets taken.

Debbie's best performance was 3 for 25 off 20 overs in the second innings of the first Test at Perth. Her total for the match was 5 for 115, and in the series overall she never failed to take a match wicket. Debbie's lively pace and impressive action is a great indicator for her future success and Australia's cricketing potential.

WILSON, Deborah
New South Wales and Australia
Batting and Fielding

	Tests	Inns	No	Runs	highest	average	Ct
1984-5 v E	5	5	4	25	12*	25.00	2

All Tests Average: **25.00**

Bowling

	Overs	Balls	Mdns	Runs	Wkts	average
1984-5 v E	198.1	1159	63	424	19	22.31

All Tests Average: **22.31**

NEW ZEALAND'S RECORD HOLDERS

PHYLLIS BLACKLER

The New Zealander Phyl Blackler had the longest Test career of any of her compatriots: It spanned 18 years. To maintain a place in a national side for such a time has to be merited and for this all-rounder whose fierce batting and beguiling leg-break bowling often succeeded at crucial times for her team, it assuredly was.

Although Phyl has several creditable performances on record, she seemed to bring out her best when answering England's challenge. It was in 1954 that she made the top team score – a rallying 46 in 69 minutes – when New Zealand had an uphill struggle to avoid certain defeat at Worcester. This followed the finest bowling feat of her career when she took 4 wickets for 22 runs off 6.5 overs.

At The Oval in 1966 she made her only half-century which, in 56 minutes, is not only the fastest for New Zealand but remains an international best. It was in that Test too that Phyl, with Carole Oyler, registered New Zealand's record 93 for a fifth wicket partnership. It took only 81 minutes.

Phyl Blackler, a strong hitter on the on-side, here shown with the Middlesex and England pace bowler Esmé Irwin during the New Zealand tour of 1954. She has the fastest Test 50 on record at 56 minutes and, a tantalising leg-break bowler, a best innings analysis of 4 for 22. In her 12 tests spanning 18 years, Phyl scored 371 runs and took 18 wickets.

BLACKLER, Phyllis
Canterbury and New Zealand
Batting and Fielding

	Tests	Inns	No	Runs	highest	100	50	average	Ct
1948 v A	1	2	—	36	34	—	—	18.00	1
1948-9 v E	1	2	—	1	1	—	—	0.50	1
1954 v E	3	5	—	144	46	—	—	28.80	2
1957 v A	1	2	—	0	0	—	—	—	—
1957-8 v E	2	4	—	56	24	—	—	14.00	—
1961 v A	1	2	—	10	8	—	—	5.00	—
1966 v E	3	4	—	124	68	—	1	31.00	1

All Tests Average: **17.66**

Bowling

	Overs	Balls	Mdns	Runs	Wkts	average
1948 v A	15.4	94	6	32	2	16.00
1948-9 v E	24	144	10	33	3	11.00
1954 v E	40.3	243	5	147	5	29.40
1957 v A	15	90	1	70	2	35.00
1957-8 v E	33.1	199	4	94	4	23.50
1961 v A	23	138	2	83	1	83.00
1966 v E	21	126	3	68	1	68.00

All Tests Average: **29.27**

BEVERLEY BRENTNALL

The highest score that New Zealand wicketkeeper Bev Brentnall ever achieved – 84 not out – was made in the second Test against England on the tour of 1966. It established a record seventh wicket stand of 90 with the fast swing bowler Joss Burley who made 46 and thus registered the highest score of her career too. That partnership 90, made in 95 minutes is still an international record.

An overall average of 32.33 in four innings for Bev, who batted a usual 6 or 7 in the order, was good going and perhaps capturing only four wickets – all caught – behind the stumps somewhat disappointing. But always remembering that a wicketkeeper's activities are dictated by the strengths in the bowling, what was remarkable about Bev's England début was that she conceded only *one bye in six innings* and that was during the second innings of the final Test. This feat has to be unique and of real merit when it is considered that England amassed a total of 1047 runs in that drawn series.

Another occasion which highlighted Bev's "stopping" powers was during the second Test at Christchurch on England's visit to New

Zealand in 1968-9. In a match which England won by 7 wickets and scored a total of 469 runs, Bev did not concede a bye. She finished that series with 5 catches and 6 stumpings which included a record 5 dismissals in the first innings of the third Test in Auckland. In this match she established the New Zealand record while rival wicketkeeper Shirley Hodges did the same for England by dismissing 5 opponents in the second innings. That match, which England won by 37 runs, owed a lot of its excitement to the skill of those two superlative keepers.

It was during her final season of Test cricket when she toured with the team in South Africa that Bev put herself in the international records once again. In the final Test at Johannesburg – which was important for either winning or drawing the series – Bev made 4 stumpings and took two catches in the first innings. Her one caught victim in the second innings gave her a record seven victims in a match to rank equally with Australia's Alice Wegemund who had performed that feat against England 35 years earlier. Bev is out on her own though by those 6 dismissals in the first innings at Johannesburg. That final Test was drawn but New Zealand triumphed in the series having won the second Test by 188 runs to which Bev contributed her fair share by making 26 in each innings.

Bev Brentnall was undoubtedly New Zealand's finest wicketkeeper. She is one of only two world class players to make 7 dismissals in a Test. Here she shows the batting style which gave her a highest score of 84 not out against England at Edgbaston in 1966.

BRENTNALL, Beverley
North Shore and New Zealand
Batting and Fielding

	Tests	Inns	No	Runs	highest	100	50	average	Ct / S
1966 v E	3	4	1	97	84★	—	1	32.33	4 —
1968-9 v E	3	5	—	87	38	—	—	17.40	5 6
1972 v A	1	2	—	21	20	—	—	10.50	— —
1972 v SA	3	5	1	96	26	—	—	26.00	7 6

All Tests Average: **21.50**

Wicketkeeping:	against England	against Australia
Catches:	9	0
Stumpings:	6	0

JOCELYN BURLEY

It was on the England tour of 1966 that "Joss" Burley made her début and not only showed her strength as an opening bowler of accuracy and pace but revealed the power of the batting. In just three years of Test cricket which meant only 6 matches, all of them against England, she took 21 at 26 wickets at 26.32 apiece. Her most impressive performance with the ball was the record 9 for 69 in the third Test at The Oval in 1966 which included 7 wickets for 41 runs off 34.2 overs in the second innings. The latter represents the most wickets taken by a New Zealander against England in any innings and an average of 7.67 the lowest in a match.

Joss hit the ball very hard indeed and her highest score of 46 was made when batting number 8 in the second Test at Edgbaston. Her 95 minutes at the crease on that occasion provided a record 90 partnership for the seventh wicket with Bev Brentnall (84★) and was brought to an end when she was clean bowled by Edna Barker. It seemed as though Edna was determined to impress herself indelibly on Joss's memory for when she herself was on 48 in the first Test at Scarborough she brought up the 50 with a six lofted over mid-wicket off a good length ball. And that bowler was none other than the luckless Joss who had never suffered such a fate before – especially when she had just taken the new ball!

In 1968-9 Joss finished the three match series 8 England wickets to the good at 36.25 apiece and though not top in the averages, this represented the most wickets taken. Her best innings bowling performance was 4 for 62 off 30.3 overs in the final Test at Auckland which England won by 37 runs.

Fast bowler Joss Burley in action in 1966. She took 9 match wickets for 69 at The Oval that year with a best innings performance of 7 for 41. A strong hitter, Joss shares a New Zealand record 90 partnership for the 7th wicket with Bev Brentnall.

During that series she clocked up another batting partnership record which was a ninth wicket 59 made in 63 minutes in the first match at Wellington. On this occasion Joss made 21, her second highest score in Test cricket, and Trish McKelvey was well on the way to her not out 155.

BURLEY, Jocelyn
Auckland and New Zealand
Batting and Fielding

	Tests	Inns	No	Runs	highest	average	Ct
1966 v E	3	4	—	79	46	19.75	1
1968-9 v E	3	5	—	31	21	6.20	2

All Tests Average: **12.22**

Bowling

	Overs	Balls	Mdns	Runs	Wkts	5/I	average
1966 v E	143.2	860	60	263	13	1	20.23
1968-9 v E	118.3	711	27	290	8	—	36.25

All Tests Average: **26.32**

JOYCE CLOTHIER

Joyce Clothier (later Powell) came to England in 1954 as an opening bat and as deputy wicketkeeper to Vi Farrell. It was the second Test at Worcester that began her reputation as a keeper of promise as well as an opener who was prepared to dig in when necessary. Doing it on that occasion – in an innings of 37 not out lasting 5½ hours – saved New Zealand from certain defeat. Hers was a talent of great use to the discerning captain who needed to shore up a failing position, and New Zealand had cause to be grateful for it more than once.

A player with a very individual stance at the crease, Joyce could be a powerful driver of the ball. This was no more evident than when she scored 49 and 63 against the Australians in the only Test played between those countries in 1957 and 1961 respectively. She was the top scorer on both occasions.

Joyce was both wicketkeeper and the number one opening bat in the two Tests played against England on their 1957-8 tour. It was in the second of these that she registered her best innings record of three catches out of the 7 wickets that fell. In her career of seven Tests she made one stumping and took 9 catches, one of which was other than from behind the stumps.

CLOTHIER, Joyce
Auckland and New Zealand
Batting and Fielding

	Tests	Inns	No	Runs	highest	100	50	average	Ct / S
1954 v E	3	5	1	73	37★	—	—	18.25	2
1957 v A	1	2	—	62	49	—	—	31.00	2 1
1957-8 v E	2	4	—	73	34	—	—	18.25	3
1961 v A	1	2	1	64	63	—	1	64.00	2

All Tests Average: **24.72**

Wicketkeeping:	against England	against Australia
Catches:	5	4
Stumpings:	0	1

JEAN COULSTON

On her début for New Zealand in England in 1954, Jean Coulston had the rare experience of opening the batting, making the top score and being a recognised pace bowler. Playing in only two Tests on that occasion, she took 5 wickets and topped the averages with 15.00. She

Redoubtable opening bat and wicketkeeper Joyce Clothier staved off a New Zealand defeat against England in 1954 by staying at the crease 5½ hours for 37 runs. Here she is shown (R) with opening partner Joan Hatcher.

Fast bowler Jean Coulston shown practising at Lord's in 1954. One of the youngest in the side, she also opened the innings on occasion. Her 5 Test match career culled 19 wickets.

also finished fourth in the batting list. It was an impressive beginning for the 18-year-old clerk from Wellington but as one of a prominent sporting family, it was obviously "in the blood".

She played in one Test against Australia in 1957 and later in the year was selected for both Tests against the visiting England side. By that time, though, her days of opening the batting had passed and it was her pace bowling that came to the force with a series tally of 10 wickets at 17.20 each. England, however, had cause to remember that Jean was no ordinary tail-ender when, in the second Test at Auckland, she held out for the vital last three balls and prevented the tourists winning by just the one wicket.

With Joyce Currie as partner, Jean formed a formidable pace bowling combination. It is a great pity that her Test career was so short-lived.

COULSTON, Jean M
Wellington and New Zealand
Batting and Fielding

	Tests	Inns	No	Runs	higest	average	Ct
1954 v E	2	3	—	51	24	17.00	2
1957 v A	1	2	—	20	15	10.00	—
1957-8 v E	2	3	1	5	5	2.50	1

All Tests Average: **10.85**

Bowling

	Overs	Balls	Mdns	Runs	Wkts	average
1954 v E	48	288	23	75	5	15.00
1957 v A	49.1	295	14	94	4	23.50
1957-8 v E	98	588	40	172	10	17.20

All Tests Average: **17.94**

JUDITH DOULL

Tireless in defence, Judi Doull was New Zealand's mainstay opening bat for almost a decade. In that time she made one century, and is thus one of a select quartet who have the achievement to their credit, as well as making five-half centuries. This latter is a New Zealand record.

Judi was among the cohort of nine players to make a début in the first Test at Scarborough on the tour of 1966, where she made a maiden half century and finished the match with an average of 107. Although she did not repeat that good performance, in fact she made a duck in the first innings of the second Test, she nevertheless hinted at things to come in a series average of 42.00.

It was in the last Test at The Oval in 1966 that Judi paired up with Janice Stead and thus formed a successful opening partnership that was to last until Janice retired in 1972. On two occasions in their 16 or so appearances together they made century opening stands. The first of these, a 128 made against England at Christchurch on the 1968-9 Tour,

With a century and five half-centuries to her credit Judi Doull ranks as New Zealand's most successful opening bat. With partner of many Tests Janice Stead, she holds the 1st wicket record of 128 made against England on their tour in 1968-9. Chris Watmough, a member of that touring party, is the fielder.

is still a New Zealand record. That was when Judi made 103 and Jan made 62. The second was against Australia in 1972, and of this second innings 104 Judi made 56 and Janice fell short of her century with 95.

No doubt that performance at the St Kilda ground in Melbourne remains a particularly memorable occasion for these two players since it was the first time that New Zealand had beaten Australia and it was by the large margin of 143 runs. After New Zealand's low scoring first innings of 89, the lead which Judi and Janice gave, together with a useful score of 66 by the number 4 bat Linda Powell, made a viable proposition of it for the bowlers.

Yet another partnership record was established in a second innings when Judi batted with Ann McKenna in the third Test at Auckland in 1968-9. This time it was for the third wicket and the 95 scored in even time saw Judi depart on 75 and Ann go on to make 60.

Although that season when England toured in 1968-9 gave Judi the highest of her batting averages, the consistency of her play on the South African tour in 1972 makes remarkable reading. In that three Test series in which she had the full six innings, her tally was: 39, 31, 10, 44, 52 and 52 not out. Finishing on a double half-century gave her that leading position of five half-centuries for New Zealand, leaving her number 2 and long-standing partner Janice Stead in second place with three.

In her final appearance in the one Test against Australia in 1975 at the Basin reserve in Wellington, Judi featured in another century opening stand. While she made 40 of the 103, Bar Bevege made the rest and eventually went on to score 96 and thus fall four short of what would have made the second century of her career. Judi finished that match with an average of 43.00 and a career average of 43.27. In 11 Tests and 22 innings this is an excellent achievement of which she may be justly proud.

DOULL, Judith
Auckland, North Shore and New Zealand
Batting and Fielding

	Tests	Inns	No	Runs	highest	100	50	average	Ct
1966 v E	3	6	2	168	74	—	1	42.00	1
1968-9 v E	3	6	1	240	103	1	1	48.00	3
1972 v A	1	2	—	57	56	—	1	28.50	—
1972 v SA	3	6	1	228	52*	—	2	45.60	2
1975 v A	1	2	—	86	46	—	—	43.00	—

All Tests Average: **43.27**

Bowling

	Overs	Balls	Mdns	Runs	Wkts	average
1972 v SA	9	54	0	24	0	—
1975 v A	4	24	0	10	0	—

JOAN FRANCIS

Housewife Joan Francis first played for New Zealand against Australia in her home city of Wellington, at the Basin Reserve, in 1948. In that single Test, when Australia overwhelmed their hostesses by the large margin of an innings and 102 runs, fast bowler Joan took two wickets for 75 off 33 overs which included 9 maidens. Since Australia made 338 for 6 declared, those two wickets attested to a promising furture for this strong player.

It was just over a year later that the 1948-9 England tourists arrived in New Zealand to play their only Test against that country. The match was at Eden Park in Auckland and once again, the visitors inflicted a heavy defeat on a country they similarly treated in 1935. Although Joan took no wickets on that occasion, but gave away only some 1.5 runs per over in her total of 39 on a somewhat variable wicket, she was top scorer in New Zealand's first innings total of 61 with a forceful 19 runs.

Joan's selection for New Zealand's tour of England in 1954 was something totally expected as well as warranted: It proved to be her finest hour.

England won the first Test in a low-scoring match on a lifeless wicket at Headingley by six wickets. Having taken 2 for 26 in the first innings, the breakthrough having been made on the evening of the first day leaving England 11 for 3 over the weekend, Joan was unable to take further part in the match after the Monday morning because of a recurrence of a knee injury. Though disappointing for her, the injury allowed the young Jean Coulston to show her paces in the post-Test matches, and in the second Test at Worcester she joined Joan in the fast bowling attack that gave England a shake-up.

With the highest tally of wickets in her Test career, 7 for 102 in the match overall was a performance that gave the lead to a determined and noble effort on New Zealand's part to force a draw. That was a Test from which the visitors gained strength of purpose and, though the final match at The Oval was spoiled by rain, it seemed to confirm the Test series as a milestone in the history of New Zealand's women cricketers. Joan herself ended her Test career as the chief wicket taker with 12 wickets overall at 18.83 apiece.

Pace bowler Joan Francis whose tally against England at Worcester in 1954 gave her the best analysis in her five-Test career.

After retirement Joan continued to do much for her country's cricketing youngsters, and is remembered with affection by friends at home and abroad.

FRANCIS, Joan
Wellington and New Zealand
Batting and Fielding

	Tests	Inns	No	Runs	highest	average	Ct
1948 v A	1	2	—	9	7	4.50	1
1948-9 v E	1	2	—	20	19	10.00	—
1954 v E	3	5	1	17	7	8.50	1

All Tests Average: **7.66**

Bowling

	Overs	Balls	Mdns	Runs	Wkts	average
1948 v A	33	198	9	75	2	37.50
1948-9 v E	39	234	8	61	0	—
1954 v E	80	480	22	226	12	18.83

All Tests Average: **25.85**

DEBORAH HOCKLEY

The very young Debbie Hockley – who was destined to become New Zealand's fifth Captain in 50 years – made her first appearance in Test cricket on her country's tour of Australia in 1979. In that one match, the final Test at the Albert Ground in Melbourne, she was run out and not out for an inauspicious average of 19. On her next appearance, another tour abroad – this time in England – she led the side as New Zealand's youngest ever Captain at the age of 21.

Whereas in 1979 she batted at number 8, she was now an established number 4 but again managed to be run out – this time in the second

Debbie Hockley New Zealand's youngest ever captain and the only player to have scored a century and half-century in the same Test. She did it against England at Canterbury, Kent, during the 1984 tour. Here she shows her defensive style. Jackie Court is at slip and England's wicketkeeper is June Edney.

innings of the first Test held at Headingley. Her average for that match was 16.5. Extraordinarily enough, the Worcester Test had her run out in both innings – though her average was on the up in a total 38.00 – but to be run out four times in one's first six Test innings had to establish some kind of record.

All this changed, however, in the final Test at Canterbury when Debbie made a century with a not out 107 in the first innings and then a half-century in a second innings 62. Certainly no New Zealander had achieved this feat before – though Trish McKelvey, Debbie's predecessor, had got near it with a 43 and 117 not out against South Africa in 1972 – and so that was both a first for Debbie and for New Zealand. Her first series as Captain, though, resulted in a draw.

HOCKLEY, Deborah
Canterbury and New Zealand
Batting and Fielding

	Tests	Inns	No	Runs	highest	100	50	average	Ct
1979 v A	1	2	1	19	14	—	—	19.00	—
1984 v E	3	6	1	278	107★	1	1	55.60	—

All Tests Average: **49.50**

INA LAMASON

New Zealand's pioneering post-war leader was Ina Lamason. She was the first to captain an official Test against Australia in 1948 when her opposite number was Mollie Dive, and in the following year she led her country against Molly Hide and the touring England team. On both occasions New Zealand received what can only be called a trouncing but she survived to fight another day. Indeed, nothing less would be expected of such as Ina and her kind and, without doubt, the present-day flourishing state of women's cricket in New Zealand owes its secure roots to those early days.

When New Zealand made their first visit to England in 1954 for a three Test series, Ina was deputy to Rona McKenzie and not only had her best series personally, but also had the satisfaction of seeing New Zealand accomplish true international status.

The 37 not out that Ina scored in the third, rain-curtailed Test at The Oval was a career highest and it produced a record partnership which lasted until 1966. Batting at number 7 in the order, she and Peg Batty put on 39 for the seventh wicket of which Peg made 24 in 55 minutes.

Ina Lamason pictured in 1954. A pioneering sportswoman, Ina captained New Zealand against Australia in 1948, and against England in 1949.

LAMASON, Ina M
Wellington and New Zealand
Batting and Fielding

	Tests	Inns	No	Runs	highest	average	Ct
1948 v A	1	2	—	13	7	6.50	—
1948-9 v E	1	2	1	29	15	29.00	—
1954 v E	2	2	1	44	37★	44.00	—

All Tests Average: **21.50**

Bowling

	Overs	Balls	Mdns	Runs	Wkts	average
1948 v A	15	90	0	58	0	—
1948-9 v E	7	42	0	22	0	—
1954 v E	15	90	4	56	2	28.00

All Tests Average: **68.00**

JACQUELINE LORD

Used as a regular leg-spin bowler and lower order bat when she made her début on the tour of England in 1966, Jackie Lord gradually established a reputation as a useful all-rounder. In a career that spanned some thirteen years, that took in three tours and meant representation against four countries, she finished with an over-25 batting average no fewer than three times.

While Jackie's first Test series was the most successful with the bat, it gave her a record tenth wicket partnership of 55 with Carol Oyler (67★) to which she contributed 25★ in 44 minutes, her last, against Australia in that country in 1979, was without doubt her finest with the ball. During that 1979 tour in which three 4-day Tests were on schedule, Jackie took 18 wickets at 17.66 apiece. On two occasions she took five wickets in an innings, giving her a New Zealand record of four such feats in a career.

The only New Zealander ever to take 10 wickets in a match, this was at the Albert Ground in Melbourne when her analysis was 10 for 137 off 55.4 overs which included 7 maidens, Jackie holds a best innings analysis of 4.80. This was against South Africa in Durban in 1972 when her 5 for 24 came off 23.2 overs including 9 maidens.

All-rounder Jackie Lord whose leg-spin bowling put her ahead of the field. With 55 wickets in 15 Tests at an average of 19.07, she is unique in being the only New Zealander to have taken 10 wickets in a match. This was against Australia in 1979, the last year of her Test career. Her best innings analysis was 5 for 24 against South Africa at Durban in 1972.

LORD, Jacqueline
North Shore, Canterbury, Wellington and New Zealand
Batting and Fielding

		Tests	Inns	No	Runs	highest	average	Ct
1966	v E	3	3	2	32	25*	32.00	1
1968-9	v E	3	5	—	20	13	4.00	—
1972	v A	1	2	—	11.	11	5.50	—
1972	v SA	3	4	1	92	39*	30.66	3
1975	v A	1	1	—	7	7	7.00	—
1977	v I	1	1	—	28	28	28.00	—
1979	v A	3	6	—	68	29	11.33	1

All Tests Average: **13.58**

Bowling

		Overs	Balls	Mdns	Runs	Wkts	10/M	5/I	average
1966	v E	80	480	24	154	7	—	—	22.00
1968-9	v E	67	402	13	201	6	—	—	33.50
1972	v A	15	120	3	51	2	—	—	25.50
1972	v SA	85.5	515	23	133	12	—	1	11.08
1975	v A	65	390	19	141	4	—	—	35.25
1977	v I	62.3	375	35	51	6	—	1	8.50
1979	v A	103.2	826	9	318	18	1	2	17.66

All Tests Average: **19.07**

Trish McKelvey batting at the Basin Reserve, Wellington where she made her first century, 155 not out, which is a New Zealand record. Here she cuts one past point. The England wicketkeeper is Shirley Hodges.

BELOW: having captained the side for 15 Tests from 1966 to 1979, Trish was Manager to the team that toured England in 1984. She is seen (R) with captain Debbie Hockley talking to HRH The Princess Anne during the series.

PATRICIA McKELVEY

It can be no easy prospect to captain one's country on making a début but that was the lot that befell "Trish" McKelvey in 1966. When, as well as that, eight others of the team were also playing for the first time and that first time was on foreign soil, then it takes some doing indeed. That Trish not only survived the ordeal but did so valiantly is attested by her successfully continuing to captain New Zealand for more than a decade against no fewer than four countries, including three tours abroad.

The result of the England tour of 1966 – in which opposing captain Rachael Heyhoe was also in charge for the first time – was a drawn series that had one team highlight in it when New Zealand had the experience of declaring a second innings at 300 for 7. This was in the second Test at Edgbaston and marked a new standard of batting for the team in that 5 players contributed more than 30 runs to establish this record score.

When England toured Australasia in 1968-9 it was again a clash between Trish and Rachael in which the latter won out with two wins and a draw. This was no easy achievement for England, however, and apart from the drawn game which was virtually a one innings affair, the matches were well-fought and exciting. During this series Trish, batting at her customary number 3, established an all-time New Zealand record 155 not out and topped the batting averages with a very good 55.75 from 5 innings. Another feature of that 155★ – which took 332 minutes – was a record second wicket partnership of 90 on 91 minutes with Janice Stead who made 54 and a record ninth wicket stand of 59 in 63 minutes with Jocelyn Burley who made 21.

In 1972 Trish led New Zealand against Australia. The one four-day Test at the St Kilda ground in Melbourne notched up two firsts. It was the first four-day Test between the two countries – and internationally – and was also the first time that New Zealand beat Australia. It was a convincing win by 143 runs.

Immediately following the match against Australia, New Zealand went on to a three-day, three match series against South Africa. Here New Zealand triumphed with a win at Durban by the large margin of 188 runs, dismissing South Africa for 89 in the second innings. It was this series that provided Trish with the second century of her career in a not out 117. Together with the 43 in the first innings, it made the drawn Test at Cape Town a memorable one with a match total of 160 and Trish remains the only New Zealander to score two centuries.

The 1975 Test against Australia and the 1977 Test against India were played in New Zealand and both were drawn. The former provided Trish with a half-century (52) and New Zealand with a highest-ever innings total of 359 setting a precedent for future 4-day Tests.

An interesting feature of Trish's last tour as captain was that it was the first time that New Zealand played a three-Test series against Australia. Each Test was scheduled for four days but, ironically, the only one to produce a result was affected by the weather and had to be reduced to three days. Australia then had an overwhelming victory by an innings and 74 runs and New Zealand thus set another precedent by having the lowest match total of 165, with a first innings 78, in 4-day Tests.

McKELVEY, Patricia
Wellington and New Zealand
Batting and Fielding

		Tests	Inns	No	Runs	highest	100	50	average	Ct
1966	v E	3	4	—	63	37	—	—	15.75	—
1968-9	v E	3	5	1	223	155★	1	—	55.75	1
1972	v A	1	2	—	26	26	—	—	13.00	2
1972	v SA	3	5	1	180	117★	1	—	45.00	2
1975	v A	1	2	—	83	52	—	1	41.50	1
1977	v I	1	2	—	34	20	—	—	17.00	1
1979	v A	3	6	—	90	37	—	—	15.00	1

All Tests Average: **29.12**

RONA McKENZIE

The captain for New Zealand's first ever tour of England was the all-rounder Rona McKenzie, who thus became the first player to lead her country in a three match series of three days duration. This showed that New Zealand was recognised as having reached full cricketing maturity, after years in which dedicated players such as Ina Lamason and her sister-in-law Joy Lamason had worked hard, with other officials, to put New Zealand women's cricket on the international map.

Although England, under Molly Hide, were victorious in that 1954 series it was only by the 6 wicket win in the first Test at Headingley. After that game, in which Rona was the most successful bowler with 5 match wickets for 33 runs off 28 overs, the tourists gathered strength. In the succeeding match at Worcester, Rona led a rearguard action in the second innings – going in at number 7 instead of her usual 5 – to

All-rounder Rona McKenzie brought New Zealand to international cricket maturity when she captained the first side to tour England in 1954. A forceful bat and useful bowler, she knew how to deploy herself and her players to good effect. Two half-centuries and a best bowling performance of 4 for 18 against England at Headingley in the first Test, were the highlights of her 7 year career. Here she is shown batting at Headingley, with Barbara Murrey at point, Kay Green at slip, Hazel Sanders at short leg and Joan Westbrook keeping wicket.

assist opener Joyce Clothier stave off another defeat. It was a successful ploy, and from that draw New Zealand seemed to gain confidence as well as a reputation for dogged survival. But Rona led them well at The Oval, sadly a rain-affected match, to see her team establish a highest ever innings total of 186 in reply to England's 281.

When England toured the Antipodes in 1957-8 with the strongest team ever sent abroad, it was Rona who captained for the two Tests. In the first, at Christchurch, her own first innings 60 – which as well as being the highest score of career to date was also her first half-century – ensured a highest innings total of 223 and was instrumental in achieving a drawn game. The sixth wicket partnrship of 40 runs between Rona and Phyl Blackler (24) on that occasion took just 28 minutes and is still a record for New Zealand on home ground.

Rona was a good, forceful bat who was particularly strong on the leg, but she was also adaptable and had the answer when stroke diagrams showed up her favourite on-side shots. Most of the 30 she scored in the second innings of the drawn Test in Auckland were scored on the off.

In 1961 New Zealand played Australia in Dunedin: It was both Rona's final Test match and captaincy. The result was a drawn game but Rona went out with her second half-century, beat her previous highest score by 1 run and also had the satisfaction of being able to declare both innings, with a highest ever first innings total of 243 for 8. She could certainly retire knowing that New Zealand was a cricketing force to be reckoned with in future international competition.

McKENZIE, Rona U
Auckland and New Zealand
Batting and Fielding

	Tests	Inns	No	Runs	highest	100	50	average	Ct
1954 v E	3	5	—	79	29	—	—	15.80	1
1957 v A	1	2	—	31	27	—	—	15.50	1
1957-8 v E	2	4	—	114	60	—	1	28.50	1
1961 v A	1	2	—	71	61	—	1	35.50	—

All Tests Average: **22.69**

Bowling

	Overs	Balls	Mdns	Runs	Wkts	average
1954 v E	47	282	16	101	6	16.83
1957 v A	22	132	6	52	1	52.00
1957-8 v E	22	132	4	53	1	53.00
1961 v A	4	24	2	8	0	—

All Tests Average: **26.75**

CAROLE OYLER

Carole was one of nine players to make her début for her country in the first Test which took place at Scarborough when New Zealand toured England in 1966. She batted at 5 and 4 in each innings, scoring a creditable 35 in the first and a good 36 not out in the second, to make a very promising beginning indeed.

Although she had the tendency to incaution at times, and this accounted for her duck in the first innings of the second Test, usually her play was attractively fluent without being aggressively active and was very reminiscent of England's Cecilia Robinson. An overall

Playing in just 5 Tests fluent bat Carole Oyler holds the record of three wicket partnerships all made against England.

average of 58.00 on that tour with a highest score of 67 not out, made in the third Test at The Oval, gave evidence of more to come.

Despite the fact that her potential was never fully realised, she played in just two further Tests which were against the England tourists in 1968-9, Carole shares in no less than three partnership records. These are: 93 for the 5th wicket with Phyl Blackler (68); 53 for the 6th wicket with Bev Brentnall (84★); 55 for the 10th wicket with Jackie Lord (25★).

They all took place in 1966 at The Oval, Edgbaston and The Oval where Carole's scores were, 67★, 36 and 67★ respectively.

OYLER, Carole
North Shore and New Zealand
Batting and Fielding

	Tests	Inns	No	Runs	highest	100	50	average	Ct
1966 v E	3	5	2	174	67★	—	1	58.00	1
1968-9 v E	2	3	—	38	26	—	—	12.66	1
All Tests Average: **35.33**									

ERIS PATON

Medium-pace swing bowler and middle order bat Eris Paton played in just two of the three Tests when New Zealand first toured England in 1954. Although she had no outstanding performances to her credit on those occasions she did very well on the tour overall – coming second in the batting and first in the bowling averages – to be of obvious Test match potential when England toured New Zealand in 1957-8.

As it happened, Eris's forceful batting was only seen in the Auckland

Eris Paton was an all-rounder dogged by injury in Test matches. She played in only four, had a highest score of 77 not out against England in 1957-8, and her most successful bowling performance was 6 for 55 in the only Test against Australia in 1961.

Test when her 77 not out in the first innings, together with 43 in the second, was a crucial part of that drawn match. Not only did her performance establish a New Zealand highest ever score and total match average of 120, but the first innings eighth wicket partnership of 40 with Caroline Sinton (10) remains a record against England. That partnership took 31 minutes.

Eris played her final Test against Australia in 1961, scoring only 32 runs but finishing with the bowling flourish of 6 match wickets for 55 runs off 42.2 overs.

PATON, Eris
Otago and New Zealand
Batting and Fielding

	Tests	Inns	No	Runs	highest	100	50	average	Ct
1954 v E	2	4	—	28	12	—	—	7.00	2
1957-8 v E	1	2	1	120	77*	—	1	120.00	1
1961 v A	1	2	—	32	16	—	—	16.00	1

All Tests Average: **25.71**

Bowling

	Overs	Balls	Mdns	Runs	Wkts	average
1954 v E	22	132	6	88	3	29.33
1957-8 v E	5	30	1	17	0	—
1961 v A	42.2	254	19	55	6	9.16

All Tests Average: **17.77**

SUSAN RATTRAY

By the time Sue toured England in 1984 she was one of the most experienced players in the New Zealand squad and yet still just 30 years of age. This useful all-rounder was the only member of the party to have played in England before, and was an obvious choice as deputy to the youngest ever New Zealand Captain in Debbie Hockley.

On her début against Australia in 1975, Sue, batting in the middle of the order, scored a maiden half-century in a total of 59. As the second highest score of the innings, this served its part in a record New Zealand first innings of 359. Australia replied with 362, and Sue took a creditable 2 wickets for 44 off 18 overs with her right-arm spin. That single 4-day Test which took place at the Basin Reserve in Wellington was drawn.

In 1979 a three-Test series was scheduled in Australia and Sue played in the first two at the Sydney University Ground and the Unley Oval in

Sue Rattray (R), all-round player and Vice-captain in 1984, is shown leaving the field at Worcester with Captain Debbie Hockley. It was an occasion when her 57 not out included a half century in 83 minutes off 83 balls. This proved something of a highlight during a seies generally marked by dour batting.

Adelaide. Her batting was a disappointment, resulting in an average of 8.75 in the four innings, and her bowling chances were reduced by the fact that Australia were only called on to bat twice in the last Test.

The 1984 series in England provided wickets that seemed to favour the medium pace bowlers, and though no one bowler did anything exceptional (the same could also be said of the England team) to bowl only 34 overs in a three-Test series does not give much chance for success. With the bat, however, Sue performed well adding another half century to her tally. It was her not out 57 at Worcester that gave her the fastest-scored 50 of the series — for either side. She took 83 minutes to do it off 83 balls.

RATTRAY, Susan
Canterbury and New Zealand
Batting and Fielding

	Tests	Inns	No	Runs	highest	100	50	average	Ct
1975 v A	1	2	—	74	59	—	1	37.00	—
1979 v A	2	4	—	35	15	—	—	8.75	—
1984 v E	3	6	1	161	57*	—	1	32.20	—
All Tests Average: **24.55**									

Bowling

	Overs	Balls	Mdns	Runs	Wkts	average
1975 v A	20	120	5	56	2	28.00
1979 v A	7	56	1	14	1	14.00
1984 v E	34	204	2	121	2	60.50
All Tests Average: **38.20**						

JILL SAULBREY

The left-arm Wellington pace bowler Jill Saulbrey played for New Zealand in 1966 against England at Scarborough. Her swing and Joss Burley's extra pace made for a good opening combination, but on her début Jill had the chastening experience of clocking up a bowling "ton". Her tally in the first innings was 1 wicket for 106 off 36 overs. Clearly, though, she was not one given to displays of temperament. Though she managed only to halve that formidable average by taking 1 for 55 in the second Test, the selectors' faith in her ability was rewarded when she took 4 wickets in the third and final Test at The Oval for an average of 15.75. In ending that drawn series with 7 Test wickets she was joint second wicket-taker with leg-spinner Jackie Lord.

Jill Saulbrey's left-arm pace bowling was her strength and provided her with a 5 wicket innings at an average of 6.4 during the 1972 tour of South Africa. Durban was the venue which also gave her a best match total of 8 for 52, and it brought off the series for New Zealand by just one win.

By the time of England's return visit to New Zealand on the tour of 1968/9, Jill had not only improved as a bowler but was beginning to work her way up the batting order. This was a three Test series in which England triumphed by two wins and a draw, but which produced four centuries – two to each country. Her bowling rate of 1 wicket for every 20 or so overs bowled may not be such as to delight, but it would be true to say that on the whole the pitches favoured the spinners.

Undoubtedly Jill's finest season was in 1972. A single innovatory 4-day Test against Australia at Melbourne's St Kilda ground, followed by three 3-day Tests against South Africa, gave Jill the best bowling figures of her career. Against Australia she took 7 match wickets which were instrumental in helping New Zealand to her first ever win against her Antipodean rival, and in the second Test at Durban she went one better. Those bowling triumphs led to averages of 13.57 and 15.13 respectively, with the latter coming off a total of 228 overs – twice as many as were bowled by any of her colleagues. It was the Kingsmead wicket, Durban, that also provided her best innings analysis of 5 for 32 off 39 overs with 23 maidens.

Jill's Test cricket finale was disappointing with the ball since she took just one wicket when Australia visited Wellington in 1975 for a single Test. In this her home town, however, Jill had the compensation of clocking up her first half-century in a top-scoring 62 in New Zealand's first innings.

Her eleven Test match appearances resulted finally in a total of 35 wickets putting her second only to Jackie Lord with 55 in 15 Tests.

SAULBREY, Jill
Wellington and New Zealand
Batting and Fielding

	Tests	Inns	No	Runs	highest	100	50	average	Ct
1966 v E	3	3	1	43	32*	—	—	21.50	2
1968-9 v E	3	5	2	46	19*	—	—	15.33	2
1972 v A	1	2	—	16	8	—	—	8.00	2
1972 v SA	3	5	1	31	14	—	—	7.75	—
1975 v A	1	1	—	62	62	—	1	62.00	—

All Tests Average: **16.50**

Bowling

	Overs	Balls	Mdns	Runs	Wkts	average	5/I
1966 v E	116	696	39	265	7	37.85	—
1968-9 v E	109	654	20	300	5	60.00	—
1972 v A	70	560	28	95	7	13.57	—
1972 v SA	238	1428	126	227	15	15.13	1
1975 v A	47.3	285	20	64	1	64.00	—

All Tests Average: **27.17**

MARY SPEIGHT

The Otago all-rounder Mary Speight (now Webb) first played for New Zealand against Australia on the tour of 1957 where the only Test was staged at the King's College Oval in Adelaide. It was a resounding win for Australia, by an innings and 88 runs, and not a startling début for Mary who was not asked to bowl her off-spinners and only managed 16 runs in the two innings. But this match was obviously a preliminary

Mary Speight was an all-rounder whose off-spin was under-used during her short career spanning 4 years and Tests. A good driver of the ball, she made her highest score of 42 against England at Christchurch in 1957-8, and also took 6-66 in the second Test at Auckland. Here she is seen (R) going in at Christchurch and having a word with Evonne Dickson the incoming number 2. At this stage the New Zealand score was 18 for one wicket.

trial for the projected visit of England and Mary's promise was sufficient to ensure her a place in both Tests later in the year.

An upper order bat of sound ability, Mary's best performance was a 42 at Christchurch when batting number 3. Her most creditable score, though, was probably the 24 compiled at Auckland when New Zealand were poised to lose after rain had delayed proceedings. On that occasion she batted at number 8 in the second innings and was eventually run out. This was a thoroughly good match for Mary who took crucial wickets in England's first innings and finished with a match analysis of 6 for 66 off 31 overs. A point of interest is that except for the run out, Mary herself succumbed to off-spin being clean bowled in each of her three other innings by Edna Barker.

Mary's last Test match appearance was against Australia in her home city of Dunedin in 1961, and although she made only 15 runs and did not bowl in what was almost a repeat performance of her début, she had the satisfaction of playing in the first Test against Australia which New Zealand did not lose.

SPEIGHT (Webb), Mary
Otago and New Zealand
Batting and Fielding

	Tests	Inn	No	Runs	highest	average	Ct
1957 v A	1	2	—	16	10	8.00	—
1957-8 v E	2	4	—	79	42	19.75	—
1961 v A	1	2	—	15	11	7.50	—
All Tests Average: **13.75**							

Bowling

	Overs	Balls	Mdns	Runs	Wkts	average
1957-8 v E	31	186	10	66	6	11.00
All Tests Average: **11.00**						

JANICE STEAD

Making her début for New Zealand on the tour of England in 1966, Janice played in two of the three Tests, made a maiden double duck at Scarborough and her highest score of 14 not out in the final Test at The Oval. This comparatively humble beginning at least saw her move from number seven to two in the batting order, and it was as an opener that she was eventually to make her mark.

Her partnership with Judi Doull during the 1968-9 tour by England

Deprived, by just 5 runs, of her century against Australia in 1972, opener Janice Stead nevertheless had the gratification of sharing another century partnership with Judi Doull and setting her team on its way to a first ever victory against Australia, by 143 runs. Here she is shown batting in the first innings against England at the Basin Reserve in 1969. She scored a solid 54 and put on a record 90 for the second wicket with Trish McKelvey. Lynne Thomas is the fielder at point.

not only proved to be one of New Zealand's most stable for many years, but led to a record score for the first wicket which still stands. Despite losing the second Test by 7 wickets, Janice played her part with a first innings 62 runs, to Judi's 66, of that 128 record. She also made the second half-century of her career and bolstered the New Zealand second innings with a second 34 runs. This good effort followed a second wicket partnership of 90 with Trish McKelvey at Christchurch when the latter was on her way to 155 not out. That 90 also remains a New Zealand record.

It was against Australia in 1972 that Janice achieved her highest match average of 60.00 and also fell only five short of obtaining a Test century. Having beaten Australia in that single Test, the first victory in 24 years, New Zealand went on to win the three match series against South Africa by one to nil with two matches drawn. Janice's highest score on that occasion was a 49 in the first innings of the first Test at Newlands, Cape Town.

STEAD, Janice
Canterbury and New Zealand
Batting and Fielding

		Tests	Inns	No	Runs	highest	100	50	average	Ct
1966	v E	2	4	1	18	14*	—	—	6.00	—
1968-9	v E	3	6	1	168	62	—	2	33.60	3
1972	v A	1	2	—	120	95	—	1	60.00	—
1972	v SA	3	6	—	127	49	—	—	21.16	—

All Tests Average: **25.81**

THE CENTURY MAKERS

ENGLAND

189	E A Snowball	v New Zealand	Christchurch	1934-5
179	R Heyhoe-Flint	v Australia	The Oval	1976
158★	C Hodges	v New Zealand	Canterbury	1984
144★	J Brittin	v New Zealand	Headingley	1984
126	H Sharpe	v South Africa	Durban	1960-1
124★	M E Hide	v Australia	Sydney	1948-9
124	E Bakewell	v New Zealand	Wellington	1968-9
119	M E Maclagan	v Australia	Sydney	1934-5
115	M E Maclagan	v Australia	Blackpool	1937
114	E Bakewell	v New Zealand	Christchurch	1968-9
113	R Heyhoe-Flint	v New Zealand	Scarborough	1966
112★	E Bakewell	v West Indies	Edgbaston	1979
112	J Brittin	v Australia	Perth	1984-5
110	M E Hide	v New Zealand	Christchurch	1934-5
110	R Heyhoe-Flint	v Australia	Old Trafford	1976
108	M B Duggan	v New Zealand	Christchurch	1957-8
105	M C Robinson	v Australia	Scarborough	1951
102	M C Robinson	v Australia	Adelaide	1957-8
101★	M B Duggan	v Australia	The Oval	1963
100	E Barker	v Australia	Melbourne	1968-9

AUSTRALIA

131	J Kennare	v India	Ahmedabad	1984
127	B Wilson	v England	Adelaide	1958
123	J Lumsden	v England	The Oval	1976
122	J Kennare	v England	Bendigo	1984-5
121	D Emerson	v England	Adelaide	1984-5
118★	L Hill	v New Zealand	Wellington	1975
117	J Stockton	v New Zealand	Sydney	1979
111	B Wilson	v England	Adelaide	1949
108	U Paisley	v New Zealand	Wellington	1948
105	P Verco	v India	Ahmedabad	1984
104★	K Price	v India	Ahmedabad	1984

104	M Jennings	v England	Edgbaston	1976
103	J Kennare	v England	Perth	1984-5
101	U Paisley	v New Zealand	Adelaide	1957
100	B Wilson	v England	Melbourne	1958

NEW ZEALAND

155★	P McKelvey	v England	Wellington	1969
117★	P McKelvey	v South Africa	Cape Town	1972
107★	D Hockley	v England	Canterbury	1984
103	J Doull	v England	Canterbury, NZ	1969
100★	B Bevege	v India	Dunedin	1977

FIVE OR MORE WICKETS IN A MATCH

ENGLAND

11 – 63	J Greenwood	v West Indies	Canterbury	1979
10 – 75	E Bakewell	v West Indies	Edgbaston	1979
9 – 58	M B Duggan	v Australia	Melbourne	1957-8
9 – 63	L Thomas	v Jamaica	Monymusk	1971
9 – 79	J Greenwood	v West Indies	Nottingham	1979
9 – 104	M B Duggan	v Australia	The Oval	1951
9 – 107	M B Duggan	v Australia	Worcester	1951
8 – 58	M E Hide	v Australia	Blackpool	1937
8 – 74	L Thomas	v Jamaica	Sabina Park	1971
8 – 86	J Davis	v Australia	The Oval	1937
8 – 124	E Bakewell	v New Zealand	Christchurch	1968-9
7 – 41	M E Maclagan	v Australia	Brisbane	1934-5
7 – 55	C Mowat	v West Indies	Canterbury	1979
7 – 60	M E Maclagan	v Australia	Melbourne	1934-5
7 – 67	G McConway	v Australia	Adelaide	1984-5
7 – 69	M B Duggan	v New Zealand	Auckland	1957-8
7 – 69	A Sanders	v South Africa	Durban	1960–1
7 – 75	A Sanders	v Australia	The Oval	1963
7 – 82	M B Duggan	v Australia	The Oval	1963
7 – 90	M B Duggan	v New Zealand	Christchurch	1957-8
6 – 53	D McEvoy	v New Zealand	Auckland	1948-9
6 – 57	M E Maclagan	v New Zealand	Christchurch	1934-5
6 – 63	C Evans	v New Zealand	Auckland	1968-9
6 – 68	M E Maclagan	v Australia	Sydney	1934-5
6 – 78	E Bakewell	v New Zealand	Auckland	1968-9
6 – 80	A Sanders	v Jamaica	Monymusk	1971
6 – 84	M B Duggan	v Australia	Birmingham	1963
6 – 84	A Starling	v Australia	Adelaide	1984-5
6 – 96	J E Partridge	v Australia	Sydney	1934-5
6 – 113	M Pilling	v New Zealand	Auckland	1968–9
5 – 17	M Spear	v Australia	Brisbane	1934-5
5 – 26	M Johnson	v New Zealand	Auckland	1948-9
5 – 28	M E Hide	v New Zealand	Headingley	1954
5 – 36	E Vigor	v New Zealand	Scarborough	1966
5 – 37	O Marshall	v South Africa	Johannesburg	1960–1

5 – 40	E Bakewell	v New Zealand	Wellington	1968-9
5 – 41	M B Duggan	v New Zealand	Worcester	1954
5 – 48	H Hegarty	v New Zealand	The Oval	1954
5 – 55	M E Maclagan	v Australia	Scarborough	1951
5 – 59	J Aspinall	v New Zealand	Headingley	1984
5 – 60	M E Hide	v Australia	Northampton	1937
5 – 68	E Irwin	v South Africa	Johannesburg	1960-1
5 – 74	E Bakewell	v Australia	Melbourne	1968-9
5 – 76	M B Duggan	v New Zealand	Headingley	1954
5 – 79	C Mowat	v West Indies	Nottingham	1979
5 – 82	H Hegarty	v Australia	Adelaide	1957-8
5 – 81	A Ratcliffe	v South Africa	Durban	1960-1
5 – 87	A Starling	v Australia	Perth	1984-5
5 – 92	A Sanders	v South Africa	Port Elizabeth	1960-1
5 – 93	A Starling	v Australia	Brisbane	1984-5
5 – 97	L Clifford	v Australia	North Sydney	1968-9
5 – 100	A Starling	v Australia	Gosford NSW	1984-5
5 – 107	M E Maclagan	v Australia	Blackpool	1937

AUSTRALIA

11 – 16	B Wilson	v England	Melbourne	1957-8
10 – 65	B Wilson	v New Zealand	Wellington	1948
10 – 107	K Price	v India	Lucknow	1984
10 – 118	A Gordon	v England	Melbourne	1968-9
9 – 62	B Wilson	v England	Adelaide	1948-9
9 – 101	P Antonio	v England	Northampton	1937
8 – 57	M Knee	v England	Scarborough	1963
8 – 65	P Antonio	v England	Blackpool	1937
8 – 68	M Knee	v England	Adelaide	1968-9
8 – 104	P Antonio	v England	Sydney	1934-5
8 – 112	L Johnston	v New Zealand	Melbourne	1972
7 – 27	A Palmer	v England	Brisbane	1934-5
7 – 47	S Tredrea	v New Zealand	Unley Oval, SA	1979
7 – 82	B Wilson	v England	Worcester	1951
7 – 95	L Fullston	v India	Delhi	1984
7 – 161	L Fullston	v India	Bombay	1984
7 – 171	S Tredrea	v New Zealand	Wellington	1975
6 – 36	D Martin	v England	Gosford, NSW	1984-5
6 – 62	B Wilson	v England	Melbourne	1948-9
6 – 66	R Thompson	v India	Perth	1977
6 – 68	L Kutcher	v England	North Sydney	1968-9
6 – 71	B Wilson	v England	Adelaide	1957-8
6 – 73	L Larsen	v England	Brisbane	1984-5

6 – 83	L Fullston	v England	Gosford, NSW	1984-5
6 – 88	T McPherson	v New Zealand	Melbourne	1972
6 – 97	R Thompson	v England	Perth	1984-5
5 – 46	A Hudson	v England	Melbourne	1948-9
5 – 50	N Whiteman	v England	Adelaide	1948-9
5 – 51	M Lutschini	v West Indies	Sabina Park	1976
5 – 52	J Bath	v England	Perth	1957-8
5 – 55	B Wilson	v New Zealand	Adelaide	1957
5 – 55	K Price	v England	The Oval	1976
5 – 61	R Thompson	v England	Bendigo	1984-5
5 – 68	K Price	v England	Adelaide	1984-5
5 – 69	R Dow	v New Zealand	Adelaide	1957
5 – 71	B Wilson	v England	The Oval	1951
5 – 82	N Whiteman	v England	Worcester	1951
5 – 82	N Whiteman	v England	The Oval	1951
5 – 102	L Kutcher	v England	The Oval	1963
5 – 109	L Fullston	v England	Adelaide	1984-5
5 – 110	S Tredrea	v New Zealand	Albert G Mel.	1979
5 – 115	D Wilson	v England	Perth	1984-5
5 – 124	R Thompson	v New Zealand	Wellington	1975

NEW ZEALAND

10 – 137	J Lord	v Australia	Albert G Mel	1979
9 – 69	J Burley	v England	The Oval	1966
9 – 85	P Carrick	v Australia	Melbourne	1972
8 – 52	J Saulbrey	v South Africa	Cape Town	1972
8 – 73	G Gooder	v England	Auckland	1948-9
7 – 95	J Saulbrey	v Australia	Melbourne	1972
7 – 102	J Francis	v England	Worcester	1954
7 - 137	E Badham	v Australia	Albert G Mel	1979
6 – 51	J Lord	v India	Dunedin	1977
6 – 55	E Paton	v Australia	Dunedin	1961
6 – 66	M Speight	v England	Auckland	1957-8
5 – 24	J Lord	v South Africa	Durban	1972
5 – 33	R McKenzie	v England	Headingley	1954
5 – 66	P Blackler	v England	Worcester	1954
5 – 70	L Bayliss	v Australia	Dunedin	1961
5 – 76	S Rattray	v India	Bhubaneswar	1985
5 – 78	J Lord	v Australia	Unley Oval SA	1979
5 – 81	J Coulston	v England	Christchurch	1957-8
5 – 89	S Rattray	v India	Lucknow	1985
5 – 91	J Coulston	v England	Auckland	1957-8

INDEX